JULIAN GWYN

Ashore and Afloat

The British Navy and the Halifax Naval Yard before 1820

University of Ottawa Press

This book has been published with the help of a grant from the Canadian Federation for the Humanities and Social Sciences, through the Aid to Scholarly Publications Programme, using funds provided by the Social Sciences and Humanities Research Council of Canada.

University of Ottawa Press gratefully acknowledges the support extended to its publishing programme by the Canada Council and the University of Ottawa.

We acknowledge the financial support of the Government of Canada through the Book Publishing Industry Development Program (BPIDP) for our publishing activities.

National Library of Canada Cataloguing in Publication

Gwyn, Julian, 1937–
   Ashore and afloat: the British navy and the Halifax naval yard before 1820 / Julian Gwyn.

Includes bibliographical references and index.
ISBN 0-7766-3031-8 (bound).   ISBN 0-7766-0573-9 (pbk.)

1. Halifax Dockyard (Halifax, N.S.)   2. Great Britain. Royal Navy – History – 18th century.   3. Great Britain. Royal Navy – History – 19th century.   4. Halifax (N.S.) – History, Military.   5. Navy-yards and naval stations – Nova Scotia – Halifax – History.   I. Title.

VA401.N6G99 2004   359.7'09716'225   C2004-900944-3

UNIVERSITY OF OTTAWA
UNIVERSITÉ D'OTTAWA

All rights reserved. No parts of this publication may be reproduced or transmitted in any form or by any means, electronic or mechanical, including photocopy, recording, or any information storage and retrieval system, without permission in writing from the publisher. Copyright clearance available from Access Copyright, 1 Yonge St., Suite 1900, Toronto, ON M5E 1E5, 416–868–1620, 1-800–893–5777, www.accesscopyright.ca.

Cover illustrations:
"HMS *Asia* off the Naval Yard c.1797," G.G. Lennock, NA, 20011073048, Peter Winkworth Collection; background, "Plan of Her Majesty's Careening Yard at Halifax, Nova Scotia, Established in 1759. Surveyed and Planned by John G. Toler in May 1815, copied by James McKenzie, 1839," Admiralty Library, Pfo B23

Cover layout: Pierre Bertrand
Copy-editing and proofreading: Carol Tobin

ISBN 0-7766-3031-8 (Bound) ISBN 0-7766-0573-9 (paperback)

© University of Ottawa Press, 2004
542 King Edward, Ottawa, ON Canada K1N 6N5

press@uottawa.ca http://www.uopress.uottawa.ca

Contents

LIST OF ILLUSTRATIONS v
LIST OF TABLES vii
ABBREVIATIONS viii
FOREWORD ix
PREFACE xi

PART ONE: NAVAL YARD COMPLEX
1 Building the Yard, 1758–1783 3
2 Development and Expansion, 1783–1819 27
3 Hospital Complex and Admiral's House 43

PART TWO: WORK FORCE
4 Officers and Their Clerks 65
5 Artificers and Labourers 101
6 The Work of the Yard 123

PART THREE: ECONOMIC IMPACT
7 Suppliers and Tradesmen 151
8 Mast Contractors and Wood Merchants 169
9 Paying Bills and Raising Cash 201

CONCLUSION 217

APPENDIX 1: Halifax Yard Establishments, 1763–1815 229
APPENDIX 2: Halifax Yard Workforce, 1761–1820 231
APPENDIX 3: Naval Yard Officers, 1756–1819 233
APPENDIX 4: Yard Returns Sent the Navy Board, 1780s 234
APPENDIX 5: Orders for the Night Watch, 1785 236
NOTES 238
GLOSSARY 321
BIOGRAPHICAL DIRECTORY 327
BIBLIOGRAPHY 348
INDEX 354

To the memory of those who toiled in the Halifax naval yard, to those who work there now, and to the officers, warrant officers, and men, both of the Royal Navy and the Royal Canadian Navy, who found a safe anchorage in Halifax harbour before stepping ashore on to the yard's wharfs.

Illustrations

Following page 238

1. "A View of His Majesty's Dockyard at Halifax 21 May 1760 ... with *Penzance* lying at the jetty head," Royal Ontario Museum, 958.97, 70CAN31
2. "Plan of His Majesty's Careening Yard at Halifax Surveyed by William Lloyd in August 1761," NA, H3/250/Halifax/1761
3. "New Store Propos'd," 1770, and cross-section of yard wall, PRO, ADM106/1179. Cross-section of painters' shed, 13 November 1807, NMM, HAL/A/1
4. "Plan and View of the Nav[a]l Yard at Halifax, Nova Scotia," inscribed on back: "Hon Hugh Palliser, 30 Sept 1771," NMM, LAD/11/51, neg. B994
5. "A View of His Majesty's Naval Yard from the Dartmouth Shore, Elevation of Buildings; View from the West Side of the Yard and General Plan," c.1771, NMM, LAD/11/52, neg. B995
6. "Halifax Harbour" J.F.W. DesBarres, *Atlantic Neptune*, II, pt. 1 #48, NA, NMC-134837 [detail of newly-erected defences at naval yard, c.1776]
7. "Halifax Harbour," J.F.W. DesBarres, *Atlantic Neptune*, II, pt. 1 #48, NA, NMC-134837 [detail of *Anson* at the careen]
8. "Plan of the Naval Dockyard at Halifax," 1784, Capt. Charles Blaskowitz, NA, H2/250/Halifax/[1784]
9. "The Careening Yard, Halifax, Oct 5–25, 1786," James S. Meres, in log of *Pegasus*, 141, NA, c-002557
10. "Plan of Her Majesty's Careening Yard at Halifax, Nova Scotia, Established in 1759. Surveyed and Planned by John G. Toler in

May 1815, copied by James MacKenzie, 1839," Admiralty Library, Pfo B 23
11. "View of Halifax from Davis's Mill, 1800," George I. Parkyns, NA, c-040311 [detail of naval hospital]
12. "View from Fort Needham near Halifax," 29 April 1801, George I. Parkyns, NA, c-000984 [detail of naval yard and hospital]
13. "Instructor's Model of Sheer Legs, Halifax Careening Yard" c.1880, MMA, M49.8
14. "Halifax Dockyard Bell," MMA, M60.6.1
15. "Masthouse, 1759–60," Naval Historical Library, DA034NHL-4-16
16. "Storehouse, 1760," Naval Historical Library, DA040NHL-1-28 [South Wing rebuilt in stone, 1768–9]
17. "Capstan House and North Wing, 1760," MCM [rebuilt 1768–9]
18. "Respective Officers" Offices, 1760s," MCM Naval Historical Library, DA034 [pitched roof added at a later date]
19. "New Storehouse, 1771," MCM, Naval Historical Library, DA034 NHL-4-4
20. "Resident Commissioner's House, 1785," MCM, Naval Historical Library, DA034 NHL-3-9
21. "Admiral's House, Halifax NS," NL, CIN, 4 August 1878
22. "Respective Officers' Tenements, 1793," NSARM, acc. 6835
23. "Boatswain's House, 1814," Naval Historical Library, DA034NHL-4-26
24. "Provo Featherstone Wallis, 1813," Robert Field, AGNS, 1979.17
25. "Jacob Hurd," William Johnston, The Metropolitan Museum of Art, acc. 64.114.1
26. Halifax Naval Yard Employment During Periods of War and Peace, 1761–1820

Tables

4.1 Clerks' Fuel Allowance, 1797 95
4.2 Those Paying Income Tax, 1809–10 96
4.3 Pay Scales for Clerks: Halifax & Jamaica, 1814 97
5.1 Halifax Retail Commodity Prices, 1795–6 & 1814 109
5.2 Yard Workers' Daily Pay Rates, 1817–18 110
5.3 Halifax Daily Pay Rates, 1814 & 1816 110
5.4 Halifax Yard Artificers' Pay Rates, 1814 111
5.5 Yard Invalid List, 1802 114
6.1 Workforce at British Overseas Bases, 1790 & 1814 127
7.1 Value of Stores Purchased by Yard, 1757–1819 (H£) 152
7.2 Halifax Prices for Paint Products, 1808 162
7.3 Horse and Cart Hire in the Yard, 1773–1804 (H£) 164
8.1 North American Sticks Exported to English Dockyards, 1772–1782 172
8.2 Naval Escorts for Mastships, 1791–1810 186
9.1 Specie Recovered from the Wreck of sloop *Granby*, 1771 203
9.2 Cash Imported into the Halifax Yard, 1775–1815 205
9.3 Sterling Bills of Exchange Sold, 1757–1814 208

Abbreviations

CIN	*Canadian Illustrated News*
cwt	hundredweight = 112 lbs
DCB	*Dictionary of Canadian Biography*
fol.	folio
HP	Hamond papers
NA	National Archives, Ottawa
NB	Navy Board, London
NL	National Library, Ottawa
MCM	Maritime Command Museum, Halifax
MHA	Member House of Assembly
MLC	Member Legislative Council
NBM	New Brunswick Museum, St John
NMM	National Maritime Museum, Greenwich
NSARM	Nova Scotia Archives and Records Management, Halifax
PRO	Public Record Office, Kew
RO	Respective Officers: naval storekeeper, master shipwright, master attendant
VB	Victualling Board, London
$	peso or piece of eight or dollar = 5s. or £0.25 sterling
£	pound sterling: 20s. = £1
H£	Halifax currency, par: H£111 12s. = £100

Foreword

When Julian Gwyn asked me to write the Foreword to this book I was highly flattered and quite delighted. Over the past thirty years we have shared a mutual interest in Halifax as a naval base. Professor Gwyn's work on the personal fortune of Peter Warren, the sailor who first persuaded the British naval establishment to show a serious interest in Nova Scotia, paralleled my own work on the growth of that colony as an element in British sea power in the eighteenth century. In an eighteenth-century study group of historians, we shared our enthusiasm for the history of that period. As our interests turned gradually to other fields we kept on exchanging sometimes diverging views on the role of the navy in Nova Scotia during the eighteenth century.

It has been my contention that Halifax – a town created in 1749 after the War of the Austrian Succession, under the auspices of the President of the Board of Trade, George Montague Dunk, Lord Halifax – was meant to be the new metropolis of Nova Scotia, the first of many towns that would finally ensure a substantial British presence in the colony. As Julian Gwyn demonstrates in this book, it was not until 1758, during the Seven Years' War, that the British Cabinet ordered the building of a naval yard, something that would make Halifax the counterpoint to Louisbourg and the essential strategic base for the Royal Navy in North America.

Halifax only became a naval yard after the failure to establish more than a handful of the planned British settlements in Nova Scotia, after the expulsion of the Acadian population in 1755, and subsequent to the ignominious 1757 collapse of the attempt to capture Louisbourg. Until 1749 the naval presence in Nova Scotia had been limited to visits and surveys by station ships and some armed vessels from the American colonies, and the escort for the annual fishing convoy from the West Country of England. After 1749, the establishment of a station ship and a "sea militia" of armed vessels based at Halifax supported the British presence, and it was only the outbreak of war that brought visits of larger naval squadrons in 1755, 1756, and 1757. Winter in Halifax, British sailors complained, lasted seven to nine months of the year. Generally speaking, they detested the place. This book argues with good evidence that Halifax, although a remarkably economical investment, was less desirable than New York during the War of the American Revolution, or Bermuda during the War of 1812, and would most likely have continued to be little more than a careening harbour in the eighteenth and early nineteenth centuries had it not been for the embarrassing failure at Louisbourg in 1757. What that would have meant for Nova Scotia and British North America is one of those "what-ifs" of history that will never be answered.

"Foreign" stations, as the Royal Navy termed them, like Antigua, Jamaica, Trincomalee, Bermuda, and Halifax – often mentioned but seldom understood – have not received the detailed and careful attention they deserve. This is the first rigorous analysis of the origins and role of a dockyard in the outposts of empire, and it is hoped that it will provide a lead for a whole series of related studies. I commend it to the reader.

W.A.B. DOUGLAS, PhD
Former Official Historian for the Canadian Armed Forces
Ottawa, February 2003

Preface

"Oh dear, those learned people who spend a whole lifetime in getting up their subjects!"[1]

This book is about the navy, not at sea, but on land. A naval yard and the squadron it serves are intimately connected. If a squadron or fleet is not much more than an elaborate gun deck, it cannot function without a base. In fast-moving operations, the base might prove to be very temporary. This was seen at Turtle Bay on Manhattan Island during the war with rebel America from 1776 through 1783. For enduring strategic reasons a base might acquire near-permanence. As the British Empire expanded, early examples of overseas yards were found in such places as Gibraltar, Port Royal in Jamaica, English Harbour in Antigua, and Halifax in the colony of Nova Scotia.

Warships, like land-based fortresses such as the Halifax citadel, needed to be maintained and supplied, while those who manned and conserved them needed all sorts of tools and equipment, as well as provisions, clothing, pay, leave, management, and training. Each yard behind its walls – wooden or stone – constituted to some extent a world of its own. Each interacted in all sorts of ways with the port town where it was established, not the least of which was economic. This is the focus of *Ashore and Afloat*, which is as much about the workforce as it is about the administration and infrastructure of an important naval institution.

To explain this interaction, this book is divided into three parts. The first section analyses and describes the history of the Halifax careening yard which sustained successive North American squadrons

xii Preface

and fleets. There is a particular focus on its spatial and physical evolution along the harbour's shore lying to the north of the growing town of Halifax. It includes discussion of the adjoining naval hospital complex and the commander-in-chief's house, prominently positioned overlooking both yard and hospital. My account of the yard ends in 1819, when it was reduced for a period of thirteen years to the status of a small depot with a skeleton workforce. Thereafter for some years, its only real work was to greet the squadron for a few weeks each summer, when the commanding admiral put in a brief appearance. Then the highlight was the annual regatta. Never again until the great wars of the twentieth century did the yard play so important a role as it had assumed before 1820.

The actual work of the yard is considered in some detail in the second part. The conditions of work for those employed in the yard, from the resident commissioner, the other officers and their clerks, to the corps of artificers, and other workers, form part of this section. The variety of work undertaken is also analysed.

The book's final section deals with the economic impact of the yard, and looks both at the extent to which it was dependent on local suppliers and its role in coordinating the supply of masts and other forms of wood products for the Halifax yard and for yards elsewhere, especially in the West Indies, England, and Bermuda. Finally, it considers the yard's role as a quasi-bank, before a banking system existed in the colony.

Between 1793 and 1815, when the British navy numbered upwards of 1,000 warships, as many as 15,000 men worked in the dockyards at home and perhaps another 3,000 more in refitting yards scattered about the British Isles and the Empire. To carry this heavy load, by 1815 the Navy Board in London employed more than 200 clerks to maintain the flow of orders to places as widely scattered as Madras, Trincomalee, Penang, Mauritius, Sydney, Capetown, Rio de Janeiro, Barbados, Bermuda, Antigua, Jamaica, Halifax, Kingston on Lake Ontario, Malta, Port Mahon, and Alexandria.[2] The Navy Board was accused by contemporaries of inefficiency, charging that it remained technologically backward and wasteful both of funds and scarce materials. Against any reforming impulses stood, on the one hand, the Navy Board's jealous defence of its London-based, highly centralized system of management and, on the other, weight of custom and traditional practice of the corps of workmen, led by the master artificers in the yards themselves. These criticisms by contemporaries have been examined and sometimes echoed by historians, especially because of the impact on the navy's ability to confront its enemies in the long wars against Revolutionary and Napoleonic France, attributed to these inefficiencies. The most scathing criticisms came from sea officers who focused their complaints especially on the inadequacies of the dockyards. Among the most strongly-held opinions were those of John Jervis, Earl of St Vincent, erstwhile First Lord of the Admiralty. The most favourable scholarly opinion, that of Roger Morriss, viewed the dockyards rather as places "of industry, enterprise and gradual improvement" bringing credit to "the Navy Board, the dockyards and the men who served them."[3]

On the world scale of the British Empire, the Halifax yard, if measured by the number of employees, was of small account. The careening yard, the largest industrial complex in North America before 1820, employed less than 300 men, even when the staff of the adjoining naval hospital is added. As the only naval yard of consequence on the North Atlantic coast, it retained obvious regional importance. As the only refitting yard in British North America until the outbreak of war with the United States in 1812 it was of evident strategic value. Of little importance to the great battles fought with France in European waters after 1793, its history has been ignored by British naval historians.[4] Twice an important irritant in conflicts with the United States, the yard has also escaped the interest of American naval historians of the War of 1812, as they focused especially on the naval war on the inland lakes, or on the single ship encounters with British warships in engagements often distant from Nova Scotia waters.

My preoccupation with the Halifax careening yard was fed in part by my earlier interest in the role of the British navy on the North American east coast and by my study of the Nova Scotian economy before Confederation.[5] That concern coincided fortuitously with the creation of the Naval Dockyards Society, an international association two of the aims of which are to foster the history of dockyards worldwide and to lobby for the preservation of these historic sites, now frequently under the threat of redevelopment and destruction by private interests.

This book is designed, in part, to appeal to those who will want to interpret the history of the harbour as fully as possible. The reduction of political tensions in Europe, upon the collapse of international Communism in the USSR in our own day, has yet to reduce, in the volatile world we have lived in since the end of the Cold War, the importance of the Halifax naval base. On the other hand, to retain it beyond the

xiv Preface

next decade or so might reflect more nostalgia than good strategy. Canada's east coastguard vessels and icebreakers, which will always have an important role, will not require an elaborate naval base of the sort Halifax now provides. Such vessels can readily be serviced across the harbour in Dartmouth or in private shipyards on the Halifax waterfront or elsewhere in Atlantic Canada. If this prediction proves accurate, then the prospect is that within a few years part of the Halifax waterfront, occupied successively by the British navy and the Canadian navy for almost 250 years, is likely to be thrown open to commercial development. It is happening elsewhere on the sites of former naval bases around the world and for the same reasons.

The Naval Dockyards Society members include, among a wide array of enthusiasts, those who have published most usefully about the English yards and established much of the intellectual framework for my own study of the Halifax naval yard. For English dockyard history, I have depended especially on MacDougall's *Royal Dockyards* and his *The Chatham Dockyard Story*,[6] *The Royal Dockyards during the Revolutionary and Napoleonic Wars* by Morriss, and *A Management Odyssey: The Royal Dockyards 1714–1914* by Haas.[7] Two theses on the Portsmouth dockyard were also especially useful. These were Knight's "The Royal Dockyards in England at the Time of the War of American Independence,"[8] much of which has been published in several historical periodicals, and Wilson's "Government Dock-Yard Workers in Portsmouth, 1793–1815."[9] Special mention must be made of Coad's *The Royal Dockyards: 1690–1850: Architecture and Engineering Works of the Sailing Navy*, which provided a rich architectural account of the English and some of the overseas yards, and Knight's valuable collection of dockyard manuscripts *Portsmouth Dockyard Papers 1774–1783: The American War. A Calendar.*[10]

None of these works did more than mention the existence of the Halifax yard, as their authors seemed unaware of Marilyn Gurney Smith's booklet *King's Yard: An Illustrated History of the Halifax Dockyard*,[11] the only publication hitherto available for this important historic site.[12]

This book has been written largely from official sources; the topics it treats reflect this. What would I have done to recover a diary or a cache of private letters by one of the yard workers, clerks, or officers! Without them the cultural history of the yard and its workers living beyond the walls is beyond recovery.[13] Who kept the goats and geese of whose noise and filth Commissioner Inglefield complained in 1807? While the master shipwright was well-housed in the yard, why was the yard's master mason housed in a shed so decrepit that, when he died, it was torn down? What went on behind the walls of the houses built for some who worked in the yard? Without a yard refectory, where did the men eat when they were obliged to work by candlelight in winter? Had they brought with them both their mid-day and evening meals when they first entered through the gate in the morning? Without a yard chapel, frequently found in other yards, were communal prayers ever led by the officers? Without a surgeon, except briefly between 1775 and 1783, who cared for yard workers, when ill or injured? What socialization occurred when seamen and their wives landed at the yard's wharfs where fishers also sold their catches? What were workers' thoughts as they trudged to work before the sun rose on a winter's Sunday morning, when overtime was ordered? Why did the officers and clerks almost always retire to England, no matter how many years they had spent in Nova Scotia? How resentful were such men to know that their salaries were always the lowest of all the overseas yards? With whom in town did they socialize? Perhaps all of the clerks aspired to gentility and were certainly addressed as "Mister" but outside their offices, did they mix with the principal officers whom they served? If the naval storekeeper, like his clerks, aspired to gentility, did the master attendant and master shipwright have the same ambitions?[14] Did any of these principal officers ever establish a first-name basis relationship with any of the sea officers or the resident commissioner? I have pondered such questions and many similar ones, without any hope of having answers for the Halifax yard.

My original ambition was to publish an account of both the naval yard and of naval operations in a single book. Owing to the original manuscript's length and anticipated publishing costs this proved impossible. Rather than forsake the project and abandon the years of research involved, I elected to publish two shorter books, one on naval operations, cited earlier, and this present monograph on the early history of the yard.

Parts of chapters 4 and 5 appeared as "The Culture of Work in the Halifax Naval Yard before 1820," in *Royal Nova Scotia Historical Society Journal*, 2 (1999): 118–44. Part of chapter 8 appeared as "The Halifax

Naval Yard and Mast Contractors, 1775–1815," in *The Northern Mariner–Le marin du nord*, 11 (2001): 1–25 and was awarded the 2002 Keith Matthews prize by the Canadian Society for Nautical Research. I thank the editors of these two distinguished periodicals for permission to reproduce this material.

For financial support to undertake the research I am deeply indebted to the Social Sciences and Humanities Research Council of Canada which, in 1996, awarded me a three-year research grant. The faith in me expressed by the anonymous reviewers of my grant application I have held as a sacred trust. This work would not have been attempted without such funds, for it enabled me to locate many manuscripts hitherto unrecognized or unstudied. These were found principally in the Public Record Office at Kew, at the National Maritime Museum at Greenwich, and the National Archives in Ottawa. The grant also permitted me to spend several months at work in the Public Archives of Nova Scotia. To the staffs of these institutions I am greatly indebted. I express my special gratitude to Timothy Dubé at the National Archives for help to gain access both to three newly-acquired Halifax yard letterbooks and to the large collection of Halifax vice-admiralty court papers. I thank Faye Kert, PhD, for making available to me her research notes for 1812–15 derived from this source. Special thanks are due as well to Carol Tobin, who edited the manuscript so efficiently. I acknowledge the help of Trish Kell, PhD, now a manager with Parks Canada, who laboured devotedly as a research assistant at the National Archives for seven months in 1996–7, and of Jennie Wraight, of the Admiralty Library, London, for help in locating several unique naval yard plans and studies of the eighteenth-century admiralty court proceedings. Others who deserve mention include Elizabeth Wallis for friendship over many years, as I lodged in her home in Kew, conveniently located only seven hundred paces from the PRO, and Marilyn Gurney, director of the Maritime Command Museum, Halifax, housed in the commander-in-chief's house, for her enthusiastic support and practical help in many directions. I thank David Jones, PhD, for making available to me several naval monographs from his personal library in Halifax. For providing platforms for some of my ideas, I thank Dan Conlin of the Maritime Museum of the Atlantic, David Flemming, and Professor Allan Marble of the Royal Nova Scotia Historical Society. Other Nova Scotia friends, who made my time among them so pleasant, whom I wish especially to mention include Barry Cahill, Professor Colin Howell, Professor Del Muise, Nancy

O'Brien, Elizabeth and Ben Pooley, Jane and Bruce Purchase, Carolyn and the late Peter Smedley, Sandra Sackett, Jenny Brickenden, and Lois Yorke. Finally, I thank a remarkable couple, Dr Zbigniew and Dr Janina Konczacki, both retired professors, for making me so comfortable in their lovely home so that, almost undistracted, I could make the final revisions to the manuscript.

I wish to acknowledge that this book has been published with the help of a grant from the Humanities and Social Sciences Federation of Canada, using funds provided by the Social Sciences and Humanities Research Council of Canada. Finally, I wish to acknowledge a grant from the Faculty of Arts at the University of Ottawa to help offset the cost of illustrations.

Ottawa
December 2002

PART ONE

NAVAL YARD COMPLEX

Chapter One

BUILDING THE YARD, 1758–1783

"I am sure the building will stand forever."[1]

If the organization of naval dockyards by the Tudors, beginning with Portsmouth in 1495, was the surest sign of England's new ambition to play a wider role in European affairs, so the decision by Pitt some 262 years later, in 1757, to build a careening wharf at Halifax represented a resolution to play a decisive role in North America. Then a "decision to construct a careening wharf was tantamount to a decision to establish a base. The logical appurtenances of a careening wharf – capstans, capstan house, storehouses – were incorporated into the original plan. It was only a matter of time before the base also acquired a forge, a masthouse, a boat yard, a cooperage, a gun wharf with magazine, living quarters, harbour defences, and perhaps a second careening wharf."[2] The building of a naval yard at Halifax merely recognized that a forward base was needed in North America to supplement the major repairs to its ships, work that continued to be completed in the dockyards in England.

Such British overseas bases first appeared early in the eighteenth century. Both Gibraltar in 1704 and Port Mahon on the island of Minorca in 1708 came ready-made through conquest. The next three were purpose-built careening yards. First came Port Royal, Jamaica, in the 1730s, then English Harbour, Antigua, in the 1740s, and finally Halifax in the 1750s.[3] None of these overseas yards was a dockyard, rather they were known as careening or naval yards. Only yards with drydocks, where ships were built, rebuilt, and cleaned, were referred to as dockyards. This remained the work of the home yards in England.[4]

Naval officers and resident commissioners appointed to the Halifax yard usually at first mistakenly wrote of the Halifax "dockyard," but after a few weeks they invariably wrote only of the "careening yard." The Navy Board, perhaps because the original overseas bases were acquired by conquest, always called the overseas bases "foreign" yards, just as it also referred to North American masts and timber as of "foreign" growth.

Eventually there were other North American sites which became temporarily important bases during the first American war. New York in 1776–83 and Rhode Island and Charleston in 1779–81 served briefly as careening yards. Indeed, the New York facilities on Manhattan Island served, until 1783, as a place for the refitting warships of even more importance to the North American fleet than was Halifax.

The outbreak of hostilities with France in 1755, not officially declared until the spring of 1756, not only transformed the navy's role throughout North America, but also had a profound impact on the port of Halifax, the newly-built capital of the colony of Nova Scotia. Concentration of naval forces of unprecedented size in the Gulf region between 1755 and 1759 indicated to some in government that a new base was needed for ships on the North American coast. In the summer of 1755 there were usually between ten and seventeen ships of the line in Halifax harbour, pointing to the need for a permanent careening yard in North America. For this Commodore Peter Warren, as commander of the newly-formed North American squadron at the siege of Louisbourg, had argued in 1745 when he suggested "establishing a dockyard under proper regulations in the most convenient of the colonies for building ships of war."[5]

Before such a decision was taken for Halifax harbour, various expedients were employed by ships on the North American station. Between 1746 and 1749, for instance, careening facilities were established at Louisbourg, and naval stores from New England and England housed there under the care of a naval storekeeper, appointed by Warren.[6] More commonly, British warships on the North American station careened at commercial wharfs in the principal termini of overseas trade. By the 1740s, this usually meant in Boston harbour,[7] at Turtle Bay half-way up the east shore of Manhattan Island, or at Norfolk, Charleston, and Philadelphia.[8] For larger ships, Charleston was useless because of the bar at the mouth of the harbour. Commodore Charles

Knowles, while attempting unsuccessfully in 1747 to careen at Annapolis Royal, using the great tides of the Bay of Fundy, warmly recommended Boston.[9] There in 1747, in Nantasket Roads, he had beached a large ship, using the hulk *Bien Aimé* as a storehouse. The establishment of a careening yard in Boston, he argued, would put an end to the arguments frequently advanced by sea captains to establish careening wharfs at their different stations.[10]

One such sea officer was Warren's contemporary, Joseph Harmar, whose ship had been demasted and had broken its rudder. Harmar informed the Admiralty that he had built a careening wharf and "suitable storehouse" on his own initiative in the winter months of 1747–8 on land he had acquired for that purpose on Port Royal Island in the Broad River, South Carolina.[11] He reported that there was water enough for ships of up to fifty guns and requested a supply of sails and other stores, explaining that Charleston's careening wharf had "quite gone to decay." When the Admiralty received his initial bill for more than £1,147 and his draft plan of the site, it requested the Navy Board to "take the whole into their consideration." When the Board advised against the plan, the Admiralty made Harmar pay the cost.[12] In reply, Harmar pointed out that his orders had been to careen twice a year while on the South Carolina station and that, without the facilities he had erected, he could not have followed his orders. He claimed that had the war continued, Commodore Charles Watson, commander of the North American squadron in 1748, had planned to winter his ships there.

Harmar overlooked the fact the Navy Board had sent out careening gear in 1746 to enable a careening wharf to be erected in Louisbourg harbour.[13] The restoration of Louisbourg to the French in 1749 meant that North American ships once again had to careen at commercial yards. When the Admiralty ordered the Navy Board to consider the best place to careen warships, even the largest, sent to North America, nothing was done.[14] As late as 1756, Capt. James Campbell was recommending that, in order to preserve the ships on the Nova Scotia station and to discourage desertion, all warships should be sent to the South Carolina station in winter where Harmar's "good careening wharf and careening gear" were still available.[15]

Before a careening yard became operational in Halifax harbour, various expedients were employed in Nova Scotia. Thus in 1753, when sloop *Albany* (14) needed extensive repairs before she could sail for England to be thoroughly refitted, the oak and other wood used in her repair had first to be cut and sawn by ships' carpenters who undertook the repairs.[16] When *Arc-en-ciel* (50) was captured off Scatarie Island in 1756, her masts and yards were so damaged that all needed to be replaced. As none of suitable size was available in Nova Scotia, they had to be imported from New England.[17] There were such shortages of other necessary stores that even by the end of 1757, eighteen months later, no repairs to her had been undertaken.[18]

Until 1755, when several ships of the line for the first time wintered in Halifax harbour, the Admiralty remained convinced that the expense of establishing a proper careening yard in Halifax harbour could be avoided. On that occasion, Commodore Richard Spry unrigged the ships and moored them as near the shore "out of the strength of the tide as could be done with safety." Before departing for England on that occasion, Vice Admiral Edward Boscawen, Spry's commanding officer, hired Barnard's wharf to moor sloops "where they are very safe and easy."[19] Spry used as many as eighty seamen at a time to overhaul running rigging, and required all available caulkers found on board his squadron to work on one ship at the same time. In this he was aided by the weather, as the 1755–6 winter proved unusually mild. Throughout December and January there were scarcely three days together below freezing. The seven-ship squadron survived the winter without damage or accident. Spry assured the Admiralty that he would "clean the ships as well as can be expected at this place and get them to sea in the spring as early as possible." This assurance and the fact that only one ship of the line, a frigate, and two sloops were ordered to winter at Halifax in 1756–7, possibly allayed the Admiralty's sense of urgency, since it first made and then cancelled plans to begin building a careening wharf near Halifax and to appoint "a proper person" to oversee the work.[20]

This decision demonstrated that the Admiralty still believed that Portsmouth was an adequate base for naval operations in the Gulf of St Lawrence region. The inadequacy of the policy was acutely felt, particularly by Vice Admiral Francis Holburne's fleet that, while blockading Louisbourg in September 1757, was battered by a hurricane – one of those which periodically come ashore in Nova Scotia about once a decade. As Commodore Charles Holmes reported of his ship when he reached England, "*Grafton* was laid on her beam's end, the tiller, pintals and rudder broke, main mast was cut away, the mizzen mast blew off, when the haze and rain cleared they found themselves almost upon the breakers. Had the weather not cleared, or had the storm lasted one hour longer, all the squadron must have been lost."[21] As it was, *Tilbury* (64) was cast away and those who survived the disaster became prisoners. When Holburne's badly-mauled ships limped back to Halifax for repairs, there was a grave shortage of necessary naval stores. Spare naval stores from the squadron were supplied to the most disabled ships, leaving all the others short of cordage and sails. Eventually *Sutherland* and *Arc-en-ciel* were careened at Barnard's wharf which was too small for larger ships.

Later that autumn, armed with an Admiralty directive to find a suitable location for a careening wharf, Holburne went with "some of the captains to look out for a suitable place."[22] He first settled on George's Island, for which the navy was given a land grant.[23] He ordered a wharf to be built "for the conveniency of careening."[24] When he departed for England in November 1757, he left Commodore Alexander Colvill in command of the ships assigned to winter in the harbour, who set men to levelling the ground there and making an abutment. It was soon breached late in December by "hard northerly gales."[25] Not expecting to complete the wharf before the end of 1758, Holburne asked that a suitable officer, "who understands this kind of work," be sent out in the spring with artificers, as none could be found in Halifax to work for less than 5s. a day.[26]

Whatever advice the admirals and captains provided upon their return to England, the Admiralty took no immediate decision, as the matter never formally came before it. Boscawen, who was a member of the Admiralty Board when not serving at sea, had already made up his mind.[27] He preferred, not an island site, but somewhere in the northern suburbs on the Halifax side of the harbour, where the water was deepest and protection from gales greatest. In 1758, when the Admiralty finally directed the Navy Board to order its construction, it quoted William Pitt as its authority.[28] Boscawen, still unable to determine the site so taken up was he in 1758 by the summer siege of Louisbourg, appointed Commodore Philip Durell to take command of the ships assigned to winter in 1758-9 at Halifax and to select a suitable location.

The selection of a permanent site was Durell's principal contribution to the history of the careening yard. By the end of November he had settled on Gorham's Point, a mile north of the town walls at the site of a small abandoned farm. With some cleared land, there was a small house and two barns.[29] Its principal attraction for Durell, after having "sounded round the harbour," was its proximity to "deep water close to the shore, and good ground to drive piles."[30] The south end of the site contained a natural body of almost enclosed water to serve as a mastpond. At the north end a vigorous brook supplied drinking water, where in 1755 Spry had erected a watering wharf.[31] The northern boundary abutted a site occupied by naval provisions contractor Joshua Mauger's distillery and storehouse. Durell failed to inform the Admiralty of another significant feature of the location. It lay immediately beneath steeply rising ground which commanded the site. Unless fortifications were established and manned on the heights above it, the yard was indefensible to attack from the land side.

The site at first was not large. In time, parcel by parcel, it expanded. In December 1758 and February 1759 two lots were bought, amounting to about five acres.[32] Also, in February 1759, seven additional adjoining acres were granted to Durell, between Gerrish and North Street. On the land side along Water Street this measured 1,240 feet. Two small additions were made in the 1760s. In 1762 Spry secured a grant of land at the north end of the yard, for which Colvill had applied, to serve as a cooperage. When Colvill departed in 1761 the plot had been disputed by Mauger. Spry claimed a prior promise from the governor when, in 1755, he had built the small wharf for watering his majesty's ships, to which this spot was contiguous. The second acquisition occurred only in January 1765, when a lot was added to the north end of the yard beyond the watering wharf. Before the end of the war against rebel American, 1776–83, only one additional piece of land was acquired. Several acres of land, beyond Mauger's distillery, were purchased on which a new naval hospital was built in 1782.[33]

As Durell was absent from Halifax for much of 1759 and too distracted to give detailed attention to the planned yard – he sailed out of the harbour on 5 May with his squadron of sixteen ships, making first for Louisbourg and then Quebec – decisions about contracts with builders devolved on the naval storekeeper, Joseph Gerrish, a New England immigrant.[34]

Winter prevented any construction except that which was required to enlarge and convert Gorham's barns at the south end of the site near the water into a storehouse. This was the first substantial structure to be readied. Of wood frame construction, it housed naval stores, including the careening gear, left there by two storeships in 1758.[35]

With spring much work was hurriedly completed. There were three principal and several secondary contractors who completed the work for less than £8,000, a paltry sum. John Burbidge made the road from the gateway across the swamp into the yard. Joseph Pierpont blasted the large rocks in what was to become the mastpond, as well as elsewhere on the site. He was paid by the blast and there were 363 of them all told. He and others moved between 20,000 and 24,000 cubic yards of soil from the higher ground to the lower in order to level the site, while he removed 5,500 cubic yards of mud from the mastpond. A very great deal of rock was carted to make land to support the foundations of the principal buildings.

Breastworks were built in several places. Pierpont was paid £596 to build two breastworks. The first ran from the waterfront facing the mastpond round the southeast corner, past the south storehouse to the little wharf, a distance of 1,438 feet. The second continued from the little wharf to the south careening wharf, at the entrance on the east side of the mastpond – a distance of 2,949 feet – and around the pitch house and boathouse slips. He earned another £485 in completing the boathouse slip leading to the harbour and the south wharf pier – some 140 feet long and fifty feet wide – adjoining the smiths' shop for fishing the crane to weigh anchors. This payment included digging the foundation of a capstan house and a trench to the mastpond, the building of a breastwork behind the stores to preserve the beach – measuring some 192 feet long, twenty feet wide and five feet high – filling it with stone and earth, and covering and levelling it with gravel. Burbidge made ground on which the capstan house and the two storehouse wings stood. He was paid £580 to construct a breastwork of timber for the capstan house. For £1,015, he built as well the north careening wharf and filled it with stones.

The principal buildings – capstan house, masthouse, and boathouse – were erected by three contractors. Joseph Marshall built the capstan house, 261 feet by forty feet, and adjoining storehouses, 190 feet by forty feet, for £1,134. The work, with its "Lutheran windows" was completed only in 1760. John Burbidge built the masthouse, 120 feet by sixty-five feet. From its south end he also built the masthouse slip, sixty-five feet by thirty feet, to the mastpond, at a cost of £465. Finally, for £292, William Ingolls built the boathouse, 120 feet by eighty feet, its roof being supported by eight large pillars. The principal buildings were erected on stone foundations enclosing a low hill; the buildings were framed in timber, initially finished in clapboards with shingle roofs. Painted with red ochre, the buildings had white window frames and doors.

Two careening wharfs, with pits to accommodate yardarms when a ship was being careened, were framed in timbers and filled with stone and earth, then covered with heavy planking. Sets of careening capstans at the side of each wharf were put in place to heave down the ships before cleaning.

The boathouse and slip, masthouse and mastpond, the smiths' shop, anchor wharf, pitch house, and brush house were all completed in 1760. A breastwork along the waterfront was also begun and a ten-foot high wooden fence was built on the land side of the yard. Near the gate was a guardhouse and porter's lodge, as well as a shed for the fire engines.

The work was performed under the eye of the master house carpenter, John Charlton, who was brought from England. In 1760 he prepared a ground plan, drawing elevations of the buildings in the yard with a perspective view.[36] Working parties of seamen, earning 6d. extra a day, did much of the back-breaking work such as moving earth and stone, unloading storeships, and stacking stores, timber, and lumber. Some artificers came from England as well as from the ships in harbour; most came from Massachusetts. There Benjamin Hallowell, the shipbuilder, concluded contracts with 187 of them, their return passage from Boston being paid by the yard each year. In these early days scarcely any such skilled workers were to be found available in Nova Scotia, when little more than boat building was undertaken and shipbuilding lay in the future. By the end of the summer of 1759, ships were at the wharf being careened, masted, and refitted.[37] Within a few years the first warship from the West Indies was refitted at the careening yard.[38]

As the war with France drew to a close in 1762, the future of the yard became a matter of concern. The Navy Board, initially dubious about the yard's creation, now became its principal advocate. "The convenient situation of his Majesty's yard at Halifax, its utility for heaving down ships stationed in North America, and supplying them with stores, and the preservation of the wharfs, storehouses, and other works erected there in the course of the war," the Board wrote to the Admiralty, "induce us to believe that the continuance of the naval officer and a very few artificers, will be of great advantage to his Majesty's service."[39] Retrenchment took the form of a greatly-reduced establishment with only fourteen places: a storekeeper and his clerk, a foreman of shipwrights and his apprentice, two shipwrights and two caulkers, one smith, one sailmaker, and four labourers who also acted as watchmen. As Halifax possessed by war's end both shipwrights and caulkers, "who may occasionally be hired to careen and refit, with the assistance of the carpenter's crew," from warships stationed on the North American coast, the Board was confident that the yard could fulfil its peacetime responsibilities.

Responsibility for the management of the yard, as no resident commissioner was appointed there until 1775, rested with successive squadron commodores. In 1762 Commodore Spry, for instance, wanted the Admiralty to order all ships on southern stations to refit at Halifax, "as nothing can be more convenient for that purpose than the King's Yard, made under the direction of Lord Colvill ... they might be supplied from hence with stores yearly without purchasing them at the exorbitant price in the colonies, which they have often been obliged to do."[40] Commodore Colvill later added to the workforce and appointed an acting master attendant and master shipwright, more for the refitting and care of his ships than for the yard buildings and wharfs.[41]

The Navy Board advised against making permanent appointments of a master shipwright and master attendant to the establishment, as "the utility of such officers must depend on the number of ships upon the station." Cost was the principal reason, "as houses must be built for them, besides many other contingencies."[42] Until the early 1770s, the yard made do with temporary appointments of such yard officers who lived aboard their ships and were paid an additional daily wage only.

Commodore Colvill witnessed the inevitable location of grog houses near the yard, when the town of Halifax still lay a mile to the south. "Drunkenness is remarkably prevalent at this place among the lower class of people," he remarked, "and seems to be encouraged by the licenses granted to the retailers of rum, whereby some addition is made to the revenues at the expense of the health & morals of the people."[43] As working parties of seamen came ashore to labour in the yard, men somehow obtained the spirits and subsequently became drunk and violent. Some were convicted of robbery, murder, and housebreaking, for which the convicted paid a terrible price. Although the yard was located almost a mile from town, at least two grog houses had been established close by the gate. "Our most notorious enemies," Colvill declared, were "Mrs Haws and Mrs Gunnel." When their licenses were revoked under their general shop licenses, they then sold rum not from inside their shops, but at the door "on Skittle Alley" nearby.

It was on Colvill's watch that the only case of theft of yard stores ever prosecuted by the Supreme Court of Nova Scotia occurred. Since the purpose of theft was resale, a fence to market the stolen property was needed and recruited. The detection and arrest of the culprits proceeded under the supervision of the storekeeper, Joseph Gerrish. On New Year's Day 1766, three marines guarding the yard stole naval slops valued at £12. Brought before the Supreme Court, they were found guilty. Pleading benefit of clergy, they were branded in turn on their left hands with the letter "T." Three weeks later they were also whipped at the cart's tail: five lashes at each of the six principal intersections in town.[44]

The crime had gone undetected for almost two weeks. Then one evening a scuttle on the upper floor of the capstan house was seen to have been left open. The store porter that evening hid himself in a vain attempt to snare the thieves. Investigation next day revealed that two bales of naval slops had been opened and as many as nineteen shirts had been removed, while two further bales were missing. Gerrish at once suspected either seamen from *Glasgow*, who were fitting her rigging in the building, or the marines on *Mermaid*, then on duty in the yard.[45] In his capacity as a justice of the peace, he issued a general search warrant. Led by the store porter, Moses Clark, the search party consisted of storekeeper's clerk Jacob Hurd, master shipwright Abraham Constable, foreman of shipwrights Elias Marshall, and a labourer. A diligent search revealed three dozen shirts, besides other slop clothes. A sergeant of marines, Michael Geasey, and a marine private, Charles Higgins, both deeply implicated, confessed and were admitted as king's evidence.[46]

Besides the three convicted, five of the accused receivers were likewise indicted, four of whom – John Fry, grog shop owner Eleanor McGregor,[47] John Jones, and tinman John Brown – were convicted as accessories and fined £5 each for buying or receiving slop clothes from seamen or marines.[48] Others were implicated, but with evidence too flimsy no charges were laid against them. They included the tailor Frazier, Walter Harkness, Henry Potter, John Williams, and merchant sailor Isaac Higgins.[49] When offered the goods, others refused to buy.[50] The store porter swore that slops had been stored in the loft of the capstan house and locked up together since 1764. None had ever been issued and the room had always remained locked except to fetch oakum, also stored there.[51] It was the naval storekeeper's opinion that the stores would be much more safely guarded by an addition of four more sober watchmen, "who have wives & children dependant on the good living which the pay ... affords them than on six marines and a sergeant, who are from home, or perhaps have no home, no families to be distressed nor any reputation to lose by anything they can do."[52]

The arrival of Commodore Sir Samuel Hood in the summer of 1767 led soon led to major renovations in the yard. The previous winter's storms and frost had been "uncommonly severe" and "wrecked havoc" on the wharfs and other buildings in the naval yard.[53] "The earth has hove up and the stones sunk so that the Yard is full of holes, particularly the wharf," he noted. "The gutters and bridges have been demolished, which has prevented the water from draining and the level part ankle deep in water all summer." He informed the Admiralty that "the greatest part of the yard is made ground, and as large stones were thrown in without being properly filled round, the frost has proved it a kind of subterraneous work."[54]

He also reminded the Admiralty that the yard was built under a high hill "from which the rains rush with great impetuosity, and the weight of it laying against the breastwork or boarded wall has occasioned it to lean in many places and must have thrown the greatest part down, if the foundation had not yielded. I have caused a deep trench to be dug from one end to the other, and in the most proper places have opened drains, which by means of gutters paved with stones will carry the water into the harbour and mastpond."[55] He was also critical of the materials used in the construction of all the main buildings in the yard. "The chief part of the wood work in the yard is hemlock ... by no means fit for buildings. But ... it was the only wood to be got conveniently," in 1759–60.[56] He first suggested that it would be much cheaper, instead of constantly repairing and painting a wooden fence, to erect a stone or brick wall on the land side.

A survey of the capstan house, the two wings which were the principal storehouses, and the range of stores at the south end of the yard revealed that the sills and much of the lower framing were decayed, with some twelve beams in the sail loft broken. Much shingling and clapboarding were needed round the so-called Lutheran windows, owing to the "sills being level with the surface and in many places underground causing them to rot sooner than if they had been above ground." As excessively hard frost had heaved the foundations, the roofs and windows let in rain and snow. The surveyors suggested that the buildings needed to be reinforced with "diagonal and perpendicular shores, taking out the rotten sills and lower floor, sinking a foundation below the depth of the frost to a point at least a foot above ground, setting the buildings on oak sills, then framing in new beams and joists." Every second Lutheran window, except in the sail loft, was to be removed. If finished in shingles and clapboard, the cost was estimated at £2,192, with a further £568 for the south storehouse, £872 for the mastpond, £1,124 for breastwork, and £574 for the anchor and careening wharfs.[57]

When the work was undertaken in 1768, ships' crews, who undertook the most arduous work of preparing the ground for the foundations, had to dig to a depth of eighteen feet before they found solid ground.[58] As Commodore Hood remarked: "Everyday experience makes me wonder how the building stood so long for want of a foundation. The north part was quite a quicksand. After digging down fifteen feet, [we] were obliged to drive 160 piles which were cut off even and were covered with thick plank to lodge the foundation on. The quantity of stones we were obliged to bury, where piles were not necessary, is inconceivable." In completing the new foundation, "the ground being so soft and miry ... the workmen have sunk by their own weight only, mid-leg deep." Finally, in order to strengthen the roof before the slating began, additional beams and posts had to be inserted. Yet these improvements convinced Hood that the new structure "will be the last, as I am sure the building will stand forever."[59]

Hood boasted that the new breastwork was so well-built that "no storm or tempest will be able to hurt it in the days of the youngest man now living."[60] He repeated the boast a year later, "The Yard is also very effectually secured towards the sea, by a breastwork sixteen feet broad and filled between the piles and plank of the two sides, with clay & gravel and I am certain no weather can affect it for the age of man."[61]

Hood returned to the theme of gradual destruction with his first despatch in 1768. The yard, he explained, "becomes more and more ruinous every week. A great part of the watering wharf was washed away in the winter. There are two great holes about 10 ft. sq. and several smaller ones, and the wharf is less than 3 years old."[62] A month later his miseries had been multiplied when a gale with hurricane force winds struck and lasted about twelve hours. The careening yard was quite considerably damaged.

> The demolition of the south breastwork exposes the whole yard, but more particularly the outer mastpond, the sea has now full scope without control, which is always very great with a south east wind ...

All breastworks and small wharfs round the yard, with platforms, sentinel boxes, and necessary houses in part carried away, the remainder much damaged. The anchor wharf much damaged and crane carried away. Great part of boathouse slip torn up and washed away. Chimnies ... blown down & shingling much damaged, 1 launch and 2 boats lost, and rest of Yard boats much damaged. Platform of the cellar for pitch & tar blown up.

In Halifax harbour more than fifty sloops and shallops were either sunk at the wharfs or beat to pieces and not a single wharf but is in great measure destroyed. This is truly deplorable in so poor a place as Halifax. Many families are totally ruined.

It was really astonishing with what violence the sea was blown against the house I live in, and though I had several men carrying away water the whole night, there was seldom less than three feet in my cellar, which has done me great mischief. I never saw so great a storm in my life. Captain Allen and several other officers in the squadron with Admiral Holburne off Louisbourgh say that this gale of wind was more violent as well as more lasting.[63]

Hood's successive reports set both the Admiralty and the Navy Board conferring on the future of the yard. The Navy Board, though shocked that "works so lately erected should be in want of such repairs, which can only be accounted for, from their being of wood, which in that country is of short duration, and built in a hurry to answer the necessities of the service at that time," recommended their phased-in repair, starting with the buildings most urgently needing attention.[64]

With the work in hand in the summer of 1768, Hood told the Navy Board that "all works of a public nature ought to be well executed. Duration is thereby given them, which they so often fail of, by being slovened over, as is generally the case when they are performed by contract, especially in such a place as this, where there is perhaps not one man capable of contracting."[65] Of the masons and bricklayers he was contemptuous. "The master himself is honest ... but the workmen are sad drunken fellows." He wanted, instead of contract labour, "to enter the workmen on the yard list, have them called with the roll, checked off every hour they are absent or idle, and have a trusty person to oversee them from morning to night."[66]

The stone, at 2s.6d. per ton, came from the Halifax side of the harbour at Chebucto Head.[67] It was dug out and moved to the high water mark.[68] Two stages were erected there to load the quarried stone to be shipped to the yard.[69] This quarrying work was undertaken by ships' crews.

The finished work greatly pleased both the commodore and the naval storekeeper. "The capstan house with the north & south wings are compleatly rebuilt with stone," Hood noted, while Gerrish wrote of the masons' efforts as "an extream good piece of work."[70] Slaters came from Boston "as none of the masons we had before understood the business."[71] Hood boasted of the "exceeding fine slate, which is dug upon the king's land directly opposite the Yard,"[72] and "superior to any in America."[73]

When the yard's wooden fence, already "quite decayed," was damaged in a week-long hard gale in November 1769, Hood recommended that it be replaced with a stone wall.[74] "A stone wall to the land side ... will give great safety to all the buildings. As the wooden fence is so dry that it might be set fire to by carelessness of a drunken sailor with his pipe. It would have been ablaze in five minutes a few weeks since had it not been for a gentleman passing by, who extinguished some shavings on fire close to the fence.[75] I am very sure stone will be much the cheapest in the end."[76] Without waiting for the Navy Board's approval, he ordered the work to begin from the midpoint between the high- and low-water-marks on the south side. "Notwithstanding the sentinels about the yard, the sailors or the people they buy rum of are almost continuously making holes in the night to put bottles through," he added.[77]

In January 1770 he recommended erecting "at the back of the capstan house" and of equal dimensions to it, a new storehouse to replace "the one too far gone to decay."[78] This work was undertaken more or less simultaneously with the building of the wall. Detached from the west gable ends of the storehouse wings, it had the same dimensions as the capstan house, 261 feet by forty feet.

Rear Admiral James Gambier, Hood's successor, only once visited Halifax harbour, on his way home in 1771. The year before he had promised to inspect the careening yard once "the present emergency ends."[79] If he wrote a report on what he found, there is no record. What survives is a drawing he had made of the yard with a proposed drydock, the first such proposal for any of the overseas yards.

This is of considerable interest and some importance. Had a drydock been built in Halifax, as Gambier appeared to have suggested in 1771, British naval control of the waters of coastal North America probably could not have been successfully challenged. In 1771 Halifax, like the other overseas bases, was no more than a careening yard; no warship had yet been built there nor any given a major refit. The building of a dockyard would have allowed for both.

Dependent only on careening yards in Halifax harbour and on Manhattan Island, naval commanders-in-chief, when ships needed major structural repairs or thorough rebuilding, were forced to order them to be patched up in one or other of these bases before making a summer's crossing to Plymouth or Portsmouth, both already heavily burdened. The construction of the drydock at Halifax would have obviated this need. The navy could have operated for long periods independently of home dockyards. To have taken the decision would have also meant that those in London intended to supply from England the necessary artificers – principally shipwrights, caulkers, and ship's carpenters to carry out the work. The limited number of artificers in the Halifax yard was the reason later given by Commodore Sir George Collier for sending home *Lizard* (28) in January 1777, even though the work could have been undertaken there.[80] In 1778 he sent home *Mermaid*, damaged in her upper works, yards, and rigging by a violent gale while at anchor in Halifax harbour, and *Fox*, much shattered when taken off Newfoundland and in being retaken off Nova Scotia. His explanation was both the shortage of necessary stores and the length of time it would take to equip each for cruising.[81]

Dockyards were later proposed for Antigua in 1795 – a double dock no less – and for Kingston, Upper Canada, in 1819.[82] In 1819 Robert Barrie, resident commissioner of the careening yard in Kingston, Upper Canada, where a ship of 102 guns was built in the 1812–14 war, sent the Navy Board an elaborate drawing of the proposed drydock to be built there.[83]

The first overseas base to have the issue seriously joined was Malta when the resident commissioner proposed it in 1806. Work began in 1811, but after seepage in the porous sandstone proved at that time an insoluble technical problem, the project was abandoned as a failure in 1816 and revived only thirty years later.[84] Before 1820 it was suggested that a drydock be built in the new yard at Bermuda, but its largely coral rock constituted a technical problem as difficult as at Malta earlier. Not until 1870 was one floated across the ocean to the Ireland Island base.[85] Oddly enough, the rocky strata surrounding Halifax harbour was ideal for a drydock, as shown when one was opened by private interests, with an annual Admiralty subsidy, north of the yard and hospital complex in 1889.[86]

With Commodore Hood's departure in 1770, his successors found themselves based in Boston, owing to political turmoil in New England. Until a resident commissioner was appointed more than five years later, the commanding officers merely forwarded the suggestions of the yard officers to the Admiralty. Rear Admiral John Montagu, for instance, in 1772, performed this small service, when Gerrish and Constable wanted to repair the masthouse slip and to rebuild the mastpond by removing its timber siding and enclosing it with brick or stone, at a cost of £1,525. In addition, they wanted, as a fire precaution, to re-roof all yard buildings with readily available slate.[87] Finally, they hoped to build a proper shed to house seamen while their ships were being careened, to be erected between the officers' lodge and the guardhouse.[88]

The Navy Board took a dim view of all this. As slate was more expensive than shingles that were already on site, Gerrish was instructed to delay slating until a new roof in any one building was needed.[89] As Montagu failed to forward the estimate the yard officers had prepared and as the Navy Board declined to act without it though Montagu had summarized its contents for them, the matter involving both the safety of the sail loft and the comfort of sailors was delayed for a year. Such was the Board's perversity on occasion! On one matter the Board took the initiative. When Montagu's successor, Vice Admiral Samuel Graves appointed a temporary master attendant for the Halifax yard in 1774 and requested a suitable office for him, it ordered one to be built at the south end of the capstan house.[90]

In another matter, Montagu responded with effective personal interest in one group of employees paid by the yard's naval storekeeper. He vehemently objected to the Navy Board's plan to replace the twenty-eight crew members – all of them Canadiens – of Joseph F.W. DesBarres's survey vessel with seamen from ships in the squadron. He doubted such men could render "every service equal to the Canadians that are well acquainted from long practice with the country, the duty required from them."[91] A year later the Navy Board, having decided to retain the Canadiens, now objected to them being paid quarterly by the yard, an initiative taken by Montagu himself. Montagu pointed out that if the Board insisted that they be paid in London, their pay would be subject to considerable loss in negotiating through agents, "which they must naturally be obliged to do, for want of connections in England, or knowledge of the service."[92] Montagu's only motive was to encourage "the people who are all tradesmen and can have constant work to continue with Mr DesBarres during the summer, as without them it will be impossible for him to get through the business in the time he proposed, and they have declined continuing upon that service unless they were to be paid at Halifax every three months, it being the only support for their familys."

An issue of far greater importance which was to disrupt the DesBarres survey and much else, was the crisis ignited by the Boston Tea Party. Halifax was stripped of warships as the North American squadron concentrated off the New England coast. Initially the Navy Board had merely assigned a storekeeper's clerk to Boston. By March 1774 the Board wanted to appoint a naval storekeeper and a muster master, as Boston was to be supplied with naval stores directly from England rather than indirectly through Halifax.[93] William Fowler was the chosen storekeeper. After Boston was relinquished and New York successfully invaded in 1776, Fowler was sent there and spent the entire war running with consummate skill what grew into the most important naval base in North America.

The first significant test of the value of the navy's material investment in the Halifax careening yard came with the outbreak of this first American war. Hostilities at sea began within days of the battles at Concord and Lexington in April 1775. Montagu's successor, Vice Admiral Samuel Graves, was concerned with the safety of the Halifax yard. It was given a marine guard "with three watchmen at night, well equipped," he assured the Admiralty, "besides a patrol from eight in the evening to four in the morning, and every other precaution is taken to prevent losses by fire or thieves."[94]

Yet he later feared an attempt to destroy the Halifax base. The "rebels from the eastern part of New Hampshire would be sure of assistance not only from the town and country people, but even from the artificers of the yard," some of whom were from Massachusetts. These he presumed were "intimately connected with rebels that barely by not working they might throw us into many difficulties. I dare not suggest what such a set of fanatics are further capable of." Such wild ideas accurately reflect the hysteria which had begun to grip the naval commander.

The first resident commissioner, Capt. Marriot Arbuthnot, appointed in 1775, assured the Navy Board of the yard's security from external attack. There were more than three hundred cannon in Halifax and not gunners enough to man one-third of them. Some were moved to the yard. The military engineers erected three blockhouses on the high ground above the yard, and established Fort Coote on the hill north of the yard beyond Mauger's distillery. For his part, the commissioner established a battery of eight 24–pounders on the yard's northwest jetty. A parapet built of butts stuffed with spruce tops and the height of two men was supposedly proof against musket balls. This flimsy affair he sanguinely believed would effectively cover the gunners from musket fire should an enemy gain the high ground.[95] If the parapet was of little protection to gun crews, it proved a perfect ladder to enable seamen to scale "the wall at night, get drunk and keep" the new commissioner "in perpetual apprehension" that they would set fire to the capstan house. He begged for a hulk to be sent to Halifax to act as a receiving ship where seamen could be temporarily housed when their ships were being careened.

Commissioner Arbuthnot's suggestion reached the Board in mid-March 1776. Five weeks later the Board ordered two hulks, *Pembroke* and *Boulogne*, to Halifax with a boatswain and carpenter, including a servant, and a complement of seamen for each.[96] For additional wages, these men were occasionally employed in the yard, under the direction of the master attendant, in unloading storeships and stowing stores. At one point in 1777 they hauled spars out of the surrounding woods to be rafted to the mastpond.[97]

Three thousand miles away in the comfort of his lodgings in Craven Street, London, Rear Admiral Molyneux Shuldham, appointed to replace Graves in command in North America, raised a crucial point which Arbuthnot had failed to mention. "There will be a very extraordinary number of shipwrights and carpenters wanted for the service in North America."[98] Five months earlier the Navy Board had reminded Graves that the "principal magazine for stores should remain at Halifax and that his Majesty's ships and vessels should still clean and refit" there. Within the month of Shuldham writing his letter and the Admiralty's forwarding the matter to the Navy Board, plans took shape to despatch twenty-four volunteers to Halifax: eleven shipwrights, eight caulkers, three smiths, a foreman of smiths, and his apprentice.[99] Their terms of employment were very attractive. Their contract was for a minimum of three years. They were to receive double pay if Sunday work was required. Shipwrights and caulkers were each to be allowed a servant, or to be allowed 6d. a day after three years in lieu of a servant. Daily pay was 2s.6d. sterling, paid quarterly, either in Halifax or to their agents in England. For good behaviour they were guaranteed work later in an English dockyard.[100]

These volunteer artificers arrived in *Chatham* early in April and were housed in a shed "run up under the wall"[101] north of the gate, built for soldiers who might be landed to defend the yard.[102] The commissioner found several of them bad characters and dismissed them; most of the rest, as they were still needed, were not permitted to return to England in 1781 when they applied.[103]

Commissioner Arbuthnot, who complained that he had written so many letters since arriving in Nova Scotia that he had injured his eyesight, quickly proved how little vision he commanded. He was a man who either saw only problems or who created them. He first of all refused Governor Francis Legge a loan of £1,000 from the naval chest, needed to equip the militia, even though *Roebuck* had just delivered £10,000 to his naval storekeeper. Next, he felt constrained by his instructions from purchasing immediately, even while at war, a much-needed thirty-ton vessel for the use of the master attendant.[104] He failed to comply with the Board's request for a detailed report on the condition of the yard. Facing the anticipated arrival of artificers from England, he remained perplexed how to house them once they arrived. As he failed to despatch a storeship promptly to Boston, the naval storekeeper there had to purchase both shoes and stockings for the fleet.[105]

Yet he grew to understand the value of Halifax as a naval base. In 1777, when Admiral Lord Howe requested that naval stores be sent thereafter only to the New York yard, Arbuthnot reminded the First Lord of the Admiralty, Lord Sandwich, that the naval commander-in-chief was poorly placed to estimate what and where such supplies were needed. He pointed out that had Admiral Howe sent ships in 1776 to the Halifax yard instead of to those in the West Indies, they would all have been cleaned and readied for sea sooner. Moreover "their crews might have been refreshed with fresh provisions and hundreds of lives saved which ... were lost by sending men from the extremes of cold to heat."[106] He believed that at Halifax "we can work as long ... in the winter as can be done to the southward."

22   Part One: Naval Yard Complex

Despite the yard's best efforts to refit the fleet in North America during the war, it acted only as more a supplement to the temporary yard established on Manhattan Island. In the aftermath of the military defeat at Saratoga, and in anticipation of French entry into the war by the end of 1777 the Admiralty, instead of planning a major increase in the facilities at Halifax with the attendant increase in the establishment, took quite a different path. It ordered the Navy Board to appoint a resident commissioner and staff with power to form an additional naval establishment at either Rhode Island, New York, or Philadelphia, as Admiral Lord Howe had advised.[107] Three weeks later the Board recommended not one establishment but three, with each being assigned a naval storekeeper, master attendant, and master shipwright with the allowances then enjoyed by the Halifax establishment. For artificers they recommended thirty: twelve shipwrights, eight caulkers, four each of smiths and house carpenters and two sailmakers.[108] The matter proved a dead letter except as it applied to New York, for Philadelphia was abandoned in 1778 and Rhode Island a year later.

At the war's end in 1783 the naval yard was without a commissioner in residence. Capt. Sir Andrew Snape Hamond, who was both lieutenant governor and resident commissioner of the careening yard, had left his post in a fit of hurt pride that January. He had been superseded as lieutenant governor by John Parr, a friend of the new administration in Whitehall that had replaced Lord North's earlier in 1782.

In conclusion, was the Halifax naval yard, started as part of Pitt's North American strategy, worth the estimated £515,000 spent there by the end of 1783? To begin to answer the question, we must remember that when Louisbourg was taken in 1758 and Quebec in 1759, it was owing only marginally to services provided by the naval yard, then under construction. Rather, it was the decision to winter over in Halifax harbour a strong naval squadron that enabled the British to be off Louisbourg in 1758 and into the Gulf of St Lawrence in 1759 unusually early. This turned the tide against France when the British repeated this early concentration in 1760 and ensured the collapse of French power in North America. Only with the completion of the principal buildings and wharfs in 1760 could it be said that the Halifax naval yard made some appreciable contribution to victory in North America.

Was the yard decisive in the war against rebel American? It could have been decisive had the Admiralty built a drydock there. There is some evidence that this was the advice in 1771 of one of its most maligned admirals, James Gambier. Had this been done and the workforce proportionately increased, it would have allowed many more warships to be repaired in North America instead of sending them across the Atlantic to the already over-burdened dockyards in England. This might have given the edge to the British in the war in American waters fought, from 1778, principally with France. As it was, large numbers of warships, temporarily worn out by continuous service in the western Atlantic, had to wait their turn to undergo major refits in the English drydocks, the only ones then in existence. That such an idea was not taken into consideration may reflect the supreme overconfidence which afflicted the navy between 1759 and 1778. As hostilities ensued, Halifax proved itself useful in supplying Boston in the year leading to the withdrawal of British forces from that port in March 1776. Once New York became the principal naval yard later in 1776, Halifax had an important but ancillary role, where a minority of the ships of the North American fleet was careened, refitted, and stored. At various times there were three other such American bases available, at New York, the most important, at Newport from 1776 to 1779, and at Charleston from 1779 to 1782. These together sustained the British naval effort. Still, whenever a French fleet chose to make for an American port from 1778 to 1782 or to enter the Chesapeake, partly to avoid the hurricane season in the West Indies, it did so more or less with impunity, notwithstanding the efforts of all the North American careening yards, Halifax included.

At the very least, the Halifax base helped to preserve Nova Scotia as a British possession. Yet so few naval units were assigned to Nova Scotian waters during the war that it was not until 1777 that Nova Scotia was free of invasion threat. Only with the destruction of the American fleet in Penobscot Bay in 1779 was the war in the Gulf of Maine carried to the rebels. That the war in Nova Scotia's waters was beginning to turn in favour of the navy based at Halifax is clear from the fact that a year earlier mast contractors for the navy began to harvest the forests in the St John River valley, a matter discussed in chapter 8. Their efforts during the war not only allowed for the adequate supply of the Halifax yard but also that of New York, Jamaica, and Antigua. Still, the navy at its Halifax base could not prevent American pirates and privateers from raiding with impunity every part of the Nova Scotian coast, especially the western shore from Lunenburg to Annapolis. Such rebel vessels even took prizes at the very entrance to

Halifax harbour itself. They took at least 225 vessels alone in Nova Scotian waters.[109]

What more specifically did the navy receive for such outlays at Halifax? Firstly, in material terms, it built and maintained a careering [yard], overseen by a naval storekeeper until 1775 when a resident commissioner was first appointed.[110] When Henry Duncan arrived in 1783 to assume the duties of commissioner, there were sixteen buildings surrounded by a mile-and-a-half of stone walls. Nearby there was a large new naval hospital that will be described in chapter 4.

Secondly, the yard regularly refitted all the ships of the North American squadron in peacetime and a minority of them in wartime, as well as those occasionally stationed either at Newfoundland or the West Indies. This was the work for which the yard had been established. The work of refitting at Halifax focused on external hull repairs of warships "limited to what could be tackled on the careen."[111] Warships with major structural defects or requiring complete rebuilding were invariably sent home. The principal refitting tasks involved careening and caulking, repairs to keels and rudders, replacing or repairing damaged masts, bowsprits, yards, orspars, rigging, and sails and, from the mid-1770s, refastening or replacing copper sheathing. It involved loading and unloading guns, powder, and shot. Working parties from ships in harbour, enabling sailors both to get ashore and to earn extra wages, were used regularly to unload storeships as well as to help the yard workforce in its specific refitting tasks undertaken by ship's caulkers, shipwrights, carpenters, and sailmakers. Other refitting tasks regularly completed at Halifax included making masts, topmasts, and yards, usually winter work for artificers.[112]

Thirdly, it refitted a variety of other government vessels. These included vessels belonging to the governments of Cape Breton – when it was established as a separate colony in 1784 – and of Nova Scotia, as well as of the Board of Ordnance and the military establishment in Halifax. In addition, there was the refitting of vessels used in the survey of the coasts of North America undertaken in the 1760s and 1770s by James Cook, Joseph F.W. DesBarres, and Samuel Holland.

To complete all this work the yard maintained a workforce, which, at its largest in 1782–3, numbered less than 200 men, including the commissioner and the three respective officers: the naval storekeeper, the master shipwright, and the master attendant. The size of the workforce fluctuated in intervals of war and peace. In peacetime both the establishment and the number of workers on the "extra" list shrank considerably.[113] Towards the end of 1762, for instance, the Navy Board suggested to the Admiralty that the "convenient situation of His Majesty's yard at Halifax, its utility in heaving down ships stationed in North America, and supplying them with stores, and the preservation of the wharfs, storehouses and other works erected there in the course of the war" required only a naval storekeeper with a workforce of thirteen.[114] Indeed, by July 1763 the workforce fell from seventy-eight to just sixteen, and in November there were only eight employed, with labourers doing double-duty as night watchmen, a most unsatisfactory arrangement. Yet two years earlier, an average of 121 were employed in the yard including twenty-seven shipwrights and caulkers, twenty-one labourers, and sixteen boatmen.[115] By 1765 the Navy Board was being pressured by the commander of the North American squadron, Commodore Colvill, then involved in an unequal battle with American colonial smugglers, to appoint a master shipwright and master attendant.[116] Colvill expanded the workforce to carry out necessary repairs to the yard structures so that in the spring and summer of 1764 employment rose to an average of fifty-five. When the bulk of his squadron returned to home waters in 1766, Colvill reduced the workforce to twenty-three including the naval storekeeper and his clerk.[117] With Commodore Hood's arrival in 1767 and the decision to reconstruct the capstan house and the storehouse wings, and then to build the sail loft to complete the central quadrangle, employment rose to an average of 180 in the spring and summer of 1769 with an average of 141 for the entire year. Numbers declined thereafter but only to an average of 120 between 1770 and 1775.

Upon the outbreak of hostilities with American rebels in 1775, owing to the shortage of artificers in Nova Scotia, smiths, shipwrights, and caulkers were recruited from the home yards at Deptford, Woolwich, Chatham, Portsmouth, and Plymouth.[118] Then the yard's establishment rose to 142, which included thirty-seven shipwrights and caulkers, thirteen house carpenters and joiners, and thirty-seven labourers.[119] The extra list included at times up to another fifty-two men; the average for 1776–83 was 159. With this and other expansions of the workforce, Halifax nevertheless would have been overwhelmed by the refitting needs of the naval units concentrated in North America from 1776 onwards, had not the Admiralty in 1777 given leave to the Navy Board to create further naval establishments, as we have noted, at Rhode Island, New York, Philadelphia, or elsewhere, as recommended by Lord Howe.[120]

If the Navy Board was obliged in the late 1750s, against its better judgment, to agree to the establishment of Halifax yard, it soon became convinced of its utility. Thereafter, to 1819, it defended its ill-begotten offspring. As it had in 1762, now again in 1782, as the war drew to a close the Navy Board recommended the continued use of the Halifax yard. In the face of the Admiralty's search for economies as the American war sputtered to its humiliating conclusion, the Navy Board supported the Halifax yard's need for the continuation of the appointments there both of a commissioner and a master attendant in peacetime. "The importance of Halifax," it explained, "under the circumstances of refitting the whole of the ships on the American station, of supplying New York and the West Indies with ... masts" was so vital that a yard commissioner should be continued there after the war.[121] Such mast contracts could only properly be concluded by a commissioner, it argued. In response to an Admiralty order of 20 October 1783 to explain why a master attendant was needed at Halifax they noted: "Being in the neighbourhood of a separate state and which may occasion large & speedy armaments being sent there. Being the only port and yard of any consequence on that side of the Atlantic. Being a boisterous coast and ships subject to disasters which may require heaving down. Having the station of Newfoundland and Quebec in its neighbourhood, and being the only port for refitting the ships employed on them. Being a considerable port in point of extent and ships requiring assistance in coming in and out."[122] The Admiralty acceded to the Navy Board's wishes; the peacetime establishment numbered 116, including twenty-six shipwrights and caulkers, forty labourers, and ten watchmen.[123]

Despite the yard's forbidding ten-foot high wall – built to keep seamen in as much as intruders out – it was no prison. It had become an important urban institution of some use to the Empire and of considerably more value to the harbour and the towns that grew on its shores. A vital pulsating organism but somewhat worn out in the extreme hurry of wartime emergencies and uncertainties, it survived and was renewed in the decade of peace that followed, and in its new roles in the long wars thereafter with France and, less traumatically, with the new republic across the Gulf of Maine.

Chapter Two

DEVELOPMENT AND EXPANSION, 1783–1819

"The men of war usually anchor off the naval yard, which a stranger may easily distinguish by the masting sheers."[1]

However demoralized by the loss of the heart of its North American empire in 1783, the British government resolved to protect what remained of its possessions. For Nova Scotia, divided in 1784 into three colonies when Cape Breton and New Brunswick became separate jurisdictions, the British navy became the effective guarantor of its defence. Lingering hopes harboured by some Nova Scotians of forming a state within the remarkable political experiment underway in the United States were thereby blasted by the presence of the Royal Navy, the ultimate instrument of British policy. The modesty of its naval base in Halifax harbour, frequently neglected and often inadequately manned for the variety of tasks required of it, effectively symbolized the North American squadron's diminished importance for a quarter-century after 1783.

This relative decline in the strategic importance of Nova Scotia was not reflected in the construction undertaken in the naval yard after 1783. The navy acquired much more land round Halifax harbour and many new buildings were erected. This expansion was undertaken at the same time as the annual struggle to maintain existing wharfs, breastworks, walls, and buildings preoccupied the yard when the workforce was not actually carrying out its principal responsibility: refitting and supplying warships based there.

The more important land acquisitions lay at the north end of the yard, both between the yard walls and those of the new hospital, as well as along the harbour shore and beyond the hospital complex, encompassing property overlooking the hospital from the height of land. In June 1785, twenty acres lying to the south of the grounds of the new naval hospital were added.[2] Almost thirty years later in 1814, for an eight-acre lot was deeded H£1,000 by Andrew Bauer, butcher, on this rising ground overlooking the hospital. It became the site of the commander-in-chief's mansion.

In 1787 Commissioner Duncan was informed that the "stream of water and the land through which it runs into the harbour," at the north end of the yard had never been granted to the navy. "As the water which at present supplies the yard and shipping is in no way sufficient for a fleet, I know of no place so fit for that purpose as the spot you now ask my opinion about."[3] Duncan thereupon asked Lieutenant Governor John Wentworth to reserve the tract for the crown.

One piece of land along the beach, privately owned, separated the yard from the naval hospital. When Henry Duncan was named commissioner in 1783, he had been given directions "to purchase the ground between the yard and hospital, if he approved of the plan to build a wharf at the northwest end of the yard, which had been proposed for the purpose of having a ship's bottom out to the southward, and that the yard artificers might be able to work better upon her in winter." As he found the plot "of little or no worth, but a distillery standing upon it of no service to government, and the proprietors supposing it was wanted for the king's use, placed a high value upon it," he made no offer for it.[4] In September 1790 some five and a half acres were added to the north end of the yard, for which the Navy Board paid £500 to the heirs of Joshua Mauger.[5] Finally in 1816, Commissioner Philip Wodehouse and Rear Admiral Edward Griffith requested the grant of a lot to the north of the yard as a potential site for an expanded mastpond.[6]

Two small additions were also made at the south end of the yard. There the town's growth, stimulated by the demands of war from 1793, brought Halifax urban development inexorably closer. In 1786 a water lot near the mastpond was reserved for the navy where masting timbers could be stored.[7] In 1815, when Commissioner Wodehouse learned that a lot adjoining the south boundary of the yard was to be escheated, he applied to the lieutenant governor on behalf of the crown for the grant. Its value to Wodehouse was as a firebreak, "as the great increase in building here, which is entirely of wood" had brought the town uncomfortably close to the yard.[8] It might also serve as a mast-

Development and Expansion, 1783–1819   29

pond, as the one at the north end of the yard was then "in a most defective state."[9] By 1817 the town had reached the yard. As a landing place had been completed at the new Halifax fish market, Commissioner Wodehouse directed that "seamen, mariners or their wives coming on shore on leave from the squadron, officers' servants going to market, and other private business" were forbidden thereafter from landing at the stairs or coming through the yard."[10]

One final acquisition should be noted. In 1800 land at Tufts Cove "nearly opposite the naval hospital" on the Dartmouth side of the harbour was suggested by Commissioner Isaac Coffin as a suitable place for depositing masts.[11] He asked Lieutenant Governor Wentworth for a lot to the depth of 600 feet on either side of the cove. Despite Commissioner Duncan's belief that a "better and more convenient" location was on the south limits of the yard "immediately under our own eye," the land was acquired.[12] This was not the first piece of land used by the navy on the Dartmouth shore. An important naval watering place situated there drew from the stream with its source in Albro Lake that came tumbling down the hillside into the harbour at a little cove which formed the northern boundary of Dartmouth Common.[13]

The principal new structures built within the yard itself after 1783 were to accommodate staff. These included the commissioner's mansion built in 1785–6, a substantial tenement to accommodate the three principal yard officers – collectively known as the respective officers – completed in 1793, and a modest house for the boatswain in 1814, erected beside the road leading from the yard north to the hospital. Finally, on the height of land overlooking the hospital, a mansion was raised between 1814 and 1819 for the naval commander-in-chief. This last structure will be considered in chapter 4.

Structures to enhance the capacity of the yard, including two new mastponds, were established both at Tufts Cove across the harbour on the Dartmouth shore and at the north end of the yard where a new wharf was also built. Beyond the yard enclosure a prison compound was built on Melville Island at the head of the North West Arm, while several buildings were added to the hospital complex.[14] In general the Navy Board instructed the yard officers "at the commencement of every year ... to send us a plan thereof properly dated and to distinguish by reference what part thereof was finished in the proceeding year, beginning now to show what was done last year."[15]

The resident commissioner's house was the first major new structure built during the decade of peace. Earlier commissioners used what had been the commodore's house.[16] Earlier still this clapboard and shingle-roofed house had been built for the naval storekeeper.[17] Alexander Colvill was the first commodore to occupy it.[18] Samuel Hood found its three parlours, kitchen on the ground floor, and two bedrooms on the second floor too modest an accommodation. As it lacked a garret, his servants, both men and women, had to live elsewhere. Hood raised a "skilling roof, by which I gain two rooms," and charged the Navy Board the cost of the improvement.[19] Hood also built a coach house and stable along with a pigeon roost and hothouse.[20] On several occasions early in the winter of 1767–8 "above two feet of water have been in the cellars of the house ... I fear I shall be the great sufferer by it, having some wines for my consumption ... which in all probability will be spoiled."[21]

Upon Commissioner Duncan's arrival in 1783, he found the house "so much out of repair" that it would be cheaper to build a new one than continue to maintain it.[22] Permission to build came in 1785 with a budget of £2,186.[23] The work was completed only in June 1787.[24] Aligned on a north-south axis, the sixty foot by forty-six foot wood-framed house was built in the classical style. Three stories high, its classical design recognized the importance of providing as much natural light as possible. It had five sixteen-pane windows on each side of the first two floors. The sloping roof held four twelve-pane dormers both front and back, with two more on each of the other sides. Two chimneys pierced the roof on either side and at some distance from a handsome cupola, erected where the roof flattened and adorned with a weather-vane.[25] A fenced circular driveway led to the main north-facing entrance, where two fine sets of steps curved upwards into the portico. Similar sets of steps led to the equally handsome south entrance of the house which looked down onto the harbour toward the town and its expanding commercial wharfs.

Extensive alterations were made to the house in 1799, when Commissioner Duncan was on leave in England. These were occasioned when the house was occupied by His Royal Highness, the Duke of Kent, before his own new military mansion was in a "fit state to receive him."[26] The duke ordered modifications made to the basement and to the ground floor by extending them into abbreviated east and west wings.[27] The work was completed by yard artificers and labourers.[28]

Under Commissioner John Inglefield a dry-stone wall was erected

Development and Expansion, 1783–1819   31

at the house to replace a wooden fence, built earlier by Commissioner Sir Richard Hughes, which had become a mere "heap of rubbish."[29] The work was completed during the yard's slow season, in part by employing Inglefield's horses and servants at his own expense.

Inglefield, incidentally, was accused of having built an icehouse at public expense for his own convenience. Calling the anonymous complaint both "ridiculous and untrue," he explained that he had put ice in the cellar of the pigeon house, and had built a partition and door as a cold storage room to keep vegetables for winter use, the greenhouse built in 1772 having collapsed.

Perhaps motivated by observing the commissioner's house under construction, the principal yard officers pressed the Navy Board in 1786 to have houses built in the yard for them.[30] They, like most other yard workers, were housed in the northern suburbs of the town. The Admiralty requested estimates, but no decision was made.[31] Later in 1790 they again applied. Their newly-stated reasons, supported by Commissioner Duncan, were the high cost of renting accommodation in Halifax, the inadequacy of their housing allowance, and the precedents set in naval yards elsewhere.[32] The Admiralty Board's approval took two years.[33] They were built only in 1793.[34]

These handsome row houses, called tenements, cost only £750 altogether. Constructed on brick foundations, and with brick-nogged walls, they were finished in clapboard with shingled roofs.[35] Each was of three floors, the front and rear façades displayed five twelve-pane windows on the second floor and two on either side of the entrance on the ground floor, much in keeping with the commissioner's house. The first two floors had three windows each, on the gable ends. Facing onto the yard road leading from the main gate down to the smiths' shop and wharf, their back gardens opened onto the area behind the "new" storehouse and sail loft.[36]

A house on a much smaller scale was built in 1814 for the yard boatswain. As he was generally employed afloat and frequently at night, Commissioner Wodehouse recommended the boatswain's proposal to the Board. As it had approved a similar request from the Cape of Good Hope yard, the Board now recommended it to the Admiralty.[37] It was a modest affair, less than half the dimensions of any one of the respective officers' tenements. With the entrance on the gable end, it also was of three floors, each pierced by two windows.

Besides these new buildings, major structural alterations were also made, after 1783, to buildings and wharfs already standing in 1783. These included the buildings in the main quadrangle: the capstan house, its two wings, and the "new" storehouse. Also included were the other important yard buildings such as the masthouse, boathouse, and smiths' shop.

The capstan house, facing the careening and anchor wharfs, substantially rebuilt in the 1760s, was subjected to searching remarks, when Commissioner Duncan arrived in 1783. "I do not see the utility of windows or frames outside the capstan house," he wrote.

> It will be better to build them up, the same as the rest of the wall. The house will be sufficiently lighted from the front. The floor of this house has for some years been wet, owing to the drains, which run under it, being choaked. These have been opened and cleaned, paved in the bottom, walls built on the sides, and covered on the top with large stones, which lie (for the convenience of getting at hereafter) within eight or ten inches of the surface. This has furnished us with clay sufficient to make good the floor in its first state, which, now that it will be kept dry, in my opinion, will be better, more durable, and attended with little expense, whereas the flooring it with wood, would be considerable and would soon decay.[38]

Fifteen years later the building again needed close attention. By 1800, the window shutters in the capstan house loft were so decayed that nails would not hold the hinges and fastenings. The careening storehouse was too small to contain the careening gear, working hawsers, and other gear. The hawsers instead were coiled in the capstan house "exposed to the frequent irregularities committed by the crews of ships alongside the wharf," in the opinion of the master attendant.[39] New floors were required at least once a decade thereafter, the iron anchor cables first having to be removed by labourers.[40]

Attached to the capstan house were the north wing and south wing storehouses, given in 1784 new stone foundations.[41] In 1786 the floors needed to be replaced.[42] As the slate roof of the sail store, built at Hood's order, failed "to prevent the drift snow from coming in," sails had to be covered with hammocks to prevent their being destroyed by the wet.[43] As a consequence the hammocks themselves became damaged. This raised for Commissioner Duncan the suitability of slate roofs in that climate. "On seeing a continual expense in keeping in repair the slating of the storehouses," Duncan put several questions to the master shipwright.⁴⁴ He learned that in 1785 some H£369 were expended on this item alone, while an estimated H£604 would suffice to unslate the roofs and replace them with shingles, which were thought to last twenty years. When he asked why the slates were laid dry rather than in lime, the yard officers told him that the roofs were not framed for that purpose and to reinforce them would cost an additional H£1,295. The officers additionally thought it ill-advised, as the severity of the weather would heave the slates and break them at the pin holes; lime would not "stand in this country under slate." It was further explained that when the storehouses had first been slated, they believed it had been a necessary precaution against fire. "The woods were at no great distance, and always set on fire every spring to clear the ground." Now that they were at a greater distance, the danger was less. Though Duncan preferred the appearance of slate, the Navy Board ordered that thereafter roofing shingles alone be employed. For some years the roofs became an unsightly mixture of slate and shingles, until the last of the slate vanished.⁴⁵

By January 1814, the joists and floors of the storehouses again needed extensive repairs. As the artificers of the yard had more than enough work in repairing and refitting the squadron, the master shipwright suggested that all or part of the needed repairs be undertaken by contract.⁴⁶ Before anything could be effected, an enormous body of supplies almost overwhelmed the yard in the summer of 1814, when naval reinforcements reached Halifax in unprecedented numbers, requiring the expansion of storage facilities. As the storekeeper informed the commissioner: "all the yard's storehouses are becoming encumbered and overloaded, and many stores have been deposited in places unfit for the due preservation thereof where they cannot be allowed to remain for long. Many of the beams of the slop loft have given way, so that additional storehouse room, which the yard officers have for some time thought of proposing is now indispensably necessary."

The solution proposed was to raise the roof of the 1771 storehouse by "adding a ten-foot high storey, and of converting the loft when so raised into a sail loft, and the present sail loft into slop, bed, colours, and bunting store. As they see all sorts of difficulties and delays caused by the usual method of issuing stores 'the oldest first' they propose without delay to fit part of the boathouse into a store for the temporary reception of the stores now in the masthouse loft."⁴⁷ Without awaiting the Navy Board's authorization, Commissioner Wodehouse concluded a contract worth £2,550 with William Finnerty, master house carpenter of the yard.[48]

The masthouse, built in 1760 in part from LaHave River timber, proved to be that rare wooden building that endured with few repairs over the decades.[49] By 1814, however, many of the joists of the masthouse loft were broken. In 1818 the masthouse required new weather boarding on the sides and ends, while the roof needed new shingling.[50] Its slip, by contrast, required regular maintenance. In 1774, for instance, this slip was ripped up and a new one built, measuring some sixty-six feet by forty-five feet, and extending ten feet further into the water than the earlier one.[51] In 1784 it was again rebuilt, and three years later £225 was set aside to lengthen the slip by yet another ten feet.[52] By 1818, the masthouse slip again needed replanking.[53]

In 1783 the Navy Board approved a new stone foundation to the boathouse; it was then substantially rebuilt, with the work undertaken two years later.[54] By 1810 the building had become so leaky "as hardly to afford shelter for the workmen employed in it, in rainy weather."[55] The Navy Board approved the repair only in 1811, although the £281 estimate had been submitted three years earlier.[56]

In 1787 when the boathouse slip was repaired and lengthened by eight feet, the Navy Board approved expenditure of £380 for the work.[57] The slip seemed to have a life span of fifteen years, for in 1803, the slip was reported to be "exceedingly decayed,"[58] and in 1818, the entire slip again needed to be rebuilt.[59]

Smaller structures were not neglected. In August 1781 the "cooperage and warehouses in which the casks, staves, iron hoops have been lodged" near the north wall were damaged by fire.[60] Demolished only in 1784,[61] it was replaced with a completely new building in 1787 with a budget of £250.[62] In 1804 a shed used to house workers then living near the watering wharf was converted into a cooperage, with a thirteen-foot picket fence erected around it.[63] This was replaced in 1806 when, on the watering wharf, a building suitable for a cooperage was built. There Vice Admiral George Cranfield Berkeley appointed James Taylor to superintend coopers from ships in port "in making, setting up, and repairing the casks of the squadron, and converting damaged staves into small casks for the cutters I expect here."[64] In 1817 Commissioner Wodehouse urged the Navy Board not to remove the yard's cooperage storehouse. As the old location of the cooperage was "not conducive to landing," it offered temptation to embezzle stores. "A

Dock Yard," he wrote, "should be made as distinct as possible from the Works."[65]

Unadorned structures like the captains' and lieutenants' lodges (1772), seamen's shed (1774) – 200 feet by fifteen feet[66] – the English artificers "long shade" (1776) all built against the west wall of the yard, continued in use after 1783.[67] Also retained were the masons' shed (1774), thirty-six by sixteen feet, which backed onto the commissioner's kitchen garden in the northwest part of the yard;[68] the painters' shop or oil store, as it was sometimes called, built in 1770 and relocated in 1783;[69] the coppersmith's shop (1782); the iron store rebuilt in part in 1803;[70] the lime shed that was rebuilt in 1783–4;[71] and the mastpond shed (1774) for the mast contractors' use.[72] After the 1775–83 war, the only new such structures erected were the watchmen's house, built in 1783, and the painters' shed built in 1807–8 on orders of Vice Admiral Berkeley.[73] Some 338 feet long, fifteen feet wide and seventeen feet high, it was used for fitting ships' rigging and for painting hammock cloths.[74] Placed in the open space between the watering tank[75] and the yard wall and recycling unserviceable masts and spars, it was built during the slow winter season.[76]

The pitch house was relocated in 1783, when a sixty-foot-long shed was built at the back of the south storehouse wing of the capstan house.[77] In 1818 it needed both many repairs and painting.[78] In 1783 the top of the venter cupola on the smiths' shop was shingled,[79] while repairs to the smiths' slip and the stone foundation of the smiths' store were approved.[80] In 1800 the stone work and the slating of the smiths' shop and pitch house needed repointing.[81] In 1806 the shop was enlarged at a cost of £221.[82] By 1818, the smiths' shop once again needed painting.[83]

By 1783 there were five fire engines in the yard.[84] As two new ones arrived in 1787, the engine house had to be enlarged. The commodore proposed "appropriating the room adjoining to the guardroom" after the doors were widened.[85] In 1802 the roof needed to be reshingled, while the hearth, plastering, and doors needed to be repaired. The floor, which was only of single boards, needed to be doubled. In 1815, when Commissioner Wodehouse proposed to make the existing guardhouses near the main gate into the engine houses, the engine house was transformed into cart sheds, "which have been much wanted."[86]

In 1812 Commissioner Wodehouse complained of the inconvenience experienced by the yard by the absence of a clock. The following year the Navy Board directed that a "Turret Clock" from Ingress

Park, an estate lately purchased by the crown, be refurbished and shipped to Halifax. Boasting a dial piece forty inches in diameter, the clock struck the hours.[87] It was erected and regulated in 1816 by James Dickman, in a specially-built cupola on the south gable end of the rebuilt 1771 storehouse.[88]

The yard was unsatisfactorily lit at night by lamps. There were several complaints, beginning in 1811, about the quality of the oil employed. The lamps went out too soon after being lighted.[89] In response to Commissioner Wodehouse's complaint about the quality of the lamps themselves, in 1815 the Navy Board directed the officers of Woolwich dockyard to supply two dozen lamps of a better quality and thicker glass.[90] Later, in 1816, Wodehouse expanded on this criticism, when he wrote of the "very bad quality of lamp oil produced in this province, the whole of the lamps being out in three hours after they are lighted during severe weather."[91] He asked the Navy Board to send out spermaceti whale oil which "if properly strained will not freeze – as is proved by the lighthouses on the coast of the United States."[92]

A new gate was erected in 1817 at the north end of the yard at a cost of H£150. Wodehouse disliked the location of the guardrooms at the yard's gate, "the soldiers constantly bringing in liquor to the working parties of the ships; and however strict the orders given to the officers, constantly going out of the gate."[93]

Besides repairs to buildings of the sort already described, regular maintenance and repair was needed at the mastponds, wharfs, and breastworks. Though kept in a mastpond, masting timbers were at first almost always afloat. This defeated part of the purpose of the pond, for if timbers were kept constantly under salt water, the sap would be forced out thus preserving the masts for longer use. This could only be done once the Board gave its permission to "clay the fences and beam the pond to confine them always under water."[94] Undertaken in 1761, thereafter regular repair was needed.

In 1783 the mastpond sluice gates, built in 1759, needed rehanging. Commissioner Duncan feared that "the frost and ice in the winter would destroy the gates, were they hung at the mastpond. As the intention of them would only be to stop back the water in the pond, to keep the masts afloat at low water, this may be done by only fixing one or two logs horizontally across the entrance, out of the mastpond."[95] The work was undertaken two years later.[96] In 1787 repairs were made to the mastpond wall with a budget of £670.[97] Further repairs were completed in 1803, when stones were hauled by boat from the North West Arm.[98]

In 1800 a second mastpond was built with the help of seamen, this time at the north end of the yard.[99] In 1809 Commissioner Inglefield ordered that thereafter all spars supplied were to be surveyed "upon the beach between the watering wharf and the south boundary of the North Mastpond."[100] Owing to the "defective state of the wharfs round the mastpond at the North end of the yard," damaged by hard southeast winter gales, by 1816 the yard officers feared it would entirely give way. Commissioner Wodehouse ordered them to drive piles on both sides of the wharf, and thereby make it much stronger than when first built in 1801. The work was done by twenty-five soldiers from the garrison, at an estimated cost of £500, but undertaken without prior Navy Board approval.[101]

Wharfs, both from their heavy use by the yard and from the pounding endured occasionally from ice and regularly from gales, proved especially vulnerable. The wharf used to land coal, firewood, and lumber constantly needed repairs.[102] In 1786 and again in 1793 estimates were sent to London.[103] In 1811 some £560 was assigned for the repair of this wharf; to take up the cap sills, three strokes below and two strokes between the neap tides, all the "lank ties within & without – the whole being decayed;" and to copper the replacement ties.[104]

The anchor wharf had largely been washed away in the winter of 1785–6. It was lengthened by adding the hulk *Boulogne*[105] and given two careening pits, thereby allowing vessels as large as 50-gun warships to careen.[106] Though in 1809 an amount of £3,000 was allocated by Parliament for its repair, nothing was done until 1818.[107] Thus neglected, by 1814 it was in a ruinous state. Wharf logs were purchased for its total repair by a contract concluded that December.[108] Incidentally, the anchor wharf's crane, acquired in 1783 and still operating in 1814, was then described as having been built "upon a bad principle, covering a large space of ground, and containing a considerable quantity of timber which is much decayed." The master shipwright wanted it replaced with a new crane built "upon the principle of those now in general use in England."[109]

By 1787 the other wharfs were in poor shape, and had "been already a subject matter of consideration." The only remedy seemed to be to carry "a breastwork totally round them, and filling up in the centre."[110] As Commissioner Duncan explained, "At present a line of battle ships cannot lay at each of these wharfs at the same time." When *Leander* was being hove down to replace part of her false keel, "the weight of her materials" so sunk the south wharf that a major repair was needed. The plan was to rebuild it with "square logs, with land ties leading into the wharfs. As high as the low water mark to be filled with nails and the inside to be made solid with earth and stones, like the anchor wharf."[111] Duncan estimated the cost at between £10,000 and £11,000. When the work was funded in 1787, in response the Navy Board allocated only £670 to construct a wharf twenty-six feet in length between the careening wharfs. A careening pit was made to enable small vessels to heave down.[112] In 1809 the wharf and breastwork on the north careening and sheer wharfs needed repair, yet it took two years to secure the Board's authorization to make two new sheers, a cap sheer, to repair the mast and capstan pits, and to fashion shells of blocks and channels for the sheers.[113]

By the end of 1813, the wharfs throughout the yard were so damaged from the constant refitting of the fleet that Commissioner Wodehouse requested the Navy Board's permission to repair them. When no reply was forthcoming after two years, he raised the matter again, proposing to employ twenty-six shipwrights for the work. This time the scheme was approved. The north wharf, for instance, which formed part of the north mastpond next to the harbour, was "so settled in one part that the high spring tides flow over it, by which means it is very probable many of the spars which have been found adrift in the harbour have escaped."[114]

Of the wharfs, few gave as much trouble, owing to constant use, as the watering wharf. When Commissioner Duncan arrived in 1783, it was "so much gone to decay that it is absolutely necessary to take it in hand" as the first task undertaken. "It may be added to and built upon in its present state, which will be a considerable saving of materials. A few gales of wind more would totally wash it away." First included in the 1786 naval estimates,[115] its repair amounted to £1,025.[116] It was again thoroughly rebuilt in 1795 for £1,397.[117]

Until 1813 there was no naval powder magazine in the yard. Rather, powder was stored in a magazine on George's Island, or in a schooner anchored either off the yard, or near George's Island and McNab's Island.[118] For years this function was performed as well by two storeships, *Success*[119] and *Inflexible*,[120] before being taken out of service in 1816.[121] A more satisfactory solution was effected in 1813 when a naval magazine, sixty feet by thirty-eight feet, was erected by the engineers to hold powder on a site near the shore to the north of the hospital complex.[122]

The magazine storeships were not the only such vessels long associated with the yard. The hulks *Pembroke* and *Boulogne*, both former ships of the line, were sent to Halifax in 1776; the first to be used as a receiving ship for officers and crew, the other to house artificers and seamen while their ships were refitting.[123] In 1799 Commissioner Duncan also requested a vessel to serve as a receiving ship, *Boulogne* having become part of a wharf thirteen years earlier. Duncan assured the Board that a "two-decked ship is absolutely necessary for the convenience of the officers, ships company and stores, while their own ships are heaving down." Yet the Board delayed for a decade, when *Centurion* arrived in Halifax. Assigned a complement of thirty-six, she served until war's end, after which she was reduced to a hulk, before being dismantled.[124]

Finally, walls and fences also needed regular attention. In the summer of 1783 carpenters erected pickets and a fence at the watering wharf "to prevent seamen getting out of yard."[125] The following spring a post and rail fence at the north end of the yard was completed.[126] In 1800 when the dry-stone wall appeared to Commissioner Coffin "very much out of repair,"[127] a survey revealed the need to rebuild the section between the north blockhouse and hospital.[128] In 1807 the yard officers were granted permission to purchase 18,000 shingles for shingling the coping of the repaired part of the yard wall.[129] In 1815 Rear Admiral Griffith received complaints from his captains that seamen were getting over the wall in the north part of the yard. The dry wall, built in 1790 with buttresses added in 1804, in the shipwright's opinion was at such risk that another severe winter would bring parts of it down. The new wall, measuring 720 feet long from the new guardhouse to the south end of the hospital wall, was built of stone, ten feet above ground level, with a foundation built four feet below ground and one above, and forty-two inches thick.[130]

On several occasions before 1819 the yard seemed to have fallen into decay from a combination of weather and constant heavy use, especially in wartime. On at least three occasions hurricanes inflicted damage on yard and ships alike: in September of both 1798 and 1811, and on 12 November 1813.[131] Hard gales, particularly between November and April, also took a severe toll, compounded by the freeze–thaw cycles of winter weather.

On numerous occasions the harbour was closed by ice. In 1783, for instance, men and boys skated from Richmond, a settlement north of the yard, to Dartmouth. Four years later ice persisted beyond McNab's Island, with teams able to make crossings for forty days. In the winter of 1805–6, in particular, the wharfs, walls, and roads in the yard were considerably damaged.[132] In the winters of 1816–17 and 1817–18, teams crossed over Bedford Basin from Fort Sackville all winter, while the Eastern Passage remained closed with ice until April.[133]

Both in 1814 and 1815 Commissioner Wodehouse described the yard houses, storehouses, and wharfs as "in the most defective state."[134] Then the proximate cause had been the extraordinary pressure to which the yard had been subject under the exigencies of war with the United States, occasioning a remarkable expansion, in the summer of 1814, of the naval force dependant on the yard. The Navy Board failed for two years to acknowledge the commissioner's request for permission to proceed, even when he assured it that the wharfs had been much damaged "by the constant refitting of the fleet." With the longed-for peace at hand that saw so few ships on station and hence the absence of working parties of seamen, the work could be undertaken, he explained, only by keeping an additional twenty-six artificers on the yard books.[135]

In 1815, when the yard could finally bask in the warmth of the general peace, the urgency to maintain the condition of buildings and wharfs greatly diminished. Indeed, the very survival of Halifax as a naval base became an issue. In pleading its cause, Commissioner Wodehouse informed the Navy Board that there were thirty-three buildings in the naval yard, excluding the hospital complex and the admiral's mansion. These totalled 2,720 feet in length, besides the 8,178 feet of wall and fence. He reminded the Navy Board that when winter "breaks up, the whole of the drains are choked up, and for many weeks after the masons and labourers are employed solely in clearing them, from the situation of the yard immediately at the bottom of a steep hill it cannot be otherwise." Besides, stone and brickwork were always in need of pointing because of the severity of winters. He argued that at least twenty labourers should be employed the year round because of the yard's situation, the size of the storehouses, and the damage that the foundations suffered if not cleared speedily of wet and snow. As there might be no more than a sloop of war in harbour for months at a time there was no prospect of getting help from working parties of seamen.[136]

Of the many repairs the yard required by 1817, the Navy Board sanctioned only three projects. Besides the admiral's house, to be dealt with in the next chapter, the anchor wharf was to be enlarged, with a budget of £3,000, first approved in 1809. The north boundary wall's budget of £1,500 was also approved.[137] The Board repeated its warning to the commissioner not to undertake any building or major repairs, except in an emergency, without first sending particulars of the work proposed, time needed, and estimated cost, in order to secure prior approval.[138]

A year later, the Navy Board requested yet another detailed report on the state of the yard buildings, wharfs, and walls. It was informed that considerable routine repairs were necessary. The capstan house, cable store, and careening room needed new floors. The smiths' shop and pitch house needed to be painted after numerous repairs were completed. Both the masthouse and boathouse slips needed replanking. The masthouse required "new weather boarding on the sides and gable ends," and the roof to be reshingled, as did the boathouse roof. The storehouses needed to be repainted, the back part of the roof on the yard officers' tenements required new shingles, and the basements needed to be pointed. Many of the drains needed to be rebuilt, as did almost all of the yard's internal fences. As the camber wharf was rotten from the low-water-mark upwards, it had to be taken down and rebuilt for a length of 635 feet, measuring from where the last repairs were made to the building slip. Finally, the north mastpond repairs were estimated at £1,055 10s. To reduce annual costs, Commissioner Wodehouse promised the Board in March 1819 that needed repairs would be undertaken only "gradually."[139] None of this work had begun when three months later came the sudden decision to close the yard and reduce it to a depot; all thought of further repairs were set aside indefinitely.

Compared to the expenses incurred for the new base at Bermuda and improvements in other overseas bases, such as Malta, Madras, and Trincomalee, those expended at Halifax from 1783 to 1819 were extremely modest. This meant that the Halifax naval yard met all the pressures of refitting a greatly-enlarged squadron during the war with the United States in 1812–15 with essentially the same facilities as it possessed at the end of the American War of Independence.

Only marginally affected by the French wars from 1793 onwards, the Halifax careening yard at first needed no great augmentation either to its facilities or to its workforce. Yet from 1807, as relations with the United States seriously deteriorated and the threat of war developed, neither the Admiralty nor the Navy Board did much to prepare the yard for the onslaught of 1812. Faith instead was placed in the construction of the new facilities in Bermuda. As these were far from completed when war engulfed North America, the burden of refitting and storing the expanded North American squadron from the Gulf of Maine to the Gulf of Mexico instead fell principally upon Halifax. The strain on yard structures was excessive, and by 1815, when peace was restored to the region, massive repairs were needed. In the financial retrenchment which characterized post-war British public finances, and with the prospect of the Bermuda base displacing Halifax in strategic importance, the Navy Board was understandably reluctant to respond quickly or positively to repeated requests from Commissioner Wodehouse for permission to undertake necessary repairs to the yard's structures.

Chapter Three

HOSPITAL COMPLEX AND ADMIRAL'S HOUSE

Associated with naval dockyards were victualling yards, ordnance yards, hospitals, and commanders-in-chief's mansions.[1] Halifax acquired most of these from the earliest days, except a hospital and an admiral's house. While the military had earlier built both a general hospital for its people and, by 1800, a mansion for the general officer commanding the troops in Nova Scotia, the navy's sick and wounded during the American war were housed on military property on George's Island, while a house for the naval commander was not completed until 1819. Both will be considered in this chapter.

The care of sick and wounded seamen before a hospital was opened for them in 1782 was varied, if not haphazard. The hundreds of sick seamen on board Boscawen's fleet in 1755 were housed ashore in tents and hastily repaired, vacant houses.[2] The small naval hospital, located on Granville Street since 1750, was overwhelmed. Yet no replacement was found until October 1776, when the navy converted a small military barrack on George's Island into a hospital. This "old building," constructed of brick and stone, was first refurbished by yard artificers.[3] In May 1777 the military commanding officer in Nova Scotia ordered the sick and wounded inmates off George's Island. Without prior notice having been given, they were loaded into boats in a heavy downpour, "some of these unhappy men were at the point of death, others with fevers ... some whose wounds were still open and dangerous." This unfortunate incident, Capt. Collier later wrote, "occasioned the pity of the whole town."[4] This was done, according to the senior sea officer "under pretense of fortifying" the island. This must have been a temporary measure, as the navy permanently evacuated the site only in 1779. In its place a naval hospital was established in an old commercial storehouse. There, artificers fashioned windows, shutters, and doors; repaired the cellar steps; clapboarded the exterior walls; and shingled the roof.[5]

To Commissioner Hamond, upon his arrival in 1781, this was indeed "miserable accommodation" for sick and wounded seamen.[6] No more than a decayed storehouse built upon piles over the water with "scarce a roof or floor to it," yet it cost H£150 a year in rent. Located between the yard and the town, it was "surrounded by rum shops." He recommended that the Board allocate £2,500 to £3,000 to construct a hospital. At first Hamond favoured Dartmouth,[7] but later settled on a three-acre site immediately north of the yard, on the harbour, away from the town and below the naval burial ground.[8]

The navy speedily approved Hamond's proposal. A plan for a 200–bed building arrived from London, calling for a flight of steps to the second storey "upon a supposition that the snow may lye too deep to enter at the lower door."[9] Before this was received, Hamond's own plan had been approved by Rear Admiral Sir Robert Digby, in command of the North American squadron at New York,[10] and advertisements for a contractor placed in the *Gazette*.[11]

With the yard's master shipwright, John Loader, superintending the contractor and paying and victualling the workers in the same manner as yard artificers, work began immediately.[12] The contractor was William Lee, the yard's foreman of house carpenters.[13] By mid-November 1782, Hamond reported that the hospital was "in such forwardness as to have part of it ready to receive patients by Christmas."[14] Built of wood and finished in clapboard with a shingled roof, it had a graceful colonnade at its west front entrance.[15] Originally there were four wards for seamen. The two largest housed twenty men each, allowing for two feet per cradle, and the other two wards, twelve and thirteen men respectively. The long garret and the upper north garret over these could hold another ten men. There were also four rooms on the upper floor, each reserved for five officers. The garrets over the officers' rooms could hold another twenty-five and nine seamen respectively. If needed, a further eighteen men could be accommodated in the large hall. Three years later an apartment was built in the hospital to accommodate the commander-in-chief of the Halifax station.[16]

Over time, a complex developed. The hospital was fenced and given a porter's lodge at the gate. A separate lunatic cabin, with double-planked rooms, was built at the water's edge. Nearby a wharf was built, where stores, provisions, coal, and cordwood could be conveniently landed. New stores were built for the hospital in 1795.[17] Later, a separate tenement was built to house the surgeon, agent, and dispenser at the hospital, while the matron was given an apartment in the hospital building itself.[18]

In 1783 with the compliance of the Sick and Hurt Board, Hamond created an establishment for his new hospital, consisting of a surgeon paid £100 a year, a purveyor, and a dispenser who doubled as an assistant surgeon. For every fifty patients, there was one hospital mate, paid 5s. sterling daily, with a nurse for every ten or twelve men, but paid only 8½d. a day, or one-seventh the rate of the mates. The matron received £52 a year; the cook 1s., the porter 2s., and each of two labourers 1s.6d. a day.[19]

The hospital appears to have been a success from the outset. In 1785 the commodore reported that his captains, who visited the hospital weekly, reported it in very good order, with "the people supplied with as good and wholesome food as the country can furnish."[20] The only difficulty surfaced in 1785 and involved the "irregularity and drunkenness of the seamen and marines" in hospital, despite a regular guard appointed to prevent spirituous liquor getting to them.[21] "Very little dependence can be placed on those they employ as nurses" who supplied the liquor, Commodore Herbert Sawyer explained. He replaced the guard and appointed a master-at-arms with the same authority as if he acted aboard a ship, an experiment which greatly reduced complaints of this sort. It was two decades before the subject again surfaced. Vice Admiral Berkeley suggested the stationing of an additional sentinel on the hospital wharf both to prevent desertion and "to put a stop to the pernicious traffic carried on by the retailing of liquor to the convalescents."[22]

For more than a decade, much of it during peace, both the surgeon and the dispenser retained apartments in the hospital. In August 1794, owing to pressure for space, Dr John Halliburton requested permission from Rear Admiral George Murray to enlarge the naval hospital by converting the surgeon's and part of the dispenser's apartments into wards. It was found that the parlours, upper bedrooms, and garret of the surgeon's apartment could each hold twenty-one men, with two more seamen in the passage. The garret over the dispenser's apartment and the kitchens could be converted into a storeroom for bedding and other supplies, while the southwest garrets over the dispenser's apartment could be converted to storerooms for medicines and utensils.[23]

The space shortage had been precipitated by the arrival in harbour of a Spanish prize filled with prisoners sick with severe ulcers. Unable to house them in the hospital, the surgeon hired a commodious house on the outskirts of town, sending all available cradles there for their reception and borrowing others from the army storekeeper. At that point, some "principal inhabitants went to the governor and represented that a great number of people with infectious diseases were about to be sent into the town and that the health of the inhabitants would be endangered" unless the governor forbade it.[24] Though Halliburton explained to Lieutenant Governor Wentworth that the vessel was free of infectious fevers and that the prisoners were suffering from open sores "of the most malignant sort, that for want of proper dressing, nourishing ... and of the necessary materials to keep them clean, the stench as well, which had saluted the nostrils of those who had the curiosity to go on board," had given rise to the report. Wentworth warned that the people, having learned of the "dreadful havoc" of the fever in Philadelphia, were greatly alarmed that the same should now be carried to Halifax. The surgeon was thus forced to hire a horse and ride about the countryside until he came upon a couple of empty houses, at a distance of two miles from the yard.[25] He felt obliged to lease them although they were in a state of disrepair.

Other buildings were added to the hospital complex. The "lunatic house" was erected near the hospital before 1802 to replace the one cell available until then in the hospital. Its windows secured with iron bars, one room was double-lined with two-inch pine plank for the safety of the inmates.[26] A second storey was added in 1809 to act as a store for beds and clothing.[27] Besides the lunatic house a porter's lodge was built, as was a shed for the hospital's one fire engine.[28] In September 1806 a small fire in one of the hospital complex buildings occasioned the building of a new guardhouse for a corporal and nine privates "to prevent a similar accident."[29] In 1810 a small house was built for the hospital clerk, James Proud, with a coal shed and necessary.[30] In 1811–12 a large necessary for the hospital and a shed to serve as a wash house were built in the field above the hospital.[31] A bedding storehouse was located at the northwest corner of the hospital grounds. A wooden building like all the rest, it stood so close to the wall that the space between was always filled with rain water in summer and snow and ice in winter.[32]

From the start the hospital maintained a vegetable garden for which a gardener was later added to the establishment. When the hospital boat was washed away in a winter gale, a problem was created. "I shall think myself much indebted to you," the surgeon explained, "for another to supply her place, as the business of collecting dung, seaweed, new earth for the garden, can be better procured by that means, than any other, and save the expenses of carting."[33] In 1806 the garden fence required rebuilding. The problem did not come from the depredations made by rabbits, but "to prevent seamen digging under," and stealing vegetables as they ripened.[34]

Water supply at the hospital proved a continuing problem. In 1804 the well near the kitchen, from which the hospital drew its water, had become "very impure and unfit for use."[35] As a drought that summer had dried it up, the well required deepening by blasting the rock down another two feet. A drought in the summer of 1811 saw the same problem reappear, as the little water in the well was "unfit to drink."[36] When the well again went dry in the summers of 1812 and 1813, water had to be brought daily from the yard until a new well was dug.[37]

Maintenance and improvement of the hospital site became a regular burden on the yard's establishment. Shingles had to be replaced to keep out the rain, while drains and necessaries needed unblocking,[38] the yard officers recommending "the hiring of black men" to clean them.[39] The entire interior needed to be whitewashed and the walls replastered,[40] the exterior repainted,[41] and chimneys and hearths repaired.[42] Heavy use, once the war with the United States began, caused constant demand for a wide range of repairs and improvements.[43]

The hospital's wharf and its adjoining wood and coal yards also needed regular attention. In 1785 the hospital wharf "from never having been completed" was nearly washed away and had to be rebuilt.[44] A room was erected on the wharf to receive patients upon landing, as earlier they had been left exposed to the weather until carried up to the hospital. This also served as the bath house that the surgeon had recommended for the convalescents. In 1796 George Grant, the hospital's agent, reported "the insufficiency and bad state of the wharf for landing the wood, and that he finds it difficult, if not impossible, to persuade the owners of vessels to go alongside the landing place, from the fear of grounding."[45] In 1813 John Albro, fuel contractor to the hospital, complained of the coal house and wood yard as "totally unfit in their present state to contain the fuel or to secure it."[46]

Walls and fences leading to or surrounding the hospital were given regular attention as well. By 1784 a succession of severe winter gales had so weakened the hospital fence that "one half of the front pickets were totally thrown down." Its purpose was to incarcerate the sick and wounded and, as the surgeon explained when three took the occasion to desert, "the sentinels cannot be answerable in its present prostrate state."[47] In 1794 a stone wall was erected from the north blockhouse to the south corner of the hospital fence.[48] A hard gale in late November 1803 so damaged the wall that buttresses were built at intervals to support it, the stones laid in mortar.[49] In 1812 Admiral Warren asked Wodehouse to see to the repair of the hospital's west wall and a "decent gate made for it ... as it is in its present state subject to every nuisance of cows and livestock."[50] As the burial ground was so full by 1813 it was expanded by one-third and additional walls raised around it.[51]

The last substantial building erected in the hospital area was a tenement of three houses for the surgeon, dispenser, and agent – the only early structures still standing almost two hundred years later![52] In 1794 the surgeon, John Halliburton, insisted that Sir Andrew Snape Hamond had intended that a house be built for the surgeon, but had left the station before this was done. Until then he had maintained an apartment in the hospital, as he explained, but thereafter lived in town. Almost twenty years later, in December 1813, the Navy Board authorized Wodehouse to enter a contract with Messrs Finnerty, Hill, and Hay. The contract, concluded in January 1815, also required them to make into wards those parts of the hospital formerly occupied by the surgeon, dispenser, and agent.[53] When peace brought a reduction of the hospital establishment, the contract was not cancelled.[54]

For the construction Wodehouse recommended "brick-nogging" and wood framing.[55] Begun in 1815 the work was completed in August 1816.[56] The plank, board, and timber for their completion was contracted for in New Brunswick with George Andrews, as wood cost much less there than in Halifax.[57]

The total cost of H£7,144 exceeded the Navy Board's approved estimate of H£4,222 by almost 70 per cent.[58] Wodehouse later explained that the contract had been concluded when high wartime prices prevailed. Moreover, it was done under pressure from successive commanders-in-chief from their "want of room in the hospital during the war." In addition, building materials from the Bay of Fundy were expected to be freighted at low rates, as there were then many transports available in Halifax looking for a cargo. Yet by the time the contract was made, there were few transports available and few artificers, owing to the demobilization following the peace with France, so that the costs of both freight and labour remained unusually high.[59]

At war's end the decision to reduce the hospital establishment was implemented in two steps, the last in May 1819. The navy's Victualling Board, then in charge of hospitals, required an establishment of only a clerk, porter, and labourer. They, with their families, were free to occupy the apartments, at the commissioner's determination.[60] The last improvement, the building of a bathing house in June 1819, had just been completed.[61]

The hospital was destroyed in November 1819. Discovered on fire on the north side, the speed with which the flames engulfed the wooden structure "baffled every effort to save any part of the building, and the whole was reduced to ashes in ... two hours." Other buildings were threatened but saved by the efforts of the navy and army as well as the town's fire engines. The fire was believed to have originated in the apartment "occupied by a woman who had been a nurse to the establishment and who in consideration of her distressed circumstances on the recent reduction had been permitted to reside, *pro tempore*, in the apartment she formerly occupied. The unfortunate woman fell victim to her carelessness."[62]

The naval hospital staff was never large. In most years there was but a surgeon, a dispenser, three mates, and four temporary assistants from the squadron clerk and agent. With the 1812 war with the United States, a hospital mate and two matrons were added and a governor appointed. The governor, a naval captain, served only from 1813 to 1815. Admiral Warren suggested adding a chaplain, as the inmates were buried without any ceremony in what he termed "an improper manner inconsistent with the rules and decency which should be observed in such an establishment and with the religious attentions which ought to be paid to the remains of the dead."[63] Nor was any service conducted for the staff and inmates on Sundays. He recommended to the Admiralty that the minister of St Paul's, Reverend Dr Stanser be appointed to visit the sick "in their last moments and to attend the funeral service of such as may die in the hospital," and to perform divine service once each Sunday. This idea became the practice.

Between 1782 and 1819 the hospital was served by several successive surgeons. The longest serving was John Halliburton who had been a ship's surgeon before settling in Newport, Rhode Island after the Seven Years' War. In 1773 he contracted with Rear Admiral Montagu to look after the sick of the squadron.[64] Later he was put in charge of the naval hospital during the British occupation of Newport. He lost most of his property when he had to flee with his family when the navy abandoned its Rhode Island base.[65] Named surgeon at the new Halifax naval hospital, he retired to England in 1807 to avoid "the severity of the winter."[66]

The only controversial appointment occurred in 1813, with that of surgeon David Rowlands, a bullying, drunken liar. An Aberdeen graduate whose family had settled in Shelburne, he was best remembered for the row occasioned when he imprudently dismissed the dispenser, Robert Hume, who had served the naval hospital since 1799. The case is worth relating as it provides a rare insight into the relationship of those working in the hospital.

Hume had entered the naval service in 1793 as surgeon's mate on *Thetis*, under Alexander Cochrane, before "going to London to complete his examination" as surgeon. He served as ship's surgeon until 1799, when appointed dispenser under Halliburton. He claimed to have assumed many of the duties of a surgeon, as Halliburton was then "an old man & living two miles from the hospital."[67] From 1802 he also attended the prisoners on Melville Island, for which duty he had to keep a horse even though he was unable to afford it, having a large family of eight children and a wife to support. His most important success as dispenser occurred in 1802 when he attended 110 men, many of them suffering from "the worst species of ulcer." Appropriate care and a change of diet allowed most to return to their ships cured.

By the first of two naval boards of inquiry, composed of three captains and held at the naval hospital in June 1813, Hume was eventually found to have used improper language against Rowlands, whose "imperious mode of conduct has pervaded the department." Hume was required to adhere strictly to Rowlands's orders.[68]

Hume's serious falling out with his superior began the evening of 13 April 1813 in ward six. Hume was asked by Rowlands why he had failed to dress the arm of a man who had undergone amputation. Hume answered that he had not been so ordered, as the amputation had been done but thee days earlier and had "already been twice dressed." Rowlands said, "You neglect your duty and I will have you removed from your situation" and used "much abusive and insulting language ... his speech was a good deal impaired and he was not sober."[69]

On a second occasion, on a June evening while Hume was dressing men in ward six, Rowlands, "who seldom saw the patients dressed in the evening," accused Hume of failing to report a newly-arrived patient and stated that as the dispenser treated him with great disrespect, he would remove him, "all this before I had made any reply." In response Hume said that he knew nothing of the man in question, but on passing his cradle, "the nurse told me he wanted dressing," a task he immediately carried out.

In a "most imperious & intemperate manner he said I must report all cases to him ... Why don't you speak, Sir? Do you hear me, speak! I will have you dismissed." Hume responded that he was not afraid of dismissal so long as he did his duty. He then asked if the surgeon was aware to whom he was using such language. Rowlands answered "Mr Hume the hospital mate and dispenser." Hume assured him that he was no mate but an officer of the hospital, serving under instructions. "After repeatedly threatening me with dismissal and using much insulting and intemperate language, he said I should not presume to leave the hospital without his permission," an order Hume ignored. Hume requested the surgeon to end his abusive language and instead "use the language of a gentleman to me." Hume later learned from the matron and the clerk that the patient in question had indeed been reported to the surgeon who had failed to visit him immediately, as had been his duty.

Less than three weeks later, near the front door of his house, while Hume was in discussion with Dawes, the naval storekeeper, Rowlands appeared and said "I want you immediately, Sir."[70] Hume had taken but a few steps when Rowlands turned to him, his face pale with rage and with the "most insulting gesture, waving his hand, he said, 'Come along, Sir.'" Hume asked him again to use the language of a gentlemen when speaking to him. Suddenly Rowlands tried to provoke a duel, saying "You have Mr Dawes here and I have Mr Campbell ... let us go out and settle it at once. I will meet you with the greatest pleasure. You will never find me backwards. I have the means within my power."

When Hume refused to rise to the challenge, the surgeon said, "Had it not been for your family, I would have removed you the first week of my arrival here." Then when told to prepare a prescription for Rowland's servant and bring it to his house, Hume replied that he would make the powder, but that he would not carry it to his house, as there were mates for that service. Furious at his inability to humiliate the dispenser, that same evening Rowlands wrote to the senior sea officer in port to request an investigation of Hume's conduct in using "threatening and intimidating language."

At the initial board of inquiry Rowlands, while accusing Hume of having used "threatening and intimidating language," also accused Commissioner Wodehouse of being "violently his enemy," which statement was treated by the court "with marked indignation." When the surgeon interrupted Hume's testimony, saying "What you said is a lie,"[71] the court abruptly rose stating that it was useless to proceed further with the inquiry and that they would await the commander-in-chief's directions.

A second board of inquiry requested by Commissioner Wodehouse was held and was composed of three different captains.[72] This board was appointed to investigate the complaints lodged by James Proud, clerk of the hospital, over the general running of the naval hospital by the agent, William Eppes. Rowlands was sufficiently intemperate also to accuse Commissioner Wodehouse of gross neglect of duty, for which the surgeon at length in January 1814 abjectly apologized.[73]

By holding this second board of inquiry, but only after a four months' delay, many of Hume's material witnesses, having recovered from their wounds and illnesses, had returned to their ships and were unavailable for his defence. Nevertheless he was able to convince the board of his innocence, and thereby "exculpate myself from blame ... and that I had not used the expression alleged by Dr Rowlands but with almost unparalleled patience submitted to insults & indignities in hopes of meeting that proper protection from the Board and commander-in-chief which I, as an officer, had a right to expect."[74] The inquiry found his behaviour deserving of not the least censure. Rather they found Rowlands's behaviour "oppressive, insolent, and overbearing to the officers of the hospital" and to Wodehouse "highly intemperate, improper, and reprehensible."[75] Great then was Hume's "astonishment" to learn that he had been superseded.

Hume felt this a double injustice as he had evidence that Rowlands, far from being a gentleman, had actually bribed his dispensary servant, John Smith, with a promise to secure his discharge from the navy if Smith would steal from Hume's house important papers relating to the disputes within the hospital, and bring them to Rowlands for his perusal.[76] The task was not difficult as Smith lodged in Hume's house. Hume secured affidavits from three material witnesses, the first of whom was Sarah Scott, an illiterate, who asserted that she was surprised to find Smith frequently both late at night and early in the morning in Rowlands's house, where before he had been turned from his door. She heard Rowlands inquire of him, "Are you sure that was wrote in Dr Hume's paper?" When Smith replied positively, Dr Rowlands then said "I thank you kindly, that will do. Very well I am much obliged to you." Mrs Scott asserted that Smith told her he would do anything to befriend Dr Rowlands, as the surgeon had promised him his discharge from the service. She also declared that Smith in the presence of Mrs Brown stated that the papers of interest to Dr Rowlands were in Hume's drawing room drawer, and that he had read them. Rowlands's servant himself told her that Hume "should take better care of his papers, she thought it highly improper that one gentleman should encourage another gentleman's servant to betray his master's secrets." Moreover Smith had "prevented Mrs Maddox from coming into the hospital" as a witness, and instead set up a rendezvous for her with Dr Rowlands.[77]

Mrs Brown, the illiterate wife of the hospital porter, agreed with Sarah Scott's testimony, and that Mrs Maddox had been offered back her place as a nurse in the hospital, as a reward for withholding her testimony.[78] The third witness, Mrs Roberts, a literate tavernkeeper, confirmed that Mrs Maddox had been discharged for helping an inmate to make his escape. One evening during the inquiry, Mrs Maddox, on her way to meet Dr Rowlands at the house of a Mrs Gardner, called in at the tavern and returned later. Maddox, Brown swore, told her that Rowlands had thanked her for not appearing against him when sent for by either Eppes or Hume. When offered her nursing position back by Rowlands she had told him "Mrs Lawlor and her would not agree and that she would rather not go back." He then offered her the appointment of matron either at Melville Island or New Brunswick, as he could procure her either position.[79]

Upon learning that the Admiralty had superseded him, Hume wrote to his former patron, Alexander Cochrane, who became commander-in-chief in 1814. Hume recounted that he had served as surgeon's mate of Cochrane's frigate, *Thetis*, in 1794 when Cochrane had last served in North American waters. Cochrane believed Dr Rowlands to be a man of "the most violent temper," made worse by liquor.[80] If he intervened on Hume's behalf, the verdict remained unchanged, probably owing to the patronage Rowlands enjoyed. Hume's dismissal cost him dearly. He lost his £300 annual salary with £15 house rent, and 2s.6d. a day for rations. He was put on half pay and entered private practice as a surgeon in Halifax, where he lived out the balance of his long life. Rowlands continued as surgeon, until the hospital closed in 1819.

If the naval hospital was a necessity, the admiral's mansion was an anticipated luxury. The arrival of Vice Admiral Berkeley to command the North American squadron in 1806 occasioned pressure to build for the naval commander a suitable residence. Before 1775 when the first commissioner was appointed to Halifax, the commodore made use of the house originally built for the yard storekeeper, as we have seen. Thereafter he either remained aboard his flagship or took lodgings, "it being impossible to carry on the king's service," as Rear Admiral Sawyer explained, "from the ship appropriated for my pendant." An alternative was made possible in 1785 when an apartment was fashioned in the hospital to accommodate the commander-in-chief of the Halifax station.[81] The apartment, as Vice Admiral Berkeley noted in 1806, was both "very circumscribed" and insufficient for "my family,"[82] even after a small office and porch were added.[83]

In 1809 Berkeley's successor, Vice Admiral Warren, recommended that a suitable residence be built "especially as every other public officer in the capital is commodiously fixed," when he failed to find suitable rental accommodation in town.[84] He selected an eight-acre site on the height of land overlooking the hospital, far enough away to avoid any stench from the burial ground.

Until the residence was built, the flag officer was expected to live on a ship in harbour. This was Rear Admiral Griffith's experience, when he was assigned to Halifax in 1813 as port admiral and lived there until 1819. He continued to live aboard *Centurion*, the wartime receiving ship, which was turned into a hulk in 1816.

Though Warren's successor, Rear Admiral Herbert Sawyer, displayed no public interest in the subject, it was during his time as commander-in-chief in 1811 that the naval estimates first mentioned the future house, allocating £3,000 for its construction.[85] Sawyer merely complained that he had to occupy the surgeon's apartments in the naval hospital which forced the surgeon to live at some distance, thereby preventing him in winter from attending properly to the inmates. Sawyer's real objection, perhaps, was that only a thin partition separated his apartments from the sick, who, if not "constantly disturbed by his comings and goings at all hours," as he stated, would in their wretchedness distract him.[86]

When Warren returned to command the fleet at Halifax in 1812, he directed Wodehouse to enter into a contract, since Parliament had now approved the project.[87] In response the commissioner reminded Warren that he had no instructions to build such a house, although £3,000 had been approved in the ordinary estimates. He could do nothing until Admiralty permission had been granted.[88] A year later when Warren asked that a plan and estimate for a house of smaller dimensions be prepared,[89] the yard officers employed John Plaw or some other "competent engineer" to prepare new designs, and to pay him £40.[90] With this plan and the elevation in hand, he reminded the Admiralty of "the impossibility of procuring lodgings at this place even of a very common description."[91] The flag officer's situation was in marked contrast to the military commander, who was "suitably and well provided" for. In March 1814 the Admiralty at length gave its consent for the Navy Board to conclude a contract to build a house based on a plan prepared, not by Plaw, but by the surveyor at the Admiralty. When the Navy Board failed to enclose the plans, confusion resulted.[92]

No start was made until the new commander-in-chief, Vice Admiral Cochrane, arrived in Halifax in October 1814. The call for tenders elicited only two offers, and as both exceeded the £3,000 ceiling approved by Parliament, neither was accepted.[93] As a consequence, the house was built without the help of an architect and without a contractor. Griffith explained that as he had been unable "to find an architect on anything like reasonable terms, under whose directions to place the conducting of this work, I was under the necessity of hiring the best workmen – one in each line – that Halifax afforded."[94]

That there were too many cooks involved threatened to spoil the broth. Normally all buildings in the naval yard or in the adjoining hospital complex came under the direct responsibility of the commissioner. In the case of the admiral's mansion responsibility was divided. The port admiral and occasional commander-in-chief, Rear Admiral Griffith, who reported to the Admiralty, was often away with the squadron in Bermuda. Commissioner Wodehouse, who corresponded with the Navy Board, never left the scene. In London the future Halifax home of the commander-in-chief of the North American squadron thus became the subject of correspondence between the secretary to the Admiralty Board and the secretary to the Navy Board. If Wodehouse was clearly the site manager for the house, he was removed from the day-to-day business of construction. Griffith appears to have appointed the leading artificer at the site, who took responsibility for the work actually performed. This was John MacKenzie, a working foreman of house carpenters, and in 1819, Isaac Rigby, a master carpenter from the Royal Engineers. Early in 1816 Wodehouse appointed the yard's master shipwright, Thomas Hawkes, as effective site manager and when he was superseded in 1816, by his successor Algernon Jones.[95]

How the building was to be finished illustrated the degree of

56 Part One: Naval Yard Complex

confusion that surrounded its construction. Cochrane ordered 150,000 bricks and a quantity of Roman cement from England.[96] When the Admiralty disapproved, the Navy Board told Wodehouse to use local stone. Before this order arrived in Halifax, Commissioner Wodehouse wrote on the matter to Andrew Belcher, an influential Nova Scotian living in London. His reply is revealing. Bricks made in Nova Scotia, he claimed,

> are certainly not of the best quality for standing the severity of that climate. They are porous and commonly made of salt water. The price three years ago was £3 10s. per 1,000. Now, from the high wages occasioned by the war, I should suppose they are much dearer. As to stone, there are very large quarries at Pictou and Merigomish, of the Portland quality, of which you know the Government House was built and of which likewise the Province House and public offices are now building and which is fully equal to any freestone in England. If it is the intention of Government to build a durable house for the Admiral, I would recommend it to be of this material, but it would take three years to complete it. If a house is wanted in a shorter time, I could recommend its being built of wood and to be brick knocked, the basement story to be of rubble stone below ground and to be faced above ground with free or Portland Nova Scotia stone. The sills and upright posts to be of seasoned yellow or red pine; sprung or condemned Riga or Canada masts would make excellent timber for the purposes and could be easily hewn, sawed and prepared in the interim.
>
> I was one of the commissioners who superintended the building of the Governor's house and had some experience in other buildings at Halifax. If you think proper to recommend a reference to me, I will readily attend the commissioners of the navy and give them all the information in my power. The front of Mr Black's house was faced with grey granite imported at a great expense from Aberdeen. The other parts of it were composed of Nova Scotia brick.[97]

Yet the Navy Board's original plan called for a wood-framed house, similar to that built for the commissioner in the 1780s. Commissioner Wodehouse ignored the Board's directive. The Admiralty plan, he explained, "differing so materially from the one already begun, that only by levelling it could the Navy Board's directions be followed." As the difference between a wood and a stone house was estimated at no more than £500, the admirals – Cochrane and Griffith – decided to build a stone house. To reduce costs, they decided not to construct the first-floor wings intended for offices. This in turn created serious problems, the determination having been given too little consideration at the time. As it turned out, the final design left office space at a premium.

When the Navy Board and Admiralty learned that the mansion was to be finished in stone rather than in wood, as they had directed, they had little choice but to approve.[98] As the building "is going on, & had probably proceeded too far to admit of alteration," they recommended that the Admiralty allow it to be completed according to Cochrane's plan.[99] The Admiralty required only in matters of design, that "the house should be built according to the usual manner of the country." This called for a house about sixty feet square and almost as lofty as the commissioner's house.[100]

The stone came from several places, but much of it was quarried at sites along the harbour. Even Portland stone was sought from Edward Mortimer in Pictou and other stone from Lunenburg Bay.[101] It was carried in the buoy boat *Hibernia*,[102] the schooner *Lively*, a sloop, and a flat-bottomed boat.[103] In March 1816 the work on the house briefly threatened to come to an unexpected halt. With the rear admiral in Bermuda, the senior sea officer in Halifax detained all the stone vessels from proceeding to sea. Commissioner Wodehouse protested that he would have to discharge masons for lack of work for them, as "the expense being very considerable, and they having worked up all the stone that has been brought here. As these people will get immediate employment elsewhere, and as they are a description of workmen not to be procured during the spring and summer months, no further progress can be made to the house this year."[104] In defending his orders, the captain explained that vessels had returned from the coast unable to reach their destinations because of ice, as the weather had been freezing or snowing constantly since. He had concluded that it was an unacceptable risk to send them out, when waiting a few days in hopes of a change in the weather was more prudent.[105] This crisis passed when the weather improved, as the officer anticipated.

That construction took so long had little to do with either the skill or the willingness of those who worked on the site. Local tradesmen did the skilled work, aided by artificers from ships and the garrison, occasionally assisted by working parties from the squadron. After seeing their finished work, Griffith wrote of their "honesty, skill, and diligence."[106] Before the onset of winter in 1814 there was little time for construction.[107] The foundation was dug and three-quarters of the basement completed. Most of the necessary materials – timber, lumber, and lime – were collected and stacked in the yard. In April 1815 advertisements were placed calling for tenders to frame the house on the foundation already built.[108] They proved so high, owing to the wartime inflation in workers' wages, that none was accepted. By late-1815 about H£3,500 had been spent, and another £4,900 was estimated, "if we purchase all the fixtures" in Nova Scotia. The sum so far exceeded the Board's original permission that Griffith dismissed the workmen, once the basement was completed, until further orders were received.[109]

In 1816, once the roof was raised and the building framed, in an effort to control costs the commissioner discharged all artificers hired from town. Thereafter he depended as much as possible on the cheap labour provided by artificers in the squadron and garrison.[110] They were paid an allowance over their naval or military wages, usually at one-fifth that of the tradesmen's wages. Still, "according to the custom of the province," upon the raising of the roof, Wodehouse paid MacKenzie an extra allowance to be shared with the other artificers.[111]

Only in the spring of 1817 did Wodehouse learn that the Navy Board had approved an additional £2,330 to complete the house.[112] However useful the men from the yard and garrison,[113] artificers from the town were indispensable to the completion of construction.[114] Besides masons, Wodehouse hired house carpenters at 5s.6d. a day, and a plasterer, William Halliburton, at 8s.[115] The sashes, sash frames, doors, door jambs, door frames, and flooring boards, purchased in 1816 by the admiral, were fitted.[116] The window panes from Woolwich arrived in 1817. In the summer of 1818, while four masons from Halifax built the stone walls on the wooden frame and flagstone steps,[117] three bricklayers built the chimneys and hearths, at 7s.6d. a day, while three painters at 7s. a day set to work.[118]

To depress these wages the Navy Board interfered directly and ordered Wodehouse to pay no more than 5s. a day thereafter. Upon this directive reaching the yard late in October 1818, the commissioner informed the painters, masons, and bricklayers that from 1 November pay would drop to 5s. a day until the work was finished. If they refused to accept this wage they were to be dismissed, Wodehouse instructed his yard officers. David Jenkins, the house carpenter, and

Thomas Jones, the painter, took their wages immediately and left the site.[119] One week later bricklayers Andrew and James Eyres were discharged, as were two masons in December.[120]

In the new year, the end was in sight. John MacKenzie, the working foreman of house carpenters, was paid off late in February.[121] That year, H£305.16.10. was paid to working parties of petty officers, seamen, marines, and soldiers employed at the site and another H£649.4.6. to different tradesmen engaged in stone cutting, painting and glazing, laying freestone, cutting steps, and finally wallpaper hanging. In addition, H£86.2.3. was spent in laying out and improving the grounds about the house.[122] Concerned that the house should be ready upon the commander-in-chief's arrival with the squadron from Bermuda, Wodehouse in mid-April gave orders to hire as many painters as could finish their work by 15 May.[123] As this last team of painters took over the carpenters were discharged.[124]

Within weeks of what had turned out to be the commissioner's final request relating to the house, Wodehouse received orders to return to England and to discharge all but a handful of employees at the naval yard. Two months later, on the last day of July 1819, he sailed from Halifax amid an extraordinary outpouring of affection and respect from the yard people, artificers, and officers of the yard and the naval hospital. Thereupon Rear Admiral Griffith assumed direct control of the finishing touches needed to the house and property. Artificers and others still employed in finishing the interior of the admiral's house, the stables, and in erecting the garden and other fences were kept at work most of the summer.[125] In the house itself, the curtains still needed to be installed. The admiral's final order related to the water closet "from the imperfect manner in which it has been fitted, having become a nuisance, which in a short time would render the house uninhabitable."[126] The master shipwright, we presume, overcame this final difficulty.

In the matter of furnishings, the Navy Board sent out stoves, none of which, in Wodehouse's opinion, was adequate "to warm the principal rooms in a climate like this." Instead, having sent the Board the dimensions of four fireplaces, he insisted on only the most efficient stoves.[127] When the Admiralty directed the Navy Board to supply the house with the usual furniture,[128] the Board first requested from Wodehouse a comprehensive "plan of each floor ... describing the doors, windows, dimensions, height from floor to top of architraves of the windows," as a guide for carpets and curtains.[129]

There then only remained the garden and walls. Still "in a state of nature," the field surrounding the house was ploughed and sown with grass in 1814.[130] In the summer of 1815 Rear Admiral Griffith had asked the Admiralty's permission to lay out a garden around the site at the cost of £100. Wodehouse had envisioned a garden enclosed with a wooden fence. Griffith proposed that the eastern wall, across which the admiral could view the harbour, the hospital complex, and the naval yard below, be fashioned of excess stone and be reinforced with mortar. "As the situation is particularly well-adapted to fruit trees, and the stone being on the spot," he explained, "I apprehend that the difference in the immediate expense will be trifling and in the end less than a wooden fence."[131] The Board awarded him £200 to complete the work. Finally, Griffith ordered that an abandoned hospital wash house shed in the lower part of the field in which the admiral's house stood, be dismantled and re-erected as a building adjoining the garden in the same field, and divided so that one part of it could be used by the gardener and the other by the marine guard.[132]

It took the navy more than three decades after the establishment of the Halifax naval station to build a suitable hospital for its sick and wounded. Until then the temporary hospitals were frequently overwhelmed in wartime by the number of sick and dying. Despite naval policy in favour of purpose-built naval hospitals being the best way to care for the sick, no one in authority, until Hamond arrived in Halifax in 1781, bothered to press the Admiralty for a large, permanent hospital building.[133] Completed in 1782 and destroyed by fire in 1819, two-thirds of its thirty-seven-year history were war years, when its value was most keenly felt.

When hostilities ended in mid-1815, ushering in a century of peace in the North Atlantic, there was little need for a large hospital establishment or structure. After its accidental destruction, the Admiralty did not replace it for almost a half-century. Only the naval emergency during the US Civil War and the heightened Anglo-American tension it created, offered the excuse to erect a new naval hospital, this time built of brick. In the intervening forty years, inmates were cared for in a succession of hulks serving as floating hospitals, the best-remembered being the old frigate *Pyramus*.

The "rude inelegant square building of stone," as Anthony Lockwood unkindly called the admiral's house in 1818, ultimately required more time to complete than it took to fight the Great War exactly a century later.[134] Construction spread over six summers, beginning in 1814 and ending only in 1819. Proposed in the midst of a war with France that seemed at times endless, decided upon at the height of a second war with the United States, its concept and construction were overtaken in 1815 by the sudden cessation of hostilities. First appearing in the 1811 navy estimates approved by the imperial Parliament, the building was assigned a parsimonious budget of £3,000. By 1814 this had been raised to £4,500, which two years later the Navy Board insisted could not be exceeded.[135] For comparison's sake it should be noted that the entire Halifax naval yard, hospital complex, and admiral's house cost less to build than the residence soon to be built for the admiral at the Bermuda base. By this measure the modest construction and maintenance costs, when calculated from 1758 through 1819, made the Halifax naval base one of the greatest bargains the British navy experienced before 1820, however unwittingly achieved.

The admiral's house, though much altered, is one of only two pre-1820 naval yard structures still standing on its original foundation. Like the other surviving building – the hospital officers' tenement – it proved for many years to be a white elephant, as a greatly-enlarged naval establishment for the Halifax yard occurred only in 1832. Built cheaply with the aid of naval and military labour, and without benefit either of an architect's plan or most unusually, a contractor, it was used for many years after 1819 only for the few weeks during the annual summer visit of the admiral with his Bermuda-based squadron.

PART TWO

WORK FORCE

Chapter Four

OFFICERS AND THEIR CLERKS

So far we have been concerned with the expansion and site development of the careening yard once the decision was taken in 1758 to establish the naval base in Halifax harbour. Our task is now to examine how the yard was managed, how the workforce was structured, and the details of the principal tasks undertaken by yard workers. Let us first consider the officers and their clerks, their roles and responsibilities, as well as their relationship to the Admiralty and Navy boards.

Studies of the eighteenth-century Navy Board, under whose direct authority all British naval bases were placed, have largely concerned themselves with examining various attempts at its reform. To Morriss, for instance, the efforts constituted a silent revolution in administration. This meant that by 1814–15 the English dockyards had become a "smoothly humming instrument of war."[1] By contrast, Haas finds no such administrative revolution; instead he believes that great energy and discussion produced only meagre results. To him, the dockyards remained inefficient, with high production costs, where "planning, organization, direction, coordination and control were feeble ... The Navy Board attempted the impossible task of micromanaging the yards, as if they themselves were actually on the spot. Information resources were practically useless; there was no control over finances, costs or inventory."[2] Peopled by lazy, undisciplined, and poorly-paid workers, many of whom were elderly or disabled, the dockyards were believed to be inefficient and indifferent to cost. To Haas, by 1815 the Navy Board seemed no closer than before war was launched in 1793 to creating what the dockyards desperately needed, namely: "clear lines of authority, individual responsibility, and full and accurate information."[3] By studying the Halifax yard, we shall attempt to assess the impact of such reforms on a foreign naval base.

The Admiralty, in the matter of dockyard policy, also regularly took detailed decisions on matters referred to it by its subordinate boards. Besides the Navy Board, these were the Victualling Board, the Transport Board, and the Sick and Hurt Board. Each such board was purely administrative and despatched its work at general meetings. Instructions were determined, accounts and contracts approved, estimates to be submitted to Parliament settled. The Navy Board had more than two thousand correspondents, a handful of whom were located in Halifax. There was no priority to the business undertaken; it attended instead to whatever matter individual board members brought before it. Without accurate and useful information such boards could not make the wisest decisions. Standing orders, among other things, required the preparation of all sorts of regular reports – monthly, quarterly, and yearly, by the yards, foreign and domestic – but their value was often reduced to merely accounting for what stores or monies were issued or received.[4] The standing orders themselves, which provided details for the management of the yards, became so numerous – more than 1,200 by 1786 – that even the most diligent yard officer fell foul of them. Such orders were often contradictory, while others were not rescinded when subsequent orders superseded them. Even the standing order to read them collectively every quarter was ignored.

Supervision of each of the separate naval yards rested in the hands of a resident commissioner – an office established in 1690 – or in his absence, by the naval storekeeper, one of the three principal officers of the yard.[5] The leading critic and foremost reformer of the Navy Board, Samuel Bentham, wanted the resident commissioner to have full authority over the business of the yard in which he resided. Yet an order-in-council of 1801 granted him full authority only to enforce obedience to the Navy Board's orders and regulations. His management powers were greatly curtailed when he was empowered to suspend but not to dismiss personnel, such power being retained by the Navy Board, or, in the matter of the principal officers, by the Admiralty.[6]

Owing to the prevailing hierarchical social structure and the paternalistic rank structure within the navy, commissioners, when issuing directions, were expected to be obeyed instantly and to the letter. The strength of their orders was additionally enhanced by the patronage they enjoyed that in the first instance had brought them to their position of authority. At the same time they were expected to obey the directives sent them by both the Admiralty Board and the Navy Board. The commissioner enforced all Navy Board regulations, orders, and instructions. He liaised with the port admiral or senior captain to determine priority in refitting warships and reported their arrivals and departures to the Navy Board. He verified the attendance records of yard employees and approved extended hours of work. He authorized purchases from local suppliers when shortages occurred and the sale of navy bills to raise cash to pay yard employees and local tradesmen. He concluded contracts for the supply of materials to build yard structures or for the supply of masts. Much of this consisted of routine formality, performed at the request of the respective officer. His position was thus less managerial than supervisory. When the Navy Board encouraged the Admiralty to appoint a new commissioner in 1783, one of the two significant reasons advanced was his role in concluding contracts to supply New York and the West Indies with rough masts; a responsibility that "ought not to be trusted to the management of inferior officers."[7]

The Halifax careening yard had seven successive commissioners, none before 1775 and none after 1819. They were Marriot Arbuthnot (1775–8), Sir Richard Hughes (1778–81), Sir Andrew Snape Hamond (1781–3), Henry Duncan (1783–99, 1800–3), Isaac Coffin (1799–1800), John Inglefield (1803–12), and Philip Wodehouse (1812–19). Each held captain's rank in the navy and had extensive experience at sea. Arbuthnot captained *Guarland* under Boscawen and Spry in North American waters in 1755. His American experience included service in 1757 on the Virginia and New York coasts.[8] Sir Richard Hughes was promoted captain in 1756, rear-admiral in 1780, and died an admiral. As captain of *Roebuck*, Sir Andrew Snape Hamond served in the Delaware and advised Howe during the campaign against Philadelphia, for which services he was knighted in 1778. As a midshipman, Dundee-born Henry Duncan served on *Nassau* with Holburne off Louisbourg in 1757. Made Howe's flag captain in North America in 1776–8, he selected the site at Turtle Bay for the careening yard established in 1776 on Manhattan Island. His appointment to the Halifax yard was also made under the patronage of Howe who, by 1783, was First Lord of the Admiralty.

Boston-born Isaac Coffin had the least distinguished naval career, but was the first of the Halifax commissioners actually to have prior experience in a naval yard, having served the previous four years at Corsica, Lisbon, and Minorca. As a lieutenant he commanded schooner *Placentia* off Newfoundland in 1778–9, and survived the shipwreck of armed vessel *Pinson* on the Labrador coast in 1779. As captain of *Thisbe*, he gave passage to Lord Dorchester to Quebec where he was subject to court martial for falsifying his muster books and dismissed from his ship.

John Inglefield, like Coffin, brought with him some yard experience. Of him John Jervis, the Earl of St Vincent, had written in 1800, "Commissioner Inglefield is honest and sufficiently intelligent, but pompous, flowery, indolent and wrapped up in official forms, staytape and buckram. He has however corrected many gross and abominable abuses and peculations practiced under his predecessor."[9] From 1794 he was made resident commissioner successively at Corsica, Malta, and Gibraltar before going to Halifax. Earlier, he was midshipman on Durell's flagship *Launceston* in 1766 at Halifax. As lieutenant he served on *Romney* at Halifax and Boston under Hood. He became Hood's flag captain in 1780, and commanded *Centaur* (74) in the September 1781 action with De Grasse off the Chesapeake and at the Battle of the Saints in April 1782. He published an account of his survival, after sixteen days at sea, when he lost his ship in a hurricane and sailed to Fayal in a pinnace with his master, midshipman, and nine seamen.

Philip Wodehouse, the younger son of John, first Baron Wodehouse, was promoted captain in 1796. After having been wounded, he was withdrawn from sea service. Made rear admiral when he departed Halifax in 1819, he died a vice admiral eleven years later, without again serving at sea.

Of these, after their Nova Scotia service, three continued their careers in other yards or as a member of the Navy Board itself. Hamond, created a baronet in December 1783, after a year as an extra commissioner of the Navy Board in 1793–4, became comptroller of the navy, the effective head of the Navy Board, until 1806. Member of Parliament for Ipswich 1796–1806, he retired only in 1811. Duncan was briefly resident commissioner at Sheerness, 1799–1800, before returning to Halifax. He served as deputy comptroller of the navy, under Hamond, until 1806. When Coffin left Halifax in 1800, under St Vincent's patronage he became commissioner of Sheerness dockyard, where he generated serious friction. At one point he threatened to have recalcitrant yard workers pressed into the navy. Created a baronet in 1804 and promoted rear admiral in 1805, Coffin was elected member of

Parliament for Ilchester in 1818. He ended his days as a full admiral and governor of Greenwich Hospital.

Only two of these men returned to command at sea, each in an undistinguished manner. A year after Arbuthnot departed Halifax, he was promoted vice admiral and named naval commander-in-chief, a position he held for almost two years. If the Admiralty "had gone through the navy list looking for a flag officer who should not be sent to New York, they could not have come up with a better choice,"[10] Syrett has written. He was at the siege of Charleston in 1780, but failed to attack an inferior French squadron at Newport later that year, and squandered his chance to defeat Destouches's squadron off the Virginia Capes in March 1781. Sir Richard Hughes commanded the North American squadron at Halifax from 1789 to 1792, without apparent opportunity for distinction.

Arbuthnot, Hughes, and Hamond combined the role of resident commissioner with that of Nova Scotia's lieutenant governor during the war years 1775–1783. Indeed, Hamond resigned as commissioner shortly after he learned that he had not been selected as governor. Three weeks later he also resigned as lieutenant governor.[11] He was a minor victim of the collapse of Lord North's administration in the aftermath of the Yorktown débâcle, the position having been granted by the new Shelburne administration to General John Parr, the first of a long post-war string of military men to assume this role. His successors, Coffin excepted, were appointed to Nova Scotia's legislative council.

Commissioners' salaries were high, about the equivalent of that of the bishop of Nova Scotia, but failed to keep pace with inflation. The prospect of a pension, much enhanced over that of a mere sea captain, helped to keep them at their posts. In 1784 Duncan received a salary of £1,000 less deductions of £75, an allowance of £100, and travel money when he was required to leave Halifax, as he did in 1785 and 1786, for instance, when he inspected crown timber reserves in Nova Scotia and New Brunswick.[12] His pension, when he retired in 1811, was £900, plus that of a superannuated captain. Inglefield was granted a pension of 75 per cent of the £1,000 paid commissioners in the home yards, plus the half pay of £219 of a senior captain.[13]

Inglefield was the first commissioner to complain of his salary. Paid in sterling, its purchasing power in Nova Scotia collapsed when wartime conditions sharply discounted sterling against Halifax currency, a matter discussed in chapter 10. He estimated in 1811 that the adverse sterling exchange rate cost him almost a quarter of his income. In addition, wartime inflation further ate into its purchasing power, as prices for necessities doubled during his residence, while clothing had risen as much as 70 per cent. His proposal that he should be allowed to add the discount on sterling to his salaries was rejected.[14] His successor echoed similar sentiments when the war with the United States caused a "very great increase in the price of every necessary of life in this place."[15] Even with the peace in 1815, Wodehouse believed himself to be "very inadequately paid."[16]

Among the resident commissioners, only Coffin regularly issued orders and he was commissioner for only six months. The only times Duncan and Inglefield were tempted to issue orders was when they went on leave to England – Duncan in 1797 and Inglefield a decade later – leaving the three principal officers in charge. Their so-called "directions" were more policy than orders. For Duncan, yard policy regarding overtime work to refit the squadron was to be followed, while Sunday work was permissible only if "the business is very pressing."[17] The joint concurrence of two officers was needed to purchase stores of any kind locally. Only with the unanimous approval of the principal officers could rounders or watchmen be dismissed except for "such reasons as may render it highly improper to continue him," the vacancies thus created to be filled in a strict order of preference. Both the master shipwright and master attendant could discharge any artificer or labourer under them, but only if they supplied the storekeeper with sufficient reason. "Replacements must be 'good and sufficient men' with proper certificates, whenever they could be obtained." When not employed on warships, yard workers were to complete a number of construction tasks in the yard. Finally, the night watch of the yard was to remain under the supervision of the duty officer who, as usual, issued the nightly password.

Inglefield left an equally short and not dissimilar list. He directed artificers to fashion masts during the winter. He ordered the officers to end "a very great nuisance" by banning hogs, goats, and geese from the yard. In contrast to these short epistles, Coffin left a New Testament-sized book of rules and regulations that "I have to the best of my judgment laid down."[18] Nothing better could contrast their management styles, the latter deeply insecure, the former quietly confident.

The commissioner's role in providing effective liaison between the naval units in harbour and the principal yard officers was often fraught with difficulties. It could have been as simple a matter as Inglefield's complaint that he lacked a coxswain for his boat, though one was on the establishment at both Gibraltar and Malta.[19] This put him in a "very awkward situation" to collect a boat's crew or steer the boat, "when it was my duty to go afloat ... to visit the commander-in-chief on his arrival that I have been under the necessity of taking the tiller myself from the man [perhaps a labourer] who had been put in by chance."[20]

The greater source of irritation occurred when the commissioner's role was usurped by the flag officer in port or by the senior captain. Immediately upon learning of Hamond's resignation in 1782 as commissioner and as lieutenant governor, the sea captains refused to take his orders as naval commander.[21] His successor, Duncan, returned to Halifax from a trip to inspect forest reserves in 1784, to find that his naval storekeeper had been superseded by order of the commodore. Coffin, Duncan's successor in 1799, immediately upon his arrival irritated the sea captains when he accused them of having issued orders to yard officers about the equipping of their ships, which "frequently deviated" from the Board's rules. Yard officers were told thereafter to ignore such orders,[22] a position subsequently endorsed by the Navy Board.[23]

This was not Coffin's only brush with the sea command. He countermanded Vice Admiral Vandeput's order to the storekeeper to supply fuel to the captains' and lieutenants' lodges in the yard, occupied while their ships were refitting. Ships' pursers had funds to purchase such fuel, the admiral was told.[24] Coffin also accused warrant officers in all the ships of embezzlement. He even identified their fences for stolen goods, "inhabitants of this town, who keep lights at the end of their wharfs, under a pretence of its being convenient for the boats to land there, but in reality to mark out those spots as a deposit."[25] When Coffin accused officers of twice storing their ships for eight months, without ever "proceeding to sea," they wrote a joint letter to the Admiralty to vindicate themselves "from the disgrace reflected on us by this unqualified charge of embezzlement." Denying Coffin's charges, they characterized his accusations as an "unprecedented insult to the service."[26]

This was no tempest in a teapot for politics were involved. Coffin was protected by his patron, the earl of St Vincent. A year later when the senior officer raised the affair with the First Lord, he departed the interview believing "the subject has made an impression on your Lordship ... not favourable to the good opinion which I am ambitious to obtain there."[27]

In 1810 the Admiralty sent to Inglefield among others, a new edition of *General Naval Instructions for the Government of the Respective Branches of the Civil Service and the Navy on Foreign Stations*, with clarifications on the relations between commanders-in-chief and resident commissioners at overseas bases. It reasserted that the resident commissioner had absolute authority over duties in the naval yard and its accounts. His cooperation in carrying out the naval commander's directions was crucial to the fleet's operation. Private or personal altercations must not be allowed to hurt the naval service. Inglefield boasted that under Admirals Mitchell, Berkeley, and Warren "not the smallest dispute, public or private has ever occurred."[28]

Inglefield was the only commissioner accused of fraud. The accusation was made to the Admiralty by John Douglas, captain of storeship *Comet*, who had for several months observed the working of the naval yard, whose people were "employed more for the conveniency of Commissioner Inglefield than for his Majesty's service."[29] Inglefield was supposed to have built for his own pleasure, at public cost, a 70-ton sloop fitted as a yacht; of building stone walls in his garden; and making an icehouse for his use, using yard masons and labourers. The sole evidence was "an unguarded expression" by the master shipwright. When the commissioner denied such intemperate accusations, the matter was dropped.[30]

Two commissioners – Hamond in 1782 and Inglefield in 1807 – resigned their posts and sailed to England without permission. Hamond was given a baronetcy and promoted, while Inglefield was obliged to return humiliated to his post. Inglefield had come to Halifax still hoping to serve later as commissioner either at Chatham or Plymouth, whichever first became available. In 1807 he suddenly departed for England, without permission, having sold his furniture, to be greeted in England by an astonished Navy Board.[31] His extraordinary behaviour arose from promises he believed he had received from Lord Mulgrave relating to his future pension. As he explained, "In consequence of having discovered such treatment and quite at a loss to comprehend from what motion it should have been considered necessary to invite me with benevolent promises to England apparently to deceive me I need not explain to you, sir, what my mind suffered."[32]

A factor of importance to the smooth running of the yard was the personality of the resident commissioner and his ability to get along with his senior managers. Modern management theorists argue that in any organization high trust tends to stimulate high performance whereby subordinate managers generally respond according to the degree of confidence placed in them by their superiors. This is usually demonstrated in them trying to justify their supervisors' good opinion by performing exceptionally well. In turn high performance will reinforce the initial trust placed by the superior in one whose expectations are being met or even exceeded. When the management culture is hostile, which it was under Coffin and at times under Inglefield, morale suffered. Communications could suffer as the protection of one's own hide from the recurrent threat of recrimination or worse discouraged efforts to focus on yard efficiency.

A resident commissioner, in the name of efficiency, could add to the misery of officers, clerks, and workers. This happened in a significant way twice, first in an acute fashion during Coffin's brief, unhappy tenure and later in 1803, when Inglefield, newly-arrived in Halifax, waged war against his acting naval storekeeper. In the earlier instance, for the six months from the time Coffin stepped ashore in mid-October 1799 until his departure for England in April 1800, he created serious difficulties for officers who carried the management burden of the yard. Coffin put his fingers in every pie, wanting to be informed about every minute matter. His intrusive style was compounded by his decidedly negative view of everyone working in a naval yard. He smelled embezzlement everywhere, having himself been found guilty by court martial of fraud. At the time, he had been dealt with leniently and merely suffered the indignity and loss of income by being removed from the command of his ship. To have been dismissed from the service ought to have been his sentence. The implementation of his bullying management style was made the easier as the naval storekeeper, who had gone mad, was absent in England on leave and the master attendant retired upon Coffin's arrival. Coffin was thus free to appoint two compliant men to act temporarily in their places.

Coffin's behaviour compared most unfavourably with that of his predecessor, Henry Duncan. Duncan was a rather easy-going administrator for whom people clearly liked to work. He delegated his responsibilities to his officers and rarely found himself in conflict with them. On those few occasions he did, it was rather at the Navy Board's insistence that one or other of his officers needed some form of censure, almost invariably relating to the tardiness or quality of the reports submitted by the yard officers to the Board. He had a patient manner with sea officers and those who complained of the yard's routine or work.

Coffin had the attitude of a reformed sinner. Blended with his naturally aggressive personality may have been his need to overcome the social inferiority of a colonial-born sea officer. Confident of the protection of his patron, First Sea Lord St Vincent, also a reformed sinner, Coffin issued an unprecedented series of orders, each prefaced by a description of the evil his measures sought to remedy.[33] As far as the squadron was concerned, Coffin directed the yard officers to refuse to approve "improper requisitions" from the admiral on behalf of his captains.[34] To avoid idleness "so prevalent among the boat crews," in future, when the squadron arrived in harbour, a priority list of ships was to be prepared with precise details about the exact stores each needed. Captains were to adhere strictly to the list drawn up by the admiral.[35] Only the yard's boats were allowed to land at the yard, as "great irregularities having arisen when the squadron's boats used the landing place by the platform ... embarking their drunken men, fresh beef, and supplies ... for their ships." None subsequently was permitted except with a pass.[36] Likewise, food for yard inhabitants should thereafter be brought by boat, as no horse was "to be entered for the use of this yard again, without the commissioner's order, the expense having been much beyond the benefit derived."[37] After studying the pay and muster books Coffin, on Christmas Eve, directed that no artificer from the squadron thereafter be placed on the yard's books unless his services were first requested by either the master attendant or master shipwright.[38] When a request was made to purchase a half-ton of oakum, Coffin refused, stating that for the "four years past that I have superintended the repairs and equipment of his Majesty's fleet under the command of the Earl of St Vincent I never heard of oakum being purchased for the use of the ships."[39]

In matters relating to the merchant community, Coffin forbade the yard from offering, as had been its habit, "immediate assistance" to vessels which ran into difficulties upon entering port.[40] Not only did this practice distract officers from their yard duties but, he argued, it wore out hawsers without compensation. Thereafter the yard would come to their aid only after written application was made together with a binding agreement to make good any losses sustained by government property. In the same vein, merchants thereafter would be provided with supplies from the yard's stores only after consulting the commissioner or, in his absence, the admiral. Otherwise such applications must accompany an affidavit sworn before a magistrate that the stores requested were unavailable in town, and that their vessel was unable to proceed to sea without the items requested. Coffin's order applied to mail packets as well as to other vessels hired by the public offices.[41] He abolished the practice of lending careening gear and other stores which were often returned damaged. Thereafter, the master attendant would make the final determination of costs payable by the borrowers.[42]

Fraud and embezzlement were the focus when Coffin turned his attention to the yard staff. Coffin ordered that the keys of the boathouse and store cabin were to be lodged in the storekeeper's office by the foreman of the yard. He insisted that all passes collected by the gate porter were to be checked each Monday morning by the three principal officers.[43] No workman could exit the yard through the gate during working hours without a pass except those at work on officers' houses or gardens.[44]

This is but a small sample of a stream of orders which issued from his pen during his twenty-four weeks' sojourn at Halifax. The effect of such micromanagement further bureaucratized the process of running the yard. It is unclear if any of these new procedures survived his departure. He directed that all orders in place at the time of Duncan's departure remain in force "which do not militate against those issued since my arrival."[45]

In the number of such directives, no other commissioner came close to matching Coffin, even those resident for a decade or more. Most of Hamond's orders, for instance, derived from his naval command over ships in harbour. Wodehouse confined himself in 1817 to forbidding ships' bands from practicing or landing in the yard,[46] while in 1819 when the new fish market opened near the yard's south boundary, to forbidding "officer's servants, seamen, mariners or their wives on their way to market, and other private business from landing at the stairs or coming through the yard."[47]

The extent to which commissioners came to know the yard's employees, other than the principal officers, is unclear. Coffin, who spent about six months in office and who created so much turmoil, formed negative opinions about a large number of the yard's employees, men he scarcely knew. Duncan with sixteen years at the helm, Inglefield with eleven, and Wodehouse with seven were afforded the best opportunities to ascertain the competencies of the yard's employees. By contrast with Coffin who was feared and perhaps hated, Wodehouse was held in high esteem. By the time he departed in mid-1819, he had seen the yard through its most active period, when more than 120 warships served in North American waters, many of which refit-

76 Part Two: Work Force

ted and stored for sea at the naval yard. The decision by the Admiralty in the late spring of 1819 to close the Halifax naval base occasioned an unprecedented outpouring of sentiment. He received several public expressions of gratitude. The town and Nova Scotia Council wrote of the "ability and zeal which have distinguished your public character and your liberal, courteous and engaging manner in private life have endeared you to all classes of society."[48] The officers and clerks, in a combined expression of regret and appreciation, wrote of "the pain of being separated from your mild command bears heavily in our minds," and of how their duties had been "rendered easy and pleasant, by your unremitted and ardent zeal ... extensive knowledge, superior judgment." They made specific reference to those "obliging acts of your condescension which have eminently tended to promote the comfort or ameliorate the condition of every individual among us."[49] One memorial was signed by ten of the senior artificers, on behalf of themselves and "the people of the yard."[50] It is significant as a rare expression of what ordinary men felt for their social betters. It was with "deep sorrow" that they saw him depart. They expressed the "gratitude of ourselves and families" for his "many acts of disinterested munificence." They assured Wodehouse that such expressions "are not merely words ... but the true and unaffected sentiments of the heart." Even if we discount their need to seize this one last occasion to seek his patronage, the tone as well as the sentiments were echoed by others for whom nothing could be expected from the departing commissioner.

This intelligent, warm, and kind-hearted man, married while commissioner and whose elder child was born at the yard, held a special place in the affections of officers, clerks, artificers, and ordinary labourers. He admired the "zeal, attention and ability," displayed by his Nova Scotians, who had toiled at times under great stress. Unable to protect them in 1819 against certain unemployment, he lobbied successfully both for their pensions and to allow those who already had houses in the yard to retain the use of them.[51]

Until the first commissioner was appointed in 1775, and in the absence of a naval commander, management of the Halifax naval yard rested on the shoulders of three men, known as the respective officers. Another officer, a boatswain, was added in 1800. In order of precedence, they were the naval officer – referred to here by his earlier title of storekeeper – the master attendant, and the master shipwright.[52]

Their actual importance to the yard was perhaps in reverse order. The master shipwright, responsible for the repair of ships and the building and maintenance of the yard structures, was the most important of the three, as his orders determined the work of perhaps six of seven foremen who worked in the yard. Reporting to him were the foreman of the yard and five other foremen: of shipwrights, caulkers, smiths, house carpenters, and labourers. At times he was also assigned a boat's crew.

The master attendant, invariably a former ship's master, acted as harbour master responsible for mooring and piloting ships, surveying and careening them, and had direction over riggers, sailmakers, and pilots. He had his own boat's crew. In wartime his department evaluated all prizes condemned by the vice-admiralty court that the naval commander-in-chief wanted commissioned into the naval service. His department was responsible for nominating a surveyor, whenever contract masts or timber were to be delivered to the yard. As the Navy Board considered his skill in piloting warships around the harbour as "a most essential part" of his duty, he made himself familiar with navigation of all harbours and anchorages in the region.[53]

The storekeeper received, stored, and issued all materials for the work of the yard. His clerks oversaw the supply of carpenters' and boatswains' stores issued to or received from warships. For this extensive inventory he was held personally responsible. Over his signature came all requests for new stores or the despatch of stores required either by the ships in harbour or at other naval yards. The Halifax storekeeper always acted as clerk of the cheque when serving as paymaster to the yard. He kept a record of service for each yard employee; he mustered them, verified the accounts of their earnings, and made out the pay books sent to the Navy Board. He maintained the cash box and advertised for the sale of navy bills to raise cash. He also requested tenders for the supply of all sorts of materials needed in the yard and for managing the contracts thereby concluded. His clerks attended the receipt of ships' stores, verified contractors' deliveries, and measured the work of contractors such as painters.

Only two of the principal officers ended their public careers at the Halifax yard. Provo Wallis, master shipwright at the New York yard during the war, held the same position in Halifax in 1783. He retired to England with a pension in 1792. Thomas Read, master attendant from 1788, also retired superannuated to England in 1799.[54]

Three others went mad while in Halifax, perhaps inadvertently poisoned by the lead-based paint that surrounded them at work and at home. Their careers abruptly ended as they returned home. John Loader, brought out in 1776, was seized six years later with a "fit of delirium ... incapable of doing his duty."[55] Titus Livie, naval storekeeper in the 1790s, "was deprived of his reason prior to his departure."[56] His successor, Thomas Oben, formerly storekeeper at Corsica, within eight months of his arrival in Halifax in 1800 fell into "a damaged state of mind."[57]

For many officers, appointment to the Halifax yard was merely a step in a continuing career spent partly in England and partly abroad. Samuel Hemmens, master attendant from 1780 to 1787, became second master attendant at Plymouth 1790–99, and ended his career as master attendant at Chatham 1799–1817. When John Jackson, made master attendant by Coffin in 1799,[58] departed Halifax, he served as master attendant in the Portsmouth yard from 1803,[59] as did Thomas Atkinson, master attendant in Halifax from 1807 until 1810.[60] Both of the last two master shipwrights – Thomas Forder Hawkes, appointed in 1813, and Algernon Frederick Jones, his successor in 1818 – came from Deptford dockyard. For each it was a promotion, after serving as foreman of shipwrights at home.[61]

Two died in office. Joseph Gerrish, the first permanent naval storekeeper and a Boston-born merchant who had come to Halifax shortly after its settlement, died in office in 1774. In the 1750s he had contracted with the Navy Board to store *Boston*, then being built at Piscataqua. A justice of the peace for Halifax county, he was successively a member of the legislative council and deputy judge of the vice-admiralty court. The other was Welsh-born William Hughes who served in Deptford dockyard for nine years before volunteering for Halifax in 1775.[62] He successfully sought the patronage of Arbuthnot, Duncan, and Hamond when Coffin dismissed him.[63] Soon reinstated, he was master shipwright for the last eight years of his life.[64]

The principal officers, who generally served shorter periods of service in Nova Scotia than their clerks, almost invariably went home to England upon retirement. Only the long-serving master shipwright, Elias Marshall, stayed in Nova Scotia. William Hughes doubtless would have also retired in Nova Scotia, had he not died in office.

If patronage was vital, competence was supremely important. Hughes would perhaps not have been reinstated had he not been so experienced and effective a senior artificer. Offered several lucrative appointments when discharged, he declined them all in the hope of returning to the yard. That John Parry, as foreman of carpenters, "grossly insulted and abused" the master attendant in 1809, did not prevent him being appointed master shipwright by Wodehouse four years later.[65] Edmund Fairfax, formerly master of the Channel fleet, was the only master attendant to be dismissed.[66] His offence was to have run *Superbe* onto Mars rock in a favourable wind when departing Halifax harbour.[67] Colvill made David Hooper his master attendant in 1763 as he had "above twenty years ... practice in heaving down ships."[68] Colvill also made James Hooper his master shipwright as the admiral could "not properly direct the whole business of the yard without the assistance of one of superior skill and genius," which he knew this man possessed.[69]

Officers were paid well when their fees and the earnings of their apprentices were taken into account. In 1763, Gerrish was paid £150 as storekeeper. By 1800 the storekeeper's salary had risen to £180, but in 1802 at the peace it was reduced to £150.[70] It subsequently rose dramatically. Until then they were paid in London and employed agents at some expense to receive and transmit pay. Only from 1807 could they draw their pay from the yard's coffers, not in cash, but by bill of exchange.[71] This meant that when sterling was at a discount, they paid a penalty, which became increasingly severe as the war lengthened. By 1811 only the commissioner and the naval storekeeper were left in this position. Dawes, the storekeeper, begged for permission to pay himself from the cash chest not quarterly, as was customary, but monthly like the yard workers.[72] By then the naval storekeeper received a salary of £480 and the master attendant £350. In 1756 George Kittoe, as the first acting master shipwright at Halifax, was paid £100 a year, while his successor, Abraham Constable, received a salary of £150, and by 1763 he was requesting a raise to £200.[73] By 1807 the base salary was £360, while the boatswain, who was paid monthly received £200.[74] Each was subjected to certain tax deductions after 1807, including a 10 per cent property tax, while in addition the master attendant and boatswain paid a 1.25 per cent widow's charity tax. Salary was paid, every three months in arrears, in London into the hands of agents with whom the officers made the necessary arrangements.

To salaries, a variety of fees or informal payments were added until the end of the eighteenth century, for instance: upon receiving new stores and selling old and condemned ones. Such behaviour, though criticized by contemporaries, was "condoned in transactions in most government departments."[75] When fees and emoluments were

80 Part Two: Work Force

abolished in the yards from 1801, they were replaced by fattened salaries and a superannuation plan. Superannuation entitled officers to between one-third of their salaries after ten to fifteen years' service to three-quarters after more than thirty-five years.[76] Thereafter officials and clerks entered into a bond "to an amount three times his salary and subscribe to an oath of fidelity not to receive any unofficial payment, act as an agent or have no interest in a ship, vessel or stores used by the navy."[77]

When a parliamentary commission enquired into gratuities, fees, perquisites, and emoluments, based in the year 1784, the yard reported none.[78] The naval officer or storekeeper, George Thomas, received a net salary of £185 and £281.8.1. in allowances. He also received £30 for house rent, another £17 5s. for receiving slops, and £15 a year for stationery, for a total of £530.8.1. The master shipwright, Provo Wallis, earned the most with a salary of £187.15.4., allowances of £335 19s. for pay and overtime for three apprentices, £30 house rent, and monthly pay for the three apprentices of 32s. each, for a total of £616.2.7. The master attendant, Samuel Hemmens, received a net salary of £185, house rent of £30, plus two apprentices worth £79 8s., £40 for extra house rent, £11 for laying buoys, and £8 10s. as a pilot, for a total of £313 18s.

Wartime inflation in the 1790s affected everyone in the yard, either waged or salaried. A month after the officers supported a petition from labourers and watchmen for improved wages, they themselves petitioned the commissioner to write on their behalf to the Navy Board. They used the fact that the Sick and Hurt Board had increased the salary of John Halliburton, the surgeon of the naval hospital.[79] Jackson in 1800 and Dawes in 1808 complained of their incomes. Dawes asked only that his compensation be placed at a rate equal to that of storekeepers at Gibraltar, Antigua, Jamaica, and the Cape of Good Hope, where salaries equalled those of clerks of the cheque in home yards, while that of Halifax was one-fifth less.[80] Jackson pointed out the obvious, as the "necessary expenses of a family in this country at all times great have been on the increase since the commencement of the war, and now become enormous."[81] He added that the "prevailing opinion in England that the officers of foreign yards acquire fortunes by agency for prizes etc. is unhappily unfounded in fact when applied to Halifax, where collectively considered a comfortable subsistence answerable to their appointments is the most they can look up to, while I, in a situation laborious, important and strongly marked with solicitude ... am left sensibly to feel the pressure of circumstances greatly narrowed." This was a sharp disappointment to him for he had brought his family to Nova Scotia "at no inconsiderable charge."

In the matter of prize agency, during the war with rebel America the Navy Board had been upset to learn that a "very great impropriety" had occurred when they discovered that two of the officers concerned in the survey of the prize frigate *Magicienne* in 1782 were also agents for the captors. Under the threat of dismissal they put an end to the practice.[82] Commissioner Hamond, who ordered in this case a second tonnage measurement as the first seemed excessive to the Navy Board, claimed he had never approved of their behaviour, "which I shall take care not to permit in future."[83] In 1793 the matter reappeared when Capt. Fisher of *Winchelsea* solicited the naval storekeeper, Titus Livie, "to become his agent for any prizes he may send in here." With Commissioner Duncan's approval, Livie sought the Board's permission to accept the offer.[84]

Until 1802 the yard officers additionally received an annual supply of coal to heat their residences, built for them in 1793. When discontinued in 1803, coal costs were charged against their salaries. In appealing this order, Inglefield argued that the climate "which has usually a seven months' winter," required houses to be properly heated.[85] He suggested at least that they not be charged for the fuel consumed the previous winter.

Suspensions or dismissals of yard officers were rare, though the Halifax yard witnessed both. Unrestrained by a commissioner before 1775, temptation to mischief could not at times be resisted. In 1775 the Navy Board learned that both the master shipwright and Jacob Hurd, the naval storekeeper's clerk, had been "vendors & dealers" in stores supplied the yard locally, contrary to standing orders. The Board warned them that if "ever they should attempt again to deal in naval stores" the master shipwright would be superseded and the clerk discharged.[86] Thereafter requirements for naval stores were to be advertised locally and purchased, after surveys had been conducted, only at the best and cheapest rates. The naval storekeeper who had "acted very properly" was exonerated.

Embezzlement of naval stores in the dockyards added to workers' incomes.[87] In Portsmouth it was "so universal and well organized as to constitute a criminal social system which extended as far as to include parts of the machinery of justice."[88] The British navy suffered more material loss, amounting to perhaps £1 million a year, in the royal dockyards than at the hands of her enemies at sea.[89] Most Portsmouth dockyard workers were involved in theft of government stores, though only about twenty a year were prosecuted.[90] Not just individuals were implicated, but groups of men working together and their families, thereby supplementing their incomes.[91] Men who left the gates under the eyes of their officers and yard guards, were shielded by their friends as they attempted to rush past in large groups. The breakfast and dinner baskets removed by wives and children might contain embezzled hemp or cordage. Boats were also used at night. To the king's naval stores for which there was a ready market, shipwrights among yard workers had the greatest access. Watchmen in Portsmouth yard proved largely ineffective, for they had little incentive to detect fraud. They were open to bribes, for their incomes were less than those of labourers as they had no chance of earning extra for overtime work. Storehouse clerks had the greatest opportunity, but had small incentive as they had to post a £50 bond, which would be forfeit if convicted of theft. Besides, they received gifts from contractors which amounts easily exceeded the net value of stores they might have stolen had they been so inclined.

The focus of embezzlement at the Halifax yard lay elsewhere, if detected crimes remain our guide. Cases were few. The most celebrated came to light in 1775 and 1800. In the first case, Abraham Constable, master shipwright, already warned about selling stores to the yard contrary to standing orders, was accused of buying timber on his own account, getting the yard sawyers to convert it to plank, and then charging the yard the valued-added cost.[92] He purchased firewood in Dartmouth, used labourers at yard expense to move it by boat to the yard, then charged the yard 55 per cent more. He greatly improved his house by using both stores and labour provided by the yard free of charge. Labourers were frequently employed in his gardens and fields to build walls round his lots, while yard masons laid stones for new hearths and built stone steps to his yard, which they then paved. Yard smiths made iron rails and banisters for the stone steps, and hinges for his gates, so that all his fencing, gates, and walls were built at public expense. He purloined the lumber from the dismantled guardhouse to build a stable on his property. He likewise made a practice of charging more overtime than was ever worked, and made "the people of the yard" refund to his office the difference. Elias Marshall, foreman of the yard, collected the money for him from "the people." He also demanded part of the pay from several yard workers. He doubled the cabin keeper's wages and kept the difference. He was dismissed and his pay mulcted upon the arrival of the first commissioner in 1775. The disgraced master shipwright applied unsuccessfully to the Admiralty both to be tried and to be re-employed.[93]

The 1800 case involved Elias Marshall, then also master shipwright, several of his connections, and two of his sons. In 1775 Marshall had escaped with a censure by making himself indispensable to Commissioner Arbuthnot who convinced the Admiralty to overlook Marshall's "past errors."[94] Now in 1800 Marshall was suspended in a new series of accusations launched by Commissioner Coffin.[95] Convinced upon his arrival that the Halifax yard was little more than a den of thieves, within three months Coffin offered rewards of H£40 to apprehend embezzlers from the yard.[96] Some twenty-seven witnesses came forward and signed affidavits.[97] Ensnared with the master shipwright were his apprentice, his clerk who happened to be his son-in-law, and his two shipwright sons, Benjamin and Samuel.[98] Implicated also were Benjamin Marshall's father-in-law, foreman of the yard William Hughes, and his apprentice.[99] The patriarch was suspended, the others discharged and denied further entry through the gates.[100]

Marshall, like Constable, had used yard stores and labour over a five-year interval for a house he owned outside the yard. Several artificers provided precise details of the work undertaken.[101] On one occasion he had removed coal from the yard for the house. Like Constable, Marshall was accused of taking bribes from a contractor, Asa Scott on the Windsor Road, a supplier of timber and spars. When Scott resisted making other such payments, Marshall "refused my supplying any more and from that time till this I have not supplyed anything."[102]

To prepare his defence the master shipwright requested copies of the charges against him and of the depositions, but this Coffin refused.[103] Unable to defend himself in Halifax, he sailed to England where, having seen the depositions, he gave what explanations he could. He offered only his sworn testimony by way of defence. In the matter of the coal, permission he said had been granted by the storekeeper, who had since gone mad. The work done on his house had been to accommodate the admiral who had leased it. He denied that he had ever accepted a bribe from a supplier. Though it was his word against his accusers, it proved sufficient.[104] When the Admiralty directed the commander-in-chief of the Halifax squadron and Commissioner Duncan to investigate Coffin's complaints,[105] Marshall was only reprimanded, "as the public have suffered very little from his irregularity."[106] Marshall and Hughes, against whom nothing had been found, were reinstated.[107]

One witness, Stephen Cullen the gate porter, who was also in charge of horse hire, claimed that the profits had been divided equally among the officers, the profits of one horse and cart assigned each to the master shipwright, the master attendant, the storekeeper, and the foreman of the shipwrights, and finally "the profits of two horses & carts to the commissioner's two clerks."[108] This matter was never investigated.

Two storekeepers found themselves involved in serious disputes with their superiors. One dispute implicated a commodore, another a commissioner, and the others the Navy Board itself. In a 1784 difference with Commodore Douglas, the storekeeper, George Thomas, was vindicated. In the battle between Commissioner Inglefield and the acting storekeeper, Alexander Anderson lost. In arguments with the Navy Board, the result was a draw.

The storekeeper's problem in 1784 arose when the naval commander, Commodore Sir Charles Douglas, overstepped his authority and interfered with the internal administration of the careening yard. Thomas had received permission for leave in England to clear his accounts when Douglas arrived to take up his new responsibility as commodore of the North American squadron. Thomas had arranged, with Commissioner Duncan's approval, to have his first clerk, John Lawson, act in his place during his absence.[109] Thomas thereupon gave up his leased house to Provo Wallis, the master shipwright, who also rented some of his furniture. He dismissed his domestics and was on the point of departing when Duncan left for the Bay of Fundy on a long-anticipated inspection of timber prospects for the navy.[110] Douglas seized the moment to insert his own candidate, Frederick Edgecombe, as acting naval storekeeper and at the same time denied Thomas permission for leave until he had carried out a general survey of the naval stores.[111] Had the temporary appointment of Lawson been allowed to proceed, this time-consuming procedure could have been avoided.[112] Thomas refused the commodore's order and, having left the cash chest and papers in the hands of his clerk, departed for Annapolis to inform the commissioner and to take ship to Boston and thence to England.[113] Infuriated, Commodore Douglas suspended both Thomas and Lawson.[114] He also suspended the storekeeper's second clerk, Alexander Anderson, who refused to cooperate in the general survey of stores.[115] In a matter of three weeks, this unprecedented behaviour utterly transformed the storekeeper's department. When Duncan returned to find the yard being run by the commodore, as he saw that there was little point in underlining the commodore's series of errors, but being unsure how the Admiralty would react, the commissioner chose to cooperate with the commodore's appointee.[116] Despite the commodore's lengthy, self-serving explanations, Douglas was severely chastised. Each of the three men Douglas had suspended was reinstated, while the commodore requested his recall "for cogent reasons,"[117] which was immediately ordered.[118]

If Alexander Anderson played a minor role in the 1784 battle with Douglas, he was at the centre of a controversy with Commissioner Inglefield, when, for the second time in his career, he assumed the responsibilities of acting naval storekeeper. The trouble began one Sunday afternoon in mid-September 1802 when Inglefield wanted the yard bell tolled to summon artificers and labourers from both the yard and the squadron back to work after their mid-day meal. When Anderson, who doubled as clerk of the cheque, would do so only with a written order, the commissioner termed his behaviour "direct contempt of my authority," and got another clerk to summon the workers.[119]

Anderson was then ordered to present his cash account immediately, with all his receipts and vouchers.[120] This was a most unusual request and implied that there was something amiss in the accounts. To pay the commissioner in his own coin, Anderson agreed, only if the commissioner provided a receipt for them.[121] Inglefield did not miss the slight and tried to justify himself: "Having given you a little time to consider your error in refusing to act in obedience to my order to send me the vouchers, I again direct you to bring to me your vouchers and receipts." He characterized Anderson's behaviour as both "disrespectful and ignorant."[122] Anderson in response pointed out that the receipts for money, then amounting to H£4,600, were "private property which I am not justified in delivering out of my charge without receiving satisfactory security for the same."[123] When asked again a month later to bring the papers to the commissioner's office, Anderson agreed on condition he retain them until a receipt for them was given him, as they were essential to passing his accounts later with the Navy Board. He denied that his behaviour was either improper or obstinate. Thwarted, Inglefield then laid the entire correspondence before the Navy Board. The commissioner found the idea of his storekeeper insisting on conditions in dealing with him both "disgusting and offensive."[124]

Unable either to suspend or return him to his duty as first clerk, as there was no one to replace him, Inglefield to his embarrassment could do nothing immediately. When Anderson requested an additional temporary clerk to help in the work of the office as his two clerks were too ill to attend to their work in inclement weather, requiring Anderson on occasion to shut his office and oversee the work himself, Inglefield ignored the request.[125] When Anderson a month later repeated his request, and specifically mentioned a former extra clerk, "who was very diligent and useful," whom the commissioner had discharged, this request was also brusquely denied.[126] Inglefield added provocatively, "if the time you had made use of in writing letters to me merely calculated to oppose my authority and the authority of government, had been employed in the essential duties of your office, the assistance you have had would have been more than sufficient for the business."[127] He then threatened to dismiss him.

Anderson utterly rejected the accusation of incompetence and formally requested an impartial investigation of their dispute. He described himself as a devoted servant who had "laboured day and frequently by night, often not allowing myself not only not the relaxation necessary to the preservation of health, but even a scanty portion of time for my meals, which themselves in some instances were given up. The society of friends or the privilege of a short walk out of town were cheerfully renounced ... I trust that it will be found that under singular disadvantages, I have carried on the duties of my department with some credit to myself." He then reminded the commissioner that two months before when they were discussing the inadequacies of the yard's establishment, Inglefield had said "you must continue to apply until you obtain sufficient assistance in the office, for the case is the same in all the yards, and the Navy Board know it," or words to that effect.[128]

The very next day, the newly-minted naval storekeeper, Daniel Butler Dawes, arrived. A ship's purser, he had never held this responsibility and knew nothing of the Halifax yard. As a consequence he depended heavily at first on Anderson who served him loyally. Dawes would eventually master the responsibilities, for he was destined to be still in this position almost seventeen years later when the yard all but closed.

The Board supported Inglefield to the extent that they found Anderson's conduct "disrespectful," from which they drew the conclusion that "mischievous consequences ... might have ensued." It was little more than a mild slap on the wrist. It ordered the commissioner first to suspend him, then, if he was sufficiently contrite, to reinstate him. Instead Inglefield, who could read between the lines, merely allowed him to go on leave to England.

The Board rarely commented on a commissioner's behaviour. Though it knew better, it always officially assumed that inefficiencies lay elsewhere, especially with the shortcomings of the respective officers. From the Board's viewpoint, the most prominent of these was the naval storekeeper whose principal task was the efficient handling of naval stores sent to the yard by the Board and the timely submission of requisitions for replacement stores. Crucial to this was the accurate and timely rendering of the so-called "demands."

In the Navy Board's attempt to micromanage overseas bases, the Halifax officers were frequently chastised. For example, something of a crisis in management occurred in 1787. The Navy Board required Commissioner Duncan to censure the respective officers as a result of a series of apparent discrepancies in the bill of lading of a storeship sent to Portsmouth at the Navy Board's direction, and laden with old naval stores from the Halifax yard. The yard officers responded in detail to each of the points made in the Navy Board's complaint which had assumed that all the errors were made in Halifax. The officers pointed out that in the matter of sails, for instance, the packages were sent home unopened, having been received in 1783 when the naval establishment was hurriedly dismantled in New York. If the tallies were incorrect, the errors had been made in New York, not Halifax. If the actual description of the sails sometimes was inaccurate, they were confidant that Halifax and Portsmouth would agree on the actual number of sails sent home.

The same cause underlay the alleged error in cordage tallies. The officers, on that occasion, assured Duncan that "the difficulty, expense, time, labour and demurrage" to measure every fathom of each type of cordage would have been expensive and wasteful. They were equally confident that the quantity tallied in Halifax "will agree with the quantity received into the Portsmouth yard."[129] Why, they wanted to know, was the English count always assumed to be correct and, by contrast, the Halifax one suspect? For instance, as the boxes of copper screws for braces and copper keel staples were returned unopened, miscounting certainly had occurred in England where they had originated, not in Halifax. The same explanation applied to hammocks, whose bundles had never been opened before being returned to England. The two men responsible for counting sheets of copper – forty to a box – were prepared, the Board was told, to declare upon oath as to the accuracy of their count which was twice done.

Having dealt with the details of the Navy Board's complaint, the officers turned to a more fundamental question. "A censure once decidedly passed," they stated in their cogent submission, "precludes and prohibits any further vindication ... the only object to which our future efforts should tend is the prevention of a prejudice, once grounded (it matters not upon how shadowy a foundation) from spreading beyond the power of diminution or erasure."[130] As a first step to effect change "some material alterations in the present internal constitution of this yard should be made." The old mode of conducting business previous to the receipt of *Printed Instructions* in July 1784, was perfectly simple: the correspondence of the Navy Board was confined to "the expeditiously transmitting of cash accounts, store accounts and progresses." They remarked that the yard was "now literally a machine, moved by a number of springs, and regulated by yourself, as the head. But if these springs are not allowed, considered, and looked up to, as acting together, irregularity must be the natural result. And, if you, who are the head, should be considered as a cypher, by a superior controlling power, that looks only to us as the inferior instruments, is it not reasonable to expect that misunderstandings will take place?" They requested that in future all orders from the Navy Board should be addressed to the commissioner and emanate from his office. The officers jointly, in turn, would make their returns to him "it being impossible for an individual to effect any part of his duty, without the connexion, concurrence, and assistance of the other two." This would make the commissioner "the voucher" for their reports, and avoid individual officers being blamed in future: "for not corresponding on subjects perhaps foreign to their accounts and duties." Duncan agreed that in future all letters on naval service "should pass under cover to me."[131] In addition, all the storekeeper's returns were also thereafter sent from the commissioner's office, with the commissioner's covering letter merely noting the title of each.

If the Navy Board was never shy about giving the officers detailed directions, still they took a year after the outbreak of war with France in 1793 to provide directions of a general nature for their guidance. War now made it necessary to "maintain considerable stores ... above the establishment."[132] As most such stores came from England, the storekeeper was to be guided in his requests by the number and type of warships, "which have been on the station of late, or to those which you may have reason to suppose would have been on it, if no alteration had happened in public affairs." Yet he was to ensure, as the "grand and principal object of your concern" that the stores in hand should never "exceed the quantities ... ordered." In view of the distance between London and Halifax and the interval needed for effective communication, this order seemed likely to be ignored. Six months later the Board, while noting that there would likely be "fewer opportunities and somewhat greater uncertainties with respect to the sending out supplies for your yard than any other," told them to request stores in the quarterly reports.[133] In particular the yard was to retain as many masts, yards, bowsprits, and rough spars as "would enable you to refit the fleet after an engagement, however severe." Above all, the Board wished the Halifax yard to make as few local purchases of those stores "usually sent from hence ... as may be compatible with the real good of the service."

Despite these general principles the Board soon expressed astonishment that the Halifax yard had ordered stores to accommodate a "line of battleships" from the West Indies. Such demands, it insisted, were both unreasonable and "utterly impossible for us to have kept up such a magazine of stores ... It must appear obvious to you that such kind of demands ... are at the best useless, but probably troublesome and perplexing."[134] For good measure, it added: "The variableness of the force in every quarter, and the contingencies and uncertainties attending almost all branches of the naval service in times like the present preclude all possibility of such a plan being executed." With some asperity it reminded the officers that "as you could not possibly look forward with tolerable certainty to the wants of the service in time of war especially for a longer period than three months, and consequently under any system of management be obliged to make a demand for stores four times a year, unless your magazines were enormously large indeed."

Though the Board ended by expressing the hope that the officers must not construe from its letter "that we are dissatisfied with your general conduct in the Store Branch," it noted that it was "exceedingly improper as well as extra-ordinary" that it had received neither monthly nor quarterly accounts of the issue of stores to warships since the end of March 1794, especially if they had never been made out and despatched in the first place.[135] As a consequence, by the time they arrived, it was "too late for any of the stores ... to be got ready in time for the ships this season." The Board bluntly wrote that officers "concerned in making the necessary provision for a squadron of His Majesty's ships, whose services may be of very essential importance, should not see the indispensable necessity of complying with our orders respecting their demands is a matter no less surprising to us and discreditable to themselves."[136]

If this was principally for the direction of the master shipwright and master attendant who had failed to submit their reports in time to the naval storekeeper, the next complaints focused on the naval storekeeper. It was his manner of completing his quarterly return that caused concern in London. The Board found its own instructions to be "so exceedingly plain that it is impossible to read them attentively and to mistake them."[137] It was a complaint reflective of an august body that believed itself always in possession of a monopoly on virtue and efficiency.

Given the management atmosphere prevailing at the yard at different times, how well did the clerks function? The clerks, whom the commissioner could dismiss, were in a position considerably inferior to that of the officers for whom they toiled. Yet the careers of senior clerks, the ones on whom the principal officers most depended, were characterized more by their length than by their brevity. This was especially true in the storekeeper's department.

The first of these long-serving clerks was Jacob Hurd, taken on in December 1758 when the site of the careening yard was determined by Commodore Durell.[138] A former ship's purser, he applied for his pension in 1794, a month short of thirty-six years in the yard.[139] Except for a few years in the master shipwright's office in the 1780s, he spent his whole career in the yard as the storekeeper's first clerk. A man of trust, he spent fourteen weeks travelling to Quebec in 1759 to secure Admiral Saunders's approval for some navy bills issued by Gerrish to raise cash, and acted as temporary storekeeper in 1763–4, when Gerrish went to England to clear his accounts.[140] Around 1760, when in Boston, he had his portrait painted. A Halifax landowner and slave owner,[141] at his death he left a large family; at least one of his sons followed him into the yard as a clerk.[141]

More celebrated than Hurd, and as long-serving, was Alexander Anderson who entered from England as second clerk in the storekeeper's office in 1783, and retired as first clerk thirty-six years later when the yard virtually closed in 1819.[143] He twice acted for absent storekeepers, in 1799–1800, and in 1801–03, a total of almost three years. Granted leave to visit England in 1804, he was absent from the yard for some months.[144] Later in his mid-fifties, when he learned of plans to erect a house for the yard's boatswain, he unsuccessfully petitioned the Board for the same privilege. He explained that "comfortable dwelling houses" could not be procured on reasonable terms near the yard, and "the weather being frequently so tempestuous or severe in the winter season as to render attendance on my duty, more especially in the night, almost impracticable."[145] Like Hurd and most of the other clerks from abroad, when Anderson retired he remained settled in Nova Scotia. One notable exception to this mould was Provo Featherstone Wallis, son of Provo Wallis, the master shipwright successively at New York and Halifax from 1776 to 1792. The son, originally a ship's carpenter, having served as a labourer in the New York yard, became his father's clerk when they settled in Halifax in 1783. When Commissioner Duncan's first clerk, John Parminter, suddenly fell ill and died at the age of thirty-three, Wallis replaced him. This was an impressive leap forward into what he later called "the most respectable office of a clerk in the yard."[146] From 1810 onwards, Wallis also superintended the naval cooperage.[147] In this position he remained until illness forced him to retire to England in 1815. Reluctant to return to Halifax, and failing to secure a new appointment in the home yards, he applied for a pension.[148] He and Hurd were the only clerks for whom portraits are known to exist.[149]

Some of the junior clerks were the sons of yard clerks or artificers. One of Jacob Hurd's sons became clerk to the master shipwright, while Thomas, son of second clerk Benjamin James, also followed his father's occupation and, upon his death in 1803,[150] succeeded him.[151] Winckworth Norwood served as the master attendant's clerk, when many of his family were yard artificers. Edward Sellon, whose father and uncle served as yard shipwrights, himself entered the yard in 1808 as a temporary clerk and acted as store porter until the yard all but closed in 1819. He retired much later as chief clerk in the quartermaster general's office. Charles Blackadar, whose family were yard shipwrights, became a clerk in the storekeeper's office, while George A. Hughes, son of the master shipwright, served as his father's clerk.

Too poor to have accumulated savings, and becoming increasingly ineffective through illness, the old junior clerks struggled on, until either they died in office or received a pension. Benjamin James had served with the commissary general's department in New York during

92   Part Two: Work Force

the revolutionary war. This recommended him to Duncan and he became second clerk in the storekeeper's office. He found that the annual salary of £50, with £10 house rent, forced him to "struggle hard to support myself and family, not without encumbering myself with debts."[152]

When a reduced establishment removed from the commissioner's office one of his two clerks, Alexander Farquharson was discharged after twenty-two years "faithful servitude ... I am the oldest clerk now alive that ever served in that office," he reminded the commissioner.[153] "I am now turned adrift to starve in a foreign country in the decline of life, incumbered with a numerous family consisting of a wife and seven children, not yet provided for, and no provision made for conveying me and my family to my native country," a service provided even to common soldiers. "These are circumstances so afflicting that I assure you, sir that I am nearly sinking under the pressure of my distress." The Navy Board recommended him to the Admiralty for consideration. John Livingston, James's successor as the storekeeper's second clerk fell into a "state of mental derangement" and filled his balance book with copious errors in 1808. Requesting a pension,[154] he went on the yard's superannuated list until the Navy Board determined his case.[155]

When the yard artificers and labourers worked overtime, frequently so did the clerks. This, in his ignorance, Commissioner Coffin found intolerable and considered it a "shameful and infamous practice."[156] This was unfair as the accounts could become excessive and the clerks forced to work at night, as Anderson explained to him.[157] When Coffin in 1799 and later Inglefield in 1803 refused to authorize the hiring of temporary clerks, Anderson applied directly to the Navy Board, so pressing was the work. "It is painful to me in the extreme that the accounts have not been transmitted from this office so regularly as the *Printed Instructions* and their other directions require," he remarked.

> They may well conceive the embarrassments I had to encounter, when in consequence of certain arrangements made in this office I was repeatedly on the point of being strip't of all assistance and left alone ... there is not an individual in the office, who is competent to the making up the Quarterly returns (No. 6), owing to the frequent discharges of the junior clerks and Mr. James, the second clerk, being fully employed in the current duties of the department, has not had

an opportunity of informing himself on the subject. No exertion on my part might be wanting to expedite the accounts. I have given my attendance early and to a very late hour as well as frequently on Sundays.[158]

This letter offers a rare insight into the workings of the storekeeper's office. It also underscores the absurdity of a system that to fill so simple a request the Navy Board in London had first to approve. Procedures had not changed a decade later, when in response to the same problem, Commissioner Inglefield threw his weight behind his storekeeper's request. This time he formulated a general request for many more clerks temporarily to be added to the department, owing to the greatly-increased workload during the war with the United States, which had broken out in May 1812.[159]

The Board's excessive economies gave way at last in the face of the huge increase in clerks' work necessitated by the increase in the North American squadron and the use of the yard by elements of squadrons stationed in the West Indies. The issue for the Board was not so much the number of clerks employed but their competence. Commissioner Wodehouse explained that they were usually entered at an early age and "brought forward according to their abilities." Frequently, when they began to be useful, they were hired away either by the commissary general's office or by merchants in town who attracted them with higher salaries. It tended to be the less competent who remained in the naval yard; "the best that can be procured in this province for the established salaries."

As clerks' salaries were not competitive in the home yards they were likewise unlikely to be in Halifax. Clerks in England were thought to have suffered, since so many of the senior ones, to maintain their living standard, simultaneously assumed private roles as agents in settling accounts for sea officers, seamen, or contractors. Hamond, as comptroller of the navy, estimated in 1804 that Navy Board clerks had seen their incomes halved by new regulations.[160] In the absence of uniform salary scales for clerks, morale remained poor for those who remained in the Navy Board's or the dockyards' wartime service.

Inflation, fuelled by war, undermined money wages for clerks, as well as others on more or less fixed incomes. Jacob Hurd's 1768 salary of £80,[161] and £10 towards the cost of renting a house, remained unchanged in 1784.[162] By then he also received an allowance of £39.11.5. The commissioner's first clerk received a higher base salary,

£100, but no allowances except the £10 for housing. The salary of the storekeeper's second clerk, which in 1784 came to £50, was the same as that for the master shipwright's and master attendant's clerks, and had remained unchanged since 1759. Their allowances and house money brought their gross incomes to just under £100.

Only in 1796 did clerks first petition for improved salaries. That year Alexander Anderson and Benjamin James felt "themselves very much oppressed by the great and unavoidable expenses of living and house rent in wartime, and especially within the two years last past." Anderson paid £30 a year for a house, which he described as scarcely comfortable, and James £24 for a house "by no means comfortable." They argued that most goods had doubled in price and many by three times. They considered their position worse than the working shipwright or even the cabin keeper, who received five shillings on days that he worked.[163] Commissioner Duncan believed that their salaries were not "nearly adequate to their services."[164]

If this petition was rejected by the Board, one in 1800 relating to overtime rates bore fruit. From October 1799, for the first time, clerks were awarded regulated overtime rates. These amounted to 4s.6d. a day for the storekeeper's first clerk, 3s. for his second clerk, and 2s.9d. each for the master shipwright's and master attendant's clerks. Previously clerks earned overtime, as Commissioner Coffin had discovered, but the pay was unregulated.[165] When the commissioner's clerks learned of this new policy, they asked for the same consideration.

Some of the clerks enjoyed an additional perquisite, a fuel allowance in the form of firewood or coal. So widespread and so extensive had their use grown that by the end of the winter of 1796-7 Commissioner Duncan insisted on capping the allowances. Expenditure greatly exceeded that of former years, and "if not settled at a fixed quantity will continue to increase to an enormous quantity."[166] To stem this "growing evil," fuel consumption reports were to be prepared.[167] As this allowance was "in lieu of chips, particular attention must be observed that no useful wood is either cut up or carried out of the Yard. Carts are almost constantly passing through the yard with fuel, which is not only inconvenient but highly improper." He ordered thereafter that "fuel to the different people shall be carried away within seven working days after the expiration of the quarter." The principal officers, whose substantial tenement houses had been built in 1793, were entitled to "whatever quantity may be necessary."[168] Unable to stem the use of firewood by the principal officers, the com-

Table 4.1   Clerks' Fuel Allowance, 1797

	Wood (cord)	Coal (chaldron)
Storekeeper's 1st clerk	10	6
Storekeeper's 2d clerk	8	4
Master shipwright's clerk	8	4
Foreman of yard	10	6
Foreman house carpenters	6	3
Mr Andrew, shipwright	8	3

Source: NSARM, MG13/6, fol. 241.

missioner limited its use for their clerks and senior artificers, as Table 4.1 shows.

When the housing allowance was cancelled in 1807, the clerks petitioned both the commissioner and the Navy Board. They observed that they could not lease "tolerable" houses for less than £25–£40 a year and needed another £20 to £25 for fuel to keep them heated.[169] Now they feared falling into debt merely to sustain their families. They reminded the Navy Board that fuel needs at other overseas yards were "very inconsiderable," while the "extreme severity" of the Halifax weather "renders fires needful for nine months" a year."[170] Noting as well that salaries for first clerks were much lower than at other overseas establishments, they wanted salaries at least raised to the level of those in the home yards.

The complaints over clerical salaries were neither unique to the Halifax yard nor, on this occasion, ignored. When the Admiralty in September 1808 approved a report of commissioners appointed to revise the civil affairs of the navy, a new salary scale came into effect.[171] Now the salaries of all the clerks, instead of being paid in London, were henceforth to be paid monthly by the Halifax yard's storekeeper. The commissioner's first clerk and the storekeeper's first clerk then received salaries of £250, the second clerks £150. The two extra clerks in the storekeeper's office and those of the other principal officers each received £120 a year. Indeed, all temporary clerks also then received £120 a year. Boys entering were paid £70, but within six months were advanced to temporary clerks, if the need existed.[172] All clerks, however, along with the officers became subject to a 10 per cent income tax. All were subject to property tax, and the master attendant's clerk to a widow's tax. The details are in Table 4.2.

96 Part Two: Work Force

Table 4.2 Those Paying Income Tax, 1809–10

	Entry	Discharge	Salary	Stopped
W. Hughes master shipwright	–	–	£360	36.00. 0.
T. Atkinson master attendant	–	25 Nov	350	22. 9. 2.
E. Fairfax master attendant	26 Nov	–	350	12. 1.10.
P.F. Wallis commissioner's clerk	–	–	250	25. 0. 0.
E. Bartlett commissioner's clerk	–	–	150	15. 0. 0.
A. Anderson storekeeper's clerk	–	–	250	25. 0. 0.
J. Livingston storekeeper's clerk	–	–	150	15. 0. 0.
G. Sherlock storekeeper's clerk	–	–	120	10.10. 0.
C. Blackadar storekeeper's clerk	–	–	120	10.10. 0.
E. Sellon storekeeper's clerk	–	11 Oct	70}	4. 8. 4¼.
	12 Oct	–	90}	
J. Fielding storekeeper's clerk	–	–	120	10.10. 0.
J. Newton storekeeper's clerk	–	6 Feb	120	8.18. 9.
H. Kerby storekeeper's clerk	1 Mar	–	120	17. 6.
E. Ward storekeeper's clerk	–	9 Oct	120	5.10. 2.
T. Mould storekeeper's clerk	16 Oct	–	120	4.16. 8¼.
J. Rule storekeeper's clerk	18 Oct	–	120	4.15. 6½.
G. Hughes master shipwright's clerk	–	–	120	10.10. 0.
J. McNab master shipwright's clerk	–	31 Mar	70	3. 0. 0.
J. Hurd master shipwright's clerk	21 Apr	1 Aug	120	2.18.10.
T. Burton master shipwright's clerk	15 Aug	–	120	6.12. 3¼

Source: 24 May 1810. NMM, HAL/E/31, fol. 178.

Before this was known, George Sherlock, then earning a salary of H£120 a year, wrote to the commissioner a letter which perhaps would have been endorsed by almost every clerk in the yard. As a single man he had been content with his salary when he entered in 1804. Since then he had married and become liable to property tax. Moreover "every necessary of life having been for a considerable time past enormously high, and still continuing so, many of them near 100% more than they formerly were, I find it utterly impracticable, though exercising the most rigid rules of economy, to support my family being six in number upon the sum of 6s.8d. currency per day, less than any artificer in the Yard."[173] He knew that many of the artificers were "earning something in addition to their pay by jobs performed in town after the working hours of the yard," whereas the clerks were restricted by the new instructions for foreign yards from having "any other occupation than the one which they hold in the yard." Both Dawes and Commissioner Inglefield endorsed these facts.

Table 4.3   Pay Scales for Clerks: Halifax & Jamaica, 1814

	Halifax £	Jamaica £	Difference %
Commissioner's Office:			
his 1st clerk	250	350	40.0
his 2d clerk	150	180	20.0
Naval Storekeeper's Office:			
his 1st clerk	250	400	60.0
his 2d clerk	150	250	33.3
his 1st extra	120	200	66.7
his 2nd extra	120	150	25.0
his 3d temporary	120	150	25.0
add'l extra	120	150	25.0
Master Attendant's Office:			
his clerk	120	180	50.0
Master Shipwright's Office:			
his clerk	120	180	50.0
extra clerk	70	150	114.3
Total	£1,590	£2,340	47.2

Source: Evans to RO, Naval Yard at Bermuda, 25 Nov. 1813. PRO, ADM106/1322.

Five years later when the naval yard establishment was being reorganized, Commissioner Wodehouse compared the pay scales for clerks in Halifax, Jamaica, and Antigua. In every comparable category he found that the least well-paid were those at the Halifax yard. The margin between them favoured the clerks who worked in Jamaica by some 47 per cent, as is seen in Table 4.3. Why the Navy Board followed this discriminatory policy is not clear.

Despite the distance between Halifax and London, the Navy Board allowed the yard officers few initiatives either in policy or practice. Excessive bureaucracy, especially after 1783, stifled initiative on the periphery of empire, as it always did, whether in backwater Nova Scotia of the eighteenth century or in India, the jewel of empire, a century later. The failure to fashion for overseas yards a significantly different set of regulations to reflect their unique situation showed what little dependence the Navy Board placed on them. It is significant that the Board always, in this era, called them "foreign" yards.

Master shipwrights attract, at the hands of historians, some share of the responsibility for inefficiency. Unlike the men who managed private shipyards, they were not businessmen. Rather "they defined themselves instead as traditional craftsmen and took a craftsman's narrow view of their responsibilities. Nor had they received an education appropriate to the high managerial functions they were called upon to perform. They were given almost no latitude to make decisions and consequently held themselves responsible for no more than carrying out their literal instructions and were little concerned in controlling costs."[174] Although they had excessive responsibilities heaped on their shoulders, the system allowed them to "shift responsibility and shield themselves from blame" when things went awry. Such men submitted false accounts both for overtime wages and materials used, neither of which were effectively audited. Before 1820 the Audit Office was often a decade or more in arrears in verifying the Navy's accounts. Parliament was as ineffective in controlling expenditures, as it invariably covered in peace or war whatever deficit in annual naval expenditures occurred.

In Halifax, failures in master shipwrights' competence seem less important sources of inefficiencies than those which stemmed from the centralized control exercised by the Navy Board, as it tried to micro-manage all yards.[175] Successive inquiries in the home yards found that planning, organization, direction, coordination, and control over finances, costs, and inventory were feeble. Organization of the overseas bases was as centralized as that of the dockyards in England. Officials were obliged to execute orders regularly received from the Navy Board in London, and from the "ever-proliferating standing orders."[176] If successive inquiries found the home yards managed poorly, could the overseas bases, never subject before 1820 to such searching inquiry, have been better managed? In the case of the Halifax yard the answer is a qualified "Yes!" Despite being hamstrung by the Navy Board, the officers and their clerks were able to act as efficiently as resources allowed. The occasional complaints by an overzealous Board of indolence by a naval storekeeper were almost wholly misdirected. Acute problems in the Halifax yard rather were occasioned by the Board's indifference to Halifax's inadequate wartime establishment especially from 1807, after Duncan and Hamond, who had both served as commissioners in Halifax and who presumably had advocated more vehemently from their experience, had retired from the Navy Board. The post-Trafalgar Navy Board, perhaps reflecting the Admiralty's own myopia, while seriously overfocused on Napoleon's reconstruction of the French navy, failed to give due weight to the United States on whose expanding overseas trade the British, at least in the Peninsular War, came to depend and whose fighting spirit at sea it would wholly underestimate. In such a climate the Halifax base was neglected.

Individual personalities and management styles of different commissioners, whatever impact it had on yard morale, seemed not to have affected yard efficiency. It is not obvious that yard efficiency rose under a gentle hand or fell under a harsh one. Commissioner Coffin's hands-on style underlay a decidedly negative view of everyone working in a royal yard. Having himself been found guilty of fraud, he smelled embezzlement both in the squadron and the yard. His domineering, almost hysterical, style demoralized staff. He pre-empted all executive power as the naval storekeeper was away on leave when he arrived, the master attendant retired upon his arrival, and the master shipwright he suspended within three months. His reign of terror began the day after he was rowed ashore, when he could have known next to nothing of the yard. Six months later when he departed, he had formed decided opinions about a large number of the yard's employees, yet they were men he scarcely knew or cared to know. By contrast, Commissioner Wodehouse held an excellent opinion of the yard workers, especially the native Nova Scotians, the predominant group, at a moment when the yard was most heavily burdened at a crucial period in 1812–15.

The three respective officers, who before a commissioner was appointed exercised effective executive control, were, as they knew, paid poorly in comparison with officers in other overseas naval yards. This might have given rise to the systematic petty embezzlement practised by Constable and Elias Marshall. It might also explain the storekeepers' willingness to pay themselves and their clerks overtime, when the artificers worked extra hours, a habit which Duncan tolerated but which Coffin found fraudulent. Their petitions for salary increases achieved little, as pay raises occurred only when the Navy Board instituted a general increase for all overseas bases.

Officers, once appointed, were not easily removed as Coffin found when he suspended the master shipwright for embezzlement in 1800. By contrast, Commissioner Arbuthnot's suspension of the master shipwright on the same charge in 1775 was upheld. Dismissal for incompetence as a pilot brought the career of one master attendant to a swift end.

The only management position to which a clerk could aspire was that of naval storekeeper. At Halifax this never occurred, though clearly Anderson and Hurd, who temporarily became storekeepers, were capable of assuming the full responsibility. Each possessed the necessary experience and skills but lacked the patronage and social prestige. Such senior clerks were not mere ciphers, as Anderson's quarrel with Commissioner Inglefield indicated. They were too valuable to dismiss, especially as their replacements, given their relatively poor salaries, were not easily found. Their importance in preparing the mountain of reports required by the Navy Board, drafting and controlling the daily correspondence, and keeping the accounts may not have been well-rewarded but was as crucial to the functioning of the naval base as it is to the writing of the careening yard's history.

Chapter Five

ARTIFICERS AND LABOURERS

If we know how the lash enforced authority afloat, how was control over workers maintained by the navy in its yards ashore? The interaction between officers, artificers, and "the people of the yard" will be central as we examine working conditions, recruitment, kinship, apprenticeship, efficiency, embezzlement, wages, superannuation, and discipline. Some of the ideas found here derive from two studies of Portsmouth dockyard workers which analysed administration as well as the social ties created by kinship, apprenticeship, and long-term employment.[1]

For yard workers, of the principal officers the most important was the master shipwright. As we have seen in chapter 4, he was responsible for the repair of ships and the maintenance of the physical site of the yard. He oversaw 85 per cent of those employed in the yard, through several foremen. He had to work closely with the master attendant who directed the riggers and sailmakers and had much to do with masting. To receive all necessary materials and tools for this work, the master shipwright had to liaise closely with the naval storekeeper and his staff of clerks and store porters. Finally, he had to keep the commissioner abreast of his labour needs, when a shortage of yard artificers made the help of both ships' artificers and working parties crucial to the repairs needed by the squadron.

The repair of warships was the yard's principal task. Refitting, as it was termed, involved careening, caulking, rebuilding, painting, and rigging. From 1781 onwards ships' bottoms were also coppered in the Halifax yard, a process introduced a few years earlier in England. Routine work included: fashioning out of the so-called sticks all the masts, topmasts, yards, and spars, and of sawing boards, plank, and deals;

smiths' work; and the sailmaking needed in the repair of ships, small yard vessels, and ships' boats.

Those who undertook this work, "the people of the yard," included skilled artificers and their apprentices on the one hand, and common labourers with working parties of seamen on the other. Of the skilled, the largest group was invariably composed of shipwrights and shipwright-caulkers. They worked side-by-side with working parties of seamen to unload and load mastships and storeships, sorting and storing the materials received. They laid out the decayed stores sold at public auction. They served as carters and fire engine crews. They acted as builders' labourers when structural repairs to buildings were undertaken by the yard. At times they maintained officers' houses and gardens and worked in the commissioner's stables and cowshed. They served as domestic servants, messengers, and watchmen. Others served as crewmen on the boats maintained for the principal officers, or as hulksmen in the sheer hulk.

One group of workmen employed by the yard were employed afloat. These were the hulksmen, whose task it was to work under the orders of the master attendant. As the Navy Board specified their numbers in the establishment, there was frequently the same sort of tug-of-war of their numbers between the Board and the yard commissioner as there was over the establishment as a whole. As an example, when the peacetime establishment was instituted at Halifax in the brief period of peace after the ratification of the Treaty of Amiens in 1802, difficulties from staff shortages manifested themselves. The reduced establishment called for six sheer hulksmen. One task normally undertaken in winter was to make small cordage for the use of the yard. So busy were they in 1802–03 that this service could not be undertaken as usual. Worse, the master attendant for whom they worked had experienced difficulty in preventing different yard craft and launches from being damaged for lack of men to secure them. An additional four men were requested.[2] Repeated requests to increase the establishment of this crucial body of men made by Inglefield during his ten years in the yard and detailed in chapter 6, were refused. As a touchstone to gauge the very limited importance of the Halifax yard in the eyes of the Admiralty and Navy Board there is scarcely a better example.

To complete its work on those occasions when the squadron was in harbour and urgently needing to be refitted, the yard made extensive use of ships' artificers as well as large working parties of seamen.[3] They came not only from warships, but from transports.[4] Even when there was no urgency, as many hands made light work, seamen were summoned to tasks in the yard's huge storehouses: to air sails, arrange stores, or to turn masts in the mast pond.[5] Requests for such working parties, usually from twenty to fifty seamen accompanied by petty officers, originated with the yard officers and were conveyed to the commissioner who then made his request to the admiral or senior captain.[6] Such parties of seamen were entitled to a half-pint ration of rum, a practice that was discontinued in 1786 at the Halifax yard two years before the Admiralty made the ban universal.[7]

To hire common labourers from the town, as extras, was the alternative to working parties of seamen. The principal officers in 1789 believed that for most tasks, hired labourers performed better than seamen. Labourers were "more manageable and compliant with the directions of the officers of the yard."[8] Working parties from the ships were useful especially in unloading storeships, on board the hulks, when warships were careened, and in aiding the master attendant when he laid down moorings.[9] They also loaded transports, storeships, and occasionally warships with cargoes of masts, spars, yards, bowsprits, and lumber for the West Indies yards.[10]

There were some unusual tasks required of the working parties. One such task required sixty seamen in 1806 to remove cables suitable for 64–gun warships, which for many years had been in storage.[11] In 1807 a party of thirty seamen overhauled and stowed old rope and removed old packing boxes and casks, "which encumber the avenues of the yard."[12] A year later spring cleaning was ordered by the senior captain, in the absence of the commissioner. A working party of seamen was directed to stow the spars, timber, and plank being delivered to the yard which had been piled on both wharfs and beach.[13] As a result of bitter cold weather in 1809, seamen towed spars which could not be deposited in the frozen mast pond and lay exposed to gales, to the north end of the yard and hauled them up the beach beyond the high-water-mark.[14] In 1818 they had to work on the admiral's house, then in the final stages of construction.[15] When the squadron was out of port and a storeship needed to be unloaded recourse was made even to the soldiers of the garrison. This occurred, for instance, in 1806 when a hired storeship, *Brothers*, needed quick unloading to avoid the costs of demurrage.[16] On later occasions in 1808, 1809, 1810, and 1815 military artificers aided the yard and the ships' artificers to refit the squadron.[17]

The Navy Board specified pay rates for such working parties and

104   Part Two: Work Force

those who superintended them. The Board announced the Admiralty's approval of a new scale in 1806.[18] The seamen then could earn 6d. a day, a boatswain's mate 9d., a midshipman 1s., and a lieutenant 2s.6d.; all to be paid by the yard storekeeper.

Hours of work were typically long and there were few holidays.[19] To describe his expectation of a reasonable workday, Commissioner Duncan explained in 1797, "As from five in the morning to seven at night is as many hours as a man can faithfully work."[20] No yard worker, he cautioned, was ever to be paid for longer hours. Nothing but necessary routine work occurred on Sundays "unless the business is very pressing indeed." The day began with the yard gun being fired. Twenty minutes later the yard bell rang to signal the beginning of the half-hour allowed for breakfast, followed by roll-call. An hour and a half for dinner was allowed at mid-day. When men could not work from six to six for lack of daylight, they breakfasted before entering the yard, to be at work by eight o'clock. Then only one hour was allowed for dinner.[21] To smoke tobacco was "strictly forbidden in any part of the yard, day or night."[22]

Prescribed overtime, called 'extra,' generally lasted from April through September. One extra hour's labour began usually early in April. In early May two and a half extra hours applied until the end of August. As daylight hours diminished so did overtime, until September 30th, when "agreeable to the custom of the yard" all overtime stopped.[23] In wartime, the squadron's needs frequently kept men at work by candlelight even into December.

Though employed in the Halifax yard, men occasionally found themselves at work elsewhere, usually when warships ran ashore or on some rocky shoal. In 1805, for instance, six shipwright-caulkers volunteered to go to Bermuda to see if they could rescue *Tartar*, which had drifted from her anchors onto a coral reef and was in danger of being totally lost. Praised for their "alacrity, cheerfulness and zeal" the six did not "give themselves a moment even to their meals" until she was again seaworthy.[24] The "Bermudans were perfectly astonished at the facility with which our people proceeded in the laborious undertaking, and at the quantity of work they performed,"[25] Commissioner Inglefield boasted when recommending them to the Navy Board.[26]

Some Halifax yardmen occasionally undertook tasks unheard of in England. In particular, during the war against rebel America when the supply of spars or timber was almost exhausted, shipwrights themselves went into the woods, then still within easy reach of the yard, to cut and haul trees to the nearest stream to be floated to the yard's mast pond.[27] A working party from a ship's company might assist them in this unusual activity.[28]

Although yard employees were excused service in the colonial militia as their work in the yard took precedence, still they were not wholly free of military service in times of crisis. Twice the yard workforce banded into a body known as the 'sea fencibles,' once in 1807 and again in 1812. In 1807 Vice Admiral Berkeley warned the yard officers that it might become necessary to defend the harbour and naval yard against the Americans, and to become familiar with the training of every man "so they may be ready to act if occasion requires."[29] Berkeley wanted to know which men, not already liable to militia duty, were fit for boat work or "capable of acting in gun boats or other armed vessels." This battalion of sea fencibles consisted of twelve-man boat crews manning four launches fitted and armed for them. They were trained both in basic manoeuvres and to load and fire the cannon each carried.[30] With the outbreak of war, they were placed under the orders of the naval commander.

With the very real threat of war with the United States in the spring of 1812, the vice admiral ordered everyone in the yard liable to militia duty to undertake military exercise "agreeably to law or find a substitute."[31] The sole exemptions granted by the town were for those from the yard who volunteered in 1807 to serve under their own officers and exercise their arms. Those yard workers who were liable to serve in the militia assembled, with their arms and accoutrements, in the yard's square the last Saturday of April to be inspected by Inglefield. From 1 May, every afternoon the yard battalion stopped work at 4:30 p.m. to spend the balance of the work time at military exercises.[32] This yard volunteer battalion was raised from four to five companies in mid-May, to ensure that one company would remain behind to command the yard's civil watch, should the battalion be obliged to march out of the yard to support the town.[33] The volunteers were outfitted in blue jackets, white pantaloons or trousers, round hat, cockade and white feathers, black neckerchief, and quarter gaiters. Reviewed by both the admiral and lieutenant governor, the battalion's initial parade took place on the evening of 23 May. The dignitaries were pleased; Adjutant General of Militia Beckwith the next day conveyed their excellencies' approbation to the corps of naval yard volunteers, as they were styled, "of their regularity and good Conduct."[34] Their training was never put to the test.

Recruits to the yard came first from Britain and New England and only later from Nova Scotia itself. For a time, British-born artificers dominated the ranks of the yard's foremen, while officers and senior clerks were generally British-born. For artificers this soon changed as few were recruited in Britain after the 1780s, except in 1815, when, as a deliberate policy, they were given post-war preferment.

The British artificers entered in four infusions. The first arrived in 1758–9 when the yard was under construction. The bulk of these departed by 1763 when the base was reduced to a mere depot. The second came when the yard was partly rebuilt in 1768–71 and the squadron enlarged to enforce British trade laws along the North American coast. The third occurred when several artificers volunteered from English yards in 1775–6 to serve five-year contracts in Halifax. Most of these chose to return as soon as their contracts expired. "I have hitherto evaded their solicitations" Commissioner Hamond explained. As he could not find replacements locally, he requested that ten shipwrights, four joiners, and a blockmaker be sent out to replace those wishing to return to England.[35] To this request the Navy Board did not comply as "our own yards" could not "keep pace with the wants of the fleet."[36] Again during the 1812–15 American war, despite serious shortages of artificers in the Halifax careening yard, the English yards could spare none. Only after Napoleon's final defeat in 1815 were ten shipwright-caulkers, four house carpenters, and a painter sent to Halifax on short contracts.[37]

As such artificers were paid in sterling, they profited when sterling exchanged with Halifax currency at a premium, but suffered when at a discount. Owing to increased wartime spending in Nova Scotia by the British government, the exchange rate favoured sterling in two years out of every five between 1758 and 1819.[38] If the English officers thus suffered most of the time at the hands of the exchange rate, they finished like fatted calves, for after 1815 Commissioner Wodehouse reckoned their wages were 25 per cent above those of the other yard artificers.[39]

Although there were many New Englanders among the first yard establishment in 1758, most left by 1763. Slaters were brought from New

England in the late-1760s. A few more entered in 1776 as loyalist refugees. More came from Charleston and New York in 1783. Within twenty years almost none of those who had worked in the New York yard before it was dismantled in 1783 remained. In this way, by 1800 at the latest, artificers and labourers native to Nova Scotia predominated.[40]

In the British dockyards service became almost hereditary, each yard being "dominated by powerful 'clanships' knit together by blood, marriage, politics, or other bonds ... Sons followed fathers, the yards often contained at any one time several generations of the same family."[41] The system of apprentices expressly favoured this development. Its ostensible purpose was to enhance the number of artificers available to the yard. In the Halifax yard nothing quite like this emerged, though apprentices were employed. In theory the only positions to which an apprentice, labourer, or watchman might not aspire were those of chaplain or surgeon. In practice at Halifax none progressed beyond foreman. The number of apprentices assigned to various types of artificers was never subject to rational analysis in the Halifax yard, while the various reforms undertaken in the home yards after 1802 were not applied to Halifax.[42] Nor did the Navy Board strictly control their numbers. The 1804 the Halifax establishment, for instance, allowed for nine apprentices, yet by 1815 no less than twenty were borne on the yard books.[43]

The Navy Board established a strict priority list in the selection of apprentices. Preference was given first to the sons of officers, shipwrights, and caulkers, then of naval officers and superannuated officers. Only then were the sons of other classes admitted in descending order: joiners, house carpenters, bricklayers, sailmakers, smiths, ropemakers, riggers, sawyers, and labourers.[44]

To have an apprentice or two was a considerable privilege for certain "deserving" artificers. These lucky few were entitled to part of the wages of apprentices. In this way family income could be augmented. Several artificer families had two generations working simultaneously in the Halifax yard. Master shipwrights Abraham Constable and Elias Marshall each served with three of their sons.

Some intermarriage occurred among several leading artificer families, including that of James Blackadar, Elias Marshall, John Dugwell, William Hughes, William Norwood, and Samuel Sellon. As examples, Blackadar's daughter, Mary, married Dugwell, while Marshall's eldest son married Hughes' eldest daughter. All were shipwrights. All, except the Blackadar family who hailed from Boston, were immigrants from England.

It was not the prospect of high wages, but their regularity, that was the chief attraction of work in the naval yard. Pay, depending on the current Navy Board regulations, either a month or three months in arrears, was always a dormant issue that but rarely surfaced. In the Halifax yard it never produced the disorders experienced in the home yards.[45] Nor were piece rates – called task work – which were so disruptive in the English yards, ever introduced at Halifax.[46] What brought pay matters into the open in Halifax was the impact of wartime inflation, when real wages significantly declined. Petitioning by workers was the preferred process. Then comparison was made with what equivalent workers earned in the town of Halifax.

If the issue did not appear during the war with rebel America from 1775 through 1783, it rose early in the war against revolutionary France. Three years into the war, in 1795, yard labourers petitioned Commissioner Duncan for a wage raise citing the "distressed situation they and their families" faced owing to significant inflation.[47] Duncan readily conceded a 10 per cent raise, which he asked the Navy Board to confirm, the precedent already having been set by the ordnance and military engineer departments in Halifax.[48]

Not only was it the sole increase for many years, despite rising inflation, but the Board's policy rather went in an opposite direction. To reduce costs between 1806 and 1809 it monetized three specific perquisites enjoyed by yard workers. These related to victuals, fuel, and "chips," which were the wastage when timber was converted to other uses. In 1806, the Halifax yard discontinued issuing victuals to any of the workers but paid them, in lieu, at the rate of one shilling per day.[49] The next year, the Navy Board monetized the fuel allowance at H£2 annually for those who enjoyed the privilege.[50] To Commissioner Inglefield it saved, "the labour expended when the fuel vessels come to the wharves, where it is piled by the labourers of the Yard with two clerks attending. A clerk attends also when it is distributed to measure it."[51] Finally, in 1809 the Navy Board directed that regulations to monetize privileges relating to chips, already in place for the home yards since 1801, were to apply to the overseas bases.[52] Thereafter chips were to be sold at auction and a daily allowance paid in compensation.[53] The subject of chips in Halifax had surfaced first in 1801, when the "People

Table 5.1   Halifax Retail Commodity Prices, 1795–6 & 1814

	1795–6	1814	% change
Beef, fresh/lb	6d.	11d.	83.3
Butter/lb	12d.	24d.	100.0
Candles/lb	12d.	20d.	66.7
Cheese/lb	11d.	16d.	45.5
Coffee/lb	8d.	14½d.	81.3
Firewood/cord	12s.	19s.	58.3
Flour/bbl	50s.	100s.	100.0
Molasses/gal	3s. 6d.	3s. 6d.	nc
Pork, fresh/lb	7d.	11d.	57.1
Potatoes/bu	3s.	3s. 6d.	50.0
Rum/gal	5s.	6s. 4d.	30.0
Salt/bu	3s.	3s.	nc
Soap/lb	11d.	13d.	18.2
Sugar, brown/lb	7½d.	7d.	(7.1)
Tobacco/lb	1s.	4s. 4d.	440.0
All (incl. tobacco)			74.7
Excluding tobacco			48.7

Note: Brackets denote a decline; 12 pence = 1 shilling; nc = no change.
Source: PRO, ADM106/2027–8, and business records, especially NSARM, RG1/306, MG1 & MG3.

of the Ordinary"[54] applied through the master shipwright for chip money on the same basis as then enjoyed by labourers, when doing labourers' work. Though the new commissioner consented, the Board first informed him that an order-in-council of 21 May 1800 gave no authority to pay chip money to artificers in foreign yards and thus wanted the practice at Halifax discontinued. When it was shown to be in error, the petition was granted.

Inflation, which Commissioner Wodehouse wildly estimated in 1814 at 100 per cent over twenty years,[55] and attendant labour shortages moved the Admiralty to approve a general wage increase of 25 per cent as long as the war lasted.[56] Before this news reached Halifax, yard labourers and watchmen pointed out that wages for Halifax labourers had risen at least 50 per cent to 6s. a day since 1795.[57] This fell short of the 75 per cent inflation noted in Table 5.1. With this second raise, watchmen earned 3s. with 40s. a year in lieu of fuel, and labourers 2s.10d. a day with 1s. for food. The details are found in Table 5.2. This was still less than in town, as Table 5.3 illustrates.[58]

Wodehouse was particularly concerned about wage rates for artifi-

Table 5.2   Yard Workers' Daily Pay Rates, 1817–18

	1817 day	overtime/hr	1818
Store porter	5s. 6d.	8½d.	–
Gate porter	5s. 2d.	6½d.	–
Foreman labourers	5s.	6½d.	4s. 6d.
Watchmen	4s.	4½d.	3s. 9d.
Hulksmen	2s.11d.	–	2s. 8d.
Labourers	3s.10d.	4½d.	3s. 6d.
Messenger	–	–	3s. 6d.
Coxswain	4s. 8d.	–	–
In charge of tank	4s.	–	–

Source: NSARM, MG13/9.3, fol. 220, 236.

Table 5.3   Halifax Daily Pay Rates, 1814 & 1816

	1814	1816
Shipwrights/caulkers	10–12s.	9s.
House carpenters	8s.6d.	9s.6d.
Smiths	7s.6d.–8s.	7s.
Painters	8s.	8s.
Sawyers	—	6s.
Sailmakers	7s.6d.–9s.	5s.
Masons	8s.	9s.
Labourers	5–7s.6d.	5–6s.

Source: PRO, ADM106/2029, fol. 199.

cers who had also presented a series of petitions requesting wage increases.[59] Even after the wartime bonus was added, a 4s. sterling gap still favoured Halifax craftsmen.[60] "I am credibly informed that there is a shipbuilder here from New Brunswick ... who would hire the whole of the shipwrights & caulkers belonging to the yard for twelve months certain, at from l0s. to 12s." a day. If not to a neighbouring province his workers, he warned, would leave for the United States "always easy to get there from here." Indeed in the twelve months to mid-1815, forty men, mainly scarce shipwrights, left the yard.

As year-round employment that the yard provided was the only reason artificers remained, Wodehouse resisted the cancellation, at war's end, of the 25 per cent wage bonus. Before he complied, he had

Artificers and Labourers 111

Table 5.4 Halifax Yard Artificers' Pay Rates, 1814

Artificer	Pay day	Extra hour	Sunday	House rent
From England:	£			
Shipwrights & caulkers	6s.3d.	8d.	8s.9d.	15
Others	5s.6d.	7d.	8s.	15
Europeans Entered on the Spot or from Ships at the Station:				
Shipwrights & caulkers	5s.	6d.	7s.6d.	15
Others	4s.3d.	4d.	6s.9d.	15
Native Artificers:				
Shipwrights & caulkers	5s.	6d.	7s.6d.	—
Others	4s.3d.	4d.	6s.9d.	—

Note: In lieu of apprentices, those from England received 1s. extra per day.
Source: Wodehouse to NB, 31 Dec. 1813. NSARM, MG13/9.3, fol. 32.

twice to be directed by the Navy Board[61] which assured him the "price of provisions and labour must necessarily fall as the intercourse between Halifax & the neighboring States becomes more open."[62] Table 5.4 provides some details. As he predicted, with yard wages still 40 to 50 per cent below those of the town, the exodus of workers increased. Some sixty-two more artificers and labourers left the yard voluntarily by mid-1816.[63]

When some English artificers arrived in 1815 on three-year contracts which included a £15 annual allowance for house rent, the yard artificers petitioned for the same. To fortify their case, the twenty petitioners with an average of twenty-five years in the yard, quoted both wages and commodity prices then prevailing in the Halifax market.[64] House rent alone absorbed one-quarter of their earnings.[65] In Halifax, "fuel and warm clothing ... are indispensable for eight months in the year ... which the people of other foreign yards require but in a very slight degree." Their patience had been sorely tried, as they went on to explain, "Your honors petitioners have patiently submitted to every privation, indulging a fallacious hope that a favorable change would take place in our markets, and that by the united industry of themselves and families they might possibly become extricated from embarrassment in which the pressure of the times, their limited incomes and large families had necessarily involved them." Their wages barely afforded them an adequate subsistence.[66]

To the Board, Wodehouse emphasized the uniqueness of the Halifax yard, with its "severe and trying climate." The native Nova Scotians as "sons of persons born in Great Britain and who have either belonged to New York or this land" should be given the house allowance. "Though these persons may be called native artificers, they are superior workmen in general, to any entered on the spot, or from the ships on the station. Their habits are the same as Europeans."[67]

In response, the Navy Board reminded Wodehouse that the principal object of their regulation that excluded the Nova Scotians from the house allowance "was to give encouragement to European artificers."[68] Nevertheless they raised the pay scale by 20 per cent and granted Wodehouse authority thereafter to set daily wages for other yard workers "when compared to the value of labour" in Halifax.[69] It was a very rare example of the Board decentralizing its control and a considerable concession.

If theft of naval stores in the Halifax careening yard, as we saw in chapter 4, ensnared two dishonest master shipwrights, it was not confined to them. Each had his creatures to undertake the dirty work. Marshall's son, Benjamin the shipwright, was accused of removing coal from the yard, of employing yard materials and labour to repair his house, and more significantly, of theft.[70] The most damning evidence against him was that given by his two accomplices, both illiterate yard labourers. He stole timber, elm, and oak boards, a large iron hoop for a ship's mast taken from outside the blacksmith's shop, and a hawser from the anchor wharf which Marshall first coiled before placing aboard a schooner. Benjamin Marshall failed to convince them to falsify their testimony. When they declined he "went away with tears in his eyes."[71] To escape justice he tried to flee the colony, but was apprehended and jailed in Annapolis. Escorted back to Halifax, he was indicted by the grand jury.[72] The dominant power of the Marshall clan in the Halifax yard, if not broken by these events, never recovered from such humiliation.

There were few other proven cases of embezzlement by yard workers. In 1810, when the commissioner received information from the Admiralty that a Halifax publican was supposedly a fence for goods stolen from the yard, the matter was investigated. A search revealed a variety of items including a block, some cord, nails, a canvas bag, and iron with the king's mark on them. Thomas Marnel, the owner, was able to produce receipts for most of them and the matter was closed. The accusation made by one Sarah Smith that he had used liquor to bribe seamen to effect the thefts remained unproven.[73] In 1812 two drunken seamen from the yard's schooner, *Hope*, made off one night with her boats. Apprehended by the watchmen and abusive to the rounder summoned to the scene, they claimed just to be borrowing it in order to get to town by water.[74] The same year Thomas Dates, a sheer hulksman, was detected at the gate carrying out a piece of copper boltstave, for which theft he was "discharged never to be re-entered or allowed into yard upon any account whatsoever."[75]

It was one thing to discharge a worker for theft, yet it was quite another to bring him to trial. The trials of the marine sentinels who stole from the storehouse in 1767, recounted in chapter 1, were exceptional. In 1817 Nova Scotia's assembly considered a bill "somewhat similar to the act of Parliament for the better preventing the embezzlement of naval stores." Though unanimously passed in council, it and a later modified bill were thrown out by the house of assembly. As Wodehouse was convinced that many in Nova Scotia "purchase government stores whenever they are offered to them," he wondered how an act of the imperial Parliament could be made to apply to Nova Scotia.[76]

A major aspiration of yard workers was to transfer from the extra list to the establishment, or ordinary. This meant tenure and employment for life upon good behaviour, with the prospect, if one's health broke down, of the invalids' list and superannuation. This is what kept men at work in the yard when their labour could always fetch more elsewhere.

In the home yards, workmen injured on the job received free medical attention and each yard retained a surgeon. Such men received full pay for the first six weeks off the job and a reduced rate thereafter.[77] No such system operated in the Halifax yard, while there was a surgeon on its establishment only in 1776–82. Though every warship at least the size of a sloop had its surgeon or surgeon's mate, until a new naval hospital was built in 1782, yard workers lacked the easy access to medical care provided by the navy. In 1782 the artificers and labourers of the yard approached Commissioner Hamond to suggest that when they were ill or accidentally hurt, they would be willing thereafter to have 4d. a month deducted from their pay in order to have access to the services provided by the assistant surgeon.[78] With the workers paying the costs,

114 Part Two: Work Force

Table 5.5   Yard Invalid List, 1802

Invalid	Age	Infirmity	Service	Invalid from
Robert Salter	53	rheumatism	20 years	1 Jan 1795
Thomas Mathews	51	rheumatism	14 years	1 Jan 1795
William Dwyer	70	violent rupture	2¾ years	1 Jan 1795
Justice Walker	72	severe bruise	7 years	3 Jan 1796
William Bryan	71	violent rupture	16 years	1 Apr 1797
Frederick Hingle	66	rheumatism	28 years	1 June 1797
Denis Maloney	60	blood discharge	10 months	18 June 1801
John Turpel	50	rupture	13 years	8 Dec 1801
John Twaddle	45	fractured leg	5½ years	1 May 1802
George Cutlipp	54	severe bruise	8 years	1 May 1802

Source: PRO, ADM106/2027.

this became the yard's medical system. It continued until 1810, when at last surgeons in all overseas naval hospitals were first permitted to treat the families of officers and workmen of the yard establishment, "whenever they can do so without interfering with their more important duties at the hospital."[79] Medicines could be dispensed by the hospital, but only if yard officers and workers paid the cost.

If a yard worker's health broke down, or through accident or blindness he could no longer work, then the invalids' list and superannuation might rescue him from indigence. When the need to accommodate invalids first arose in 1782, no invalids' list had been approved for the Halifax careening yard. The boatswain of the hulk *Pembroke*, John Flint, "incapable of doing his duty through lengthy illness," and "worn out and unfit to continue in that station" was merely discharged.[80] A warrant officer for many years and with a large family, Commissioner Hamond recommended him for a pension. Later Commissioner Duncan assigned such men to the extra list of *Pembroke* as ordinary seamen for pay and provisions. "People who have grown old in the service," he suggested to the Board, "or rendered incapable of duty by accidents, cannot be continued as part of the establishment nor can they be turned out to starve."[81] A year later there were five men in that situation including a shipwright, aged 57, worn out after seventeen years. Also worn out were two labourers, aged 66 and 71, with sixteen and fifteen years' seniority respectively. Two others had been in the yard only three years, a watchman, aged 58, suffered a fractured skull and was rendered incapable of duty and a blacksmith, aged 43, placed temporarily on the list "during severity of the winter."[82] By 1802, with ten invalids, the list had doubled as Table 5.5 shows.[83]

Later additions included Henry Rhodes in 1807, ill from severe asthma after thirty-one years,[84] and Farquhar McLean in 1810, a labourer, aged 60 with almost twenty years in the king's service, "rendered incapable of Work by age and Infirmity" when he moved to Pictou.[85] Still another example is that of Frederick Muhlig, a shipwright, in the yard for more than twenty years but by 1814 "totally incapable of performing a day's work in consequence of rheumatism."[86] He had lost the use of his lower limbs and attributed his illness "to exposure to wet & cold while working on stages alongside" warships.[87] The yard officers were to ensure that he picked "the proper quantity" of oakum.[88]

Wodehouse also supported the petition of two watchmen to the invalid list. The first had served thirty years in the yard following seven at sea, and the other had twenty-three years of service. Storey, born in 1754, had a family of five children. From a fall and severe rheumatism he became feeble and incapacitated, with only partial use of his right hand from an injury sustained at sea.[89] Mallon, born in 1747 and illiterate, was married, and in 1814 four of his ten children still lived. He had become progressively enfeebled as a consequence of a groin rupture suffered a decade before and which frequently rendered him incapable of his duty.[90] Both received annual pensions of £15. Among the youngest was Alexander Stewart, a 39-year-old watchman, who had been a private soldier in 1800–05 and then a yard watchman. Seized by a palsy while on yard duty in February 1813, he lost his speech and the use of his limbs.[91] Also afflicted with palsy was the 52-year-old house carpenter, Christopher Blackadar. With a wife and seven children he had served but eleven years in the yard before becoming an invalid in May 1811.[92] Another was Hugh Blackadar, a shipwright aged 38, who suffered a serious thigh injury in 1812 while on board *Milan*. His bone failed to heal keeping him confined. Thomas Wils requested entry to the invalids' list in March 1800, upon his discharge. A soldier with twenty-six years' service, he settled in Nova Scotia after the American war, when invalided from the army. Offered work in the yard as a slater and then as a labourer, the father of a large family then "in very indigent circumstances," he successfully begged for a place on the invalid list. Awarded a monthly allowance of £1.2.6. with provisions, he reported every Saturday afternoon to help sweep the yard.[93] Few were available to sweep. A discharged shipwright,

Thomas Riley, had been blinded nine years earlier when particles of verdigris lodged in his eyes from copper on a ship's bottom. Unable to work, he hoped in vain for the return of his eyesight, while he waited another two years for a vacancy on the invalids' list.[94]

Among those who first applied for a pension was the long-serving foreman of house carpenters and builder of the naval hospital, William Lee. He had entered the service forty-two years earlier as volunteer on the 1758 expedition against Fort Ticonderoga and Fort Frontenac. He entered the yard under Colvill who made him foreman of house carpenters, a position he had held since. In 1800 "subject to many infirmities incident to old age, in addition to his having a large family to support yet unprovided for," he requested superannuation from Commissioner Coffin.[95] He withdrew his application upon Coffin's departure as commissioner and retired only in 1814.[96]

By then sixteen men were on the list. Their average age was 60, one third of which had been spent in the yard's service. They had toiled till they could work no longer, driven out of the yard by injury or by a general collapse. They had either become blind or crippled with withered or otherwise useless limbs, and unable to do any sort of yard work.

In 1814 the Navy Board discovered that the Halifax yard allowances for invalids far exceeded the superannuation rates granted in the dockyards at home.[97] Those on the invalid list were now removed and examined by the surgeon of the naval hospital in the presence of the commissioner. When judged unfit for further service and entitled to superannuation, their pensions now conformed to the lower English rates. These ranged from £20 down to £10 a year, while exceptional service might be rewarded with a pension of £4 to £5 higher.[98]

Those recommended for a pension at Halifax included an illiterate labourer, with only six years in the yard, who had become blind when driving a hoop off an old mast injuring his left eye by some rust particles. Infection led to blindness.[99] Recommended also was a watchman, who was unable to work from incessant "sciatical and rheumatic pains," after forty years a soldier and twelve in the yard.[100] In 1810 John Cook, a literate sawyer, petitioned for a pension, having served in the 70th Foot Regiment for ten years, including the entire American war. Continuously employed since 1785 when he entered the yard, in consequence of "hurts he has received and from the cold and damps of the laborious trade of sawing timber," he wrote that he "has become feeble, with pains in the breast, indicative of an approaching consumption."[101] In 1814 John Brush, foreman of smiths, found himself in a similar position; his case was supported by Commissioner Wodehouse. After thirty-five years in service, twenty-eight years of them in the yard, at age sixty he applied for a pension. Born in Westchester, he served an apprenticeship as blacksmith. He attached himself to the British when war broke out in America and joined the Regiment of Orange Rangers as a sergeant in 1776, until he was disbanded in 1783, much of which time he was employed in the engineers branch. A foreman in the blacksmith shop in 1786 when he entered the navy yard, a decade later he was made foreman of smiths. Struck down by a severe illness in 1812 he was thus unfit for duty. He was awarded a pension of £50 a year two years later.[102]

To begin to rid the yards of the elderly and infirm workers, superannuation had been introduced in 1764, the scheme being at first restricted to shipwrights and caulkers. The initial rate was two thirds of income, paid to those after thirty years of continuous service, or to those injured in the yard. Coinciding with the establishment of the Halifax naval yard, the regulations provided a significant comfort for those few who qualified. When the Halifax yard virtually closed down in 1819, all the remaining artificers, as well as other long-serving yard workers, were granted pensions based on the 1814 rates.

The most serious threat to a reliable income from naval yard work and the later possibility of getting on the invalids' list or receiving a pension was discharge or dismissal. Those on the extra list were the first to be let go, when peace reduced work in the yards or when winter weather greatly restricted outdoor work. In winter, unless the squadron was in need of refitting, workers on the extra list were discharged, usually by mid-December and were not rehired until at least mid-March. Discharge also occurred because men wanted to leave the yard's service voluntarily at the end of a pay period. In theory the resident commissioner could only recommend dismissal. If this rule operated in the home dockyard, at Halifax successive commissioners themselves clearly exercised this executive power over artificers and "the people."

Men were commonly dismissed for absenteeism or some other infraction. In 1785, as an example, Nicholas Wall had pleaded to be reinstated to his old job at the yard. Wall had been employed as an artificer in Boston, had come to Halifax with Gage's army in 1776, and had worked in the yard until the fall of 1784, when "without a thought" he went to Shelburne to see his brother, a loyalist refugee whom he had not seen for ten years. Dismissed upon his return, he remained unemployed all winter "to the great distress of his family," and begged re-entry.[103]

If absence went unexplained, it usually meant that the men had found work elsewhere, probably in Halifax or Dartmouth. Such men were dismissed and frequently ordered, "not to be re-entered." In June 1809, for instance, after studying the May monthly pay lists, Commissioner Inglefield found five men who had been absent between six and eleven days. He required an explanation "for their very great apparent neglect of their duty."[104] Shipwright James Turpel, who "having absented himself from his duty without leave, and employed himself in the town, when his services were most wanted," was discharged in 1813 and his pay stopped.[105] In 1818 when Patrick Savage, an unsatisfactory labourer, was "so often absent lately," Commissioner Wodehouse merely sought an explanation from his master shipwright.[106] He avoided dismissal on this occasion but suffered it some months later. For "idleness whilst at work" Thomas Muhlig, an experienced shipwright-caulker, in avoiding dismissal for absenteeism, suffered being mulcted half-a-day's wage.[107]

Insolent behaviour usually brought quick dismissal. In 1800 James Condon, the pitch boiler, was discharged by Commissioner Coffin for this reason,[108] as was John Dingle for behaving "in a very insolent and disorderly manner" in Coffin's presence.[109] John Purcell, a labourer, was discharged in 1805 for insolent and improper conduct in an altercation with the master attendant.[110] The most serious case occurred in 1803 when Anthony Vincent, a shipwright-caulker who had served his apprenticeship in the yard, while employed on *Leander* had uttered words "calculated to excite mutiny and disaffection, by treating the usual ceremony and respect shown to the commander-in-chief, when passing with his flag, in derision in the presence of the officers and ships' companies." Commissioner Inglefield ordered him immediately discharged "for such disloyal and ungrateful conduct, as a man unworthy of being fed and protected in any employment under the king's government."[111] This statement reveals rather more about the commissioner's view of work in a naval yard than on the shipwright's motives, about which we are left ignorant. Michael Riley, a labourer, was ejected from his yard house for drunkenness while on duty and insolence to John Parry, the foreman of shipwrights.[112] In 1810 Master Attendant Edmund Fairfax complained to the commissioner about a pilot, Rackstraw, who went aboard *Pallet*, weighed her anchor, and took in moorings without advising him, while knowing someone else was to pilot the vessel out of harbour. When Fairfax threatened to inform Inglefield, Rackstraw replied "he had lived without the assistance of the Yard and would again" and left the office. As Fairfax explained, "As I full well know many persons principles are more independent than their circumstances, I waited 'till this morning in expectation that he would make some apology." When none was forthcoming a complaint was lodged.[113]

To disobey orders usually resulted in instant dismissal for common labourers, while artificers were treated less harshly. When shipwright Michael Donovan and labourer William O'Brien disobeyed orders, however, they were only publicly reprimanded at the one o'clock call and warned that for their "next offence of a similar kind they will be discharged also."[114] Jasper Rhodes, the shipwright who was charged by the master shipwright with refusing to obey the order of the foreman of the yard to work on board *Eurydice*, avoided dismissal by apologizing, "being sensible of the impropriety of his behaviour."[115]

Men were also dismissed for bad behaviour, the most frequent example of which related to spirits. For bringing liquor into the yard, expressly forbidden, workers paid heavily when caught. Although there were taphouses in all the home yards, and one had existed when the Halifax yard was under construction, no later reference is found to such a place in the yard. Spirits, especially rum, were readily available, as several grog shops established themselves outside the yard walls. It was introduced both by boat and by being smuggled into the yard through the gate. In 1806, as we saw in chapter 3, an extra guard was posted to prevent spirits from being retailed to inmates of the naval hospital. When caught "bringing liquor to the yard for the purpose of disposing of it to seamen of *Hogue*," shipwright John Ripley, whose services were needed, was discharged and mulcted his pay.[116] John Moore, a labourer, caught in 1815 bringing spirits to artificers from sloop *Rifleman*, was also discharged.[117] In 1817 Abraham Coleman, a labourer, was discharged "for bringing liquor into the yard" contrary to regulations.[118] The last man to be discharged for a similar infraction

120 Part Two: Work Force

was James Devit in 1819. A labourer, he was discharged and mulcted four days' pay for bringing liquor to the working party from *Forth*.[119]

What conclusions come from this array of evidence? First, the voices of the ordinary workers and artificers were rarely heard except when disputes or difficulties arose. In the absence of labour unions or physical confrontation over pay and working conditions, workers voiced their concerns through joint petitions, a process widely employed in dealing with the colonial government of Nova Scotia and other jurisdictions. Rarely used in the yard, and always couched in moderate language, they were articulate, persuasive, and proved effective. In the navy such behaviour among seamen amounted to mutiny.

Second, unlike those who served the navy afloat, yard workers were free to leave and seek work elsewhere. Owing to the regularity of their pay, few left voluntarily once they found a place on the yard establishment. This probably led, as in England, to too many older men remaining on the yard's pay lists, when their health and strength were impaired. In the absence of a medical system in Halifax of the sort found in the English dockyards, many must have answered the morning's bell and attended the roll-call when actually too ill to put in a proper day's work.

Third, if Halifax yard workers were embezzlers, they went almost wholly undetected. An effective system of fencing stolen goods was crucial to the illegal activities in the contemporary Portsmouth dockyard. The failure to develop in Halifax such a system may have been a contributory cause to the apparent lack of embezzlers. As yard workers were as keen in Halifax to supplement the family income as those elsewhere, the greater virtue of yard workers in Halifax cannot be established. That the navy never built a chapel or assigned a chaplain in the yard, may indicate that in Halifax there was less perceived need of it than in England, where every dockyard built a church and retained a prelate.

Fourth, there was an unwritten race and colour bar in the yard. If Acadiens were employed in the naval yard – I encountered none in the pay lists – certainly none ever reached foreman rank. Few blacks found work in the Halifax yard and then only briefly, unlike the yards in Jamaica and Antigua, where African slaves were regularly employed as the "King's Negroes." Records refer to black workers only on two occasions. Blacks undertook work others would normally avoid, as when in 1802 the state of the hospital's necessary was such that it "required black men to clean it."[120] In 1815 for eight weeks six blacks – John and Henry Thomas, John Baptist, John Lewis, Pierre Peter, and Christopher Joseph appeared on the pay list.[121] When they absented themselves without leave a few days later, all were discharged.[122]

Fifth, in England where the warships were built, labour was "on average much less productive in the dockyards than in private yards."[123] However long their work day it was less than in merchant yards, where the pay was considerably higher. As the Halifax yard built few vessels before 1820 and as no study has been undertaken of labour efficiency in privately-owned shipyards in early British North American history, a similar comparison cannot be made. Historians assign part of the blame to shipwrights, the principal class of yard worker, who varied greatly in skill. In 1805 at Deptford, for instance, only a little more than one in five was classed as good or superior, the rest being old, disabled, or idle.[124] Attrition alone never freed the yards of "the old, the infirm and the refractory."[125] The same can also certainly be said of the Halifax naval yard.

Finally, the yard and the hospital complex were largely a male preserve. Though women were present in the yard as wives of officers and of those who were housed there, the yard never had a woman on its pay list. In the hospital were found a matron and nurses, some of whom were certainly women. Women were also found in the kitchen and wash house.

In these ways the naval yard is a historical microcosm illustrating the limitations of personal freedom imposed both by the need for work and the prospect of a pension. Its study allows us to understand something of the culture of work and the operation of social authority within a complex industrial workplace.

Chapter Six

THE WORK OF THE YARD

"this remote and frozen part of the world."[1]

Earlier chapters have occasionally addressed, in a general manner, the type of work undertaken in the yard. We have seen that some of it involved erecting buildings and other structures as well as their renovation and maintenance. These were mere means to an end, for the principal responsibility was to maintain the Halifax squadron at sea, and to refit and store those warships from other stations which might put into port.

Before we consider in some detail the type of work habitually carried on in the yard, something must be said about the fluctuating size of the workforce, which reflected the differing pressures on the yard. In the years of peace following the Seven Years' War and before 1769, there were on average only forty-five men employed. In the seven years between 1769 and 1775, when many of the yard's main structures were substantially rebuilt, the average rose to 124.[2] As throughout this interval the yard's establishment numbered only fourteen, the additional workers were noted on the extra list. To some extent it was also during these pre-war years that the considerable value of the yard was first proven. It was then that the enlarged North American squadron began to be used against colonial port towns in a vain attempt to control American smuggling. With the outbreak of hostilities with rebel America during the War of Independence, the Halifax base became extremely busy. In 1776, the yard's establishment was raised to 163, a number never exceeded before 1820. Even though the establishment was reduced after 1783 to 124, owing to a new building programme in the years of peace between 1784 and 1792, an average of 186 men were employed.³ This post-war establishment was more than adequate to handle the usual size of the Halifax-based squadron then consisting of one 50-gun fourth rate, three frigates of 32, 28, and 24 guns, two 16-gun sloops, and two lightly-armed brigs.⁴

When war with France broke out in 1793, the Navy Board, instead of expanding the establishment at Halifax, reduced the establishment to 111 in 1797, and to sixty-six in 1802, when the false Peace of Amiens came into effect. The Admiralty's apparent neglect of Halifax meant that, with war, the number of men employed was inadequate even for the needs of the North American squadron, without considering the other types of work undertaken by the workforce. Even in the 1790s, when the Western Atlantic was a minor theatre of war, the size of the yard's workforce on occasion proved too restricted to accommodate quickly the burdens placed on it. As early as 1795 Vice Admiral Murray remarked that "notwithstanding my endeavours to cause the arrival and refitting of the different ships of my squadron at Halifax to be in as regular a tour as possible so as not to bring too great a quantity of work on the naval establishment there at once ... delays often must happen in spite of the greatest zeal and execution in Commissioner Duncan, and the officers and men under him."⁵

To ease the burden on the Halifax yard, Murray contracted with private shipyards in Bermuda to refit his smallest warships and claimed that the experiment was successful. "Had the Bermudian vessels been taken [to Halifax] to refit," he explained, "they must either have been laid-by for some time while other ships were refitting, or have prevented these other ships from service by coming in their way. They would also be far removed from the scene in which their lordships wished them to be employed on." Between 1793 and 1801 on average 184 people worked in the Halifax yard, under four officers. This was an increase of only 12.5 per cent when compared with the decade of peace before 1793. It meant that those on the establishment only supplied two thirds of the workforce. It was thus a false economy for the Navy Board to maintain an establishment wholly inadequate for the work undertaken at the yard.

The resumption of war in 1803 at first changed nothing. It was 1805 before the Halifax establishment, at 125, was restored to the level of the pre-war years. Commissioner Inglefield pressed the Board on several occasions to increase the establishment which had been reduced at the Peace of Amiens to sixty-six. Yet in 1802–03 on average

107 were employed, only two thirds of whom were on the establishment. Wodehouse argued that the Halifax yard shouldered additional heavy responsibilities which the Board could not ignore. Not only had it repaired the ships of the Barbados squadron, but it also had refitted in a few months forty-seven warships, as well as several transports and storeships which had recently undergone refitting and had been loaded with stores by the yard. Between 1804 and 1807 on average the yard employed 165 men, or even below the peacetime average in 1783–92. With the additional task of building a sloop and gun brig, as well as about a dozen flat-bottomed pettyaugers – fifty to eighty-ton boats – the yard was seriously undermanned. In the heightened tension with the United States in 1808–11, the number of yard workers rose on average to 194. With the workload almost doubling, this was still only a 17.5 per cent increase.

Curiously, the Navy Board failed even to press the Admiralty to augment the Halifax establishment during the thirty-two months' war with the United States, begun in June 1812. It took no account of the huge increase in the number of warships dependent on Halifax. In 1813 Admiral Warren warned Commissioner Wodehouse to expect the squadron to be "considerably increased." Not only were masts to be readied but moorings laid down for five ships of the line and three frigates, as ships entering harbour "experience much inconvenience from being obliged to ride at their own anchors & cables."[6] As the port admiral told the Admiralty at the peak of this pressure, the strength of the yard was "so unequal to the necessary repairs of the ships and vessels which come here, since the augmentation of the naval forces on this station ... that it has of late frequently happened for a ship to be detained a considerable length of time after being replenished, and, in all other respects refitted, waiting for caulking or other repairs to be done to her." The establishment then represented only about half the number of workers in the yard, or 125 out of an average of 247 employed in 1813–14. For six months in the autumn and winter of 1813–14, an average of 267 men were at work, the highest totals ever reached by the yard in this era. At its most extensive in 1814, the fleet in American waters had grown to about 120 warships of all sizes. That year on average every month almost 250 officers and men worked as employees of the yard.

The commissioner at times during the war with the United States was unable to hire artificers in Nova Scotia "to such a height has the price of labour risen,"[7] and even the augmented wages offered by the yard proved an inadequate inducement for skilled artisans to enter the service. Wodehouse recommended that if the war continued in 1815, fifty shipwright-caulkers should be sent to the Halifax yard that spring. While the war with France and the United States lasted, no artificers were sent to Halifax from England. The explanation was the shortage of artificers in the home yards and uncompetitive wage levels for suitable skilled yard workers in the labour pool of British North America.

The peace of 1815 eventually had an impact on the yard's establishment. By November 1815 the commissioner dismissed dozens of men from the establishment and extra list. The new peace establishment, at sixty-seven, was similar to that of 1802.[8] This again failed to reflect the real needs of the yard when on average to mid-1819 about 145 were at work in the yard, a one-third decline from the late war years. This meant that workers on the establishment numbered a good deal less than half the actual workforce. In 1819 an average of 114 men still worked in the yard as the officers rapidly discharged workers from July onwards, preparatory to the virtual closure of the yard by January 1820, when there were only nineteen men employed.[9] By then, the Halifax yard had virtually ceased to function in a manner of any real use to the North American squadron.

The Navy Board had received plenty of warning that this would result from their orders. However reduced the squadron after 1815, yard workers had responsibilities other than to refit warships, as Wodehouse had informed the Board. Owing to the number of specialized vessels used by the yard and to the number of buoys to be maintained in the inner and outer harbour, Wodehouse wanted to retain eight sheer hulksmen whose duties included maintaining buoys that were "subject to heavy eastern swells, frequently carried adrift by sea and ice," he explained. It was six miles from the yard to the nearest buoys and seventeen miles to those off the lighthouse. Besides that, they were needed to man the four yard craft – the pilot sloop, a buoy boat, and two mooring lighters – in addition to keeping them clean, dry, and ready for service. They had also to maintain the sheers and other careening gear. Wodehouse also thought that the yard needed at least twenty labourers year-round, as every spring the drains needed unblocking, when "for many weeks after the masons and labourers are employed solely in clearing them – from the situation of the Yard immediately at the bottom of a steep hill it cannot be otherwise."[10] Stone and brickwork were always in need of pointing because of the

Table 6.1   Workforce at British Overseas Bases, 1790 & 1814

	1790	1814	% Change
Halifax	4+136	5+241	75.5
Jamaica	3+250	5+309	24.1
Antigua	3+103	5+327	226.0
Malta	–	5+378	–
Madras	–	4+516	–

Note: Officers + men distinguished.
Source: NMM, ADM/BP/34b.

severity of winters. Unless snow was cleared immediately in winter, damage to foundations occurred. As the squadron had been so greatly reduced after 1815, dependence on working parties of seamen to help was no longer possible.

If the size of the establishment thus bore no obvious relation to the number of workers actually on the yard's pay list, it was nevertheless a good indication of the relative importance in which it was held by both the Admiralty and Navy Board. Within the developing world of British naval power, the Halifax base, by 1815, had the smallest establishment and smallest workforce among the larger overseas bases, as Table 6.1 illustrates. Though its workforce grew between 1790 and 1814, its numbers failed to keep pace with the Antigua yard and never overtook that of Jamaica, even as its own work rapidly multiplied, especially between 1807 and 1815, the years of repeated crises with the United States. From this perspective the Halifax careening yard appears as the misbegotten child of the elder Pitt's enthusiasm in the early stage of the Seven Years' War.

The principal use of the Halifax yard was to refit and store the squadron, whatever its size. Its ability to undertake this satisfactorily depended in part on the level of skill of the artificers, the size of this skilled workforce, and the availability of working parties of seamen to assist the labourers, especially at times of intense activity. The ready availability of suitable stores was also crucial.

If refitting the squadron was the central responsibility of the yard, it was obliged to undertake a great deal more. The first post-war autumn of 1783 witnessed quite unusual activity in Halifax harbour of a very different sort. Transports arriving with loyalists and disbanded

128   Part Two: Work Force

troops who chose to settle in Nova Scotia and Cape Breton were either redirected back to New York to collect the remaining regiments still occupying the town, or ordered to carry troops from Halifax to England.[11] Each had to be unloaded, stored, provisioned, and watered before being sent again to sea. Other transports were despatched with cargoes of flour for refugees settling at Port Mouton, Shelburne, Country Harbour, around Chedabucto Bay, at the mouth of the St John River, Annapolis Royal, and various other points on the Bay of Fundy as far up as the Cumberland shore.[12] By the following spring, those who had wintered at Port Mouton had found the soil "so exceeding bad and sterile" wished to settle elsewhere; transports were provided to carry them to Digby and Passamaquoddy.[13]

By contrast, the yard's normal peacetime routine, when few ships needed attention in any given year, was comparatively unhurried. This was the situation between 1764 and 1774, when on average some thirty-seven warships of all sizes were stationed on the North American coast. Hood's squadron for instance, in 1768-9, numbered only fourteen vessels which the careening yard could easily handle. In the years 1783-4, on average twenty-two ships and vessels were surveyed and refitted at the yard each year.

There was little winter work in peacetime. As the squadron was not required to cruise, it was moored near the yard, the topmasts removed, the exposed decks boarded, and additional stoves brought on board. Towards the end of March, these unsightly winter coverings were removed, and the ships readied for their summer cruise in the Gulf of St Lawrence, or wherever the commodore or admiral wished to direct them.

In wartime, there was no question of mooring the squadron in harbour over the winter months. The warships were at sea, either alone or as a squadron, for as much of the year as possible. In the war against rebel America, the main problem at first related only to rebel privateers. When France entered the war as an ally of Congress in 1778, the issue was far more serious. On more than one occasion the navy lost command of the sea off the French coast, failing to prevent French naval squadrons from gaining access to the Western Atlantic. This caused consternation even in Halifax, where attack was anticipated but never endured. In the wars against revolutionary and Napoleonic France from 1793, the Halifax-based squadron found itself blockading French warships which sought the safety of American ports; patrolling the coast as far south as Florida; ranging well east, north, and south of

Bermuda; picking up French privateers whenever opportunity presented itself; and stopping, searching for contraband, and seizing American merchant ships off their major ports. All such cruising took a heavy toll on masts, yards, sails, and rigging and, when ships struck a ledge or shoal, on their copper bottoms. Even under normal sailing conditions a general caulking was needed regularly, while the salt and sun bleached and wore off the paint and varnish.

An example of the pressure on the yard can be found in May 1809, when the yard employed some 214 men. There were three pettyaugers still on the stocks when the squadron arrived with ships to be refitted. Typically, when the squadron had been at sea for more than a few weeks, the yard officers adopted a tone of resignation in their progress reports.[14] Two months later, under increasing pressure from the admiral, Commissioner Inglefield explained that though the refitting was "progressing as expeditiously as is possible" using all available labour in the yard and with the assistance of the squadron's own artificers, the squadron would not be ready for sea until mid-July. Just to load masts in a transport to ship to Bermuda would take sixteen men a week to complete. Unless the men worked two successive Sundays the admiral's proposed date of departure could not be met.[15] It was a case either of excessive expectations by the admiral, or the failure of the yard, despite working every available pair of hands both long hours and Sundays, to complete its most important work speedily enough.

If Inglefield was feeling pressure from the admiral, his own officers wrote urgently to him, especially the storekeeper. That July several shipments of coal were received at the coal yard at the same time that timber, spars, and lumber were delivered to another part of the yard. Simultaneously two storeships, *Inflexible* and *Zephyrus* and transport *Ajax* arrived with orders to be unloaded "with all possible dispatch."[16] To oversee this the storekeeper, independent of the clerk routinely receiving and issuing stores, reckoned he was five clerks too few for all these tasks, as well as those concerned with the ships and the yard offices. Seamen from the squadron, helping to unload and working in the stores, had constantly to be watched. Delays ensued, sea officers and warrant officers as well as merchants became impatient with the delays. Of his clerks, one was absent sick and the other at work but so ill that he could accomplish little.

The inadequate establishment was not a new problem. Three years earlier in 1806, to provide another example, Vice Admiral Berkeley had politely suggested to the commissioner that he might hire more artificers. As all the shipwrights and caulkers were then at work refitting his squadron, the construction of the sloop *Halifax*, still on the stocks, had stopped. Unless the ship was launched before winter, she would be unable to join the squadron until 1807.[17] Inglefield, in response, informed the commander-in-chief that there were already forty-six artificers above the establishment.[18] Indeed, there were that month 173 men on the yard's pay books. The commissioner might have used this opportunity to encourage a joint appeal to the Admiralty and Navy Board greatly to increase the size of the yard's establishment. If this occurred to Inglefield or Berkeley there is not a scrap of evidence to show it.

Two years earlier still, in 1804, in correspondence with Vice Admiral Mitchell, the commissioner had written of the yard's "very inadequate establishment."[19] Yet he never made an issue of it in his official correspondence to the Navy Board or raised it directly with the Admiralty. The establishment had been set the year before at 114, up from 111 in 1797, but down from the pre-war level of 125, and far below the 165 existing at the end of the War of American Independence. That Duncan, Inglefield, and Wodehouse on no occasion ever lobbied for an increased establishment perhaps indicates that they could meet every emergency simply by adding to the extra list and hiring artificers in Nova Scotia when they were needed.

The closest Inglefield came to drafting such a letter occurred on two occasions, once in 1806 and the other in 1811. The first instance happened while explaining to the Navy Board why he had entered four additional men to serve on the sheer hulk: "On the arrival of the dismasted ships in the fall of last year," he wrote, "which were also careened to shift their keels, it was evident to every man of judgment on the spot that the establishment of Sheerness would not have been more than equal to the work." Sheerness employed at that time four times the workforce then employed in the Halifax yard.[20] When consulted, the Admiralty flatly refused any increase in the hulk's establishment.[21]

On the other occasion, in 1811, when explaining to the Navy Board why extra hulksmen had been hired, Inglefield retorted that he could use four times as many hulksmen as he actually possessed in the yard, that during "the hurricane we experienced here on the 30th September, and when his Majesty's ships have been since coming in dismasted with signals of distress flying, I had not hulksmen sufficient to man the launches or to bring the ships to their moorings." The Navy Board expressed its alarm and immediately responded by encouraging him to hire as many extra men as the service might in future require, but all as extras, and none to be added to the establishment.[22]

As another expedient to make up for the serious shortages, especially among skilled artificers which the very restricted yard establishment dictated, recourse was made to employing men on warships, transports, and even from the garrison. The first recorded occasion when carpenters from the transports were used occurred in June 1808, when the number of artificers was inadequate to refit the squadron.[23] When the squadron was again in harbour five months later, the commissioner mustered on shore every artificer in the squadron to help in the refit of their ships.[24]

A surviving series of monthly reports to the Admiralty from August 1808 through January 1810 offers a rare opportunity to view the amount of work this small yard managed to complete in wartime, despite the shortage of workers and space at the careen. We learn from the first monthly report that ten ships had been recently refitted and had sailed and an eleventh was ready to sail.[25] Of these, one was schooner *Adonis* based in Newfoundland, another was sloop *Dispatch*, based in Jamaica.

Most such refits took at least a month to complete, between the time the ship entered harbour and the time she again sailed. Of those waiting to be repaired two were from the Leeward Islands squadron and one from the Jamaica squadron. Two months later in October 1808, there were eight warships to be refitted, two of them 74-gun third rates. One sloop had been there for more than two months and was only then preparing to heave down at the careening wharf. Besides the warships there were two storeships and several transports being fitted to embark troops. In addition to all of this there were six pettyaugers still under construction.[26] A month later, at the end of November 1808, Commissioner Inglefield reported no progress on the pettyaugers, as Admiral Warren insisted that the entire yard workforce devote itself to refitting his squadron.

Among those that were much longer in port was storeship *William* (John Foxton, master), which with great difficulty had been floated from a ledge where it had gone aground in Canso Harbour on its passage from England. She had a cargo of sails, canvas, hammocks, and slops both of linen and wool. All were salvaged and brought to Halifax to be dried and cleaned. The sails, canvas, and hammocks were first kept in the water, secured to the wharfs to prevent them being frozen.

Linen slops were washed under contract, while those of wool dried by means of airing stoves placed in the masthouse loft. Hats and shoes suffered the most damage.[27] Three months later the commissioner still hoped *William* would be ready to sail before the worst of the winter storms played havoc with shipping in the North Atlantic.[28]

In May 1809, when the Halifax squadron of fifteen warships had been in harbour but a day or two, Inglefield was able to provide the admiral with estimates of the time required to undertake the necessary repairs to six of the smaller warships.[29] This amounted to six days for *Hussar*, eight days each for *Ferret* and *Squirrel*, twelve days for sloops *Columbine* and *Halifax*, and sixteen days for *Colibri*. The rest had yet to have their defects surveyed.

The August 1809 report listed twenty-eight warships. Of these, *Centurion*, which was serving as a permanent receiving ship, had her masts removed. Another, *Inflexible*, served as a floating powder magazine. Of the remainder, twelve had already departed, leaving fourteen in some stage of repair. Of these, six had arrived with Admiral Warren two months earlier, two others were from the West Indies squadron and one, *Comet*, came from the Newfoundland station. Each of the six that came in with Warren in May had received extensive damage, two – *Horatio* and *Junon* – had timbers shot away. Still it seems reasonable to conclude that the restricted capacity of the Halifax yard to handle but two ships at a time at the careening wharf and the limited number of artificers, were the principal causes of the yard's lengthy turn-about times.[30]

As more ships from the West Indies squadron arrived in September, as well as several ships sent by the Admiralty on different assignments, Admiral Warren became concerned for his own squadron. Knowing that nine or ten of his squadron would join him there in October to refit, he urged Inglefield to order the yard to work overtime for the next five weeks.[31] The commissioner responded by noting that "working the artificers by candlelight" was unproductive.[32] To accommodate the admiral he stopped work on storeship *William* which was still refitting at the end of the year, to concentrate all the yard's efforts on refitting the squadron.[33] Of the thirteen warships and storeships in harbour, five were from Warren's squadron. *Cleopatra* had run onto Thrum Cap Shoal as she came into harbour and needed a new false keel, her bottom recaulked and general recoppering, while *Driver* required a "large repair." Sloop *Little Belt* had been dismasted in a storm, and needed both new masts and a thorough refit. The yard workers saw no end to their toil. Yet when Inglefield sent the Admiralty his final report for 1809, the yard seemed to have accomplished almost all that had been asked of it and much of it on schedule. With a larger workforce and an additional careening wharf or drydock much more could have been accomplished. Such ideas, if considered by the Admiralty and Navy Board, never were put on paper.

Additional wartime work was created for the yard not just through the gradually increased size of the squadron using Halifax as a base. In 1805, for the first time the Leeward Islands squadron, to escape the hurricane season, refitted in Halifax.[34] No remark seems ever to have passed between the Admiralty or the Navy Board to augment the yard workforce to accommodate this important and useful initiative. In 1808 Admiral Warren, then in Bermuda, casually mentioned that Cochrane would sail to Halifax during hurricane season for refitting.[35] How the extra naval stores that would be required were to be supplied he did not explain.

In addition, ships owned by other branches of the navy,[36] the Ordnance department,[37] the separate governments of Nova Scotia[38] and Cape Breton, as well as packet boats, storeships,[39] and transports[40] were regularly refitted in the yard. In 1812 and 1813, for instance, transports had to be converted by the yard artificers into cattle boats to ship bullocks and hay from Halifax for the use of the squadron then using the Bermuda base.[41] Occasionally a ship on the Newfoundland station, whose home base was either Plymouth or Portsmouth, was refitted in the Halifax yard. An example of this last kind occurred in 1809. When *Comet* arrived from Newfoundland to have her defects repaired, Admiral Warren expressed the wish that such work "may not interfere with the repairs of the ships already in this harbour."[42]

A second major task regularly imposed on the yard was the unloading of storeships, usually from England, and the depositing of the cargoes of naval stores in the appropriate storehouses. There was also the task of the reloading of naval stores being returned home or distributed to other bases, or to accompany the squadron on one or other of its several wartime expeditions.

Every year the Navy Board sent out its storeships filled with naval stores which had been ordered the year before by the Halifax yard's principal officers. Frequently such storeships loaded unserviceable stores for the return voyage to England,[43] or occasionally timber for masts and other sticks for the home yards.[44] Before 1788, Navy Board policy aimed to ensure that an eighteen months' supply was on hand at any one time in all overseas bases. That year the Navy Board inaugurated a two-years' supply policy.[45]

The Navy Board generally held the view that naval stores, except some significant examples, were better supplied from England as they were both less expensive and of more reliable quality than those obtainable in the colonies. In view of the seriously underdeveloped manufacturing capacity in British North American colonies before 1820 and the restrictions on trade with the United States from 1775 onwards and with foreign colonies and states under the Navigation Act generally, this policy was well-founded.

Significant exceptions to this policy were perishable items and wood products from the still largely unsurveyed forests of the maritime colonies. In the 1780s the timber wealth of Quebec was still largely unimagined! Their policy in the 1790s for masts was clear enough: Halifax should largely supply its own needs, and maintain a supply sufficient "to refit the fleet after an engagement however severe ... [and] to replenish your store before such another event could be supposed at all likely, or even possible, to take place."[46] Items of a "perishable nature beyond what may be reasonably expected to come into use in the course of the war," would also not be sent, and could be purchased locally.

Besides the usual duties of an overseas base, the Halifax yard acted as a distribution centre for all sorts of wood products needed at foreign bases. In 1809 alone Commissioner Inglefield estimated that 11,000 spars of different sizes and large quantities of deals and timber were loaded that year from the Halifax yard and shipped to England, Jamaica, Antigua, Barbados, and Bermuda.[47] This topic will be considered in some detail in chapter 8.

The key to success in implementing this storage policy was effective communication between the London headquarters and all overseas yards, the Halifax yard included. It implied an effective organization within the home yards from which Halifax drew its supplies, especially Woolwich and Deptford. In wartime it meant the safe and timely despatch and arrival of storeships, both owned by the navy and hired from contractors.

To effect this system the Navy Board attempted to control the overseas bases as tightly as those in England. As we saw in chapter 4, it felt free to criticize those yard officers who failed to understand their directives, or complete accurately and on time their numerous monthly, quarterly, and annual returns.[48] Inventory control, as in all large enterprises, was a particularly difficult administrative problem, and problems caused irritation, at times, on either side of the Atlantic.

As it has been repeatedly noted, Halifax, and indeed British North America in general, was clearly off the Admiralty's beaten track, and hence the Navy Board's as well. To these august bodies the strategic sea lanes included, beyond the waters off the coasts of northern Europe and the Bay of Biscay, those to and from the West Indies and the Mediterranean. The Navy Board explicitly referred to this early in the French wars. In 1794 it noted that "there are fewer opportunities and somewhat greater uncertainties with respect to sending out supplies for your yard than any other."[49]

The general principle guiding the yard at the outbreak of war with France in 1793 was spelled out by the Navy Board only two years later. Though war placed additional burdens on the navy, Halifax yard's requisitions aimed only to supply a squadron both in number and type of warship then on the station.[50] In a word, as the war was evolving, Halifax remained a backwater – as if Britain was still at peace. Thus it continued, more or less, until the Admiralty altered its strategic concerns. This occurred finally only in mid-1813, and then only lasted for about eighteen months.

The process of unloading a storeship and placing its cargo in the appropriate places within the storehouses was labour-intensive. It could take labourers days to complete, even when aided by working parties of seamen. When this occurred at times when the yard's capacity was already stretched in refitting and provisioning the squadron, stress within the workforce and on the officers rose dramatically. July 1809, as has already been noted, found the storekeeper begging for extra clerks when two storeships, *Inflexible* and *Zephyrus*, arrived in the midst of just such a situation.[51] In 1806, on average three warships every month were stored for either four or eight months' duration, while in 1808, the number had doubled to six a month.[52] As the squadron expanded thereafter until 1815, the number of ships drawing stores and provisions correspondingly increased, and with it the amount of work to be completed, always "with the utmost dispatch." Earlier in this chapter we saw how the size of the workforce, whether skilled artificers or common labourers, failed to keep pace with the yard's increased workload. The storekeeper's office felt this pressure as much as those repairing ships. For example, in 1807 it took the yard thirteen days to unload the storeship *Hewson* and in 1808 eight days to unload the smaller hired brig *Hazard*.[53]

Some of these stores, when they became unserviceable after use by the ships or the yard, were then sold at public auction. It was one of the few ways by which the yard could earn revenue. The first storekeeper, Joseph Gerrish, held seven such sales in fifteen years.[54] Sale items usually included old and decayed cordage, junk, old canvas, hammocks, slops, chips,[55] and other articles "which are fit only to be sold in this country,"[56] and which were "likely to sell to more advantage here than in England."[57] For such auctions, permission had first to be obtained from the Navy Board. The Navy Board specified that no item bearing the king's mark was to be sold; instead it was to be shipped to England or destroyed.[58] The manner in which such sales were conducted was laid out in the *General Instructions*. Sales included wood ashes saved from the pitch house and steam kiln,[59] wood chips, and on a couple of occasions limestone brought from Bermuda as ballast.[60] When the hospital was virtually closed down in 1816, its remaining stores were sold by the yard staff.[61]

Sales of ships also occurred occasionally, once the Navy Board's authorization had been given. In 1783 the prison ship *Jersey*, after being thoroughly aired, was sold.[62] In 1785 two schooners were sold.[63] The galley *Hussar*, the former armed tender *Felicity*, a pilot boat *Mackerel*, and the yard's anchor sloop sold in the spring of 1786 when "people are fitting out vessels for the fishery."[64] In 1795 two schooners, *Chatham* and *Diligent* were paid off and after lying at the wharfs, one was sold and the other converted into a hoy for watering and carrying stores on board the squadron.[65] A third paid-off vessel, the armed cutter *Prince Edward*, beyond repair, was sold a few months later.[66]

There was a flurry of ship sales after the general peace in 1815. The receiving ship, *Centurion*, used by Rear Admiral Griffith, along with six of the unemployed pettyaugers and the frames of three brigs were then sold.[67] Between 1817 and 1819 further sales were effected: the frigates *Niger* and *Success*, the survey sloop *Examiner*, and finally the buoy boat *Hibernia*.[68] These sales reflected in Halifax the situation throughout the British Empire, as the Navy scaled back and reduced its size as it returned to a peacetime establishment. With a much-reduced workforce in the post-war English dockyards, such ships were no longer even to be sent home for major rebuilding. With the sale of the buoy boat in the summer of 1819, as it coincided with the drastic reduction in the yard's establishment, the navy signalled that it would no longer maintain the buoys in Halifax harbour.

The conditions of all auction sales conducted by the yard were pretty much the same. The storekeeper placed advertisements in the newspapers giving about ten days' notice. He then sold the items in small lots by weight, the highest bidder deposited 20 per cent with the balance due when the goods were removed, which had to be within three weeks or the deposit was forfeited.[69] The sales were conducted by the commissioner's chief clerk, who until 1809 received a 5 per cent commission for acting as auctioneer. Thereafter, if an auctioneer was needed, the naval storekeeper, or one of the clerks "must perform that duty, as we do not approve of an auctioneer of the Town being employed for the purpose," the Navy Board explained.[70]

The sale of the three brig frames in 1817 was organized somewhat differently. To attract higher bids the auctioneer allowed the purchasers from six to twelve months credit. Under such conditions the auctioneer, while receiving his usual commission, was alone "answerable for the money."[71]

One of the Navy Board policies that helped to define the work of the Halifax yard related to shipbuilding. After what the Board considered an unsatisfactory episode in the 1740s, when the Admiralty forced it to agree to build two warships in New England, it held to the view that American timber for shipbuilding purposes was inferior to available species in Britain and the Baltic, its traditional sources.[72] In 1773 when the Admiralty received an offer to build two frigates in New York, the Navy Board was decisive in its reply: "having experienced the badness of the materials and workmanship by two ships, *Boston* and *America*, built in North America, we cannot recommend the proposition."[73] It took the ship timber crisis after 1802 to trigger a new policy. Then the Navy Board, desperate for new sources, began importing timber and other wood products in large quantities from British North American colonies, a matter to be discussed in chapter 8.

It was during this emergency that the Admiralty ordered a sloop and a gun brig to be built in the Halifax yard. It came at Inglefield's suggestion. He had remarked that a shipbuilder's slip could be erected at "trifling expense," owing to the natural slope of the land into the harbour, and the presence of bedrock so close to the soil surface.[74] He said nothing about the need for additional skilled workers, a thought which never occurred to either the Admiralty or Navy Board. He felt confident that William Hughes, foreman of shipwrights, "whose diligence I cannot say enough of ... will with all the skill and art of ship building prove himself capable in the construction of these vessels." Received in London at the end of September 1804, the decision to use the Halifax yard for the first time in this manner passed without objection from the Navy Board.

When the order reached Halifax, Hughes prepared a report on the practices employed by shipbuilders in Nova Scotia. He found that grey oak, black birch, beech, and maple were used for the heels, floor timbers, and lower futtocks, and dead wood for keelson and places where the timber "is always kept damp with salt water."[75] Red pine, sapling of pine, white pine in small logs, and black spruce were used for decks, topsides, quick-work, futtocks, tops, timbers, and futtlings among others. Juniper was preferred for treenails "being proved from the least subject to decay, and the turpentine in juniper a proof against leaking." The insides of the plank and the timber were then painted with a mixture of tar and oil to prevent mildew collecting and to preserve the timbers, a process widely practised both in Nova Scotia and New Brunswick.

As a result, sloop of war *Halifax* and gun brig *Plumper* began construction.[76] Both were built by the yard's artificers with wood supplied by Forsyth & Smith and Fraser & Thom.[77] The sloop carried twenty-two guns and a complement of 121 men.[78] Launched on 11 October 1806, she was broken up in January 1814. The gun brig carried twelve guns, with a complement of fifty men.[79] Launched on 29 December 1807, she was wrecked five years later in the Bay of Fundy.

The only other wartime shipbuilding undertaken for the navy in the Halifax yard occurred in 1807 when the Navy Board required the construction of a dozen so-called pettyaugers, already noted, for use in an expedition against Spanish possessions in the Caribbean. Flat-bottomed and at first of fifty tons, they were later increased to eighty tons. Inglefield described them as having "decks large enough to carry two traversing guns in midships and four light carronades along the waist."

To build them, wood was purchased in 1807 and 1808.[80] Additional artificers were hired, while others were loaned by the garrison.[81] Within a few months, as the yard ran out of "crooked" timber, building stopped.[82] The commissioner was skeptical of them from the outset;

with extensive service in the Caribbean, he could not see what purpose such flat-bottomed vessels would serve "where trade winds prevail, and where the more essential quality in a vessel is fast sailing & plying to windward."[83] Delays multiplied as the yard concentrated on its main task of refitting the squadron.[84] Construction was still underway in 1809 when, owing to Spain's withdrawal from her French alliance, offensive plans against her in the Caribbean were cancelled. Prior to this, three of the pettyaugers had been completed and loaded with stores for the Leeward Islands squadron.[85] With Navy Board approval, two others were sent to Bermuda to act as watering boats for the squadron when anchored in Murray's Passage, and another served the Halifax master attendant as an anchor boat.[86] The balance were sold in 1815 at war's end. It was an inglorious finale to the yard's shipbuilding efforts for the naval service in wartime.

Another of the yard's responsibilities was to survey and estimate the value of ships or vessels, captured and condemned as prizes of war by the Halifax vice-admiralty court and then commissioned into the navy. Once the value was determined payment was received by the captors' agents. Before the 1797 *Naval Instructions*, such payments occurred only when prize ships arrived in England. There they were valued according to the price paid for ships built by contract, with their age and other factors taken into account. When the captors themselves ordered an evaluation on the spot, the Navy Board always examined and revised the initial evaluation. This method ensured that payment was delayed for years.

The new edition in 1797 of *Naval Instructions* was meant as a reform. Now naval storekeepers abroad, upon a survey and valuation, could draw bills for 75 per cent of the amount, the balance being a reserve dependent upon the final valuation by the Navy Board.[87] As the initial valuation reflected costs abroad, which might be inflated above prices in England, the Navy Board considered this a major concession.

The only remaining issue for the captors, once the court's decision was known, was what rate of exchange would govern the payment. The practice hitherto had been for the yard's storekeeper "to draw bills in the prize agent's favor for three-fourths of the amount in sterling, leaving them to negotiate the bill upon the best terms in their power." After 1800, as the rate of exchange, as we shall see in chapter 9, turned sharply against sterling, exchange was so unfavourable for drawing at Halifax, that captors wanted the discount on sterling bills to be added to the prize valuation.

The Navy Board's prejudice against North American-built ships made less and less sense in view of the quality of ships capable of being built in North America, first deployed in the American War of Independence and used against the British navy and merchant marine. Frequently enough rebel warships, letter-of-marque ships, and privateers were purchased into the navy before the 1783 peace by a succession of commanders on the North American coast, beginning with Peter Warren in 1745. Many of these were smaller vessels, acquired for their speed and sailing characteristics, and used as advice and despatch boats. A few others, more commodious, became prison hulks. By the 1770s the Navy Board expressed few reservations of the sort expressed earlier about rapid deterioration of ships' timbers.

During the wars with the United States, several captures were commissioned. In the first war against rebel America, the largest American-built ship commissioned at Halifax was the 30-gun frigate *Hancock*.[88] Other smaller vessels were American privateers and merchant ships. Of these the three largest were the ship *Rittenhouse*, renamed sloop *Albany*,[89] and the brigs *Amsterdam* and *Chabot*.[90] The rest, not all of them prizes, were small enough to serve as tenders to warships or as naval yard boats.[91] Evidence also survives for a number of American ships taken during the 1812–15 war and commissioned in Halifax. These included the brig *Nautilus*, which became in 1812 brig *Emulous*,[92] while an American private armed brig *Curlew* became brig *Columbia*.[93] In 1813, when the frigate *Chesapeake* was taken, the Navy Board rejected as too generous the Halifax yard's valuation, and it underwent a second survey later in England.[94] In 1814 several smaller prizes were commissioned, including sloop *Frolic*, renamed *Florida*,[95] sloop *Rattlesnake*,[96] brig *Anaconda*,[97] schooner *Lynx* renamed *Musquodoboit*,[98] and *Racer* renamed *Shelburne*.[99] The difference in valuations carried out in Halifax, when compared to those undertaken in Portsmouth, was rarely more than 1 per cent, hardly worth the Board's trouble!

In the French wars the first commissioned prizes were taken from the Americans. They were small merchant ships condemned by the court for carrying contraband, and included *Little Republican* renamed cutter *Prince Edward*, and *Friends Adventure* renamed schooner *Chebucto*.[100]

The navy was usually delighted to commission any captured

French ship which was proposed by naval commanders. In the American revolutionary war 36-gun French frigate *Magicienne* received the highest valuation of any prize ship at Halifax.[101] Evidence survives for twelve such French ships having been evaluated and commissioned in Halifax, the first in 1795.[102] These included *Espérance*,[103] 36-gun frigate *Prévoyante*, and 24-gun frigate *Raison*.[104] In 1805 France lost privateer *Matilda*,[105] and frigate *Ville de Milan*.[106] In 1806 corvette *Observateur* was fitted up as a brig sloop. In this instance the valuation done at the Halifax yard was rejected as inadequate and drew from the Board the observation that thereafter each survey of ships to be purchased into the service must include details of age, general condition, place where she was built, and whether the prize was copper fastened or sheathed. In addition, the Board wanted to know the moulding and "siding of the knees, beams and such parts of the frame as you can ascertain, also the length and diameter of the masts and yards."[107] A list of serviceable naval stores had also to be compiled, together with the weight of such metal objects as anchors and chains.

The final French prizes were taken in 1808–10. In 1808 schooner *Voltigeur* was purchased by the Ordnance department after the yard's artificers surveyed her.[108] In 1809, French 38-gun frigate *Junon* and corvette *Colibri*, with 300-men and 110-men complements respectively, were purchased into the naval service.[109] In 1809 sloop *Bonne Citoyenne*[110] was purchased along with *Furieuse*, fitted out as a 38-gun frigate with an initial complement of 284 men.[111] In 1810 the French cutter *Peraty* became cutter *Barbara*.[112] The last French vessel commissioned into the British navy at Halifax was letter-of-marque ship *Fantôme*.[113]

The presence of the naval squadron and the increasingly elaborate military fortifications adequately deflected from Halifax harbour any threat of invasion. Indeed, it was clear that the North American squadron would have to have been mauled at sea before an enemy force could risk such an expedition. Yet the 1807 incident involving *Chesapeake* and *Leopard* meant that for months afterwards heightened tension lingered at the yard. Even a year later the senior sea officer warned the yard officers to exercise "the greatest vigilance ... in guarding his Majesty's naval yard ... against every species of danger."[114] Fearing sabotage, he warned them "to give the most positive direction to the gate porter and watchman to be constantly on the alert, especially those stationed at the gate." They were to deny access to strangers, unless by appointment, when they were to be accompanied at all times.

To guard against fire, riot, or theft successive standing orders emerged, of which one in 1785 may serve as a model.[115] The main responsibility rested with the principal officers, who acted in turn as duty officers of the night. When a fourth officer, a boatswain, was appointed in 1800, the onus on the respective officers was thereby reduced. It was to the duty officers that the password was given.[116] Under them came the rounders who were selected from among the artificers and drew an extra honorarium for this arduous duty. Rounders were appointed in strict seniority and apparently the position was much sought-after. In 1785 there were nine, one of whom acted as spare, while the others served in pairs on successive nights. The password was communicated to the rounders when the duty officer saw the night watch properly installed. Once the password was announced, rounders on duty could not quit their posts. Only the rounder, in whose territory the gate was located, had the authority to order its opening. At work for them were the watchmen. Forming part of the yard establishment, they were hired specifically for the task. Unlike almost all the other waged workers in the yard, they had no opportunity to earn additional income through overtime. The number of watchmen varied according to circumstances of war and peace. Their numbers were frequently augmented in wartime by marines from the warships in port, or in their absence, occasionally by soldiers from the garrison. The watchmen assembled every evening after bell ringing, and received the password from the rounders. In 1785 there were five watch posts, and the watchmen were relieved every four hours on the personal orders of a rounder. In wartime each watchman was armed with a musket and bayonet, with three cartridges of powder.[117]

With the night watch in place, announced by the firing of a gun, boats could neither depart from the yard, nor come to the wharfs, nor alongside ships tied there. Only sea officers whose ships were already at the yard wharf for refitting or to be stored were allowed to enter the yard, and they were furnished with the password, after applying to and registering with the yard officer on duty. From 1812, while the war lasted, no one was admitted after 10:00 p.m. except captains.[118] At each watch in the night, the rounders on duty were given the list, and submitted them to the duty officer the following morning after sunrise.

In case of a crisis in the night, arising either from fire, or alarm, or riot, the duty officer of the night woke the commissioner. If fire, a general alarm was given, and the engines employed once the key to the engine house had been fetched from the gate porter's lodge where it hung.

The fear of fire persisted as a matter of concern. The destructive power of fire was witnessed several times in the town, and annually in the forests, albeit rarely in the yard itself. Not until 1799 was there cause for any anxiety, when deliberate attempts to set the yard on fire formed a rather bizarre episode.[119] In August 1799 the commissioner's stable was found to be on fire. This was the first of several small fires, all apparently deliberately set, and all extinguished before much damage was done. Three years later, Bartholomew Cullen, the son of the defunct long-serving gate porter Stephen Cullen, freely confessed his role in the failed attempts at arson. He made this confession while being held on a charge of robbery. That summer he admitted seeing the late Elias Marshall Jr, the son of the master shipwright, kindling a fire in the boathouse. Cullen took a dollar bribe and small presents of gingerbread and fruit to say nothing of the incident, when Marshall begged him to keep silent as it would ruin him and disgrace his family. Shortly afterwards he accepted matches, lint, and tinder from Marshall to set fire the next day to hay in the stable. Marshall would then himself set fire to the cable store while the yard was distracted. As Cullen failed to light the hay as instructed, the fire was soon extinguished. Marshall then paid him 3s. to set fire to the masthouse. As the military guard had been increased, Cullen made no attempt. He threw the matches, lint, and tinder into the harbour, but not before, of his own accord, he set fire to his bedroom in his father's house. Elias Marshall, who suffered fits of insanity which brought on his mischievous behaviour, attempted to cut his own throat and subsequently died insane.[120]

Under repeated examination Cullen stuck to his story, and was believed by the justices. Without corroborating evidence he could not be convicted. It seems the rest of the Marshall family had suspected nothing, which also was Cullen's view. To Inglefield, the "means made use of were so ill contrived for the diabolical purpose that it is most probable to have been imagined by a madman and attempted by the mischievous boy in question, who I am informed has on various occasions given proofs of almost vicious and depraved mind."

These revelations had come at a most awkward moment for the commissioner. In receipt of the Navy Board's orders to reduce the yard's establishment, owing to the 1802 peace treaty with France, Inglefield retained fifteen watchmen. As he explained, "several attempts having been made to burn the town of Halifax he has conceived it necessary to adopt precautions of vigilance to prevent such malicious attempts in the Naval Yard, and as it appears to him absolutely necessary in the present alarming moments, and for the protection of the Naval Yard," he did not reduce the number of watchmen. These he considered "barely sufficient to guard so large a space as there is between the North and South Mast Ponds in the former of which there are spars to the amount of about £15,000, and in the latter upwards of £10,000."[121]

To help extinguish fires was one tangible means the yard was of assistance both to the town of Halifax and to the military establishments in the neighbourhood. Forest fires in the vicinity of the yard alarmed the respective officers. "In June the woods were on fire and a fresh wind from the northward blew many sparks into the yard, but as they were carefully watched did no damage. However accidents may happen by fire & buildings covered with wood are not safe, besides the covering of them are so decayed, they soon must be covered in wood or slate."[122] As an example, in June 1786 when a forest fire threatened the military powder magazine, the artificers and labourers under their officers gave immediate aid. Major General Campbell, in thanking Commissioner Duncan, wrote of the men's "cheerfulness and alacrity," and their "powerful aid." It occasioned his decision to use a gun fired from the Eastern Battery to signal such a danger in future.[123]

In 1789, as a result of a fire in Halifax, Commissioner Duncan developed new orders for the yard. He informed Governor Parr, that "on an alarm of fire the people shall be collected and the engines got out. They will have no directions to move from the yard, without an application by a reasonable messenger from you for that purpose. Then the men will be ordered to obey their own officers." He added that "if at any other time you think the people of the yard on any other occasion can be serviceable I am to request that you will signify your wish in the same manner, and will always find us ready."[124] In March 1797 the governor had occasion to express his gratitude for the yard's help to suppress a fire which threatened devastation of the town. He mentioned especially Elias Marshall Sr's conduct and "the steady, enterprising, powerful exertions of the men."[125]

As with every other subject that came within his purview, Coffin had a view on the role the yard should play when the fire alarm was raised. "A great assistance may be given by the officers, artificers, ordinary, and labourers from this yard in the event of an alarm of fire ... Instead of a confused crowd, order and regularity may attend their efforts."[126] His directions required all belonging to the yard to "repair to the yard, when Mr Hughes, the foreman, will march at the head of the shipwrights and labourers, the former taking such tools as may be judged necessary, and ... the master attendant at the head of the ordinary. The boatswain of the yard bringing up the rear. The people to march three abreast," with the commissioner at their head.

If the Halifax yard avoided destruction by fire, it barely survived the Admiralty's 1809 decision to build a new naval base at Bermuda with its almost fatal impact on the careening yard.[127] The remote cause was the decision of the Admiralty to survey the Bermuda Islands and the consequent discovery in 1795 of a safe anchorage at Murray's Anchorage leading to Ireland Island. Admiral Murray's understandable enthusiasm for the Ireland Island site rested on two undeniable, but quite different, assertions. Firstly, in contrast to Halifax, Bermuda's winter weather allowed regular outdoor work. Secondly, as the war with France unfolded, the naval service in the western Atlantic demanded that "great attention be paid to the southward ... to destroy that swarm of marauders out of Charleston." By contrast, for almost five months each year, sailing to Halifax was achieved only with extreme "difficulty, and hardly to be effected without much wear and tear to his Majesty's ships and their furniture."[128]

The Navy Board created a small naval establishment at the site, which was disbanded and the stores shipped to Halifax in 1802 following the Peace of Amiens.[129] The naval presence at Bermuda was re-established three years later with the appointment of a storekeeper and a few artificers. The decision to create a full-fledged base resulted from the growing difficulties with the United States in 1807. When Admiral Warren pressed the government in 1809 to act, the only matter to settle was the location.[130] Built against the Americans and still under construction as the war with the United States drew to an end, it continued for years to attract huge sums from the naval estimates. If Navy Board parsimony characterized the Halifax yard, largesse distinguished its behaviour in Bermuda. The commissioner's house there and at Halifax made for a suitable comparison. Still uncompleted in 1827, the Bermuda stone mansion's costs had reached £42,500,[131] while the wood frame house in the Halifax yard had cost less than £2,200 in 1785–7, and the admiral's stone house under £6,000 in 1814–19. Price inflation to 1815 and deflation thereafter cannot account for the huge difference in expenditure.

The Bermuda naval yard also benefitted when the Halifax yard arranged contracts for building a number of prefabricated structures for it in Nova Scotia. These included a storehouse built of white pine, plans for which were sent from London.[132] A Nova Scotia contractor, Alfred Gordon Adams, also prefabricated in Nova Scotia the first Bermuda naval hospital.[133] As the site was wholly undeveloped, shelters had to be constructed for the construction workers who were sent from Halifax on warships. Vice Admiral Sawyer suggested that the houses for the Bermuda yard officers and artificers should also be contracted for in Halifax and the wood houses sent "in frames from Halifax."[134] The Halifax yard also shipped oak timber for the careening pits and procured a transport to freight from the Miramichi "hemlock piles for the wharf" and "pine timber & deals for the capstan house & other buildings."[135]

The peace of 1815 not only brought in its wake a reduced establishment, but the dismantling of the yard's cooperage establishment and the reduction of that of the naval hospital.[136] Thereafter management of the cooperage was entrusted to the purser of the flag ship, assisted by such competent person as was selected by the naval commander.[137]

As we saw in chapter 3, early in 1816 the hospital staff was reduced in peacetime to include only a surgeon, agent, dispenser, hospital mate, chaplain, matron, and porter. The hospital governor, among others, was discharged.[138]

In May 1819 the Admiralty decided that the Halifax yard, like that of Gibraltar, was surplus to the peacetime needs of the navy. Reduced to a depot, a few buildings were maintained and minimal stores housed. Stores sufficient for six months for one ship of the line, two frigates, and three sloops were to be kept on hand. The excess was shipped to England and to Bermuda. Anchors and other imperishable articles were retained for future use at Halifax.[139] After transport was arranged for Wodehouse and his family,[140] the commissioner's house was appropriated for the use of the remaining officer.[141] With the departure of the principal officers and discharge of the clerks, artificers, their apprentices, labourers, and watchmen, the master attendant now superintending the depot complained loudly to the Navy Board. He begged for a horse, cart, and a labourer as "absolutely necessary to be employed, particularly in the winter, principally for the purpose of clearing away the snow which accumulates so much in various places, as will otherwise render the yard impassable and have the most ruinous effects when it dissolves in the spring." Without a clerk-messenger "to communicate with the other public departments, to carry vouchers into the town for signatures as prescribed by the *Instructions*, to clean out the office, to get coals and light the fires" he wailed, he could not carry out his duties even in the yard itself, let alone in harbour. Moreover, as the "chest with the public money is deposited in the office," the clerk "must be a man of tried integrity."[142]

The yard, then almost abandoned, immediately suffered a predictable fate. By June 1820 Rear Admiral Griffith had reported all sorts of depredations had already taken place under the military guard at the yard. It was reminiscent of the events of 1767, but without the series of criminal prosecutions. As the soldiers could not be trusted, he appointed watchmen.[143] As he could not arbitrarily add them to the establishment, he proposed first discharging the four boatmen who were suspected of stealing from the yard, and who were found to be "very unwilling and inefficient labourers."[144] An opportunity to lease one of the houses in the yard arose in 1822, when Thomas Maynard, a retired sea officer, asked permission to house his "large family" in the substantial naval storekeeper's tenement, then unoccupied.[145] This the Navy Board rejected as "the admission of strangers within the gates might lead to inconvenience." It seemed a sorry ending to what had been a useful yard, and a bitter pill for "a very old commander." Like Gibraltar, however, Halifax as a naval base, though a shadow of its former self, would not altogether vanish.

For the variety of tasks required of the Halifax yard, in war years it was frequently seriously understaffed. Even for its principal task – the refitting and storing of the North American squadron – the yard was never provided with an adequate workforce in wartime. This was especially the case after 1807, when the hostility of the United States led to war in 1812. Such a policy reflected the marginal importance given by the Admiralty to the yard after 1783. If, from the Admiralty's viewpoint, the east coast of North America became something of a backwater, when war broke out with France in 1793 there was no excuse to retain, after 1807, such a small establishment. The construction of a new base in Bermuda, begun late in 1809 and not fully operational until after 1819, may have been part of the explanation for the prolonged underdevelopment of the Halifax yard. This was especially acute when war with the United States engulfed the region in May 1812. At first reluctant to assign large naval units to the American theatre, it was late in 1813 before the careening yard bore the full brunt of the war as it attempted to refit the bulk of the 120 or so ships which then constituted the fleet off the North American coast. Stretched to the limit for the next eighteen months, the coming of peace saw the hasty reduction of the workforce as the number of ships on station declined rapidly.

Had the yard's workforce not been required to undertake so many additional tasks, it might have been able to refit the squadron's warships at a faster rate. These responsibilities included especially the repair of an assortment of vessels not belonging to the naval department, the construction and maintenance of yard structures, and the building of several small warships. All this and more was undertaken in a climate variously described, admittedly mainly by Englishmen, as possessing a winter that lasted for seven or eight months.[146] This work was undertaken by men who received, in years, the lowest levels of pay and who enjoyed the fewest public amenities of any of the king's overseas yards, facts that were well-known to many of them. Yet all the work was undertaken by men who never downed tools and who came to be described, when their numbers were dominated by native-born Nova Scotians, as workers of the highest calibre and devotion. If these facts were known to the Navy Board, they were never acknowledged.

PART THREE

ECONOMIC IMPACT

Chapter Seven

SUPPLIERS AND TRADESMEN

Though the Navy Board aimed to supply almost all the needs of the Halifax yard, as we saw in chapter 6 the policy proved unrealistic. Yet it was 1788 before this was acknowledged officially. Then the Board for the first time listed the sorts of goods that the principal officers were permitted to purchase. The commissioner's approval of the requests made to him by the respective officers would be granted so long as such local purchases were "to the advantage of the service." Included in the initial list were mainly items made of wood. Besides sticks there were boards, plank and deals, wooden anchor stocks, boats, oars and fletches for boats, boat hooks, ash rafters, treenails, dead eyes for stays, crosstree and trestletree pieces, wooden wedges, birch brooms, and handspikes.[1] In time the list of items frequently supplied the yard from Halifax greatly expanded. It especially included coal, bricks, firewood, ranging boards, timber, capstan bars, clapboards, shingles, staves, barrel headers and hoops, handspike staves, candles, fearnaught fabric for greatcoats, white linen for signal flags, kersey for colours, sail needles, fish-hooks and lines, lime, and rat-traps. Appearing also was hardware of all sorts: files, auger bits, handles, bolts, boltstaves, locks, springs, hinges, nails, spikes, and knobs. Additionally the list contained pitch and tar, turpentine, train and seal oil, paint and paint brushes, glass, and printed forms of all kinds used in the navy. From the 1780s, all such items the yard regularly purchased.

The primitive nature of the Nova Scotia economy, with its thin and scattered population before the arrival of American loyalist refugees, effectively prevented the colony from producing many of these commodities.[2] The bulk of the manufactured products originated in England or continental Europe and, until 1776, many were imported

Table 7.1 Value of Stores Purchased by Yard, 1757–1819 (H£)

Years	Annual average	% of total expenditure
1757–62	5,835	32.3
1765–71	3,054	23.7
1773–80	4,119	30.2
1780–90	5,800	22.2
1784–5	1,638	10.5
1790–9	7,152	24.9
1799–1803	2,947	16.9
1803–19	8,516	21.6

Note: missing months: October 1763 through December 1764, August 1800 through July 1801.
Source: Gerrish accounts, 1757–73; Williams accounts, 1773–80; Thomas accounts, 1780–90; Edgecombe accounts, 1784–5; Livie accounts, 1790–9; Anderson accounts, 1799–1803; Dawes accounts, 1803–19.

from colonial ports especially in New England. In filling the needs of the yard, for items not supplied from the English yards, the squadron and careening yard thus created an important internal market for enterprising merchants and tradesmen. When war stopped the supply from New England in 1775, opportunities arose for merchants who swarmed into Halifax, several of the better-known among them from Scotland. These were the first to profit from the wartime expansion of the careening yard. After the war, as the population of Nova Scotia expanded, especially with the arrival of loyalist refugees and disbanded soldiers in 1783, Nova Scotians became the principal suppliers to the yard. Then the bulk of the wood products needed in the yard came from Nova Scotia's mills.

The magnitude of supply of so-called naval stores, of the sort listed above, is illustrated in Table 7.1. Not included there are tradesmen's and artificers' accounts when they supplied services to the yard. Also excluded were materials they might bring into the yard to complete their work. Such stores represented between a fifth and a third of all annual expenditures. In the years of heaviest spending by the yard, such as between 1806 and 1816, expenditure on stores was almost one-quarter of all costs borne by the yard. The annual amount required by the yard greatly accelerated in 1809 when extensive purchases began to be made on behalf of the new facilities launched at Bermuda. Tenders were frequently advertised, such as for wood products, pitch, tar, and turpentine.³ The supply of so-called sticks and other wood products drew in suppliers from New Brunswick and eventually even from Quebec, a matter to be considered in the next chapter.

Among the items never furnished from home was the supply of fresh meat and vegetables to the Halifax squadron. The yard became involved with such contracting when by the 1808 edition of *New Instructions for the Officers of Foreign Yards*, the resident commissioner became responsible for all pecuniary matters relating to the navy's Victualling Board and Transport Board.⁴ Inglefield, then commissioner, had first to familiarize himself with local wholesale commodity prices and report them in detail to the Victualling Board. "From the late accommodation with America there is a certainty that all the articles usually or frequently obtained from thence will fall in price," he predicted and added: "intercourse having recommenced with that country, provisions have already fallen considerably, particularly the article of flour, which sold here during the last winter as high as $19 a barrel."⁵ He explained that the difference between the cost of salted beef and pork was owing "to the one being Irish and the other American the former being preferred from its superior quality and weight to the latter." Fresh beef before embargo had sold wholesale for 4d. to 6d. a pound, during non-intercourse when commerce was suspended unilaterally by the United States, beef went as high as 10d. and mutton as high as 14d.⁶

In the matter of the squadron's supply of rum, the price depended "greatly upon its flavour and proof." As for locally-made butter, its price – normally 10d.–11d. per pound – rose during non-importation by two-thirds. In general, Inglefield concluded that during the American embargo the West Indies, Bermuda, Newfoundland, and other markets, normally supplied from the United States, instead got provisions from Nova Scotia. Thus with the easing of Anglo-American tensions and the threat of war receding, he found prices sharply falling.

Inglefield's next task was to conclude a contract for the supply of beef, an important item as Admiral Warren's squadron lacked fresh meat "except in very small ... supplies during the whole time they are absent from this harbour."⁷ The good health of his crews depended in part on the regular supply of such beef.⁸ The supplier, Capel Hians, with a new two-year contract, was supposed to own "most of the livestock" in the region of the harbour.⁹ Hians had negotiated one significant change in the new contract, as he insisted that an end be put to the "practice of surveying meat once it has been taken" to the ships as this "sometimes attended with loss to him in consequence of its being a good deal handled, trod upon, and dirtied in the boats, and thereby rendered unfit for sale."[10]

Later that year Hians was warned about the certainty of a civil suit, unless he ensured that only fresh beef was supplied, as a result of a 9 December 1809 incident, when beef sent on board the ships was "in a putrid state," obliging crews once again to devour salted meat.[11] Instructions were issued to purchase fresh meat directly from the butchers in town, "let the price be what it may." If such meat was ever again produced, Hians was threatened with a suit to recover the difference between the contract price and the market price of beef so purchased.

Upon the contractor's sudden death two years later the contract was awarded to Andrew Belcher, one of Hians's guarantors. The new contract was on the same terms as the old, that is for 5d. sterling per pound. As customary, to terminate the contract six months' notice was required and, in the event of war, the contract could be opened to allow for any price inflation.[12] Within a year Belcher had become the navy's general contractor to supply naval provisions not only at Halifax, but also at Quebec, at Norfolk in Virginia, and at Bermuda.[13]

Belcher sold the meat to the navy for the same price he paid the grazier. His profit came from two sources. The first, as Inglefield explained, was termed the fifth quarter, which included hide, horns, and tallow. "In buying from the farmer or grazier here it is very common to pay the same price and sometimes higher than the butcher afterwards sells the beef for in the market on account of this advantage."[14] The more important part of his profit came from the 5 per cent commission charged on all his purchases.

Under the terms of the contract, upon the outbreak of war in May 1812 Belcher had to submit a new tender along with others. His bid was unsuccessful.[15] So fierce was the competition that no merchant house dominated this supply. By 1817 it was held by Andrew Wright; when his contract ended that May, it was won by Frederick Major & Son with a bid of just under H£1 10s. per hundred pounds weight. This proved too low to be profitable and they gave up the contract after only a year. The new contractor, Messrs Bauer & Harry, bid three farthings per hundred higher than had Major a year earlier.[16] This was classic cut-throat competition, with merchants scrambling to supply an ever-diminishing market as the number of seamen on the station continued to shrink.

One other provisions contract which formed part of the commissioner's responsibilities related to the supply of fresh vegetables to the squadron. Until September 1811, fresh vegetables were purchased by individual ship's pursers. James Proud was one such purveyor. He sold large quantities of potatoes, turnips, carrots, beets, cabbage, and onions.[17] He received no allowance for decayed vegetables, or those accidentally frozen in winter, for store or cellar rent, or for advance money. In 1811, though the Victualling Board suggested that public contracts were preferable, it left the matter to the resident commissioner and the naval commander to determine.[18] When tenders were submitted by eight suppliers, Peter McNab emerged successful. Upon the outbreak of war in 1812, unlike the meat contract, McNab's merely applied for an allowance to accommodate the newly-inflated wartime prices.[19] McNab continued to supply vegetables to the squadron in peacetime when prices dropped considerably, reflected in a subsequent agreement.[20]

Besides provisions, the yard regularly needed supplies of coal that were furnished from Nova Scotia's mines. Used to heat houses and other yard buildings, as well as fuel for the foundry, it was also supplied to warships. Coal, mined at first in Cape Breton and later in Pictou County, had been used in the yard ever since the fortress of Louisbourg had been captured in 1758. Thereafter the exploitation of Cape Breton coal, first developed under the French, was jealously guarded by the imperial government in London. Before commercial mining was permitted, a limited amount was mined to furnish the needs both of the military and navy at Halifax and elsewhere in North America.[21] It was not an exclusive supply, for every year British coal, frequently used as ballast, was exported to Nova Scotia.

During the war against rebel America, the colliers in Cape Breton were protected by a contingent of soldiers, and the annual coal convoy protected by a naval escort. One such convoy was attacked and scattered in 1781. On 21 July, inward-bound to Spanish River and Quebec, a convoy of eighteen sail including nine colliers and four victuallers was attacked by two French frigates. The escort – a frigate, two sloops, and an armed ship – was severely mauled.[22] But, as the coal was eventually loaded at Spanish River and safely transported to Halifax, the

French attack was hardly significant.[23] Cape Breton coal was subsequently exported for both naval and military establishments in New York as well as Halifax.[24] Coal was then not mined under a monopoly, which from the 1820s characterized the history of coal mining in Nova Scotia until 1858. Rather, the naval storekeeper's accounts noted payments made to various coal suppliers such as John Clarke, John Fraser, and George Smith, as well as to other small contractors who shipped as few as twenty-four chaldrons at a time, when the yard's normal annual consumption was ten times that amount.[25] In this early supply, individual ships were hired to freight the coal to the yard and garrison from where first it had been mined by soldiers. Ships, through their pursers, were individually supplied a hundredweight or a chaldron at a time from the coal and wood wharf in the yard. This same source also provided the hospital complex its supply.

The coal at first arrived without much planning. In 1785, for instance, William Forsyth offered the yard 150 chaldrons for 40s. a chaldron,[26] even though Commissioner Duncan had contracted with the brig *Lilly* to freight a shipment from Sydney at 5d. less.[27] He wanted only the best coal "as the inferior kind is so foul and full of sulphur" it was useless for "working iron," as he informed the Cape Breton governor.[28] Later that summer *Rebecca*, with Forsyth as broker, unloaded her coal at the yard for 21s. a chaldron.[29] When the coal vessels arrived at the wharf, all the labourers and even the sheer hulksmen, if not otherwise busy, undertook the dirty task of unloading "with the greatest dispatch."[30]

So large was the military and naval expansion in Nova Scotia during the French wars that coal shortages, by late spring, occasionally became acute.[31] Under such conditions, the yard had either to borrow coal from or lend to the military garrison.[32] In addition the yard had to arrange shipments of coal to supply the Leeward Islands squadron from 1807,[33] and Bermuda once the naval base there began to be constructed in 1809.[34]

By then the navy depended on contractors to maintain its supply. In 1808 the naval contractors, Messrs Jonathan and John Tremain, voided their agreement when they claimed they were unable to purchase any coal, so great was the "demand for the army." In response, the senior sea officer simply despatched available naval transports to Sydney to load coal for the yard.[35] In June of the next year the yard placed advertisements inviting tenders for 230 chaldrons for the ensuing year's supply, that "being the best season of the year for providing a store of that article."[36] When all the tenders were rejected owing to the "extravagant prices" quoted, the commissioner despatched the yard's schooner *Hibernia* (Thomas Robinson, master) and the naval transport *Lady Delaval* to Cape Breton to collect a cargo.[37] By 1814 so great was the demand that it had become a cash business, the funds carried in an escorting warship to Sydney.[38]

In 1815 when peace descended on the Atlantic, the subsequent diminution in the size of the squadron and the military garrison caused demand to collapse. Wholesale prices fell by two-thirds from a peak of 120s. a chaldron in February 1815 to 40s. by August. Thereafter until 1820, coal was supplied the yard by sending naval transports or hiring vessels to sail directly to the mines. It was in 1816 that for the first time this supply originated in Pictou County, where, owing to the shorter haul, the coal supply proved cheaper.[39]

The more common form of fuel was firewood, sold by the cord, a measure which varied from place to place. In Halifax the measure was eight feet wide by four feet high and four feet deep.[40] Time-consuming to cut and haul, ship, unload, cart, and stack, demand grew as the population around Halifax harbour expanded. Involved in the supply of firewood in 1784-6, for instance, were John Creighton, John Lawson, and John Stairs, all of them well-placed merchants, whose tenders then ranged between 19s. and 20s., and James McNamara, Nicholas Glawson, and Josiah Davis, whose tenders ranged between 13s. and 15s. Some 250 to 400 cords were then burned every year by the yard.[41] In addition, with two stoves on each ship, in peacetime the crews burned an average fifty-one cords during the seventeen weeks between December and March when the warships were immobilized at anchor.[42]

Supply was by contract based on the usual competitive tendering process. Occasionally the local contractors failed to supply the firewood promised. In 1801, as an example, Samuel King was very long in explanations and decidedly short in supply. A succession of persistent contrary winds prevented the usual supply coming to market, he explained that August, "which raised the price of the article fully thirty per cent." Claiming that firewood was "never known so scarce as it has been this season," King had been allowed to supply half his contract to the garrison with coal, and requested the same "indulgence" from the navy. He sweetened his proposal with the offer "to cart it, free of expense, to the doors of such of the officers and men as should be induced to accept of such an equivalent. This would be a great relief to

158 Part Three: Economic Impact

us. At the same time, we shall exert ourselves to the utmost to get the whole quantity of wood contracted for, part of which we have already secured and shall deliver as soon as it can be brought, having purchased a vessel for that purpose."[43] Five years later, when the contract was held by J. & J. Tremain, coal contractors, they blamed a severe fire during the summer which consumed their supply as the cause for their inability to deliver the quantity promised. It is strange that they waited until late October to offer this explanation. By that time an acute shortage was felt in the yard which then had to purchase cordwood at the much higher price then prevailing in the Halifax market.[44]

Average annual costs for the yard rose from H£147 in the 1770s to H£560 in the 1790s. Storekeeper Williams in the seven years after 1773 purchased 145 cords annually. The average price was about 20s., with actual prices ranging from 7s.9d. to 30s.5d. a cord. Some of this was cut by yard labourers on Cornwallis Island, for which Jacob Horne earned £16.8.8. for truckage to the waterside, and Richard Bulkeley a fee of £5.14.9. for access to the site. Williams's successor as storekeeper in the 1790s, Titus Livie, paid H£5,604 for firewood, when prices topped out at 30s. a cord.[45] During the war with the United States from 1812 to 1815, Halifax wholesale firewood prices reached 40s. in February 1813 and peaked at 55s. a year later.[46]

Vessels were frequently hired by the yard for a variety of tasks other than to ship coal and firewood. Gerrish's accounts between 1757 and 1762 noted H£2,584 in such costs, most of it to do with yard construction and naval operations.[47] In the 1776-1783 war, vessels were used as cartels for the exchange of prisoners of war, as prison ships, as a hospital ship, and for carrying despatches. Some H£8,346 was spent to hire sixteen such cartels, four others to carry despatches, and a dozen others on various services. Commissioner Hughes concluded a contract for the schooner *Dispatch* to carry correspondence to New York at H£40 a month.[48] Depending on the vessel's size, the monthly rates could be higher.[49] Among the cartels was the brigantine *Jeannie*, owned by Messrs Wallace, hired to take prisoners to St Malo in exchange for British seamen who were conveyed to Glasgow.[50] They sailed with neither cannon nor firearms on board, and with a white flag at their fore topmast-head, day and night. Other vessels included *British Queen* and *Betsy* which acted as cartel ships to carry American prisoners to Boston.

One of these many cartels was seized by the 100 French and thirty-five rebel prisoners aboard. The 170-ton ship *Ann* (John Barker, master), chartered on 5 October 1781 to carry them to Boston, was forcibly seized, and carried out to sea in a hard wind and thick weather, and was never heard of again. The yard compensated her owner the appraised value of H£1,500, as the charter allowed.[51] Another payment was to Claude Carte for the loss of his shallop requisitioned to ship "rebel prisoners" to Boston, but seized by them.

The bulk of such expenditures benefited the owner of the prison ship *Stanislaus*, Winckworth Norwood, clerk to the master shipwright.[52] The decision was Commissioner Hamond's, as Halifax then had no prison capable of holding more than 100 prisoners. When great numbers arrived in 1781, he hired a suitable transport at a low price, fitted out at the yard to hold 400 prisoners without being crowded.[53] All her small cabins were removed, a steward's room built with bins for bread, peas, and oatmeal. Guard beds were fashioned fore and aft between decks, under the half-deck, and in the great cabin. A bulkhead, with doors and loop holes, was erected, thus separating prisoners from the guard. Stoves with chimneys were installed and a fireplace for the guards. As a result of complaints, the main deck was covered against the weather, while the necessary house also was roofed.[54] Destitute, the captured seamen had clothes and blankets bought for them.[55] The owner quietly awaited his payment at the rate of 8s. sterling per ton each month. This came to a tidy £197.16.7. By May 1783 he had grossed £4,252 without having to worry about stress of weather, wages, or provisions for crews or any of the other usual worries of a shipowner.[56] The military guard, who did not prevent eleven prisoners escaping one night in November 1781 and stealing a longboat, was suddenly withdrawn in January 1782, and was replaced by seamen.[57]

One other fortunate shipper was the owner of the 378-ton storeship *Lion* (John Davis, master) which in 1782 having unloaded her stores at the careening yard, was hired to ship masts from the St John River to England.[58] To help in this heavy and difficult work, the careening yard paid H£83 10s. to hire several gondolas for ten months in 1784-5 to load her and other privately-owned ships at the mastpond located at Fort Howe at the mouth of the St John River.[59]

In another matter, the need for the yard to build or repair ships' boats was constant. In slow times, such work was undertaken by the yard itself. "Great inconvenience having arisen in the careening yard from

160   Part Three: Economic Impact

boats belonging to the squadron being indiscriminately hauled up for repair," Coffin complained in 1800.[60] Thereafter when boats required light repairs, the master shipwright or his foreman, having inspected them, made available the necessary materials for the carpenters to effect the repair. Wartime conditions rarely permitted such work. By 1805 much of this work was undertaken outside the yard by contractors, of whom the most reliable was Seth Coleman of Dartmouth who also built cutters for the yard.[61] In 1807, as an example, Rear Admiral Cochrane, then in command of the Leeward Islands squadron but with considerable earlier experience with the Halifax squadron, requested sixteen jolly boats to be built by Coleman.[62] Usually between sixteen and twenty feet in length, the wartime cost was often only 22s. a foot, or half the West Indies price of £40. In 1812 Coleman was given a contract to build six cutters and six jolly boats, to replace those lost to bad weather by the squadron.[63]

Connected with boat building was oar-making. In 1802, the only oarmaker in Halifax was Enoch Wiswell. For some years before he had supplied the yard with oars, made usually of ash but occasionally of spruce. Then the contract price for delivering oar rafters to Halifax was 5¼d. per foot, when Wiswell supplied them for 4d., and spruce oar rafters for 3½d.[64]

As we have seen earlier, many of the yard buildings were of wood construction. To preserve them regular painting was undertaken. Navy Board regulations, needless to say, were characteristically detailed. All exterior woodwork had to be painted once a year, between one and three coats depending on exposure to weather. In 1809 the painting of all stonework was discontinued. Inside woodwork had to be painted once every eight years, with two coats if necessary. Any four rooms in houses occupied by the commissioner and any two by other yard officers were painted on average every four years. If repairs were carried out, painting was always undertaken for the affected surfaces. Expensive colours were forbidden the officers if the cost was borne by the yard. This, the Navy Board explained, meant no lilacs, pink, and bright green, "nor any dead white."[65] If the officers selected wallpaper instead of paint, a price limit per square yard was specified.[66] Wallpaper was forbidden for rooms in officers' houses when used as servants' apartments or domestic offices.[67] For all but the officers' houses, whitewash was standard interior painting for yard buildings.

The regulations stated that none but "common" colours were acceptable on the external walls of officers' houses. The colours were those used in the dockyards in England, a mixture of tar and red ochre, with white paint powder mixed with linseed oil for the windows and doors.[68] Painted when they were first constructed, in the spring of 1762 Commodore Colvill thought "the houses, fences ... should be payd and painted again."[69] This then included the capstan house, the north and south storehouses, guardhouse, porter's lodge, engine house, masthouse, boathouse, and smiths' shop, as well as the storekeeper's and master shipwright's offices. That autumn the fences were also painted with tar and red ochre.[70] Commodore Hood ordered the next repainting in the summer of July 1768.[71] Duncan in 1783 issued the same orders.[72] In 1800 Commissioner Coffin ordered the yard officers to ensure that "such parts of the yard buildings as require it to be painted in the course of the ensuing summer employing Mr [William] Lawlor who appears to have done this business for many years."[73] Lawlor's proposals were white and red for the yard and black and yellow for the warships.[74] In 1808, John Douglas the senior sea captain, in the absence of the resident commissioner in England, directed yard officers to have the yard buildings again painted.[75]

Until 1814 painting continued to be done by contract when it was held by John Merrick. This contract, first given him in 1806, was both to supply paint, oil, varnish, and turpentine to the yard, as well as to undertake painting in the yard and of warships. In 1808 he claimed that he could no longer furnish linseed oil and turpentine at the rates stated in his contract, owing to the great price rise in England from whence he imported his supply. Inflation in England had been caused by a scarcity of supplies both from the Baltic and from the United States, the one resulting from Napoleon's trade policies to exclude Britain from direct trade with the continent, the other from the self-imposed American trade embargo. In response, the commissioner directed his yard officers to ascertain the prices then prevailing in Halifax and compare them to Merrick's.[76] The details are found in Table 7.2. From the accumulated evidence it became clear that Merrick's prices remained competitive. As he had supplied products "of unexceptionable quality," the commissioner agreed to his request.[77]

So acute had the shortage of linseed oil become by the spring of 1809 that Inglefield, on Merrick's behalf, requested permission for him to import it directly from the United States.[78] The Navy Board directed that only in case of absolute necessity should linseed oil thereafter "be

Table 7.2   Halifax Prices for Paint Products, 1808

	Halifax prices	John Merrick
White lead paint (cwt)	75s.7¼d. to 90s.	63s.
Black paint (cwt)	– to –	66s.
Yellow paint (cwt)	66s.7½d. to 61s.	61s.
Varnish, black (gal.)	4s. ¾d. to 5s.10½d.	3s.9d.
Linseed oil (gal.)	9s. to 12s.10½d.	10s.

Note: No quotation for ochre; low price for yellow paint 66s.7¼d.; upper price for black varnish 5s.4½d.; high for linseed 12s.4½d.; and two new items: lamp black 1s.1½d. to 2s.8½d. and turpentine spirits 7s.2½d. per gal.
Source: Inglefield to RO, 21 Oct. 1808. NMM, HAL/E/37, HAL/E/40, fol. 133. Yard officers' prices, 19 Oct. 1808. NMM, HAL/A/1.

purchased for the purpose of mixing with paint." Instead, substitution with train oil was mandated as soon as the contract for linseed oil with Merrick expired.[79]

Further dispute over prices in 1814 encouraged the yard to amend Merrick's contract. During the war with the United States, heightened demand caused havoc with the paint contract. As Merrick did not import white lead in kegs, but ground "dry, in lumps ... in oil," the yard officers began to fear that he might be tempted to adulterate his paint. Furthermore the contractor lacked sufficient oil to meet their demand without risking running out of it before the spring shipment. Increased demand and hence pressure on supply arose from the yard's need to send paint for ships on the lakes in Canada. As the contractor did not hold himself bound to provide for any other than the yard and the ships in port, and as they were not free, under an order of 21 October 1808, to purchase it elsewhere, the officers insisted on alterations to Merrick's contract.[80]

Inflation affected Merrick's employees as well. His journeymen, employed to paint both the yard and warships in July 1814, requested an increase in wages and refused to work. Merrick told the yard officers in July 1814: "unless the prices allowed me ... are augmented, I must give up the employ as it would be productive of inevitable ruin to me was I to continue in it ... When it is considered that I receive less for my services than was given thirty years since, when wages and expenses of living was not half the present price, I trust that the expediency of this application will be acknowledged, and that I cannot possibly be accused of an attempt to take an unfair advantage of government."[81]

The yard officers unanimously recommended against this. Instead, as an experiment, they hired some painters at 12s. a day and 8s. a day for journeymen "a sum by no means unreasonable, when the high price of every article of life, and the pernicious effect of such an employment are considered." This cost them 2d. a square yard, from which they concluded that Merrick, if his proposal was accepted, would make a "clear profit of 50 per cent, which in our opinion is at least 35 per cent more than any tradesman has a right to expect, when his payments are certain, and made so frequently, as Mr Merrick has been accustomed to receive them."[82]

Merrick withdrew from his contract; yard painting was undertaken by hired men, paid by the day. The yard hired John Boles and John Sullivan, who entered as extra men "for painting the yard buildings" with the wages of house carpenters.[83] The next year a sheer hulksman was transferred from the extra list of the yard, to assist in painting the yard boats and buildings.[84]

The weather's impact on all wooden buildings was relentless. By 1818, the last year the subject was mentioned before the reduction of the yard in 1819, most of the buildings again needed to be painted.[85] Thereafter they were neglected.

To assist in the work of the yard, horses and carts were hired every year to undertake all sorts of haulage. They were used in unloading storeships and carting stores to different parts of the yard. They dragged timber and rough masts, yards, topmasts, and spars from the woods to the waterside. They removed rubbish from the yard. They were also hired to haul earth and stone when work on wharfs, buildings, and breastworks was undertaken, and countless other tasks. They also loaded coal and firewood at the wharf, drawing it to the yard buildings.

Forming a small item in the annual yard budget – Table 7.3 provides some of the spending details – in theory it was under the control of the resident commissioner. Coffin pretended that, in his absence from the yard, the Navy Board had first to be consulted before horses and carts were hired.[86] This, of course, was nonsense. Still, when the commissioner was in residence, permission had to be obtained from him before such services could be employed. As a typical example, in March 1806 Commissioner Inglefield, when observing that the yard's wharf walls and roads had been "considerably damaged" in winter,

Table 7.3 Horse and Cart Hire in the Yard, 1773–1804 (H£)

Years	Total	Daily rate	Monthly Ave	Annual Ave
1773–80	450.19s.	8s.	5. 5s.	62.18.5.
1780–90	4,345.10s.	8s.	39. 3s.	469.16s.
1784–5	395. 4s.	8s.	49. 4s.	590 8s.
1790–9	5,180. 8s.	8s.	49. 6.9.	592. 5s.
1799–1803	969. 0.3.	7s.	22.10.6.	270. 6.6.
1803–04	192. 2.3.	–	8. 8s.	100.16s.

Source: Williams accounts, 1773–80. PRO, ADM17/150; Thomas accounts, 1780–90. ADM17/151; Edgecombe accounts, 1784–5. ADM17/150, Part F; Livie accounts, 1790–9. ADM17/151; Anderson accounts, 1799–1803. ADM17/152; Dawes accounts, 1803–4. ADM17/153.

required his officers to hire a second horse, cart, and driver to help in the spring clean-up.[87]

In 1803 Inglefield asked the yard officers, after the death of Stephen Cullen who had served from 1787 as the yard's gate porter, to provide details on the policy relating to the hire of horses by the yard. It seems that Cullen virtually monopolized the business; his death presented "an insurmountable obstacle to our furnishing a more particular account of the disposal of the money after he had obtained possession of it," as no separate account was maintained by anyone else in the yard.[88] From the storekeeper's office they only recovered vouchers for nine years – up to mid-December 1799, amounting to H£5,484 at a monthly cost which averaged about H£50.

A motley group of suppliers provided other goods and services to the yard. From time to time slops – seamen's clothes – were unavailable in the yard's storehouse. The shortfall was made up by making purchases locally. Most of these orders consisted of pairs of woollen mittens, called handskoons, woollen caps in their thousands, and pairs of shoes in their hundreds[89]. In July 1811 alone, when the yard stores ran out of seamen's shoes, some 860 pairs were purchased in town.[90] In addition there were frocks, hats, and shirts, blue cloth trousers, and gaiters for marines, in their hundreds.[91]

As another example, every year or two the yard supplied fearnaught fabric to those who undertook piecework to fashion overcoats for the yard's watchmen and sheer hulksmen. The surviving accounts indicate that men alone were paid for this work, though perhaps the task was partly performed by women.[92]

All such small tradesmen's bills and suppliers of goods purchased by the yard were normally paid in cash. At times severe cash shortages made this impossible, as we shall see in chapter 9, and for months at a time those owed £100 or more had to accept sterling bills of exchange. As these bills were heavily discounted when converted into dollars or Halifax currency, sharp unanticipated losses had to be absorbed.

During such periods of cash shortages the commissioner received lists of the suppliers yet unpaid, prepared by the storekeeper's office. In 1806, as an example, Inglefield was told the yard was then indebted to some thirty-nine local suppliers, amounting to £6,129.8.1., or an average of £157 3s., ranging from £1 1s. to £1,454 14s.[93] This was still a period of moderate spending by the yard, before the heightened tension that characterized relations with the United States from 1807 onwards with the resultant increased size of the squadron and the decision to build the Bermuda base, elevated spending to an unprecedented level.

Storekeeper Williams, between 1773 and 1780, paid out H£1,192 15s. while his successor, George Thomas, between 1780 and 1790, paid out H£2,054 19s. for a great variety of work performed by artificers outside the yard, for which jobs the people of the yard either lacked the skill or the time to undertake themselves. This involved such tasks as repairing pumps, ships' compasses and lanterns as well as those of the yard; overhauling and fitting new standing blocks; cheaving and pinning topmasts, yards, catheads, and careening blocks; touching and polishing needles; rebuilding fireplaces and hearths; such coppersmithing and tinsmithing as making new scuppers and tinning surgeons' pots and kettles; heading up casks and puncheons in the store and providing iron hoops for them; trimming barrels for pitch, tar, and turpentine; and repairing fire engines.[94] As well, every year men were paid to trim the yard's lamps and sweep the chimneys. Tasks such as bookbinding and printing forms were also frequent tasks undertaken in town on behalf of the yard.

Other beneficiaries of the yard's presence were those who received gratuities. One of the first noted in the account books was James Cook, master of *Northumberland*, who received by Colvill's order £50 above his "common pilotage" for "his indefatigable industry in making himself master of the pilotage of the river St Lawrence, and for his service in conducting the squadron up and down that river, at a critical juncture, when the skill of the French pilots was of no service."[95] Twenty years later William Fullerton of Cape Breton received H£7 10s. for canoeing from Spanish River to Halifax to report the attack by two French frigates in July 1781 on the coal and provisions convoy.[96] It had taken him seven days.

The navy was happy to pay those in Nova Scotia who caught and returned deserters and so-called straggling seamen. The Admiralty had a specified rate, adjusted from time to time, that was greater for able seamen than ordinary seamen, while those who snared landsmen and marines received lesser rewards. For instance, such services amounted to less than H£40 a year under storekeeper Williams between 1773 and 1799, when deserters were valued at £2 and stragglers between 10s. and 20s. each.[97] Some of those who profited in this way came from the military garrison. In wartime, payments were unusually frequent. Typical was one made in 1808 to James Carmichael who conducted two deserters from *Latona* to Halifax from Pictou. He received H£4 10s. for expenses, "deeming it necessary," in Admiral Warren's words, "that the utmost encouragement should be given for apprehending the said men in order to check the very frequent instances of this kind which occur at this port."[98]

Others were paid gratuities along with their expenses when coming to the aid of warships in trouble. In 1784 for instance, Roger Pye, his mate, and three men from sloop *Virgin*, who for six days successfully assisted *Vestal*, "when on shore in the Gut of Annapolis," received H£15.[99] Two years later six vessels, three of them shallops, worked for four days to get sloop *Weazle* off a shoal in Canso Harbour, by landing her stores to lighten ship.[100] More than twenty years later, also in Canso Harbour, when storeship *William* went aground, several local vessels were rewarded for similar help.[101] When *Tribune* tragically was wrecked as it entered Halifax harbour in 1797, J. Herron received H£23.17.9½. to bury the bodies of forty-three men "belonging to her and for saving nine men from the wreck and for the board for fourteen days of one of the men saved."[102] Daniel Kelly and his crew received H£7 10s. for his sloop *Betsey* hired for three days while searching for the wreck. Another recipient was John Cowen, "an industrious inhabitant of Prince Edward Island, master of a coasting sloop" who received £20, though he asked for only £16 10s., for coming to her aid when sloop *Atalanta* went aground in the fall of 1807.[103] "He was the only person who came *of his own accord* ... Had it not been for the assistance derived from his vessel," Captain Hussey reported, "a great part of the provisions and stores" would have been lost. Still another was the master of the schooner *Caledonian*, Samuel Kelly who, "at a moment's warning," assisted sloop *Forth*, aground on Thrum Cap Shoal in 1815. For his "great alacrity and chearfulness" he received H£7, and five men who volunteered to assist him each received 10s.[104]

Still others received compensation and rewards for helping distressed crews from warships. John McGarry of Yarmouth had little choice when *Blonde* broke up on Seal Island as her captain, when rescued, requisitioned supplies from him worth H£230.6.4.[105] George Bellows, a pilot of Prospect Harbour, risked his life and boat in a gale and thick fall of snow and boarded sloop *Little Belt*, which had lost her main mast and bowsprit. He was rewarded with £5 5s. It was likely that the safety of the sloop "depended in a great measure on having at this inclement season and in her situation a skillful pilot on board," according to her captain.[106]

For her "humane attentions & services" to survivors of gun brig *Plumper*, wrecked at Dipper Harbour near Saint John in 1812, a Mrs Dowson received £20, and her husband £70.[107] She supplied them "with poultices, bandages" and housed them for two days.[108] A year later, after sloop *Fantôme* was wrecked near Prospect Harbour, Hannah Power received £7, while John Wagner was paid £3 for the use of his cart.[109]

Thomas Turpel turned an accident into a small advantage. Normally when the yard's mastponds were full, mast timber was "deposited in Tufts Cove." When some of these went adrift in 1810, Turpel retrieved and secured them. As he lived nearby, he was retained by the yard at 10s. currency a week to keep watch both against theft and to ensure that they remained in the cove until they were brought to the mast ponds.[110]

In another incident, George Doyle received 10s. for picking up a launch that broke adrift from the yard. The sum was to be taken from the pay of the three watchmen on duty, with the warning that if it happened again they would be dismissed.[111] In such small ways did some of the taxes raised in Great Britain funnel their way into the hands of ordinary Nova Scotians.

The presence of the naval yard at Halifax, along with the military garrison, created an important internal market in Nova Scotia. I have argued elsewhere that together such public spending by the British government was crucial to the early economic development of the colony.[112] That such invisible annual transfer payments from Great Britain were not entered in one single ledger in the manner that the customs house accounted for almost every item of visible overseas trade did not make them less important.

In addition, it can be shown that naval yard and squadron demands stimulated, among the more important supplies needed annually, early coal mining – first in Cape Breton and later in Pictou County – and expanded overall the market for cordwood. This provided a market for vessels that relied on coastal trade for their freight. Agriculturists were marginally better off, under successive contracts, because of the need to supply fresh meat and vegetables to the squadron. Some of the expansion of grazing might have occurred anyway, but instead of feeding the navy, it might have been directed into the export market in Newfoundland or the Caribbean.

The principal local beneficiaries were those who successfully contracted on behalf of the naval yard and squadron. Among the larger contractors were William Lawlor and John Merrick who successively held the contract to paint the yard buildings and to repair broken window panes, grossing several hundred pounds annually for many years, and keeping skilled men at work.[113] The unique skills of others was so useful that the yard and squadron turned to them year after year without calling for tenders. Here the Dartmouth boat-builder, Seth Coleman, and the oarmaker, Enoch Wiswell, stand out.

On the whole, the names of very few women appear as suppliers to the yard. Mary Salter, Hannah West, and Margaret Fuller earned £10.11.6, £8.4.3., and H£6 8s. respectively between 1807 and 1810 to repair damaged beds.[114] When damaged linen and cotton slops were brought to the yard in 1807 from storeship *William* which had run aground in Canso Harbour, all had to be laundered, work normally undertaken by women. If women supplied this and other petty services for the yard, it was their fathers, brothers, or husbands in whose name the accounts were paid.

Chapter Eight

MAST CONTRACTORS AND WOOD MERCHANTS

The people here are not wealthy eno' to provide much upon speculation [in timber]."[1]

One issue that ought to have been discussed thoroughly in 1775–6 by both the Navy Board and the Halifax yard officers under their newly-minted commissioner, Capt. Arbuthnot, was the supply of sticks. This was the naval jargon for masts, bowsprits, topmasts, yards, and small spars. "The business of maintaining an adequate supply of timber and other stores in the dockyards," Morriss reminds us, "was fundamental to the navy's existence."[2]

Dependence for part of the navy's needs since the seventeenth century had been on the supply from New England.[3] The river systems to the Maine coast and from the New Hampshire interior proved the most promising, though the Carolinas also possessed impressive stands of pine. Since the first recorded shipment of New England timber to England in 1639, exports were stimulated by the Anglo-Dutch wars. Trade centred at the mouth of the Piscataqua River, which Joshua Mauger described in 1760 as being "neither sea nor shore ... a most disagreeable damn'd country."[4] In theory, New World supplies were so abundant that the monopoly hitherto held by the Baltic ought to have been broken. Yet, whatever was imported from New England remained, until the mid-eighteenth century, a small fraction of Britain's requirements, whether for warships or merchant vessels. The Navy Board, believing that American hardwoods were inferior to those of the British Isles and the Baltic, had little use for them. Their interest was largely confined to pine masting timber. To effect this import it established a system whereby merchants in England would bid for an exclusive contract, frequently of several years' duration. The contractors then employed local agents in New England or sent them from England to oversee the work.

The process was similar to that operating in the Baltic. Cut and hauled to river banks in winter by oxen, the masting timbers were then 'twitched' into the water when the ice melted and were carried down water courses with the heavy spring run-off. Before they reached the river's mouth, the timbers were driven into a mast pond where mastwrights began to set about their skilled work of mast making. Such work the agents superintended until the masts, bowsprits, yards, and spars were loaded for the English dockyards, their final destinations.

By mid-eighteenth century the New England contract contained terms long-established. For instance, it noted if "by reason of open winters or for want of snow, the masts, yards & bowsprits cannot be brought down at the appointed times, they shall be received the following year." In wartime mastships were given naval escorts. An allowance for demurrage, at twelve shillings a ton per month to begin a fortnight after the first fair wind, was part of the contract.[5] In addition, the English contractor John Henniker, his agent, and his workmen were given leave "without any interruption to travel into and search His Majesty's woods in the Province of Maine and other of His Majesty's colonies in New England, there to fell and cut down so many good and sound trees as may answer the number and dimension mentioned in the said contract." Throughout Massachusetts this was possible under its 1691 Charter, whereby all trees at one foot above the ground with a diameter of two feet or greater were reserved for the king's use on land not yet granted. In addition, a 1729 Act of Parliament entitled *An Act for the Better Preserving of his Majesty's Woods in America and for the Encouragement of the Importation of Naval Stores from Thence, and to Encourage the Importation of Masts, Yards and Bowsprits from that Part of Great Britain called Scotland* noted among other things that thereafter no one within the provinces of "Nova Scotia, New Hampshire, the Province of Maine, the Massachusetts Bay, Rhode Island and Providence Plantation, the Narragansett country of King's Province, and Connecticut in New England, New York, and New Jersey in America ... shall cut, fell, or destroy any white pine trees except those on private property, without a royal license for so doing."[6] Though such grasping laws were no longer found in Great Britain and were widely resisted in North America wherever timber abounded, they remained the basis of the navy's claim to the best American mast timber. It is probably fair to say that through this policy, that of the so-called broad arrow, the navy occasioned more irritation among American colonials over a longer period than any other British institution.

A vain attempt to challenge this New England monopoly was made by William Duer of New York. In 1773, Duer suggested to the Admiralty that four mast yards be established for the navy in North America. With other shipbuilders in New York he was prepared to build frigates for the navy at a time when they were greatly needed. The Navy Board responded that they were well-supplied with as many masts as they needed from New England, for their contractors had "never failed to deliver the quantity agreed for." As to shipbuilding, having experienced disappointments, as they claimed, at the hands of New England shipbuilders in the 1740s they would not recommend this new experiment.[7] There the matter died. Within a few years the navy was pleased to commission many American-built vessels, when they became prizes of war.[8] There was then nothing but reference to their beauty and fine sailing qualities.

Of this misplaced complacence the Navy Board was soon disabused. A month after the battle of Lexington in April 1775, the surveyor general of the woods, John Wentworth from New Hampshire, reported that Edward Parry, the London-born agent for the mast contractors – since October 1768 Messrs Durany & Bacon, who undertook to supply three or four loads annually of North American white pine masts, yards, and bowsprits[9] – had been seized and held in custody on the Kennebec River by the "country people."[10] There his mastwrights were hewing the huge pines into masts both for the home yards and for the Halifax yard. This was very serious, as the agent had readied cargoes for at least three mastships – fully a year's harvest – at the mast dock on Pierce's Island about sixteen miles from the mouth of the Kennebec River. As a result of this rebel action, the navy lost some sixty-five large masts and twelve smaller ones, twenty-six yards, nineteen bowsprits between twenty-five and thirty-one inches, and thirty-four pine logs, eighteen inches square.[11]

When events in 1775 evolved into the prolonged war with rebel America, the British government found its supply of American masts, bowsprits, small spars, and yards suddenly severed. The impact of the war on this necessary supply is well illustrated in Table 8.1. It shows that the American supply to the home yards vanished in 1776. In 1777–80, less than ten per cent of the usual peacetime supply reached the

Table 8.1 North American Sticks Exported to English Dockyards, 1772–1782

	Portsmouth	Plymouth	Deptford	Woolwich	Chatham	Totals
1772	3,789	6,602	3,532	–	–	13,923
1773	–	–	569	–	–	569
1774	–	–	–	4,269	3,869	8,138
1775	–	–	6,476	–	–	6,476
1776	–	–	–	–	–	–
1777	–	585	–	–	–	585
1778	–	–	109	–	–	109
1779	–	856	–	–	–	856
1780–2	–	–	–	–	–	–
TOTAL	3,789	8,046	10,707	4,269	3,869	30,680

Source: NB to Stephens, 2 Jan. 1783. NMM, ADM/BP/3.

English dockyards. For Portsmouth, the largest of the dockyards, the last deliveries of North American masts occurred in 1772. Had the Navy Board shifted its mast contracts to Nova Scotia as soon as its New England supply was cut off, "an ample stock of the largest American sticks could have been secured within a year."[12] The nation paid a severe price for this grave error, for there is a correlation between timber shortages in the English dockyards and Vice Admiral John Byron's failure to stop Admiral D'Estaing's squadron from reaching American waters in 1778. The British squadron was dismasted and dispersed by summer gales owing to bad masts and rotten timber.[13]

In time, one of the important roles played by the Halifax yard was as a supplier of sticks to other naval yards in North America and the West Indies during the American War of Independence, and to the home yards and elsewhere in peace and war from the 1780s. Though the timber resources of Nova Scotia were imperfectly known, as settlement was so sparse and scattered, some timber suitable for masts was shipped from Halifax in most years between 1750 and 1775.[14] In 1760 the naval storekeeper, Joseph Gerrish, informed the Navy Board that in the LaHave River were available "mast trees of considerable dimensions."[15] Three years later Philip Peake, foreman of shipwrights, went to Chester and Mahone Bay in search of black birch, trees suitable for oak and pine timber for capstan barrels, catheads, knees, standards, and cheeks as well as masts, spars, yards, and bowsprits. He returned with a rather discouraging report, having found only a few black birch fit for capstan barrels between thirty and thirty-three inches in diameter, some small oak, pine, and spruce from sixteen inches and smaller, but very straight and tall. There was no oak timber for ships above 150 to 200 tons, some pine fit for masts of up to 20-gun ships, and yards and topmasts for 40-gun and 50-gun ships, but at a great distance from the rivers, the ground being rough and rocky.[16] In 1774 Surveyor General of the Woods John Wentworth set aside extensive forest tracts in Nova Scotia, even including the upper St John River valley, for the navy.[17] Yet for years the Navy Board ignored this information, so that by 1776 its knowledge of the timber resources of Nova Scotia had scarcely deepened in the quarter-century its yard had been based in Halifax harbour.

Upon the outbreak of hostilities with the American rebels, so great was the shortage of spars and topmasts that yard artificers had to spend time in the woods felling trees around Halifax harbour, and then hauling them out to the water's edge. Commodore Collier noted that the forest in the 1770s was but two or three miles distant from the town of Halifax, while the rest of Nova Scotia was "one wild desert, thick wooded as possible with trees, which principally consists of what they call hemlock."[18] For yard labourers and working parties of seamen to toil in the woods happened frequently during four successive winters of 1776–7 through 1779–80. Only in the autumn of 1779 did some artificers design and build a "pair of stout wheels for getting masts out of the woods."[19] Such work as lumberjacks was a unique experience among Britain's dockyard workers, for which none of them had been specifically engaged.

So adequate was the New England supply to the home yards and to those in the West Indies and Halifax, that it never occurred either to the Navy Board or to Arbuthnot to consider appointing an agent specifically to look for suitable timber in Nova Scotia. It is arguable that as the navy was hardly able to hold its own in the waters around Nova Scotia in 1775, 1776, and 1777, it could not undertake a search for mast timber through the forest preserves of Nova Scotia. Only when the threat of invasion from New England had subsided, and with it the fear of aboriginal raids, was it safe for contractors to roam the woodlands of Nova Scotia with impunity.

Entrepreneurial initiative, when it came in 1777, immediately caught the Board's attention. A Mr Gray offered to supply spruce and pine masts from thirty to twenty-four inches in diameter from the Bay of

Fundy. "If a supply could be obtained from thence," the Navy Board responded, "it would be of the greatest advantage to the service." The Board urged Arbuthnot to contract with anyone else who could furnish masts both for Halifax and New York. As Arbuthnot was recalled, negotiations were left to the new resident commissioner, Capt. Sir Richard Hughes. When Hughes reported in September 1778 a new offer from a John Cort of the Miramichi River, the Board remarked especially on the shortage of large masts caused by "the troubles in America" and welcomed "the prospect of being furnished from ... Nova Scotia."[20] In fact Cort, a Scotsman, had been on the Miramichi since 1765, and knew the extent of its pine forests. The Board sent Hughes a list of the last pre-war contract prices. They doubted the accuracy of Cort's assessment of the size of the trees he had seen, "knowing by experience how greatly persons are deceived therein when trees are standing, as they seldom hold the sizes required by the contract at the several quarters, which must ascertain the diameters at which they are to be received and paid." In May 1779, after Hughes wrote about locating masts in Cape Breton, the Board again asked only for samples.[21] When that first shipment reached England in 1779, the Board found them "so knotty" they declined any more of similar quality.[22]

The supplier was William Davidson, with whom Hughes had concluded a contract in 1779.[23] Originally a partner of Cort's, he had brought out settlers to the Miramichi, established a fish trade to the West Indies, and a modest fur trade to London, employing vessels which he built on the Miramichi.[24] As Davidson later explained,

> Great pains had been taken prior to that period by different persons in exploring the woods in the province in order to compass the same end, but without effect. Hence it was deem'd a thing impracticable, as well from the want of timber of the requisite dimensions as from the danger apprehended from the enemy who held the post called Machias removed only a few leagues from the River Saint John where the masts &c were found by your memorialist who could not for some time draw any security from Fort Howe being between fifty and sixty miles distant from the tract that produced the sticks.[25]

No payment was to be made until the sticks, suitably trimmed, had been inspected in the mast pond he had erected at Fort Howe. He concluded his contract by March 1783, but not without difficulty, because the surveyor sent from the yard, the shipwright George Andrew, rejected many of them, while several more, when worked on by the yard artificers, were found to have hidden defects.[26]

When Capt. Sir Andrew Snape Hamond superseded Hughes as commissioner in 1781, he concluded a contract with Messrs Francklin, Hazen, and White also to supply masts from the St John valley.[27] The same problem with quality which plagued Davidson was experienced by the new contractors except on a larger scale. Almost 200 of their sticks were rejected. Both sets of contractors were required to make up the deficiencies before final payments were made, a problem that continued for them well after the end of the war. In addition, the two contractors competed both for labour, several of whom were Davidson's Acadian axemen, and for suitable standing timber to fulfill their contracts.[28] This led to disputes and confrontations on the banks of the St John River in 1782. Francklin claimed to have held conversations with Hamond to complain of Davidson's behaviour.[29]

Whatever the difficulties he experienced in locating the sticks, getting them out, sorting them for quality, shipping them first to Halifax and then to England, and receiving payment, Davidson had demonstrated that an important new source of masts could be harvested, even on a threatened frontier.[30]

With the permanent loss of the New England source for sticks, the Admiralty and Navy Board now needed to become properly informed about the extent of suitable timber found in what remained of British North America, especially in the new colony of New Brunswick, which was carved from the former frontier territories of Nova Scotia. Quite enough interest had been raised in London, where the Navy Board urged the Admiralty to appoint a surveyor general of the woods for what at war's end remained of British North America. In 1783 it appointed John Wentworth, the talented and hard-working pre-war surveyor. His orders were to survey first those tracts of forest growing "nearest to the best & most commodious shipping places, and particularly on the River St John, from whence were drawn the late supplies for New York and Halifax ... and those which grow in the neighbourhood of Halifax, and the Bason above it, as the supply of that yard will become a material object in the future."[31] Shipwright George Andrew, who since 1781 had inspected and approved all sticks cut for the navy, suggested various New Brunswick locations along tributaries of the St John River.[32] At the same time the Board ordered Capt. Henry Duncan, the first post-war resident commissioner of the naval yard, to make a quick survey of them on his own.[33]

The initial reports both of the surveyor general and the commissioner were each so encouraging that the loss of the New England sources now was no longer even mentioned. As a result, the Navy Board thereafter concluded a further series of contracts which continued until the end of the wars against Napoleonic France and beyond.

The next year the Board directed Commissioner Duncan himself to inspect the hinterland of Halifax for naval stores, masts, and timber suitable for shipbuilding. Instead of reporting on the Halifax region's potential supplies of naval timber which he thought in the 1780s were limited, the commissioner sailed instead to Passamaquoddy and returned via the southwestern coast. In the region of Passamaquoddy Bay and the St John River he found "white pine for masts sufficient to last the navy of Great Britain for any length of time. Nor do I think the destruction that naturally must follow from such numbers of people settling there will deprive us of that resource."[34] He was equally enthusiastic about white oak, which could then be purchased for twenty shillings a ton. He believed the Shelburne area would produce an abundance of deals, though he saw few pine over eighteen inches in diameter. He advised that contracting was the cheapest method, while freighting was better done by the ton delivered in England than hiring ships at a monthly rate. He warned the Navy Board that in any such contract the "first freight should be lower as they will have secured a freight out and home. If not, they will accept of lower terms here rather than go home in ballast."[35]

The following spring he concluded his estimate of the timber potential of the colony by visiting the eastern regions of the province for the first time.[36] He cut across the peninsula by the Shubenacadie River to the Minas Basin, where he saw many white pine fit for masts. The rapids on the river presented no great barrier to float large timbers. He also visited Chedabucto Bay, sailed through the Canso Strait, to Pictou, Saint John Island, and most of the ports on Cape Breton, commenting favourably on Merigomish oak and Pictou masting white pine.[37] Everyone had assured him that at Miramichi large pines fit for masts were available in great quantities.[38] When he visited it in 1788 such prospects were amply confirmed. He thought the best oak of Nova Scotia, although "very good sound wood, is not the real white oak, like that of Great Britain, but I believe as the master shipwright says, better than the Staten [Island] timber" with which he had become familiar during the late war.[39]

Duncan wrote almost lyrically about the harbours, especially of

Nova Scotia. In all of them a ship would find wood or timber to repair the common damages afflicting ships and, in many harbours,

> a fleet might be amply supplied with masts ... This country at present can produce for the use of the navy more safe harbours fit for a fleet than there are in the same space in any part of the globe. Timber of all kinds, firewood, coals, water and fresh provision, lime and brick, and if it is thought advisable to give encouragement, the country will produce, for I have seen it, hemp and flax, and there is iron all over the province. These last articles would require Parliamentary encouragement, to bring them forward in quantities, but the country is capable of it. I do suppose that in a few years, grain of all kinds will be plenty here. The tar and turpentine are the material articles which will not be found in this country.[40]

The Navy Board dismissed much of this. However useful for the supply of the Halifax naval yard, the English yards needed neither North American masts nor deck timber, it then believed. Interested though they were in samples of white oak sent them,[41] as late as 1784 the Board remained "hopeful it will not be necessary to apply to America for that or any other for ship building" materials.[42] If such myopia was astounding, it seems also a naive expression of hope at least for the next generation about the future course Anglo-French and Anglo-American relations.

When Duncan's enthusiastic report was matched by the first annual reports from the surveyor general of the woods, the Navy Board, under pressure from the Admiralty, changed its mind. Now in 1787 it wanted to establish a firm "ground for the supply of masts" and sought advice for the best mode of contracting for masts.[43] It undertook to provide a priority list for the exploitation of the various regions which Wentworth had identified. A hint of its future plans came later when it inquired about the dimensions of masts if ever there was a need to supply the Jamaica and Antigua yards.[44] In response Duncan and Wentworth assumed that letting of contracts would be made in North America through advertisements placed in newspapers. Duncan reminded the Board that, with a license, a contractor could take white pine for masts on any land, not just crown-reserve land. They believed that both the St John and the Miramichi held the greatest reserves of the largest timber.[45]

More specifically, in 1788 the Board consulted Duncan about the suitability of North American fir for topmasts to be supplied to the West Indies' yards.[46] Again Duncan responded warmly, assuring the Board that Nova Scotia's white pine was of "very good quality and I esteem it the best for ships above the class of frigates. For frigates and all under I should prefer black spruce. It is lighter and tougher and equally durable as the white pine, but would not answer so well when grown to a greater size."[47]

In the meantime, Duncan oversaw the shipping of sticks awaiting in the mast pond at Fort Howe, near the mouth of the St John River. By the end of 1783, about 3,000 tons of shipping were needed to load the assembled timbers. Loading could rarely occur in winter at Fort Howe, as thick ice froze the masts in the mastpond.[48] The site was also poorly protected from gales, which in 1784 "broke all the ropes & threw the masts ... one over the other."[49] Navigation was much more difficult, in part owing to the considerable tides, than getting into Halifax harbour. If mastships got into difficulties, as had *Britannia* in 1783, they had to be beached in order to be repaired, as had *Medway* which ran onto a ledge the following year.[50] So large were the sticks that some ships proved unsuitable to load the larger timbers, such as *Keppel*, which proved so short she could load no masts between decks, only shorter yards.[51] Still, in 1784 Duncan was able to send both *Holderness* and *Selina* to load masts.[52]

Duncan also had to deal with the first two wartime contracts which remained incomplete as a result of defects or incorrect measurements found when delivered to the Halifax yard. William Davidson, who had pioneered the supply under hazardous wartime conditions and had cut down, through his inexperience, many trees which proved unsuitable, had at the end of his contract in March 1783 many rejected timbers still on his hands. As a consequence he received £396 less than he had anticipated.[53] The deficiency was covered under a new contract, at prices reduced by 20 per cent.[54] The new contract allowed him to deliver two-thirds of the sticks left on hand in 1783, provided he made up the deficiencies in his 1779 contract.[55] Owing to the lack of snow in the winter of 1785–6, and the consequent "very short time for hauling the masts out of the woods with oxen, and the uncommon lowness of the freshets in the spring that prevented the sticks cut and trimmed on the small streams from being got onto the main river," he needed until the spring of 1787 to complete his contract.[56] With insolvency threatening, he began to draw bills on the yard to pay his workers, in anticipation of his future contract payments.[57] In effect he was using the naval yard as a bank by being granted credit, secured on the future delivery of sticks, something not anticipated by his contracts.

The second wartime contract, awarded to Francklin, Hazen, and White in 1781, was concluded in September 1783. Yet as in Davidson's case, so many timbers were found to be defective or wrongly measured, that payment was reduced by £416.[58] In anticipation of a second contract from Commissioner Hamond, though none had actually been signed, the consortium had unwisely gone ahead and cut another 200 sticks. When hostilities ended in 1783 without a subsequent contract having been negotiated, they managed to ship only about fifty to Lisbon. In April 1784 they begged Duncan to be allowed to deliver the remaining sticks to Fort Howe. To this the Navy Board consented,[59] if the price was lowered by 20 per cent.[60] When Hazen and White agreed to these conditions,[61] Duncan concluded a new contract with them,[62] principally "to encourage and enable the undertakers to refund the deficiencies on former engagements."[63] It required them to deliver by 1 July 1785 at the mouth of the St John River at the cove under Fort Howe some 100 white pine masts, yards, and bowsprits ready to be surveyed by a yard shipwright. When one-half were cut and hauled to the frozen river ready to be carried in the spring thaw, they were free to draw on the yard storekeeper for half the value of the contract.[64]

When the Navy Board underwent its change of heart about the potential importance of North American timber, it also decided to assume control of the contracting process, by removing it from the hands of the resident commissioner. This was to revert to a procedure which had become standard in the twenty years following the first such mast contracts for American masts given to Henniker in 1755. Though entrepreneurs from the colonies were given the opportunity to submit tenders on the same basis as those from Great Britain, by moving control to London, British merchants were necessarily favoured, owing to their much deeper pockets.[65]

A draft advertisement reached the yard to be placed in newspapers both in Halifax and neighbouring colonies. Inserted toward the end of August, 1788, it stated "the Navy Yard will issue a contract for yards in England for a supply of North American white pine masts, yards & bowsprits, also at yards at Antigua and Jamaica. It is not intended to confine the tenderers to any particular spots, but to extend to St John's River, Lake Champlain, or any other parts of the British territories there." Contract conditions were made available both in Quebec and from Commissioner Duncan at Halifax.[66]

Doubtless one of the reasons the Navy Board in 1788 looked beyond the North American colonies for a contractor may have been the lack of suitably large colonial-owned ships for the task of freighting the sticks either to England or the West Indies. This implied a lack of sufficient capital to carry on the sort of task the Board now had in mind. Hazen and White on the one hand and Davidson on the other, from their scrambling always to be paid, conducted businesses far too limited and too precarious to be entrusted with this new and larger task. Duncan was explicit on that point, "There are no shipping here, or that come to this place, fit to carry masts."[67] Indeed, just to clear the masts still at Fort Howe he needed a 700-ton ship, which in 1787 could not be found in the colonies, so had to come from England.[68]

Before the results of the contract tendering process were known in Halifax, Michael Wallace, formerly of New York, and Benjamin Mulberry Holmes, a refugee from Boston, formed a consortium with Davidson to tender a bid.[69] With their business acumen and Davidson's personal experience as a contractor tramping and canoeing the inland rivers of New Brunswick from the headwaters of the Miramichi to the Northumberland Strait and from the upper St John Valley to the Bay of Fundy, they believed they had reasonable expectations of success. To support their cause Wallace and Holmes planned to travel to London to present their tender, but were prevented from doing so by the lack of London-bound shipping from the port of Halifax.[70] Though the Navy Board assured them that their tender had been considered, it concluded an agreement in 1788 "on much lower terms than their proposals."[71]

The Greenock firm of George Robertson, James Hunter, and William Forsyth won the competition to supply the navy with "North American masts, yards, &ca."[72] Only William Forsyth lived in Nova Scotia, where he had arrived less than five years earlier, but whose scale of business, owing to the wealth of the Scottish company, probably equalled that of any other Halifax merchant. Forsyth first evinced an interest in supplying masts to the navy when the contracts, held by Messrs Hazen and White on the one hand and William Davidson on the other, came to an end in 1787. Their remaining sticks, then gathered into the mast pond at Fort Howe, awaited delivery to the English yards. Through his London agent Robert Livie, Forsyth offered to deliver all the masts either to England for £2,000 or for £2,500 to the West Indies.[73] Nothing came of this though his name became known to the Navy

Board. Fourteen months later Forsyth was destined to arrange the actual work in the forests, to deal with any problems relating to loading and shipping and, in wartime, convoying home the mastships.

A month later a second contract was awarded to Alexander Blair of London and James Glenie of Fife and Goldsborough, New Brunswick,[74] to supply several English yards and those of Antigua, Jamaica, and Halifax with white pine masts, yards, spars, and bowsprits, on the same terms and in the same dimensions as those in the contract with Hunter, Robertson & Forsyth.[75] By July 1789 Glenie was in Saint John to implement his contract to supply at least twenty shiploads of masts. His first two ships, *Admiral Parker* and *Amphion*, loaded for Plymouth and Portsmouth respectively, where they were needed immediately.[76] So began a new phase in the supply of the naval masting needs by exploiting the forests of British North America, the later history of which has been so well-studied.[77]

This invasion of forest tracts by agents of the British navy, which these and later contracts precipitated, led to renewed conflict with private landowners, similar to experiences in New England until 1775. Several parliamentary acts specified white pines for the masting of the fleet. This crown right could not be alienated by any provincial patent to private persons. Such patents were void *ab initio*, as Wentworth reminded the Admiralty in 1791, and were inconsistent with the 1729 statute enacted for the express purpose of preventing larger white pines from becoming private property.[78]

A balance had to be struck between the legitimate development of a lumber trade in the colonies that threatened mast timber and the exaggerated claims of the contractors to all the pine timber to fulfil their contract, whether it proved fit or not. They claimed the right to any tree they cut down or which broke upon felling and which proved defective for masting purposes, as compensation for the expense involved. As this wastage was part of their contracts with woodcutters, the workers also laid part claim to such felled timber. Wentworth, the surveyor general of the woods, explained the process. "The workmen claim an interest in the timber hawling on to the River St Johns, being, as they said, unpaid for their labor."[79]

Such claims were inadmissible, as they would have given the contractors virtually a monopoly of the market. At the same time they would have removed any incentive to the landowner to nurture his woodland. Rather he might lay waste his wood, if he could not find a ready market for the timber, before the contractors arrived on his grant.

Another problem faced by the contractors related to the crews on their mastships. As certain ships were granted special protection from the press, the contractors frequently had to apply for this privilege. A naval escort sent to the Bay of Fundy to convoy the mastship *Earl of Mansfield*, which lacked such protection, pressed seven men from her. When only four were returned upon the merchant captain's complaint, the rest of the crew fled, fearing impressment. Before the matter was cleared up, an eleven-day delay had ensued,[80] which resulted in a demand to the Navy Board for demurrage.[81]

On occasion, North American mastships arrived in an English harbour only to become so short of crew through pressing, the ship could scarcely be navigated with safety. In other instances, ships hired in the colonies to load masts for the Halifax yard could not find crews unless protected from the press. In 1805 the problem was experienced acutely at Saint John when only some of the pressed men from mastship *Governor Carleton* were returned.[82] When brig *Busy*, assigned to escort mastship *Lilly*, came into port, the labourers loading mastships, to avoid the press, went into hiding and soldiers had to be hired to complete the work.[83] In 1806 in Saint John harbour *Cambrian* pressed four men from a mastship, again contrary to the express conditions of the contract and to the protection granted by the Admiralty. "The injury is the greater that one of them is an officer, whose services on board are indispensable," explained the contractors.[84] A similar incident occurred in 1808, when the escort, gun brig *Plumper*, pressed five men from the mastship *America* while they were in the process of loading her.[85]

The mastships originating in England sailed directly either to Saint John, St Andrews, or Miramichi, then were escorted either to a rendezvous at Halifax or directly to England, Antigua, or Jamaica, wherever the masts, yards, bowsprits, and spars were destined. In the summer of 1797, for instance, mastship *Trelawny* sailed from Halifax to the Bay of Fundy, having arrived from England. Once loaded it was escorted from the Bay of Fundy directly to Jamaica.[86] Meanwhile mastships *Britannia*, *America*, *Earl of Mansfield*, and *Princess of Wales* arrived from England. The first two of these then returned to England from the Bay of Fundy under convoy, while *Earl of Mansfield* brought mast cargo to Halifax, before returning to the Bay of Fundy to load a second cargo for England. *Princess of Wales* sailed directly to Miramichi before sailing for England.[87]

Occasionally, the commander-in-chief and the commissioner redirected a mastship from her original to an alternate destination. Thus when Admiral Berkeley learned in 1806 that a hurricane had dismasted "three line of battleships" at 21°30'N 63°40'W, while the mastship which sailed earlier bound for Antigua had been captured, he directed that the mastship then loaded and bound for England should instead be sent to Antigua to aid Cochrane's squadron, which be believed had been devastated by the storm.[88] The only cautionary note came from the contractors, Forsyth & Smith, who pointed out that since the insurance did not cover this diversion, which was not contemplated until she was *en route* from the port of loading, the contractors had to pay the full premium to the insurers. The additional expense of a new insurance policy would have to be absorbed by the Navy Board. Moreover, as they still intended to send a ship's load of masts to England, *Rosina* would require a return escort out of danger.[89]

Once the Navy Board assumed control over the major masting contracts, the resident commissioner was confined to making contracts solely to supply the Halifax careening yard. The accumulated numbers of sticks involved could be enormous. In August 1801, for instance, when the squadron was still of moderate size, after a load arrived from the mastship *Duke of Kent*, in the Halifax yard there were 347 masts, yards, and bowsprits and 1,106 spruce spars.[90] As their number was so large and the mastpond could not accommodate them, Inglefield shipped many to Gibraltar, where he knew there was a great shortage, especially of smaller spars.[91] In 1803 when next a significant surplus accumulated at the yard, two storeships, one on its way from England to Jamaica, and the other homeward-bound from the Mediterranean, were routed home via Nova Scotia to load whatever the yard could spare.[92] It was 1807 before, for the first time, a brief shortage of masts and spars occurred in the careening yard. It was large-sized masts with which they were principally concerned "in case of the arrival of ships from other foreign stations disabled in their masts considerable delay to the injury of the service might be occasioned."[93]

When Forsyth claimed that his firm could not deliver sticks unless the yard ordered the equivalent of a full load, the Navy Board insisted that there were sticks enough in the yard's mastpond, according to information in the yard's quarterly reports.[94] This was yet another example of micro-managing the yard's routine business from a distance of 3,000 miles. The Board went further by reserving for itself the power to supply the Halifax yard with those masts requested in their quarterly returns. This was not the response Inglefield wanted, as he had hoped to be able to order such items locally, without going

184   Part Three: Economic Impact

through London, when a response might take six months to reach him from the time the yard requested the items.[95] The first such supply came from the contractors selected by the Navy Board late in 1807.[96]

Inglefield's direct intervention helped to define the limits to the mast contractors' monopoly. Until the end of 1807 Forsyth & Smith of Greenock held the contract for masts. Inglefield thought any new contract should exclude the supply of all smaller spars used in the careening yard, that is those of twenty-two inches diameter and less, as they could readily be supplied from Nova Scotia.[97]

When Forsyth & Smith saw his advertisement calling for tenders for small black spruce spars to be supplied to Barbados and Bermuda they protested, claiming that by their 1805 contract they alone should fill the order. Since 1788 spruce and pine sticks suitable for topmasts, from eighteen inches to fourteen inches inclusive, had always been inserted in the contract. The expense of supplying such items differed from yard to yard, yet the price hardly varied between the Thames River and Plymouth, Halifax, and the West Indies, as the deductions in Nova Scotia and the West Indies were subsequently countervailed by the duties payable in England. In their 1805 tender they had aggregated all costs, thus blending the benefits of one with the disadvantages of another. "For some of the smaller spars we are paid little more, after transporting them to England, than they cost in the woods in North America. In the case of the *Hamilton* and *Governor Carleton* last year, the whole amount of their cargoes would hardly pay a common freight at the present rate of tonnage."[98]

The Navy Board eventually agreed with Inglefield's interpretation, that the mast contractors had no right to the small spar supply either to Bermuda or Barbados. The Board's earlier scheme to supply Bermuda with spars and other stores from New York and the Chesapeake ports had fallen foul of American foreign policy. The American embargo of 1807 followed in 1808 by non-intercourse brought all supplies from the United States to a virtual standstill. Now the Board endorsed a proposal made by Inglefield, whereby smaller spars would first be delivered to the Halifax yard, before being shipped on board warships bound for Bermuda. Some would sail directly to Cochrane's squadron at Barbados.[99]

The task of assigning escorts for mastships became a continuing responsibility of the North American squadron, upon the outbreak of hostilities against France in 1793, as the admiral considered the ever-increasing needs of the yards at home and in the West Indies. Nevertheless, shipping masts, spars, yards, and bowsprits to the home yards continued uninterrupted throughout the war. One or two mastships sent home yearly were usually escorted by the ship on station which most needed extensive repairs in a drydock. The mastships sailed from Saint John to Halifax often without escorts. At Halifax the mastship found ordinary merchant ships awaiting her arrival in order to make up a small convoy of perhaps five to eight vessels with the escort. In 1793, with "a superior fleet now upon the American coast," and a number of privateers cruising to intercept the British trade, William Forsyth's mastship, *Earl of Mansfield*, then loading in the Bay of Fundy, ran "a great risk of being captured" before reaching the safety of Halifax. Commissioner Duncan with but one frigate in port was unable to help.[100] Table 8.2 provides the details of mastships and their escorts thereafter until the end of the war in 1815.

Between 1795 and 1801 storms frequently separated the escort from the mastships, but none was lost. In 1795, when letter-of-marque mastship *Brunswick* was on the point of sailing from Saint John, part of her crew deserted. Reaching Halifax only in mid-January, she struck a shoal. Delayed for a further three weeks by unfavourable winds and weather from sailing for England, she was partially manned by invalids and French prisoners. Escorted by 44-gun *Severn*, she proved so leaky from her accident that, even when she threw all her guns overboard, water rose almost three feet above the ceiling of the lower deck. She had to make for Antigua instead.

Details of one 1795 convoy will serve to illustrate the difficulties for escorts, especially in winter crossings. When *Thisbe* escorted three mastships and five other merchant ships to England in November 1795, convoy orders required mastship *Earl of Mansfield* to lead, followed by the two other mastships abreast with the two escorting frigates on either flank, with the rest of the convoy following as closely as possible.

> No ship to show any lights except when seeing a strange sail, except to hoist lights and make every possible effort to warn convoy. On parting at night and meeting again, hoist three lights in inverted triangle. Within hailing distance, ship hailed to cry "King George" hailing ship to respond "Old England." No ship to pass one carrying a light. From Sambro lighthouse SE x S by compass 130 miles then ESE

186   Part Three: Economic Impact

Table 8.2   Naval Escorts for Mastships, 1791–1810

Year	Escort	Mastship	Destination
1791	Resistance	Earl of Mansfield	Plymouth
1793		Earl of Mansfield	England
1794	Ceres	unknown	Portsmouth
1795	Severn	Brunswick	Antigua
	Thisbe	Princess of Wales	Portsmouth
		Admiral Parker	Portsmouth
		& Earl of Mansfield	Portsmouth
1796	unknown	unknown	England
1797	Espérance	Princess of Wales	England
	& Raison	Earl of Mansfield	England
		Britannia	England
		Trelawny	Jamaica
		America	England
1798	Resolution	America	Portsmouth
		America	Plymouth
	Lynx	Lord Macartney	Portsmouth
1799	Dasher	unknown	England
1800	Lilly	Camel	England
1801	Cleopatra	Duke of Kent	England
1802		Camel	England
1803		Chichester storeship	Portsmouth
		Camel storeship	England
1804	Boston	America	Plymouth
	Amsterdam	Rosina	Jamaica
1805	Eagle	unknown	Portsmouth
	Busy	Lady Parker	Antigua: captured
	Busy	Lilly	Jamaica
	Busy	Caledonian	Barbados
		Duke of Kent	England
1806	Tartar	Duke of Kent	Portsmouth
	Milan	Caledonian	Plymouth
		America	England
	Cleopatra	Governor Carleton	Antigua
	Cambrian	Rosina	Antigua
		Hamilton	England
1807	Cambrian	unknown	England
1808	Bellona	Rosina	Portsmouth
		America	England
		Eisdale storeship	England
		Diligence	England
1809	Hussar	Elk	Plymouth
		Pallas	England
		Dawson transport	England
		William storeship	England
	Horatio	Eliza transport	Portsmouth

Table 8.2 (Concluded)

Year	Escort	Mastship	Destination
1809	Bonne Citoyenne	Ajax	Portsmouth
	Bellona	Rosina	England
		British Tar	England
		Pallas transport	Plymouth
1810	Prospero	Ariel	Plymouth
	Harpy	William storeship	Downs
		& Robert transport	Downs
		Diligent	England
	Cleopatra	Diana	Plymouth
		Penelope	England

Sources: PRO unless otherwise noted. Robertson to O'Bryan, 2 Oct. 1791. ADM106/2473, 48; Hamilton to Stephens, 10 July 1794. ADM1/1911; Milne to Tripp, 19 Jan. and 13 Feb. 1795. ADM1/2596; Murray to Tripp, 19 Dec. 1794. ADM1/2596; Hardy to Nepean, 25 Nov. 1795. ADM1/1913; Forsyth & Co. to Duncan, 15 May & 17 May 1797. Duncan to Forsyth, 30 May 1797. NMM. MG13/6. fol. 235, 242; Vandeput to Marsden, 4 Aug. 1797. ADM1/494, fol. 70; Vandeput to Lechmere, 18 Aug. 1798. ADM1/2064; Lechmere to Nepean, 12 Sept. 1798. ADM1/2064; Vandeput to Marsden, 8 July and 18 Oct. 1799. ADM1/494, fol. 177, 211; Tobin to Nepean, 19 Aug. 1799. ADM1/2599; Skene to Nepean, 11 Nov. 1799. ADM1/2500; Murray to Nepean, 3 Aug. 1800. ADM1/495, fol. 128; Pellens to Nepean, 26 Sept. and 27 Oct. 1801. ADM1/2322; Inglefield to RO, 22 Aug. 1803. ADM106/2027; Douglas to Marsden, 11 Nov. 1804. ADM1/1726; NB to Marsden, 19 Nov. 1804. ADM/B/217; Colby to Marsden, 18 Oct. 1805. ADM1/1643; Forsyth & Smith to Inglefield, 10 May 1805. NSARM. MG13/9.1, fol. 295–6; Forsyth & Smith to Inglefield, 3 June 1805. NSARM. MG13/9.1, fol. 318–9; Forsyth & Smith to Inglefield, 2 & 14 Sept. 1805. NSARM. MG13/4, fol. 143, 158; Forsyth & Smith to Mitchell, 23 Nov. 1805. NSARM. MG13/4, fol. 242; Mitchell to Inglefield, 24 Nov. 1805. ADM106/2028; Forsyth & Smith to Inglefield, 8 Aug. 1806. NMM. HAL/A/3b, fol. 150–1; Inglefield to NB, 18 Sept. 1806. ADM106/2028; Berkeley to Marsden, 10 Oct. 1806. ADM1/496, fol. 478–9; Poyntz to Marsden, 5 Nov. 1806. ADM1/2331; Forsyth & Smith to Inglefield, 26 Aug. 1807. ADM106/2028; Forsyth & Smith to Inglefield, 24 Sept. 1808. NMM. HAL/E/39a, fol. 5; Warren to Erskine, 21 Nov. 1808. ADM1/1731; Forsyth & Smith to Inglefield, 26 May & 7 June 1809. NMM. HAL/E/39a, fol. 156, 176; Inglefield to Warren, 8 June 1809. NMM. HAL/E/39a, fol. 177; Warren to Pole, 13 June 1809. ADM1/499, fol. 120; Warren to Scott, 1 Aug. 1809. ADM1/2521; 8 & 21 Aug. 1809. NMM. HAL/A/4b, fol. 201, 208; Warren to Inglefield, 16 Aug. 1809. NMM. HAL/E/35b, fol. 51; Inglefield to RO, 20 Oct. 1809. NMM. HAL/E/37; Pechell to Inglefield, 3 Jan. 1810. NMM. HAL/A/4b, fol. 295–7; Warren to Crocker, 17 June 1810. ADM1/500, fol. 82; NMM. HAL/A/2, fol. 62.

60 miles, then make a 74°E course for 1,280 miles which leads you into the 47°N 30'W and about 21 leagues to the westward of Lizard and so between 49° and 49°20' degrees, the convoy to keep by that means should I unfortunately part company I may be enabled to join them.[101]

One week out from Halifax a violent gale, which lasted several days, dispersed the convoy; the escort reached Spithead alone.[102] Three years later when *Resolution* acted as escort, outside Halifax harbour mastship *America* was taken in tow, the sea captain intending thereby to ensure her safety. Within five days the hawser broke in a violent storm, separating the mastship from the frigate which reached Spithead alone.

Losses inevitably occurred at the hands of the enemy. In 1803–04 when two of Hunter, Robertson & Forsyth's mastships were captured by privateers, Inglefield recommended that the use of armed storeships was the only safe way thereafter to send such "valuable cargoes of masts." He wanted the Navy Board to assign such a ship armed with forty-four guns to ply regularly between Halifax and England with a cargo of masts.[103] The policy was not implemented. Later, in 1806, despite the gallant action fought by sloop *Busy*, a French frigate took the mastship *Lady Parker* that she was escorting to Antigua.[104]

Halifax yard, when not excessively busy, repaired the mastships damaged by stress of weather in their crossings. This was the case in 1801 and 1802, for instance, involving *America* and *Lord Macartney*.[105]

In 1807, Forsyth & Smith lost the masting contract to a consortium of London entrepreneurs: Christopher, John, and George Idle, Thomas Coates & William Haynes.[106] Their Halifax agent was Andrew Belcher, a Nova Scotian, then living in London until this opportunity brought him back to Halifax in January 1809. Belcher incidentally immediately irritated the yard officers by disputing the accuracy of their mast measurements, held in his absence, and by requesting a second survey with an independent timber measurer.[107] This brought a sharp reaction from Dawes, the naval storekeeper. "The professional officers of the yard need no information from any individual," he wrote, adding "we imagine if the Navy Board thought a timber measurer necessary they would not leave the nomination of a person to that office with the agents of their contractors. Upon the whole we are of opinion that another survey is not necessary, that Mr Belcher is not entitled to it, and that to comply with his request would be introducing a practice that on future occasions might tend to the hindrance of the service."[108] Belcher, for his part, begged to be forgiven for "having asked what appears to be contrary to the practice of the yard ... I likewise hope I may be the more justified in the application when it is observed that almost all the masts fall short of the measurement at Quebec."[109]

This occurred in a crucial era, when the Baltic supply closed to the British, and an extraordinary scramble occurred as the Navy Board extended its range of suppliers from the shores of the Aegean to the Ottawa River valley in search of needed shipbuilding timber. The urgency of the situation was not lost on the yard where every reasonable offer of spars was accepted. Advertisements appeared in the papers for topmasts and topsail yards for the use of the Halifax yard[110] and spars and timber for the home yards.[111] This anticipated wishes both of the new commander-in-chief, Vice Admiral Sir John Borlase Warren,[112] and the Navy Board's later orders.[113] All complacency vanished. In 1807 an offer of spars available at Miramichi had been rejected, when the tender called for delivery in Halifax. A year later Warren changed his tune. Owing to shortages of wood at the yard, a naval transport was despatched unhesitatingly to Miramichi for a shipload of spars, pine timber, and pine deals.[114]

Reliance was placed increasingly on Lower Canada, New Brunswick, and Nova Scotia in descending order of importance. To the prejudice of the traditional Baltic supply, Parliament imposed duties in 1809-10 to favour the British North American supply.[115] Not only was an unprecedented amount of timber thereby soon exported to England, but large ships of 500 tons and more, boasting raft ports up to thirty-eight inches wide, were built on the St Lawrence, of a size not constructed in Nova Scotia until after the war's end. Mure and Joliffe, the Quebec agents for the London contractors Scott and Idle,[116] with whom Admiral Warren opened a correspondence, themselves alone anticipated shipping between 16,000 and 20,000 tons in 1808.[117] It was in the years 1808 to 1812 that the supply of wood products entering the British market from British North America for the first time exceeded that of the Baltic.[118]

Also for the first time, in 1808 the Halifax careening yard was supplied with masts from Quebec, a memorable year for British North America. When transport *Dawson* brought masts as well as 116 spruce spars at contract prices six time higher than such spars could be had in Halifax from Nova Scotian suppliers, the commissioner sent Mure and Joliffe a stinging rebuke for the inadequate quality of this first load.[119] The "service would be much embarrassed if a ship of the line or large frigates should arrive here dismasted not having spars of proper dimensions for making large masts."[120] Their next shipment satisfied him no better as it included masts only between twenty-three and twenty-seven inches, as the ship could not load masts of longer size.[121] In 1810 their ship *Dorset* carried the next cargo of masts, bowsprits, oak timber, and a few logs of pine timber.[122] In 1811 they delivered no masts whatsoever, which breakdown Inglefield characterized as a failure to "manifest the zealous attention to the conditions of the contract that might be expected." As a result he pictured his yard virtually devoid of masts yet having to refit a line of ships disabled by storm.[123] Two weeks later the North American squadron was indeed overtaken by a hurricane, not at sea but in Halifax harbour itself. The damage inflicted on masts and topmasts proved to be extensive.[124]

Inglefield's complaints about the dilatoriness of the contractors might have been accurate, but the underlying problem had arisen from the ineffective system established by the Navy Board which, without consultation as we have seen in many instances, centralized in London the control of masts shipped between Quebec and Halifax. Until then the Halifax yard had proved quite capable of making its own arrangements to keep itself supplied. The new procedure resulted in the Board, among other things, ordering thousands of oar rafters for Halifax, when local supply was more than enough, and at one-third the contract price, a point which the commissioner was quick to underline both in Quebec and London. The Navy Board accepted his logic and immediately left him once again free to purchase masts or whatever else he needed, without using the contractors, until alternative arrangements were made.[125]

Throughout his remaining three years in Halifax as the resident commissioner, Inglefield spent a significant part of his time overseeing the shipment of spars, timber, and plank to the English yards. During one twelve months' interval in 1808–09, he boasted that ships calling at the Halifax careening yard shipped to the home yards and other overseas bases some 11,945 spruce and twenty pine spars, thirty-three bowsprits, 194,787 feet of pine plank, 263 tons of timber, three made masts for schooners, fifty ship's sweeps, 2,832 oar rafters, ninety-five capstan bars, 180 serving mallets, and 200 wood wedges.[126] In addition the yard shipped 938 barrels of pitch, tar, and turpentine and 218 gallons of train oil. In the absence of mastships, these products were freighted in a somewhat unorthodox manner by using nine warships, three storeships, and nine transports.[127] How the warships were to engage the enemy, with their decks so encumbered, was not clear. As it turned out, none faced such an encounter.

In 1810–11 Inglefield contracted with James Fraser of Halifax to ship cargoes of red pine timber and plank, red pine and spruce spars fourteen inches and less from Miramichi.[128] He stowed over 2,000 spars into the captured French frigate, *Furieuse*, and other warships returning to England.[129] Much of her cargo he purchased from small local suppliers around Halifax, including M. and A. Archibald, John Clark, and Godfrey Schwartz of Windsor Road. He used available transports for the same purpose[130] and appointed naval escorts for as many of these as needed them.[131]

Inglefield's successor as resident commissioner of the Halifax careening yard and the last officer to hold this post, Capt. the Hon. Philip Wodehouse, scarcely had to concern himself with the question. In 1813, when Wodehouse wrote to the Quebec agent to order the masts needed in the Halifax yard, he was first informed that the war with the United States had completely interrupted the lumber trade with Upper Canada.[132] Later he learned that some large masts and bowsprits would be sent as soon as the navigation on the St Lawrence River opened.[133]

That year he was surprised to receive a shipment of Riga masts and yards from England.[134] Though valued by the Navy Board at between £125 16s. and £180, Wodehouse quickly assured the Board that "sticks of equal quantity and diameter and 70 feet long" could be cut within twenty-five miles of Halifax and delivered to the yard for no more than £18 each.[135] Upon the advice of his master shipwright, Wodehouse ordered the mastships, still loaded, to return to England.[136] As a result, the Navy Board ordered that a dozen spruce spars of twenty-two inches diameter be ordered for the Halifax yard and inspected for their suitability as topmasts. These were fetched not far from Halifax off the Windsor Road.[137] Before the results were known in London, the Navy Board by March 1814 had reversed its position and informed the commissioner that it would continue to ship to Halifax from England either Riga or red pine masts for topmasts, while Nova Scotia spruce were to be used only when necessary.[138] No further such shipments were made to Halifax before the wars with the United States and France came to an end in 1815.

That the supply of sticks even to the Halifax careening yard had almost entirely been removed from the initiative of the resident commissioner there, is seen in some surviving correspondence in August

192 Part Three: Economic Impact

and September 1813 between a London merchant and the Navy Board. In response to the Board's advertisements for spars and handmasts placed in the London newspapers, one Fenchurch Street businessman was moved to write to their lordships. "The woods on the banks of the Bay of Fundy in the province of Nova Scotia ... abound with that species of fir which yields the handmasts and the other spars used for the ... navy." He noted: "There they may be had of all the dimensions usually required at the dockyards and of a quality equal to any imported from America being generally considered as inferior to none in toughness and durability. I intend to form an establishment in that part of Nova Scotia, and to turn my attention in particular to the cutting down and sending to Britain of those spars." If favoured with the Board's encouragement, he would furnish handmasts and spars "upon better terms than any they have yet been offered at." He planned to purchase directly from the woods, and would supply ships to carry them to the English dockyards for a commission of 5 per cent to compensate him for the cash and credit advances needed to undertake the work. Though he guaranteed that the Board would only be charged the actual price contracted for with other suppliers plus the commission, he was informed that it would not be "expedient to adopt the plan he suggests."[139] The centralizing process of the London-based Navy Board in the matter of contracts for sticks was complete long before peace descended on the Atlantic Ocean in 1815.

The wood merchants hovered around the edges of what remained once the mast monopolists fulfilled their contracts. Three significant avenues were still open to them: the supply of materials when yard structures were either erected or repaired, the supply of materials needed when ships were refitting, and the supply of stowage for warships, transports, and storeships, when used to ship wood products to England, Bermuda, or the West Indies. The usual method was for the yard officers to request the commissioner's permission to place advertisements calling for tenders for whatever types of wood were required. Tenders were then submitted, placed in a chest, locked with three separate keys, each held by one of the officers, then opened before witnesses, the tenders read, and the supplier selected. When no tenders were received in response to a particular advertisement, the commissioner felt free to authorize the purchase of parcels of the wood products needed as they became available, paying either in cash or with sterling bills at par.

In the early years, before shipbuilding began to take hold in Nova Scotia with the loyalist influx, the needs of the naval yard were rivalled only by those of the garrison. In a limited internal market, to supply the careening yard was the only considerable business open to wood merchants and traders. Once the surge of yard building had subsided in 1761 and the brief period of rebuilding under Hood in 1768–70 ended, there was very limited demand for wood products. The period of the war against rebel America opened a new phase when the needs of the squadron considerably expanded, while the building of the naval hospital in 1782–3 heralded a new era of yard construction. The decreased demand, occasioned by the reduction of the squadron after 1783 until the renewed war with France in 1792, was partially offset by the building of the commissioner's house and extensive improvements and repairs to buildings, wharfs, and breastworks, all of which required both timber and lumber in considerable quantity. If the wars with France saw relatively few new structures erected – the tenements for the principal officers and the hospital managers, as well as the admiral's house – the demands of the squadron produced a steadily increasing market for wood merchants. This demand was greatly elevated when coincidentally both the Baltic supply of naval stores stopped, temporarily as it transpired, and tensions with the United States cut off most American supplies upon which the West Indies bases had partly depended. This inaugurated a vastly heightened demand as the Halifax squadron grew with war in 1812 into the size of a fleet, with all its attendant requirements for wood. Then the yard had to compete in the wood market with Nova Scotians who were carrying on commerce with a renewed vigour, investing in privateers, and building or purchasing ships condemned as prizes of war by the Halifax vice-admiralty court. Thus at the very moment when the navy's need was the greatest, private demand also peaked, causing a price and wage spiral which was generally characterized as a brief wartime economic boom.

The total quantity supplied annually between 1783 and 1819 is not known, nor is the cost. Yet the initial tender called for 1,500 wharf logs, 2,000 wharf layers, 800 tons of pine, and squared hemlock timber. The successful bidder, Joseph Scott, grossed between H£1,375 and H£1,500 on his initial contract in 1784.[140] The advertisements appeared in the New Brunswick newspapers as well as those of Halifax at least from 1785 onwards, when the yard needed another 100 tons of oak timber and 100,000 feet of white pine plank, from 2½″ to 3½″ thick and of extreme length.[141]

Commissioner Duncan did not hesitate to encourage tenders by writing to men of known experience, like the former Philadelphia shipbuilder, David Thomson, a Shelburne resident in 1786, from whom he solicited 200–300 tons of squared pine timber. "I do not know whether you or any of your friends may be concerned in the saw mills or cutting down timber in the neighbourhood of Shelburne; but should that happen to be the case and convenient for you to send it to this port, I would take 200–300 tons of square pine timber, the larger the better, but not shorter than 24 ft. It has been offered to me from your port @ 18s. I would give that or even 20s. to have some soon ... I will contract for 300 tons @ 18s., if this will serve you or any of your friends. The sooner the timber is sent the better."[142]

The 1788 contract concluded with three Halifax businessmen, Samuel Mercer, Leonard Dunn, and Asa Scott is the first for which all the details are known. It required them to supply 250 tons each of pine and black spruce timber, sixteen inches in diameter between thirty and forty feet in length, "clear of wanes and other defects" at 20s. a ton. Next it included 1,600 hemlock or black spruce wharf logs, a foot in diameter at the top end and twenty-eight feet in length, at 5s., and an additional 1,400 wharf logs of the same length but only nine inches in diameter at the top end, at 4s.6d. apiece. The contract specified three successive delivery dates, when one-third payment became due, except that H£100 would be held as security against the completion of the contract.[143]

In searching for ways to supply the English yards, in 1788 Duncan proposed shipping oak treenails, already employed in the careening yard.[144] The Navy Board was less impressed when it considered the samples sent home. "Altho' the Nova Scotia treenails may be made use of for temporary purposes," they wrote, "we do not think it right to encourage a general use of them on his Majesty's ships."[145]

During the American war, some lumber and timber had been shipped along with masts, both to the navy's New York careening yard and to those in Antigua and Jamaica. To these were added in the 1790s those of the Cape of Good Hope and Gibraltar, and from 1807, Bermuda. In this way, the market for wood merchants and traders resident in Nova Scotia and New Brunswick was considerably and most interestingly expanded.

In February 1796, Vice Admiral Murray received a request for all sorts of wood products from the commander-in-chief at the Cape, the colony having just been seized from the Dutch. As wood was "extremely scarce" he requested a shipment of timber, spars of all dimensions, oak and fir plank and deals, staves, pitch, and tar.[146] The vessels involved were authorized, as part of the contract, to reload with exports a return cargo. In the admiral's absence, Duncan opened the letter and arranged with William Forsyth to hire a vessel, while suggesting that a mastship be despatched to the Cape in the spring.[147] For H£1,100 Forsyth chartered *Camilla*, the "largest vessel then in Halifax harbour."[148] Her owner, Robert Ross, who was jointly concerned with Forsyth in the cargo, went to purchase the return cargo, the principal business objective of the venture.

The venture to Gibraltar was equally rare. In 1799 owing to shortages there, the Navy Board directed acting commissioner Coffin to assemble a cargo of deals, knees, and fir timber up to eighteen inches square to be loaded into a ship of between 150 and 200 tons.[149] As at the Cape so too at Gibraltar the purpose was to repair ships and their boats. Shipped under American colours, the Navy Board reasoned, these would be far less expensive than if shipped from England, so a Boston merchant was selected to undertake the supply.

In 1807 the Halifax yard began purchasing materials for the newly-planned Bermuda naval yard, and for the small repairs to the squadron to be undertaken there.[150] This included principally timber, plank, and spars, much of the supply originating in New Brunswick.[151] Earlier, a plan to ship small spars from the Chesapeake became stillborn with the greatly increased tension with the United States.[152] By 1812 the yard began shipping masts from New Brunswick, under a contract concluded with Forsyth & Black. "The quality of the spars is likewise preferable to the spruce cut in the neighbourhood of Halifax," thought Inglefield.[153] At war's end in 1815 the pace of building the Bermuda base increased. The shipwright, Samuel Sellon, was sent with a clerk, James Ritchie, to St Andrews to survey and ship the timber and lumber ordered for Bermuda under the contract with Alfred Gordon Adams for the first naval hospital at Bermuda.[154] At the same time the Navy Board gave permission to Commander Evans, who superintended the site construction, to import timber from the United States, now again open to commercial traffic.[155] So high were the freights at first demanded by shipowners in Halifax that Commissioner Wodehouse decided instead to employ a naval transport, *Adventure*, to freight the needed materials to Bermuda.[156] With lower freight prices in the post-war era, cargoes of wood products for some years flowed from both Nova Scotia and New Brunswick to the Ireland Island naval base.[157]

There was never a dispute over tendering until 1804, when evidence indicated the commissioner's partiality unfairly favoured one merchant house over others. The complaint by Jacob Miller and his son, Garret, provides a useful and rare insight into the details of the tendering process. The Millers were well-known for their "probity and efficiency" as lumber merchants, who annually supplied the military with lumber and timber, which in 1800 amounted to £10,000, "to the entire satisfaction of His Royal Highness the Duke of Kent.[158] They have in every instance acted with honour and fidelity and that they are men in whom I can place confidence but as to their fairness as merchants and as to their ability to perform any contract they may enter into with me as an agent of his Majesty."[159]

In December 1804 they bid on a contract to supply the careening yard with timber to build sloop *Halifax* and gun brig *Plumper*. Though they were the only Halifax firm to offer to supply the entire requirement, they were "wholly excluded from any share" in the supply.[160] Instead the contract was given to Forsyth & Smith, and Fraser & Thom, each separately for a part and jointly for the remainder. Curiously, the prices at which Inglefield had let the contract were higher than those proposed by the Millers. The decision, which they believed to be "totally preventing all future competition in matters of a similar nature," was inexplicable. They informed the Navy Board in their complaint that they had been "the principal contractors supplying government with timber and boards for the public works carried on in the army departments of this garrison, and also furnished considerable supplies to the naval yard. In every instance they have performed their contracts with the utmost fidelity and punctuality."

They provided a detailed statement of the case, including the fact that they were told on the day they submitted their tenders that the delivery date for timber had been considerably extended, information which Inglefield had given earlier to the winning bidders and to no one else. When the bids were taken by the commissioner into his office, Miller retired with William Smith and John Black of Forsyth & Smith and James Fraser of Fraser & Thom. At about 2:00 p.m. Miller was told that though the lowest bid had yet to be ascertained, his bid was "lowest for a considerable part."[161]

On 29 December Miller again called on Inglefield "who was just preparing to get into his carriage." He was assured that he would have a large part of the supply. When they went into his office his clerk, Provo F. Wallis, handed him an abstract of the tenders, with Frederick Major's name coming first, with Miller's name either on the second or third line, as follows: "Major. 300 pieces birch timber, birch compass knee timber, birch for breast hooks, birch knees, birch or spruce boots, birch plank; Miller. birch timber (straight & curved), red or yellow pine timber, 380 pieces oak timber, oak knees, white pine plank & boards, red or yellow pine plank."[162]

In the presence of his secretary, Inglefield stated that he was very pleased that the Millers had "come forward to make offers on this occasion as he knew they were able to fulfil their engagements." He was invited back on the following Monday with the others, when the whole business would be settled. Before departing, Miller was told by Mr Wallis that he might be asked to supply other items, especially oak plank "as the person who had offered that species of lumber resided at Manchester, and it might be found inconvenient to deal with them."

At the appointed hour of 11:00 a.m. on New Year's Eve, Miller walked to the yard, intending to wait on the commissioner later at noon. Frederick Major was there on the same business. A half hour later the naval storekeeper informed him that the contract had been settled on Forsyth & Smith and Fraser & Thom. Whereupon both Miller and Major immediately went to the commissioner's house. "Mr Miller," said the commissioner, "the contract is settled. I have given it to Forsyth, Smith & Co. and Fraser, Thom & Co."

When Miller protested in view of their conversation the previous Saturday, Inglefield replied, "Yes, sir. I am not to account to you for what I do. I do as I please." In further conversation he was told that Forsyth & Smith would supply seasoned timber from New Brunswick. They had refused to supply any, unless they supplied the whole. Miller wondered how the commissioner could know that Miller did not have on hand sufficient seasoned timber, without having asked. His firm wanted, not favour, but "justice." The commissioner repeated that he could act as he pleased, stating that he was not to be called to account by memorialists, who were dissatisfied merely because they had failed in obtaining the contract.

Major then pointed out that he had been informed by Dawes, the naval storekeeper, that his tender was the lowest for several articles, especially birch timber. To this the commissioner answered: "I know, sir, it was but the reason of my giving it to Forsyth, Smith & Co. that they are to furnish seasoned timber."

In reply, it was observed that it was not essential that the keels and floor timbers of ships should be laid with seasoned timber. Miller suggested that between Saturday and Monday the commissioner's change of decision "must have been occasioned by some intermediate influ-

198 Part Three: Economic Impact

ence." The distinction he now made between treating with persons making proposals – as found in the advertisements – and a promise to accept the lowest tender was not in his mind the previous week.

In the matter of seasoned timber from New Brunswick, Miller observed that Forsyth & Smith, since they secured the contract, had employed people near Halifax to cut some of the very timber intended for the contract, when it could only have been wet, not seasoned. Miller assured the Navy Board that he would have supplied seasoned timber had the advertisements specified it, without any advance in his price. To his firm's detriment the commissioner seemed determined to prefer the others. The Millers never again wasted their time tendering for a naval yard contract, though it is known that in the period of much-heightened demand owing to the Baltic crisis in 1809 they supplied, without tender, 30,000 feet of pine lumber.[163]

If Forsyth & Smith were well-known contractors to the navy, Fraser & Thom had never sold anything to the yard until two months before they became successful joint-tenderers. In October 1804 they had sold, without benefit of a tender, about 7,000 feet of plank and board, with Inglefield's approval.[164] Inglefield also accepted an offer for a rather larger consignment from Forsyth & Smith for boards and plank to repair *Cleopatra* and *Tartar*.[165] Again this was done without tenders, when they were already three months into their joint contract. It seems obvious that the agents and principals in each firm had easy access to the commissioner's drawing room, while the rest of the world had to make do with his secretary's office.

The consortium failed to complete their contract on time, and begged in September 1805 for an extension, while seeking payment for the portion then delivered. They claimed that as they had given preference to Nova Scotia growth, only a small proportion of oak timber was cut "owing to the lateness of the season & uncommon depth of snow, which here, and in all the northern parts of America exceeded anything that has been known for thirty years past."[166] They turned to the American market where they bought a consignment of white oak at 40s. a ton more than the contract stipulated for grey oak. Their second excuse also described as "equally unexpected and unprecedented in these colonies, tended very much to retard and thwart us in the delivery of the timber, and caused nearly a suspension of all business on or near the waters namely the vigorous system of pressing which took place last spring and summer on shore as well as afloat." When the navy pressed the entire crew of their brig *Sophy* when she arrived in

Halifax from the Bay of Fundy, laden with timber and plank, the "whole country was thrown into consternation. When it was known that no regard was paid to persons employed immediately in the service of the navy yard, it was vain to attempt by any encouragement to induce men to come near the harbour of Halifax." The plea succeeded and the delay was granted. Their mismanagement effectively delayed by several months the completion of the only two warships ever built by the naval yard before 1820.[167]

Whatever the contract did for the house of Forsyth & Smith, it seems to have launched Fraser & Thom, who between 1806 and 1811 became important local suppliers to the yard. They maintained a connection with the Miramichi and several ships were sent there from the yard to fetch their timber and plank.[168] They were awarded another contract in December 1806 which included pine and spruce plank.[169] In 1808 they had to be reminded to deliver "with despatch" the consignment of yellow pine plank they had agreed to supply.[170] They also shared in an 1808 contract to supply timber.[171] The following year they sold a small cargo of white pine lumber from New Brunswick,[172] having earlier delivered 20,000 board feet of New Brunswick white pine plank, destined for the English yards.[173] In 1811 they offered another small cargo of red pine plank from Miramichi, at one-third the price of Canadian deals.[174] It was the last evidence of their role as suppliers to the yard.

Besides the usual activities of an overseas base, the Halifax yard acted as a distribution centre for all sorts of wood products needed not only in the English dockyards but also at foreign bases. It became a major entrepôt from 1778 for the procurement and shipment of masts, bowsprits, yards, spars, deals, and timber for the home yards as well as the naval establishments permanently based in the West Indies or temporarily established elsewhere in North America during the War of Independence. This was unique to Halifax among all the Empire's overseas bases before 1820.

Supplies sent to Jamaica, Antigua, and later Bermuda were coordinated by the commissioner and successive commanders-in-chief. Their task was principally to determine how the supplies were to be shipped: either stowed on warships or by hiring suitable vessels in Nova Scotia.

That the British navy was already dependent on masts supplied with the help of the Halifax yard before the crisis created when the Baltic became closed to the British in 1808 is little appreciated. By 1801, the Navy Board estimated that it then needed about 18,000 tons of timber, 13,000 tons of hemp to make about 15,260 tons of cordage, 1,400 tons of iron, 949 tons of copper, 200 tons of copper boltstaves, 18,000 barrels of tar, 5,500 barrels of pitch, 371,000 deals, 500 masts, and 111,000 wooden blocks.[175] The cost was £2.9 million; half the masts came from North America.

It quickly became apparent that the timber resources of Nova Scotia, in so far as they were known by 1783 or even by 1815, would not suffice. Those of New Brunswick and, after 1808, of Upper Canada and Lower Canada, came to dominate this supply. It is noteworthy that in 1815 when the naval yard at last turned to the task of repairing its anchor wharf, which the Navy Board had authorized as early as 1807, and the new set of tenement houses erected for the hospital officers that year, the wood came, not from Nova Scotia's forests, but from New Brunswick, the price being half that prevailing in the wood market at Halifax.[176]

This meant that Nova Scotia's wood merchants had to maintain business contacts both at Saint John and on the Miramichi, if they were to compete for the supply either of the careening yard and squadron on the one hand, or the garrison on the other. The New Brunswick partners or agents of such Halifax-based enterprises not only had to keep their principals abreast of rapid wartime price changes for wood products and labour costs in order to bid successfully on a contract, but also to ensure the timely supply either of timber or lumber once a contract was won. If the supply of the naval yard and garrison remained a significant part of the Halifax wood market, wood merchants also supplied the expanding private wholesale market either for ship building or repair in the maritime colonies, or for timber export to the burgeoning English market, based especially in London and Liverpool.

Finally, it seems reasonable to conclude that the opening of the timber market in England from British North America by the British navy initiated the process of familiarizing the English with Nova Scotia's wood products. British North American timber, an insignificant English import commodity before 1800, by 1808–12 became more than 60 per cent of total British timber imports, and by 1830 more than 82 per cent. If the impact on the Ottawa, the Gatineau, the St John, and the Miramichi river valleys was especially important, it was no less so on select regions of Nova Scotia.[177]

Chapter Nine

PAYING BILLS AND RAISING CASH

"I have heard some say that if it were not for the troops and navy about Halifax, that we would have no money in circulation."[1]

The naval yard, when paying both wages to its workers and the invoices from local contractors, acted as a quasi-bank. In this way it resembled the activities of the British army in North America, which helped fuel the money markets wherever their deputy-paymasters established themselves.[2] Like them, the Halifax naval storekeeper was responsible for keeping the cash box adequately supplied. To do this he advertised in the Halifax newspapers for those who possessed cash surpluses and who wished to exchange some cash for sterling bills of exchange. This navy bill of exchange, drawn on the naval pay office in London, was usually at thirty days' sight, at which point it began to earn interest. The bill became part of the navy's unfunded debt, guaranteed by government. These newly-drawn bills of exchange then became instruments of exchange in the Halifax money market. The final holders sent them to London to be redeemed, using the proceeds for a variety of purposes, but usually to pay off commercial or private debts owing in England. The navy bill, like those drawn by the army abroad, was usually considered an excellent form in which to hold liquid capital.

Approval for such bills of exchange being drawn had first to be obtained from the yard's resident commissioner, or in his absence the commander-in-chief, or senior sea captain. The procedure was spelled out in successive editions of the so-called *General Instructions*. Thereupon the naval storekeeper contacted the postmaster, the collector of customs, the receiver for Greenwich hospital and, from 1807, the registrar of the vice-admiralty court, "or other offices in the practice of remitting money to England on account of government" to inform them of the yard's cash needs.[3] This was done before the storekeeper tested the local money market which was dominated by the import merchants of Halifax.

By the time the navy established itself in Halifax and began to construct a careening yard in the 1750s, an impressive and successful system of public finance had been flourishing in Britain for decades. The British government from the 1690s had acquired a reputation, unsurpassed by any other European state with an extensive colonial empire, for both borrowing money and in paying interest regularly on its accumulating national debt. The size of the debt, which occasioned excessive and needless political anxiety and thus helped trigger the revolt in America in the 1770s, became an expanding instrument for investment by capitalists, a subject now understood well.[4] It enabled Britain in wartime to put far more battalions into the field, subsidize many more foreign troops, and equip and man more warships than would otherwise have been possible.

In the earliest days of Halifax, frequently the naval storekeeper could not raise enough cash in the colony, so rudimentary was its early economy and so dependent was it on government spending. He had to resort to the Boston or New York money markets, in the same manner as his military counterpart. The only loss ever experienced in shipping specie to Halifax occurred when sloop *Granby* with an experienced crew was lost at the mouth of Halifax harbour. Much of the cash was recovered, despite the fact that the poor fishers nearby secreted some of it.[5] The details in Table 9.1 provide, among other things, a rare view of the variety of coins then in circulation.

This American cash source dried up in 1775 with the outbreak of hostilities along the American coast. Thereafter the cash needs of the careening yard were filled elsewhere, principally in Jamaica but occasionally also from England. Later, in the first decade of the nineteenth century and beyond, when the cash demands on the yard were extreme, cash had to be imported from Jamaica in large quantities.

When purchasing coin elsewhere, officers faced several problems. The most important related to the exchange rate obtained for sterling bills, an issue imperfectly understood by many sea officers. The navy, like all institutions of the British government, dealt in sterling. Yet each of the colonies, Nova Scotia included, developed a different currency

Table 9.1   Specie Recovered from Wreck of sloop *Granby*, 1771

	Rate	Rate	Value
	£	H£	H£
Bag of gold unmarked			
161 half-joes	36s.	40s.	322. 0.0.
488¼ guineas	21s.	23s. 4d.	569.12.6.
75 pistoles	16s. 6d.	18s.	67.10.0.
9¼ moidores	27s.	30s.	13.17.6.
3 French guineas	20s.	22s.	3. 6.0
Bag No. 1			
1,847 pistareens	10¾d.	1s.	92. 7.0.
410 half-pistareens	5⅜d.	6d.	10. 5.0
3 quarter-$	4s. 6d.	1s. 3d.	0. 3.9.
Bag No. 2			
$1,109	4s. 6d.	5s.	277. 5.0.
34 half-$	2s. 3d.	2s. 6d.	4. 5.0.
275 quarter-$	1s. 1½d.	1s. 3d.	17. 3.9.
225 eighth-$	6¾d.	1s. 7½d.	7. 0.7½.
1 pistareen	10¾d.	1s.	0. 1.0.
Bag unmarked			
$1,489	4s. 6d.	5s.	372. 5.0.
Bag unmarked			
$1,579	4s. 6d.	5s.	394.15.0.
			2,151.17.1½.

Source: Gerrish accounts, 1757–73. PRO. ADM17/150, fol. 338.

of account that exchanged with sterling at par, and that varied from colony to colony. In Nova Scotia, H£111 12s. were the equivalent of £100 sterling, or par of exchange. This Halifax currency was also employed as the local measure of value in all other Gulf of St Lawrence colonies, as well as in Quebec, and later in Upper and Lower Canada. Yet the par of exchange was very different both in Massachusetts,[6] in New York,[7] and in the Caribbean colonies where Nova Scotia merchants principally traded. At the same time, the rate of exchange between each of these colonial currencies and sterling at times rose above or fell below this theoretical par of exchange. However varied and confusing it might appear to a later age, contemporary merchants were well-familiar with the phenomenon and remained untroubled by oscillations in exchange rates. To that extent it was very useful to the yard that its first naval storekeeper, Joseph Gerrish, had been a competent New England merchant.

204 Part Three: Economic Impact

The naval yard, like the Halifax military garrison, to pay its accounts and its workers, imported into Nova Scotia cash in the form of Spanish pesos, known as dollars. Surviving evidence indicates that, between 1775 and 1780 and between 1803 and 1815, dollars worth almost H£283,000 were imported by the Halifax naval yard. The cash came principally from Jamaica, where public bills of exchange generally sold at a premium, arising from the island's extensive trade with Spanish America. As the balance of that commerce generally favoured Jamaica in most years, a great influx of coin, mainly pesos, occurred. This meant that both the navy there and the army had access to as much cash as was needed locally. Indeed, there was sufficient cash to export, without eroding the exchange value of sterling. Merchants of Jamaica, in making remittances to England, seldom risked sending cash to settle their accounts abroad. Instead they procured "good bills on London, upon ... tolerable terms."[8] No better bills of exchange could be found in the money market than those supplied by the army and navy.

This situation contrasted markedly with Nova Scotia, which, owing to its feeble and unprofitable trading links, was always chronically short of specie.[9] Before 1820, the colony traded favourably with no part of the world. It was able to balance its accounts only because the British government every year spent such comparatively large sums in the province. In addition, the colony's economy limped along through credit extended to merchants principally by their suppliers in Britain and the United States. This in turn fuelled the colony's imports.

Commissioner Inglefield pointed to one such avenue of trade when he offered an explanation of the continual financial problems he encountered in 1811. "The principal cause of it," he believed, "is attributed ... to the balance of trade between this province and the States of America being decidedly against the former." He explained:

> The growth of wheat being very precarious as yet, flour for the use of the inhabitants, the navy and army, is almost entirely imported from the States where it is considered a ready money article and therefore, dollars and gold coin are generally sent from hence to pay for it ... It might be presumed that specie, flowing into the States from this and various other and greater sources, would be in abundance and the merchants of that country having remittances to make to England, would be anxious to purchase our government bills at par, or even at a premium but the East Indies trade carried on by them to a great

amount operates with respect to them as the flour trade does with respect to this province as a constant drain for dollars.[10]

The net cost of flour to Nova Scotia's economy, he claimed, exceeded the annual export earnings from fish and gypsum together.

Of the H£283,000 in cash imported by the careening yard, about 46 per cent arrived between 1812 and 1815, when spending peaked during the war with the United States. Always carried on a warship, for which the captain earned 1 per cent freight money, during war years the cash was brought first to Bermuda in one ship and from Bermuda to Halifax in another. The details are in Table 9.2. The urgency to import cash arose from the exchange rate which moved against sterling when the cash needs of the navy and army in Nova Scotia became excessive. A slight discount, of perhaps 1 or 2 per cent, however disagreeable to the commissioner or the Navy Board, was barely tolerable. When the discount rose to 15 and 17 per cent, as it did in 1811 and 1812 and then to 22.5 per cent in 1813 a policy of importing cash was adopted. If it stemmed the increasing discount at which sterling exchanged, it failed to return the exchange to par, as military and naval spending continued at an unusually high level. Once spending subsided as it had by late-1815 and throughout 1816, sterling for the first time in years sold

Table 9.2   Cash Imported into the Halifax Yard, 1775–1815

	H£	Exported from
1775–6	22,222	England
1778	5,555	England
1780	5,556	England
1803	10,278	England
1806	42,692	Jamaica
1808–9	33,002	Jamaica
1810–11	31,600	Jamaica
1812–13	78,727	Jamaica
1815	53,250	Jamaica
TOTAL	282,882	

Note: 85 per cent from Jamaica
Sources: Anderson accounts, 1799–1803. PRO. ADM17/152. Dawes accounts, 1806–13, 1815. PRO. ADM17/155–160, ADM17/162.

at a premium against Halifax currency. By 1817 the premium was between 3 and 6 per cent.[11] Thus the commercial weakness of Nova Scotia led to a perennial shortage of specie in the Halifax money market, that in turn added to the British cost of war in North America.

As I demonstrated in my earlier study of Vice Admiral Sir Peter Warren, in 1745 the first commander of the North American squadron, well-informed sea officers serving on foreign stations could become as well-placed as any merchant to understand these money matters.[12] So great were the needs of a naval force sent to serve on a distant coast that it was incumbent upon squadron or fleet commanders to become familiar with such affairs, or at least have business-minded and discreet secretaries on whom they might depend.

When Rear Admiral Montagu assumed command of the squadron in 1771 and based himself, not in Halifax, but in Boston, he assumed the responsibility for securing cash for the Halifax yard with bills of exchange. The negotiations were undertaken by his secretary, who charged the Navy Board 2.5 per cent. The sea captains tried to charge 2 per cent freight to convey the cash to Halifax. When the Navy Board complained of these excessive charges for freight money, they insisted that the business remain in the hands of the naval storekeeper at Halifax, as less costly. Stung by this implied rebuke, and believing his honour to be involved, the admiral sought clarification from the naval storekeeper about the rate for freight money paid the captains, the rate of commission for his agent and if a 1.5 per cent commission was habitually paid the merchant for negotiating bills at Boston. "It was your duty Sir, to have pointed out to me if any unusual charge was made in freight or negotiating bills. I tryed many merchants but none would undertake to transact it at less ... In future you may take such methods of getting your money matters transacted as you think proper, I desire to have nothing to do with it."[13]

In response Gerrish provided Montagu with a brief history of and lesson in currency exchange. Noting that Halifax navy bills had been negotiated at Boston and New York for the first time in 1765, he remarked that the merchant's commission was then 1 per cent and the captain's freight money 2 per cent. By 1768 the commission had risen to 1.5 per cent though in 1769 Commodore Hood negotiated with commissioners of the customs at Boston for no fee. Under Gambier in 1770–71, the commissions reverted to 1.5 per cent.[14] He also explained the advantages of dealing in Boston, where par was M£133 33s. for every £100. This meant that when the Spanish dollar cost 4s.6d. sterling, it cost 6s. in Massachusetts currency and 5s. in Halifax currency. Thus $1,000 in coin purchased in Boston for £225 could be paid out in Halifax for £250, a gain to the crown of £25 or 10 per cent. If sterling fell against Massachusetts currency, as it did by 7 per cent in 1771 for instance, a loss could occur as "the price of the dollar will be advanced in proportion to the deficiency and consequently so much less will be gained in paying it away at Halifax."[15]

With these details, Montagu went on the offensive, telling the Navy Board that he was fully "capable of judging which is the properest way of sending public money to Halifax. I own I am much hurt, that, after many years' practice of sending money to that place without any fault found with the exorbitant charge of freight that it should be altered during my command. Be assured, gentlemen, my proportion of the freight does not make it an object worth my attention."[16]

Montagu misinformed the Board by stating that in almost every year cash would have to be raised outside of Nova Scotia as Gerrish could never raise more than £3,000 or £4,000 in cash by issuing navy bills in Halifax. Gerrish's successor, Williams, found that he was able, by the end of 1773, to raise in Halifax as much as £10,000 or £15,000 in cash at or about par, and no longer needed to compete in the Boston or New York money markets.[17]

With hostilities in 1775 these hopes were soon blasted. By August 1775 sterling was selling at a 15 per cent discount, and threatened to fall further, making it difficult "to procure money at any rate."[18] Even had the yard staff consulted the accounts for the previous war, they could have no clear notion what the new war would do to exchange rates. Between mid-July 1757 and the end of September 1762, for example, when Gerrish had drawn bills valued at H£93,395, only 30 per cent were at par and the balance at a premium. Of the 70 per cent which sold at a premium, almost one-third were issued at between 2.5 and 5 per cent premium, a quarter at 5 to 8 per cent premium, and the balance ranged up to 15 per cent premium.[19]

Then, at the outbreak of a new war, the Navy Board asked that £10,000 in coin be shipped immediately to defray the contingent expenses of the Halifax yard.[20] This occasioned the purchase of an iron chest in which to store the cash in the storekeeper's office.[21] By the end of the year the new commissioner, Arbuthnot, reported that less than £2,300 remained.[22] In March 1776 a second shipment of £10,000, also in Spanish dollars, was sent from England to Halifax.[23] The next shipment occurred in 1778 when £5,000 was shipped to Halifax.[24] By 1780

Table 9.3 Sterling Bills of Exchange Sold, 1757–1814

Years	Annual Average
1757–71	£12,900
1790–9	£22,770
1800–2	£ 7,234
1803–14	£20,333

Note: no data for missing years.
Sources: Gerrish accounts, 1757–73. PRO. ADM17/150; Thomas accounts, 1780–90. ADM17/151; Anderson accounts, 1799–1803. ADM17/152; Dawes accounts, 1803 to 1814. ADM17/153–61, NMM. HAL/E/34, fol. 20, NMM. ADM/BP/25a, fol. 26, 30b, 31b.

there was renewed pressure on the rate of exchange and Commissioner Hughes suggested a further shipment of £4,000 or £5,000. Though he had been cautious in the yard's expenditures, he blamed his difficulties on the military. As "the considerable sums of money, on demand, for the use of the army, will, sometimes, enable the merchant to make his own conditions, and if we want cash at that time, we are obliged to comply with them."[25]

The end of hostilities, a reduced squadron, and the withdrawal of much of the military force in Nova Scotia by mid-1784, saw the exchange rate return to par. Of the bills valued at H£10,523 18s. issued by Edgecombe, in the eight months he acted as storekeeper in 1784–5, almost 60 per cent were tendered at par, and the rest at a 2.5 per cent premium.[26] By 1785 sterling was selling at a premium of between 2 and 3 per cent[27] and in 1786 and 1787 between 1.5 and 2.5 per cent.[28]

When cash shortages were acute, the yard borrowed cash from the garrison and repaid it, without interest, when next able to do so. In like manner, on occasion the military borrowed cash from the naval yard. The first such recorded instance occurred in 1794, when Commissioner Duncan requested a loan from Major General Ogilvie for £2,000 or £3,000 "as soon as money can be procured."[29]

The dimension of the need can be illustrated by tabulating the annual value of the bills drawn at Halifax, and making comparison with all overseas bases. In 1803, when the Halifax yard issued bills of exchange worth £8,850, it represented 11.8 per cent of the total for all foreign yards, while in 1805, at £37,326, it had risen to 18.8 per cent of all such issuances, as Table 9.3 indicates.

On occasion, the yard's advertisements for cash did not produce the results intended. In September 1803, for instance, when the yard advertised for £2,000 in cash, no offers were received. Dawes, the naval storekeeper, placed a second advertisement for £3,000, in which he reminded merchants that as the New York packet, expected shortly, was the last bound for England from Halifax that year, they should make use of the opportunity to secure a draft on the Navy Board by purchasing one of the yard's bills.[30] Only £400 in cash was proffered, which Commissioner Inglefield found "so inadequate and the discount so exorbitant" that the offer was rejected "as it might establish the exchange."

To solve the longer-term problem, the commissioner requested a shipment from England of milled Spanish dollars in the amount of £15,000 to £20,000. Upon receipt of this news, the Navy Board arranged with the Admiralty, as the price of silver was then so high in London, to ship them from Jamaica in the spring of 1806, even if they had to pay 5 per cent above the usual price for dollars.[31] This shipment, amounting to £28,279 in silver dollars, arrived safely the following April.[32]

Dawes next discontinued the practice of paying all tradesmen's bills in cash. Thereafter those of £100 or more were paid, not in cash, but by bills of exchange at par.[33] The effect was to force those with larger accounts to accept a reduction in their invoices to the amount of the current exchange discount against sterling then in effect.

Faced with the immediate need to pay H£3,700 in monthly wages, bounties to naval volunteers, and tradesmen's bills,[34] he then accepted an offer of £2,500 from Forsyth & Smith at a 7.5 per cent discount.[35] By the end of the year, with less than H£170 in his cash balance, the storekeeper again advertised for a new £3,000 infusion in return for bills of exchange.[36] The arrival of the cash from Jamaica, and even more for the army, finally restored the rate of exchange to acceptable limits.[37] The rate remained steady when another H£11,267 in dollars reached Halifax before the end of 1806. Within a year the yard's cash balance had again fallen below £1,000 and advertisements were repeatedly inserted in the Halifax newspapers for cash to be tendered.[38] Some £3,000 was required in August, and £4,000 in November.[39] As cash was again tendered only at discounts, Vice Admiral Berkeley, in the absence of Inglefield who had returned temporarily to England on leave, ordered the prize agents for captors and claimants in the cases before the vice-admiralty court to supply the yard with dollars at par to the value of £10,000. In return, the admiral offered them sterling bills of exchange when sums were to be remitted to England.[40]

Discount, Berkeley explained to the Navy Board, had been as much as 10 per cent

> especially at those times when it was known the service was most in want. A considerable portion of my publick life having been dedicated to the investigation and final remedy of this very evil at another board, will perhaps serve as an apology for thinking it my duty to state it to you. Whenever the public services at this place have been supplied with money from home a premium has been given for good private bills. I cannot therefore see why the same should not be offered for those on government account. The peddling traffic of the United States with the East Indies however soon takes away the bullion and reduces the rate of exchange to par, and sometimes to a discount.[41]

Supplies of money from Great Britain or elsewhere alone provided "opportunities of getting it at par." Berkeley wanted the naval storekeeper to be given greater latitude to draw his bills for the ensuing quarter beforehand, "when the exchange is at par, or when a premium is offered." By this means he would avoid in future becoming "the victim of speculative avarice." Before he learned of the Board's reaction to this novel idea, he was forced to resurrect Inglefield's policy of paying tradesmen's and suppliers' accounts over £100 with bills of exchange.[42]

Help was at hand, for the Admiralty took up part of Berkeley's suggestion, with the Navy Board's agreement, to send to Halifax regularly – twice a year in dollars if available – £10,000 in cash. As in the spring of 1808, sterling in Jamaica was at a 20 per cent premium, the Board hoped to make a profit of £1,300 for every £10,000 sent to Halifax, if Halifax currency remained at par.

Their purpose in 1808 was the same as in 1795. Cash from Jamaica would defeat "the combination among the merchants" in Halifax, by reducing the exchange rate to par.[43] Captains involved in this freight were limited to a one-half per cent gratuity.[44] Crates packed with $42,000 in coins began to arrive the following August in Halifax.[45]

Some of the cash received from Jamaica was rerouted to Bermuda. Thus in November 1806, some dollars to the value of £800 were sent there, the first time such an entry is found in the Halifax yard correspondence or accounts.[46] In June 1808 Inglefield received a further order from the Navy Board to despatch another £1,500 to the small naval establishment.[47] Indeed it became the policy for Halifax to supply Bermuda on as regular a basis as possible with £3,000 in coin annually.[48]

This obligation forced the yard back into the money market in January 1809, when cash reserves had again evaporated. By May £10,000 had been raised by drawing bills[49] before a new infusion of cash reached the storekeeper's money chest.[50] As the sum received represented only half the sum promised by the Board and sterling remained at a discount in Halifax, for the first time recourse was now made to the Bahamas in search of £5,000 in dollars.[51] This scheme proved a failure as only £1,000 was raised. Dawes, the storekeeper, was placed again in the unenviable position of having to re-enter the money market with sterling at a 2.5 per cent discount and "likely to become still lower."[52] Before the next shipment arrived from Jamaica in December,[53] he had not only failed to raise cash from the vice-admiralty court,[54] but was forced to borrow £1,000 from the military chest, even as the balance sheet showed the yard to be indebted to its storekeeper in the amount of £3.4.9¼.[55]

For the previous eight years of Inglefield's tenure as commissioner, the exchange rate was "almost invariably against government," varying from one to ten per cent discount.[56] Only on two occasions had sterling bills sold at a premium, once at 1.25 per cent in 1807 and on another occasion at 0.5 per cent in 1809. The solution to the yard's ability to meet its financial obligations at the end of 1809 seemed as distant as it had been at the outbreak of war almost seventeen years earlier.

Like most sea officers ignorant of the principles of supply and demand, the commissioner railed against the "combinations which merchants sometimes enter into for keeping up a high rate of exchange."[57] To circumvent this, in 1810 he again appealed to the Navy Board to ship either from England or from Jamaica £25,000 to £30,000 once or twice a year. Until $63,000 arrived that October from Jamaica, the yard survived on bills of exchange.[58] Of this sum the army immediately borrowed £3,000.[59] A further $63,000 arrived in March 1811 and had the desired impact on the exchange rate, but only for a few weeks.[60] By July, as the discount had risen to between 7.5 and 10 per cent, he begged again for £15,000 cash every six months, but this time, instead of going through the Navy Board, he wrote directly to Jamaica's resident commissioner.[61] When the Board learned of this it gave the necessary directions to the Jamaica yard officials.[62] By November the exchange rate for public bills in Halifax ranged between 12.5 and 15 per cent, and private bills between 20 and 22.5 per cent.[63] This forced Inglefield to beg money directly from England "to prevent the service from suffering," a proposal rejected by the Navy Board.[64] In December 1811 he was forced to sell bills at from 16 to 19 per cent discount, an unprecedented level.[65] In February 1812, he managed to borrow £2,000 from the army,[66] a month before his precious shipment of coin arrived from Jamaica.[67] This brought the exchange rate down, but only to an 8 to 10 per cent discount range and only for the months of April and May.

By June, public bills, triggered by the outbreak of war with the United States and the anticipation of huge public spending in Nova Scotia by the British government, sold at a staggering 20 to 25 per cent discount. Before the next shipment of coin arrived in October, Inglefield found himself again begging shipments directly from England "to prevent the service being distressed or embarrassed by a want of specie to pay the workmen, or for the purchases of necessary stores."[68] Again the Navy Board rejected the scheme, placing its reliance on Jamaica.[69]

It thus became clear that losses to government on the exchange in Halifax were but one of the inevitable costs of the war. However greatly this offended the principles of the Navy Board and its officials, shipping silver coins to Halifax from England, in view of the other pressing needs which the war threw up in 1812, was a solution never to be adopted in this era.

The crisis continued to deepen. In August 1812 wages, normally paid monthly, had not been paid for three months. Advertisements to raise cash received no tenders.[70] When at length Jamaican coin arrived in mid-October, two-thirds was already committed in wages and purchases of stores for the yard, as Inglefield described in his very last letter as resident commissioner.[71]

The new commissioner, Philip Wodehouse, once he was fully briefed, refused all tenders for cash above 15 per cent. As he could borrow none immediately from the military, his naval storekeeper could propose no other expedient than raising their demands for coin shipments to £40,000 a year for the balance of the war. He reminded the commissioner that the impact of the cash shortage struck hardest at the "families of people who work at the yard," when for many weeks they were denied their monthly wages.[72]

For his part, Wodehouse informed the Navy Board that for lack of cash the yard was unable to pay its pilots or seamen their bounties as volunteers. Furthermore, frequently they received offers of "small cargoes of very useful timber," and as the "owners are too poor to take bills," the merchants purchased them up with cash and then inflated the cost of the timber, making it impossible for the yard to purchase them with bills of exchange.[73] He failed to understand that the inflated prices offered to the navy were designed to compensate the vendors against loss as they had to convert the bills into sterling, when it was heavily discounted already.

When the next shipment from Jamaica arrived in February and March 1813, the £1,500 borrowed from the army was refunded them.[74] The situation remained grim for the balance of 1813 and into 1814, as bills remained at a discount of between 15 and 20 per cent.[75] Two large shipments of specie arrived from Jamaica in 1815 but only after the war's end, when pressure was already diminishing on the yard's resources.[76] Owing to the decreased demands at the yard, in April some £15,000 of this was immediately loaned to the military.[77] In June another $45,000 were sent to the military chest, by way of a loan, as surplus to the needs of the yard.[78]

In this whole matter, the only administrative reform introduced during the war was to centralize the raising of cash. Instead of having different services competing with one another, from June 1813 onwards the chief officer of the military commissariat was made responsible for the army, the Board of Ordnance, the naval yard, and the navy's Victualling Board and Transport Board. Each separate department, both army and navy, thereafter submitted annual estimates of their cash needs.[79] This spared the yard the need to advertise for tenders. Now the naval storekeeper merely applied to the deputy-commissary for whatever was immediately needed. In 1817, for instance, Dawes estimated that £21,500 would be needed for the following year.[80]

This particular reform the contractors to supply beef to the squadron, Messrs Starr and Shannon, found inconvenient and complained to the commissioner. Unable to secure payment when it was due them from the deputy-commissary, they begged to be allowed to revert to the earlier system, that of drawing bills on the Victualling Board, described in their contract. "When we have bills on hand it often happens," they explained, "that we can dispose of them readily by giving the merchants a short credit for a part of the sum."[81] Their proposal was rejected by the deputy-commissary, despite Wodehouse's advocacy of their proposal.[82] This procedure thus remained in force until the yard's virtual closure in 1819.

The one area of business which went profitably related to prize vessels purchased into the navy at the request of the commanders-in-chief. These were always paid for in bills of exchange at par, no matter what the current exchange might have been. If, owing to the heavy wartime discounts of sterling bills, this saved the government when purchasing such ships, it was a loss to the captors as their net proceeds, if converted in Nova Scotia, were reduced significantly by 10, 15, or even over 20 per cent owing to the exchange rate current at the time of payment.[83]

Thus, by selling bills of exchange to raise cash for the careening yard's expenditures, the naval storekeeper expanded the colonial money supply, wherever the bills circulated. In an average year between 1757 and 1771, the naval storekeeper issued such bills to the value of almost £13,000. The ability to issue bills of exchange was equally important to the operation of the careening yard, where, on the eve of war in 1772–74, for instance, such a sum approximated the total annual expenditures by the storekeeper.[84] In the absence of cash shipments from abroad, the capacity to raise funds locally kept the yard functioning. Cash crises developed only when expenditures rapidly rose, as they did on occasion in wartime when pressures on the Halifax money market from the navy, army, and the demands of commerce created serious cash shortages. The result was severe pressure on sterling and the consequent exchange losses sustained by the agencies of the British government in Halifax. When recourse was then made to large cash imports, especially from Jamaica, the effect was invariably temporary. Only with the restoration of peace in 1815 did sterling recover its value and once again sell at par or even at a premium. The ordeal of the Halifax yard was thus no different from the contemporary experience of the army in Halifax or elsewhere in places like Quebec.

In the severely restricted early Nova Scotia economy, before the outbreak of the war against rebel America, the role of the Halifax naval storekeeper and that of the several deputy-paymasters and commissaries in North America was probably crucial to the colony's commercial survival. For Nova Scotia, in the absence of important exports, British government spending there sustained the colony to a degree greater than any other economic activity before the arrival of loyalist refugees in the 1780s. Thereafter it helped fuel wartime inflation which led, during the war with the United States in 1812–15, to the colony's first full-blown economic boom. It was remembered during the economically stressful era of peace which followed. "Halifax may yet become in peace," a committee of the house of assembly announced in 1839, "what it was in the years of 1812 to 1815, during the American war."[85]

Conclusion

"The ship that ploughs the angry waves, what trace is left of her passage?"[1]

The need for continuous British naval involvement with Nova Scotia in the 1740s and 1750s surprised both the Admiralty and the Navy Board. Until the advent to power of the elder William Pitt, they successfully resisted such pressure for as long as possible. To accept the logic of the "Americans" in either Pelham's or Pitt's administrations required a fundamental change in thinking about North America. Before the 1740s most often the area was viewed as merely an appendage to Britain's primordial interests in the Caribbean and in Newfoundland. If Newfoundland bred seamen and increased commercial wealth from cod, and the West Indies generated even greater wealth from sugar cane, Nova Scotia promised only expense and trouble without much prospect of commercial wealth. Hostilities with France after 1755 triggered the need for a thorough reassessment of naval strategy in the North Atlantic. This was led less by the serving officers at the Admiralty Board than by politicians elsewhere in government.

Yet to newly-located settlers and colonial officials in Nova Scotia in the 1750s, the presence of a British naval squadron, however small – and not merely a station ship as elsewhere on the coast from Newfoundland to Georgia – was of crucial importance to its preservation as a crown colony. The navy had ensured the defeat of the French at the siege of Louisbourg in 1745. Later, when the British abandoned the fortress-town, the navy together with the military supported the new settlements of Halifax, Dartmouth, and Lunenburg, and attempted unsuccessfully to overawe the Acadiens and Mi'kmaq. The navy, which alone was able to carry the war to the French in America, transported and sustained the troops who won the crucial land battles.

The navy's presence in Halifax was given concrete form in the establishment of two important institutions, first the vice-admiralty court in 1749 and then the careening yard in 1758. The former gave an additional gloss to the range of public institutions established when Halifax became the colonial capital in the hectic summer of 1749. The latter helped to define the navy's new dependence on Nova Scotia as a base for its entire North American squadron. Built initially to confront France, the careening yard was still under construction when the French menace evaporated in mid-1760. The sudden collapse of French ambitions in North America in 1759–60 robbed the yard of its principal initial purpose. Thereafter, as long as that war lasted, naval strategy was directed to other theatres, especially in the West Indies, for which the Halifax base was only remotely useful.

With the dozen years of peace beginning in 1763, the new base was not dismantled though its establishment was drastically reduced. Instead, it continued to refit the North American squadron increasingly employed against the king's subjects in North America in the failed effort to impose imperial trade laws on recalcitrant colonists. As the navy's focus thus shifted south and west along the American coast, the northerly location of the yard in Halifax harbour proved less useful. Prevailing winter winds made beating up the coast from either other American ports or the West Indies almost impossible without sustaining great damage to masts, rigging, and sails. A new base, perhaps at New York or Newport, both of which were as ice-free as Halifax but far more accessible in winter, probably should have been established, as Commodore Colvill suggested at the time.

Cycles of war and peace had a powerful impact on the amount of work provided by the yard which otherwise was impervious to the boom and bust cycles of the maritime economy. War expanded employment opportunities at the yard, while peace required less labour as warships were paid off and laid up and the Halifax squadron drastically reduced.

The war with rebel America, underway in 1775, gave new purpose to the Halifax naval yard. Had a drydock adjoining the naval yard in Halifax been constructed as appears to have been first imagined in 1771, and the yard's workforce proportionately increased, this would have allowed many more warships to be repaired in North America. This might have had a decisive impact on the naval war in American waters fought principally with France from 1778. This in turn could have altered the military outcome. To have taken up the idea would have heralded a commitment by the Admiralty Board to a forward strategy in the Western Atlantic of far greater significance than it was prepared to recommend at any time during the war.

Perhaps as a consequence, when war was waged against rebel America, Halifax played a subsidiary role to that of New York in refitting and storing the ships on the North American coast, once the site at Turtle Bay on Manhattan's east side was expanded. The value of the Halifax naval base, at its least, was that it helped to preserve Nova Scotia as a British possession – a matter of peripheral importance in the overall shape of British strategic thinking before 1783. Yet during the first American war, the few warships in the waters around Nova Scotia failed to protect coastal settlements. American rebels raided even into the Bay of Fundy and along the Northumberland Strait. Halifax yard itself was never threatened, but the navy at times could not prevent American privateers from hovering off the very entrance to Halifax harbour or from targeting the western shore from Lunenburg to Annapolis Royal. From 1778 mast contractors for the navy began to harvest the forests in the St John River valley, as the war expanded in the Gulf of Maine, sufficient evidence that the navy had secured Nova Scotia from invasion. This had the significant effect of permitting a flow of masts, yards, bowsprits, and small spars to supply both the Halifax yard and those of New York, Jamaica, and Antigua, and from 1782 the English dockyards.

During the decade of peace which followed the first American war, the navy continued to treat the Atlantic Ocean as a British lake. When the great division rendered asunder the British political experiment in North America, the British navy, for its part, fell back on its Nova Scotia base. After 1783 the Americans, unwilling in peacetime to maintain a navy because of the cost, disposed of their warships in part as gifts to France and thereby no longer constituted a threat to British North America. During the decade which followed, when the British navy was without an enemy in the region, the Halifax careening yard was not only maintained but expanded as new structures were erected on the site.

It slowly became obvious that Halifax's northerly location remained a serious defect in the altered circumstances occasioned by the birth of the United States. Until 1794 there seemed no alternative. From the time in 1794 that the Admiralty became aware of the deep water passage at Ireland Island, the prospect of building a new, larger base at Bermuda was raised. Bermuda as a naval base was not an alternative to Halifax, but an inferior substitute for what New York had been between 1776 and 1783.

Bermuda had many disadvantages. It proved to be far more expensive to build than the Halifax yard, as many of the building materials had to be imported. There was a perpetual water shortage and the existing technology for a long time precluded the building of a drydock in its porous rock. The warmer climate hastened rot in ships and death among the crews. Navigation to the anchorage was quite difficult for larger ships, while the anchorage itself was exposed to gales. Its only advantage – its strategic location – proved crucial to the Admiralty. American hostility from 1807 onwards led directly to the decision taken two years later to build a considerable careening yard there. In the war of 1812–14 against the United States, its value was borne out as an ancillary site to Halifax to refit the fleet, even if it was still not fully operational as a naval base at war's end.

In the early stages of the long wars against France from 1793 to 1815, the Halifax squadron and hence the naval yard played a rather minor role. Thus, despite the onset of a period of apparently endless campaigning, the size of the yard's workforce scarcely expanded. The main activity of the modestly enlarged wartime squadron was to seize usually unarmed American vessels thought to be carrying contraband to France, a matter of small strategic importance. The constant patrolling along the United States coast nevertheless wore out the warships and their rigging. Their refitting thus made the existence of the Halifax yard a matter of real importance in maintaining a policy of trade interdiction. The alternative for the North American squadron, to have been based at a British or West Indies port, would no doubt have made the Admiralty's task of defeating the French and their Spanish allies at sea the more difficult.

As for his Majesty's enemies, few French or Spanish warships ventured into the waters off Nova Scotia. Between 1793 and 1815 the squadron took less than eighty French and Spanish ships, none of them in Nova Scotia waters. Of these, three were French frigates, one was a French sloop, and two were French corvettes. The rest were merchant ships. Such occasional successes could not prevent French warships, either from France or the West Indies, from readily getting into American ports to refit, a privilege not accorded the British. As there were no naval engagements of consequence, the work of the yard was the repair of routine damage resulting from single-ship engagements or sustained by stress of weather and constant cruising.

It was only in the heightened tension in Anglo-American relations from 1807 that Halifax became of crucial importance as a naval base. Yet, as increased naval scrutiny focused on coastal states from New York south, Halifax was increasingly seen again as being located too distant from the strategic centre.

The Admiralty between 1807 and 1814 remained so myopic, with their eyes fixed on the French fleet rebuilding in many continental ports – hence the disposition of English resources to sustain the bloated size of the fleets in home waters – they failed to build up the capacity of Halifax base in the face of the growing threat to peace posed by a bellicose American administration. Then, by deciding in the midst of war to build the base at Bermuda, the navy jeopardized its ability to sustain the fleet off the North American coast by using two underdeveloped bases, instead of one properly equipped and manned.

Thus, the resumption of war with France in 1793 eventually raised the profile of this isolated northern base, yet only when that war merged with the one launched in 1812 by the United States. In the long war with France, the Halifax yard was never of great strategic importance. Only during the unexpected war with the United States did the yard, largely neglected for two decades by both the Admiralty and its creature, the Navy Board, prove its worth. So great was the British naval response, by 1814 the yard at times seemed almost overwhelmed by an acute shortage of skilled workers. This, as we have seen, was partly the result of competing labour demands in the town of Halifax from private commercial interests whose wages the Navy Board failed to match.

By 1819 the careening yard had cost British taxpayers £1,550,000 or £25,000 a year, certainly a modest sum. This included the costs of building and maintaining the yard's structures, as well as the pay and allowances for all those who worked in the yard, including the frequent working parties of seamen. The sum included all the invoices submitted by suppliers to the yard and to workers brought from town to undertake a variety of tasks, from cleaning chimneys to horse and cart hire, as well as the cost of importing coin from England and Jamaica to pay these bills. When the last commissioner, Philip Wodehouse, departed in 1819, there were thirty-three major buildings, whose overall length, he proudly reported, was 2,270 feet, with a dozen minor structures all of which were surrounded by two kilometres of stone walls. There were also nine wharfs. There was a naval hospital and a newly-erected tenement of three spacious homes for the hospital's officers. Finally, overlooking the hospital and yard there was a controversial new mansion for the commander-in-chief. No longer a year-round naval base, it seemed then little more than a white elephant, even if a modest one by the standards of the home dockyards. It was not the last apparent folly financed by the Navy Board, as additions to the new Bermuda base and to other overseas bases after 1819 were to prove.

The yard from 1759 onwards regularly refitted most of the North American squadron in peace and wartime. It also occasionally repaired those stationed at Newfoundland or in the West Indies. In 1802 it refitted eight ships of the line and some frigates of the Jamaica squadron and, in 1805, the entire Leeward Islands squadron. The numbers annually in North American waters varied greatly, from the lowest in 1784–92, when about a dozen ships used the Halifax yard as a base, to 1814, when the yard was overwhelmed trying to refit the 120 ships and vessels of all sizes on the coast.[2] Refitting was confined to the external hull, and less serious internal repairs. Lacking a drydock, Halifax sent home warships with major structural defects or those needing complete rebuilding.

The great variety of labour required was undertaken by a workforce, which, at its largest in September 1813 and February 1814, employed 267 men, exclusive of the hospital and other naval establishments around the harbour. Among the skilled workers, shipwrights and caulkers dominated other classes. There were few officers. Until 1775, when the resident commissioner was first appointed, the naval yard was managed by the naval storekeeper, the master shipwright, and the master attendant, working through various foremen.[3] A fifth officer, a boatswain, was added to the establishment in 1800.

By 1820, the yard was reduced to a mere depot, as it had been briefly in 1763–8. In 1819 the establishment was reduced to nine: a boatswain, a gate porter, a painter, and six shipwrights. They were permitted to occupy the yard's houses, so long as they maintained them. The yard, the hospital complex, even the newly-furnished admiral's house became surplus to needs. Nor were the nine buoys at the harbour entrance and four in the inner harbour any longer maintained by the yard staff. Snow was left uncleared in winter, and drains left

Conclusion 223

unclogged in spring.[4] Wharfs and breastworks, battered by winter storms, fell into disrepair. Shingles torn off roofs and siding off yard buildings by gale force winds were not replaced. The paint, formerly so generously applied, was soon bleached away by the salt spray.

In the absence of any official inquiry into the operations of the Halifax yard, it is difficult at this distance to estimate its efficiency. Neither the officers, from either the yard or the squadron, nor the Navy Board ever complained of inefficiency, while complaints from sea captains usually related to the priority given individual ships brought in for repair. There is some evidence that efficiency may have been influenced by the role of the Navy Board, which desired to manage all overseas yards as if no ocean separated them from the Naval Office in London. This bore more heavily, not on the workers, but on the officers. At times the Board heavily criticized them for their perceived inadequacies, but only regarding the regularity and accuracy in completing reports. The subject of efficiency was never raised. Only on rare occasions was this highly centralized system challenged from Halifax. Confronted by effective leadership from Commissioner Wodehouse, the Board, among other things, conceded some local autonomy over wages paid in the yard.

Perhaps because the original overseas royal naval dockyards were acquired by conquest, the Navy Board continued to think of and refer to them as "foreign." This seems consistent with a general naval mentality. The Navy Board also referred to North American timber along with that of the Baltic as "foreign." That the overseas dockyards were considered by the Navy Board to be quite different is obvious whenever there was a matter where the Navy Board wanted the expert opinions of the principal officers at the royal dockyards – as in the case in 1783 when the relative merits of using copper or iron bolts for fastening copper sheeting to ships' bottoms were an issue – it consulted those in England alone, while ignoring the opinions from those they might have received abroad. Navy Board commissioners considered places like Gibraltar or Halifax to be very remote and quite different from those within the commissioners' relatively easy reach in southern England.

What was unique to the Halifax naval yard, among all the overseas yards, was its role from 1778 as an entrepôt for the procurement and shipment of masts, bowsprits, yards, small spars, deal, and timber for the home yards as well as the naval yards in the West Indies, and New York during the War of Independence. The importance of Halifax in supplying both New York and the West Indies with wrought masts during the war, as well as the need for an officer with the appropriate experience and authority to conclude suitable contracts were both issues so vital to the war effort that the Navy Board was able to argue successfully in 1782 that a resident commissioner should be continued there once peace had been negotiated.[5] By 1807, when the matter had become strategically important to the navy, all but local contracts were thereafter negotiated in London.

Not intended for shipbuilding – only two modest warships were built in the Halifax careening yard, both begun in 1805 – the yard's establishment never exceeded that assigned it in 1776–83.[6] Additionally, in 1808–10 about eight or so pettyaugers of fifty and eighty tons were built, though a dozen were initially ordered, to be employed in amphibious operations against the Spanish, the original Trinidad builder being sent to the Halifax yard to instruct the master shipwright and yard foreman in their design and construction.[7] Some of the vessels ended life ingloriously as either yard boats in Bermuda or Halifax, the rest being put up for public auction in 1815.

Two other special roles should be noted. First, to a limited degree, the naval yard helped man and supply the naval yards and squadrons established on Lake Champlain during the War of 1812, as well as those in Upper Canada especially in 1812 and 1813, before these establishments were largely supplied directly by the Navy Board. Second, it organized the supply of building materials for the construction undertaken from 1809 of the new naval base at Bermuda.[8] A prefabricated storehouse, small office, three houses fifty by twenty feet, and a naval hospital were provided from Halifax, all by contract.

Was the Halifax naval yard worth the £1.55 million spent by 1820 to sustain it? As it was not a yard for the construction of warships, its value must be judged principally by its utility in wartime. If Halifax was built against the French to ensure that a fully-equipped fleet could be ready early in the season, it was useful principally against the Americans. Bermuda was designed against the Americans, but it had little subsequent value until the Great War of 1914–18, as Britain, after 1815, followed unswervingly a foreign policy that would never again allow it to become involved in a maritime war with the United States.

That from the worldwide perspective of the British Empire, the Halifax careening yard was of marginal importance, except occasionally in war, is clearly seen from the size of its establishment. Of all British overseas naval bases before 1820 it was one of the smallest, with far fewer workers than Antigua, Jamaica, Gibraltar, Madras, Malta, and Trincomalee. It was only larger than the bases in Upper Canada and in the Cape Colony of South Africa. Ironically, the harbour was perhaps never again as important for the British navy after 1759, when yard construction began, than it had been during the five previous years.

Finally, what value was the naval yard to Halifax and Dartmouth? Its active presence doubtless elevated the status of the town and harbour. It helped put as much of a stamp on eighteenth-century Halifax harbour, unique to the maritime provinces, as did the later building of the military citadel there by the army between the 1820s and 1850s.

As the largest industrial complex in British North America, the yard conferred on the region a degree of wealth it would not otherwise have attained. Naval yard spending was important to the local economy and influenced patterns elsewhere, especially in New Brunswick. Added to this were the annual expenditures incurred in the region by other naval departments drawn to Halifax by the careening yard: the Sick and Hurt Board with its naval hospital, the Transport Board, and the Victualling Board. To this must be added spending by sea officers and seamen. Halifax and Dartmouth were probably content to pay whatever social costs arose from the presence of the navy in their midst. The funds annually entering the Halifax economy gave the region a marginally higher standard of living than would have been the case if the yard had not been maintained after 1763. Its replacement by Bermuda was an economic blow as naval spending in Nova Scotia quickly evaporated after 1819.

Naval spending at the yard at the best of times gave permanent employment to several dozen artificers, watchmen, and labourers. Its apprenticeship system offered tenure to a few shipwright families. It provided seasonal employment to two or three horses, carts, and their drivers. It helped sustain a number of neighbourhood grog shops. It paid blacks to clean the necessaries, women to convert fearnaught and kersey fabric into overcoats for the watchmen, and to repair hospital beds. It purchased annually twenty or thirty dozen birch brooms and innumerable ballast baskets, probably made by Mi'kmaq women.

The yard was both a producer and a consumer of goods. As a producer its workers built boats and small vessels, and repaired ships and government vessels of every sort. The yard sold, not only to commercial customers but to other government departments as well, an increasingly wide variety of materials from its stores, from anchors and spars to specially-cut pieces of ship's timber.

Those who did business with the yard were best-positioned to profit. The range was large, from those who painted the yard buildings in their characteristic red ochre and tar mix, with the window frames and doors painted white, to the bookbinders, stationers, and newspaper proprietors who printed a stream of advertisements.

Although the bulk of the naval stores needed in the yard came already manufactured from England, shipped by hired or naval storeships, a great array of commodities were purchased from local suppliers. These included coal, bricks, stone, and sand to every sort of locally-produced wood product from firewood to boats with oars. Imported goods such as pitch, tar, and turpentine, sheathing paper, lamp oil, linseed and train oil, paint, paint brushes, and hardware of every possible description were also provided the yard by town traders and merchants. Agricultural commodities such as corn, oats, bran, and hay for the government horses were also locally supplied.

The yard stimulated business by attracting capitalists who supplied the most valuable services and products. These were mast contractors, wood merchants, and provisions contractors. They included shipowners who leased their vessels to the navy, especially in wartime. Then they were used to transport naval stores, house enemy prisoners, serve as cartel ships, freight sticks from the St John and Miramichi river valleys, and to ship coal from Cape Breton and Pictou collieries to the yard.

These same entrepreneurs also profited from the naval storekeeper's role as paymaster, when the yard acted as a quasi-bank. To pay yard workers and ships' crews who earned extra wages in working parties ashore, as well as small tradesmen's bills, there was a constant demand for cash. The yard in effect printed commercial money in the form of navy bills of exchange. If occasionally shipments of coin were ordered from Boston and New York before 1775 and afterwards from England and Jamaica, the yard's cash demand was principally met from local sources. Those who tendered for navy bills constituted the capitalist class in the colony. In return, the successful seller of coin acquired an interest-bearing sterling instrument, the best form of transferable security available. This was then exchangeable in any commercial transaction in town, or used to make remittances wherever commerce was conducted by them: in the British Isles, the West Indies, the United States, or in other Gulf of St Lawrence colonies. The cash in the hands of the workers and suppliers soon circulated back into the hands of the capitalists – some of them women – that allowed them later to sell coin again to the yard.

First in importance, among those who did well out of the yard, was William Forsyth. He arrived in the colony shortly after his fellow Scot, Henry Duncan, became resident commissioner in 1783. With Duncan's support and his own acumen, Forsyth understood that at Halifax at least, government business alone commanded the commercial heights. Combining private commercial ventures in fish with the contracting for the navy, he found an agreeable place at the public trough. Within five years, Forsyth ran the Halifax business end of a mast contracting partnership based in Greenock and London, an arrangement which endured in various forms long after his death. To lobby the government and retain personal contact with his partners Forsyth found himself crossing the wartime Atlantic. He was merely the most prominent of those who frequented the commissioner's mansion and the naval storekeeper's office.

The reputation of the yard, as distinct from the fleet, is uncertain. In every conflagration of any consequence in the town, teams of yard workers with their primitive pumping fire engines gave assistance both to the town and the military. It was a kind of human insurance policy against a disaster which might one day afflict the yard. Before 1820, on this account the yard never had to call in its many credits. The one major fire, that of the naval hospital in November 1819, could not have been contained no matter how many fire engines the town could have despatched.

Examples of public charity by the yard were rare. One of the few recorded occurred in 1817, when blankets, beds, and slops, at the request of the Earl of Dalhousie, were donated to a "Committee of a Charitable Association, formed in consequence of the great distress of the Poor at this time."[9] Ship's bells were provided first to the Catholic chapel in Halifax,[10] and then to the Anglican church in Windsor.[11]

If the navy was despised for the press gang, the yard gained merit by paying regular sums to those Nova Scotians who assisted in retaking naval deserters and stragglers. Payments were also made to those who found volunteers for the naval service. The yard also rewarded those willing to help in naval disasters, paying not only out-of-pocket expenses, but giving rewards as well for exceptional service.

Any unpopularity associated with the yard would likely have related to its workforce, many of whom were recruited around the harbour. It dismissed many workers regularly for neglect of duty which usually meant absenteeism. It dismissed others for minor infractions, especially relating to the use of liquor. It rarely hired an Acadien or an Afro-Nova Scotian. It was intolerant of those who stole or who fenced embezzled goods. When the sloop *Granby* went on the rocks near Sambro with cash for the yard acquired in Boston in 1771, yard officers organized its recovery from the sums secreted by fishing families in the nearby woods.

However important it was to the town, the Halifax yard never became more than one of "several minor refitting yards around the coasts of the British Isles and scattered around the globe."[12] When the Halifax yard employed almost 270 men during the war with the United States, Portsmouth – the largest home dockyard, employed twenty times as many workers, while Deptford – the smallest of the dockyards, employed eight times as many men as Halifax. Larger than either Jamaica or Antigua during the American War of Independence, Halifax was outstripped by both thereafter. Other overseas yards such as that at Malta employed a third more and at Madras twice as many yard workers.[13] Its relative neglect after 1815 simply reflected Britain's naval triumph over its European enemies and the British government's determination after 1815 never again to risk a maritime war with the United States. This made the naval yard in Halifax harbour as well as the new base in Bermuda, still under construction in 1819, largely redundant.

Thus the Bermuda base became a pleasant residence for the commander-in-chief of the North American squadron to winter, before he took his squadron north to Halifax for a few weeks each summer. "The arrival of the Admiral ... is always looked forward to with anxiety and pleasure, as it at once enlivens and benefits the town," as Thomas Chandler Haliburton noted, before adding, "The Admiral is always popular with the townspeople, as he often renders them essential services, and seldom or never comes into collision with them."[14] There, from the 1820s, he oversaw the annual summer regatta in Halifax harbour and, with his wife, helped set the tone to the social season. Besides this policy of showing the flag to the loyal colonials, the admiral, when not getting up a cricket game against the military or the locals, confined his squadron to fisheries' protection against Yankee depredations, the principal irritant on the coasts of Nova Scotia, until the Great War, a century later, transformed almost everything.

Appendix One

HALIFAX YARD ESTABLISHMENTS, 1763–1815

	1763	1775	1776	1784	1797	1802	1805	1815
Officers:								
Commissioner	–	1	1	1	1	1	1	1
Naval storekeeper	1	1	1	1	1	1	1	1
Master attendant	–	1	1	1	1	1	1	1
Master shipwright	1	1	1	1	1	1	1	1
Boatswain	–	–	–	–	–	1	1	1
Surgeon	–	–	1	–	–	–	–	–
Clerks:								
Commissioner's	–	–	2	2	1	1	2	2
Naval storekeeper's	1	2	2	2	2	1	2	2
Issuing	–	2	2	–	–	–	–	1
Pay office attendant's	–	–	1	–	–	–	–	–
Master attendant's	–	1	1	1	–	–	–	1
Master shipwright's	1	–	1	1	1	1	1	1
Artificers:								
Foreman shipwrights	1	1	1	1	1	1	1	1
Foreman caulkers	–	–	–	1	–	–	–	–
Foreman of shipwrights afloat	–	–	1	–	–	–	–	–
Shipwrights & caulkers	4	37	34	26	26	16	26	12
Foreman of house carpenters	–	1	1	1	1	1	1	–
House carpenters	–	13	14	4	4	3	4	–
Foreman of smiths	–	1	1	1	1	1	1	1
Smiths	1	5	14	4	4	3	4	2
Foreman of sailmakers	–	–	–	1	1	1	1	1
Sailmakers	1	1	4	–	1	1	2	2
Sawyers	–	2	2	2	2	2	2	2
Painters & plumbers	–	–	–	–	–	–	–	1
Blockmakers	–	–	1	1	1	1	1	–
Master mason	–	1	–	–	–	–	–	–
Masons & slaters	–	6	10	1	1	1	1	–
Apprentices:								
Master attendant's	–	–	2	3	2	–	2	–
Master shipwright's	–	3	2	3	3	–	3	–
Foreman of shipwrights'	1	1	1	1	1	1	2	–
Shipwrights'	–	2	–	4	5	5	5	–

230 Appendix 1

	1763	1775	1776	1784	1797	1802	1805	1815
Apprentices: (continued)								
Foreman of shipwrights afloat's	–	–	1	–	–	–	–	–
Foreman of house carpenters'	–	1	1	1	1	1	2	–
Foreman of smiths'	–	1	4	1	1	1	2	–
Foreman of sailmakers'	–	–	–	1	1	–	1	–
Blockmakers'	–	–	–	1	1	–	1	–
Masons'	–	–	–	1	1	–	1	–
Boatswain's	–	–	–	–	–	1	–	–
Cabinkeepers'	–	–	–	–	–	–	–	–
Other People of the Yard:								
Steward[†]	–	1	1	1	1	–	1	–
Store porter	–	–	–	1	–	–	1	1
Cabinkeeper	–	1	1	1	1	1	1	1
Shipwright's storekeeper	–	–	–	–	1	–	–	–
Foreman of labourers	–	1	1	1	1	–	1	1
Labourers	4	37	20	40	26	10	30	12
Gate porter	–	–	–	1	1	1	1	1
Watchmen	–	9	13	10	13	6	15	15
Coxswain	–	–	–	–	–	–	1	1
Commissioner's crew	–	–	6	–	–	–	–	–
Naval storekeeper's crew	–	6	6	–	–	–	–	–
Master shipwright's crew	–	5	5	–	–	–	–	–
Runners/messengers	–	–	1	–	–	–	1	1
Totals:	16	145	163	124	111	66	125	67

Sources: NB to Admiralty, Dec. 1762, NMM, ADM/B/170, HAL/F/1, fol. 132–3; Duncan to NB, 24 Jan. 1784, HAL/F/2, fol. 81–6; 1797, PRO, ADM42/2171; NB to Nepean, 10 May 1802, NB to RO, 31 May 1808, NMM, HAL/C/1, fol. 58; NB to Wodehouse, 2 Oct. 1815, HAL/C/2, fol. 81–3; Wodehouse to RO, 20 Nov. 1815, NMM, HAL/E/41, fol. 233–4, NMM, ADM/BP/22a; NB to Marsden, 24 Feb. 1804, ADM/B/213, NSARM, MG13/1, #486; Inglefield to RO, 30 Mar. 1805, NSARM, MG13/9.1, fol. 235, PRO, ADM36/15490; Anderson accounts, 1799–1803, PRO, ADM17/152; Dawes accounts, 1805–7, ADM17/154–5.

Appendix Two

HALIFAX YARD WORKFORCE, 1761–1820

	Jan	Feb	Mar	Apr	May	Jun	Jul	Aug	Sep	Oct	Nov	Dec	Ave
1761	–	–	–	–	–	128	110	124	127	118	111	120	121.1
1762	105	89	85	84	79	82	84	92	83	83	83	83	85.5
1763	81	82	81	88	81	78	16	16	16	15	8	16	47.5
1764	45	42	58	59	55	57	52	58	53	37	33	31	48.3
1765	31	32	29	36	40	40	36	33	43	39	36	35	35.8
1766	33	32	33	33	34	35	34	37	25	25	25	25	30.9
1767	24	26	28	28	33	36	57	57	54	55	54	54	42.2
1768	43	45	46	57	52	54	67	76	88	95	93	70	65.5
1769	67	68	69	99	153	163	184	192	190	202	193	110	140.8
1770	40	40	40	105	136	144	140	145	149	145	120	110	109.5
1771	89	86	87	142	154	160	168	194	179	181	152	114	142.2
1772	107	102	118	127	127	119	137	139	121	134	150	112	125.3
1773	114	117	117	116	117	124	126	121	115	117	117	117	118.3
1774	87	87	87	140	140	140	139	139	139	111	111	111	119.3
1775	89	89	89	126	126	126	132	132	132	108	108	108	114.5
1776	–	–	–	–	–	–	146	146	146	140	140	140	143.0
1777	–	–	–	129	129	129	157	157	157	133	133	133	139.7
1778	128	128	128	149	149	149	159	159	159	155	155	155	147.8
1779	150	150	150	167	167	167	160	160	160	168	168	168	161.3
1780	160	160	160	152	152	152	167	167	167	164	164	164	160.8
1781	160	160	160	180	180	180	182	182	182	175	175	175	174.3
1782	175	175	175	179	179	179	188	188	188	194	194	194	184.0
1783	187	187	187	163	163	163	169	169	169	180	180	180	174.8
1784	169	169	169	169	169	169	133	133	133	132	132	132	150.8
1785	140	140	140	149	149	149	176	176	176	167	167	167	158.0
1786	172	172	172	189	189	189	191	191	191	184	184	184	185.3
1787	155	155	155	154	154	154	168	168	168	158	158	158	158.8
1788	148	148	148	163	163	163	168	168	168	163	163	163	168.0
1789	155	155	155	174	174	174	–	–	–	193	193	193	174.0
1790	155	155	155	159	159	159	179	179	179	179	179	179	168.0
1791	169	169	169	171	171	171	165	165	165	164	164	164	167.3
1792	159	159	159	188	188	188	193	193	193	180	180	180	180.0
1793	179	179	179	142	142	142	186	186	186	174	174	174	171.5
1794	169	169	169	191	191	191	204	204	204	193	193	193	189.3
1795	191	191	191	187	187	187	206	206	206	207	207	207	197.8
1796	207	207	207	195	195	195	199	199	199	197	197	197	199.5
1797	207	207	207	200	200	200	188	188	188	188	188	188	194.0
1798	190	190	190	196	196	196	207	207	207	206	206	206	199.8

Appendix 2

	Jan	Feb	Mar	Apr	May	Jun	Jul	Aug	Sep	Oct	Nov	Dec	Ave
1799	199	199	199	200	200	200	203	203	203	190	190	190	198.0
1800	127	127	127	159	159	159	203	203	203	175	175	177	166.2
1801	172	172	172	165	165	165	203	203	203	160	160	160	175.0
1802	146	146	146	114	114	114	100	100	100	90	90	90	112.5
1803	120	120	120	99	99	99	94	94	94	96	96	96	102.5
1804	97	97	97	104	104	104	121	121	121	128	128	128	112.5
1805	115	115	115	163	163	175	181	192	196	189	205	220	169.1
1806	182	160	177	161	154	170	168	173	165	166	163	163	166.8
1807	162	170	164	162	158	156	159	155	155	159	158	156	159.5
1808	155	156	157	167	170	168	171	180	194	194	194	192	174.8
1809	192	196	203	214	214	211	211	215	215	215	215	213	209.5
1810	213	209	210	205	204	207	207	201	202	200	197	195	204.2
1811	194	196	196	198	199	198	198	200	197	193	198	197	197.0
1812	195	197	197	209	201	209	210	213	220	225	213	233	210.3
1813	235	231	233	236	233	234	233	254	266	268	266	266	246.3
1814	266	268	239	235	248	246	245	247	246	247	243	243	247.8
1815	230	237	223	231	218	210	245	231	231	210	174	235	222.9
1816	171	171	180	173	172	157	152	153	151	136	139	135	157.5
1817	–	–	–	–	–	–	–	–	–	–	–	–	–
1818	140	140	140	140	140	140	135	135	135	132	132	132	136.8
1819	136	136	136	147	147	147	135	135	118	55	55	23	114.2
1820	19	–	–	–	–	–	–	–	–	–	–	–	–

Appendix Three

NAVAL YARD OFFICERS, 1756–1819

Resident Commissioners:
Capt. Marriot Arbuthnot, 1775–8
Capt. Sir Richard Hughes, 1778–81
Capt. Sir Andrew Snape Hamond, 1781–3
Capt. Henry Duncan, 1783–99, 1800–03
Capt. Isaac Coffin, 1799–1800, acting
Capt. John N. Inglefield, 1803–12
Capt. the Hon. Philip Wodehouse, 1812–19

Naval Storekeepers:
Lewis, George, acting, 1756
Gerrish, Joseph 1756–74
Williams, Richard, 1773–80
Thomas, George, 1780–90
Edgecombe, Frederick, acting 1785–6
Livie, Titus, 1790–9
Oben, Thomas, 1800–01
Anderson, Alexander, acting 1799–1800, 1801–03
Dawes, Daniel Butler, 1803–19

Master Attendants:
Hay, Charles, acting 1757–8
Hamilton, Richard, 1759–63
Hooper, David, acting 1764–5
Holman, John, acting 1774–5
Kilworth, John, acting, 1773–4
Prowse, Richard, 1775–80
Hemmens, Samuel, 1780–7
Read, Thomas, 1788–99
Jackson, John, 1799–1803
Patterson, George, 1804–05
Fernie, David, acting 1805–06
Atkinson, Thomas, 1807–10
Fairfax, Edmund, 1809–15; dismissed
Douglas, John, 1815–19

Master Shipwrights:
Kittoe, George, acting 1756
Constable, Abraham, 1758–63, 1771–5; dismissed
Hooper, James, acting 1763–5
Johns, William, acting 1767–70
Willison, Thomas, acting 1770–1
Loader, John, 1776–82
Wallis, Provo, 1783–92
Marshall, Elias, acting 1776; 1793–1800 suspended; 1800–05
Andrew, George, acting 1800
Hughes, William, 1805–13
Parry, John, acting 1813
Hawkes, Thomas Forder, 1813–17
Jones, Algernon Frederick, 1817–19

Boatswain:
Ridgeway, David, 1800–19

Appendix Four

YARD RETURNS SENT THE NAVY BOARD, 1780s

Monthly:
1. Progress of works carrying on in the yard
2. Cash accounts & vouchers: account of ships' books left to be transmitted
3. Accounts of warrants unexecuted & abstract of letters to the Navy Board unanswered
4. Abstract of yard musters
5. Abstract of ship musters
6. List of all ships & vessels on the station, including those that occasionally arrive
7. Men discharged from the yard, with reason
8. Account of works carrying on by contract
9. State of anchors
10. Cables, cordage, hemp, sails & canvas in store

Quarterly:
1. Account of old, unserviceable stores sold
2. Charges incurred on ships & works in the yard
3. Issues and remains, including masts
4. Store accounts
5. Naval pay books: yard
6. Demands of stores, accompanied by remains
7. Received and expense of muster, pay & other forms, paper
8. Men discharged
9. Expense on the head of extra [discontinued in 1788]
10. Slops issued and remaining in store
11. Issues to boatswains and carpenters [added in 1788]

Annually:
1. Works & estimates proposed for ensuing year with the state of the works in hand at that time
2. General annual demand, accompanied by remains
3. List of artificers entered, dead, or discharged

4. Return of Negroes
5. List of advertisements, tenders, bargains & hire of artificers
6. Monthly rate of exchange & bills drawn within the year
7. Particulars of the value of stores received within the year
8. An account of the total quantities of every species of stores issued or expended in the yard [added in 1788]

Appendix Five

ORDERS FOR THE NIGHT WATCH, 1785

1st. The naval storekeeper, master shipwright, & master attendant are in succession officers of the night.
2nd. There are nine rounders selected from the artificers sent from English yards. They do duty in pairs.
3rd. The number of watchmen is thirteen, assembled every evening after bell ringing.
4th. The number of posts is five, relieved every four hours by one of the rounders in person.
5th. Every watchman has musket & bayonet, receives three cartridges of powder. (not in force)
6th. The lodge next the gate is the guardroom, the arms are there deposited.
7th. The rounders do not quit their posts, on any consideration, after the watchword is given.
8th. No seamen sleep in the yard.
9th. No lights are admitted in the warrant officers' storerooms.
10th. The parole is given by the commissioner to the officer of the night.
11th. When the officer of the night has seen the watch properly set, he gives the parole to the rounders, and they communicate the same to the watch.
12th. No boats go from the yard, nor are suffered to land therein, after gunfire.
13th. Officers belonging to ships at the wharf wanting admittance are furnished with the parole, upon their application to the officer of the night. Upon their being admitted they give their name and that of the ship to which they belong, which must be given in at the time of their admittance.
14th. A List of those people who are admitted after the setting of the watch is delivered to the rounder of each watch, to the officer presiding over them, the next morning at 8 o'clock.
15th. No boats to go from, or come alongside of ships at the wharf, after gunfire.
16th. In case of an Alarm in the night proceeding either from fire or riot, the officer of the night is informed by one of the rounders, and if the officer deems it of consequence, he informs the commissioner immediately.

17th. The rounder to which the charge of the gate is committed by the officer of the night gives particular injunctions to the watch not to open the gate without his previous assent.
18th. The rounders and watch are to take particular notice of the persons whom they admit.
19th. The key of the engine house hangs in the porter's lodge under his charge.

Notes

Preface

1. *The Autobiography of a Saint: Thérèse of Lisieux*, tr. Ronald Knox (London: Collins, 1958), 109.
2. Roger Morriss, *The Royal Dockyards during the Revolutionary and Napoleonic Wars* (Leicester: Leicester University Press, 1983), 3–5.
3. Morriss, *The Royal Dockyards*, 9.
4. Typically, neither Brian Lavery, *Nelson's Navy: The Ships, Men and Organization 1793–1815* (London: Conway Maritime Press, 1989) nor Jonathan G. Coad, *The Royal Dockyards, 1690–1850: Architecture and Engineering Works of the Sailing Navy* (Aldershot: Scolar Press, 1989), discuss the Halifax base.
5. *Frigates and Foremasts: The North American Squadron in Nova Scotia Waters, 1745–1815* (Vancouver: University of British Columbia Press, 2003); *Excessive Expectations: Maritime Commerce and the Economic Development of Nova Scotia, 1740–1870* (Montreal: McGill-Queen's University Press, 1998).
6. Philip MacDougall, *Royal Dockyards* (Newton Abbot: David & Charles, 1982) and his *The Chatham Dockyard Story*, rev. ed. (Rainham, Kent: Meresborough Books, 1987).
7. J.M. Haas, *A Management Odyssey: The Royal Dockyards 1714–1914* (Lanham: University Press of America, 1994).
8. R.J.B. Knight, "The Royal Dockyards in England at the Time of the War of American Independence," (PhD thesis, University of London, 1972).
9. David Wilson, "Government Dock-Yard Workers in Portsmouth, 1793–1815," (PhD thesis, University of Warwick, 1975).
10. R.J.B. Knight, *Portsmouth Dockyard Papers 1774–1783: The American War. A Calendar* (Portsmouth: Portsmouth Record Series, 1987).
11. Marilyn Gurney Smith, *The King's Yard: An Illustrated History of the Halifax Dockyard* (Halifax: Nimbus, 1985).
12. As it is replete with errors in its treatment of the pre-1820 yard, Brent Raymond, *Tracing the Built Form of HMC Dockyard*, Curatorial Report 88 (Halifax: Maritime Museum of the Atlantic, 1999,) proved to be worthless.
13. Think of such marvelous books as Robert Darnton, *The Great Cat Massacre and Other Episodes in French Cultural History* (New York: Basic Books, 1984).
14. Though the title naval storekeeper was changed to naval officer late in the eighteenth century, I have retained the former throughout, to avoid confusion with other officials given the same title.

1 "A View of His Majesty's Dockyard at Halifax 21 May 1760 ... with *Penzance* lying at the jetty head," Royal Ontario Museum, 958.97, 70CAN31

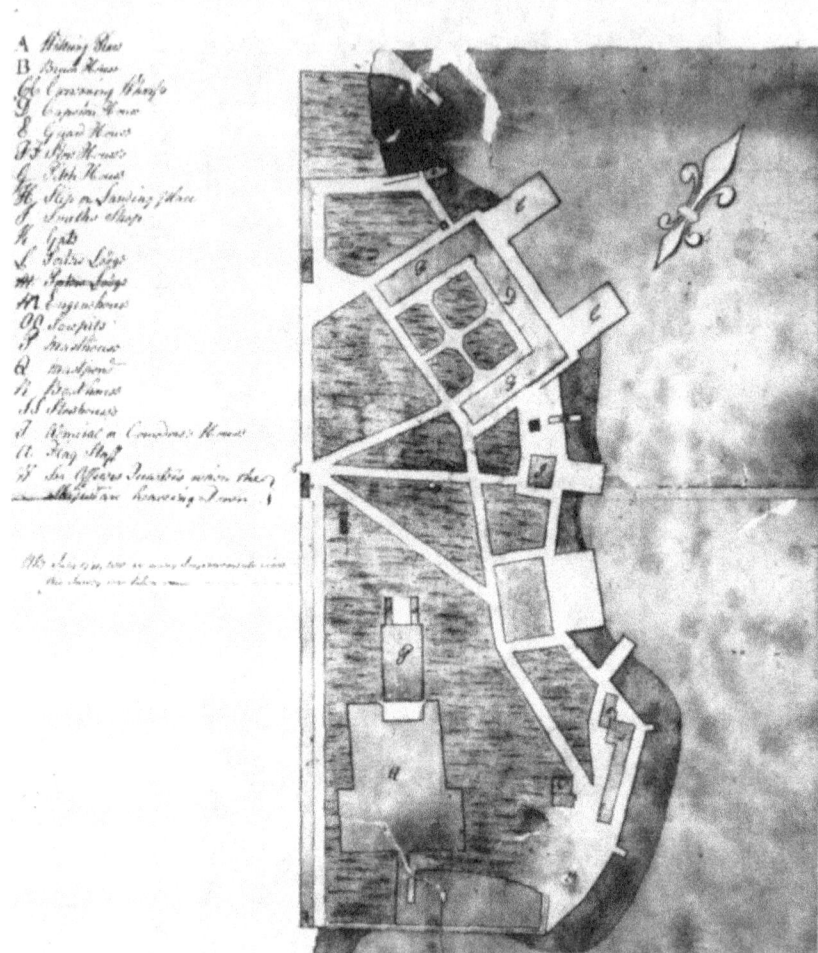

2 "Plan of His Majesty's Careening Yard at Halifax Surveyed by William Lloyd in August 1761," NA, H3/250/Halifax/1761

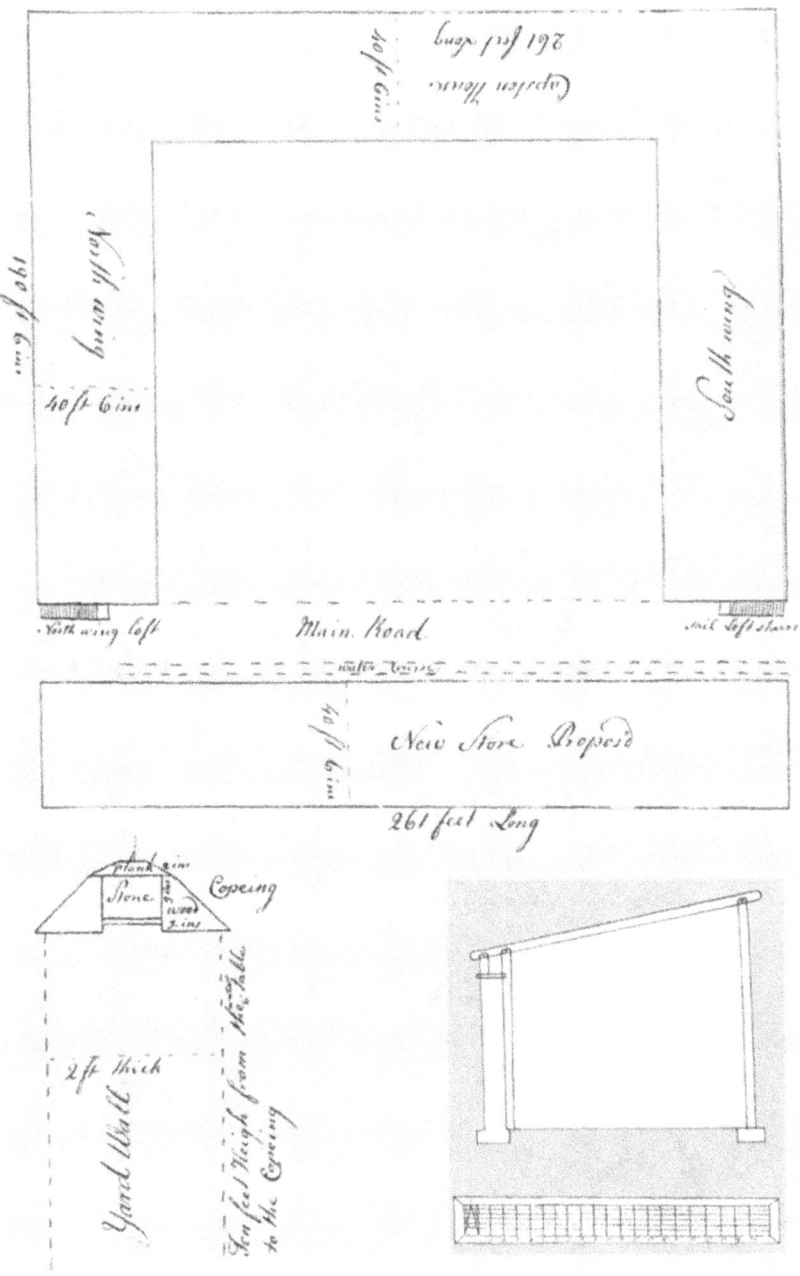

3 "New Store Propos'd," 1770, and cross-section of yard wall, PRO, ADM106/1179. Cross-section of painters' shed, 13 November 1807, NMM, HAL/A/1

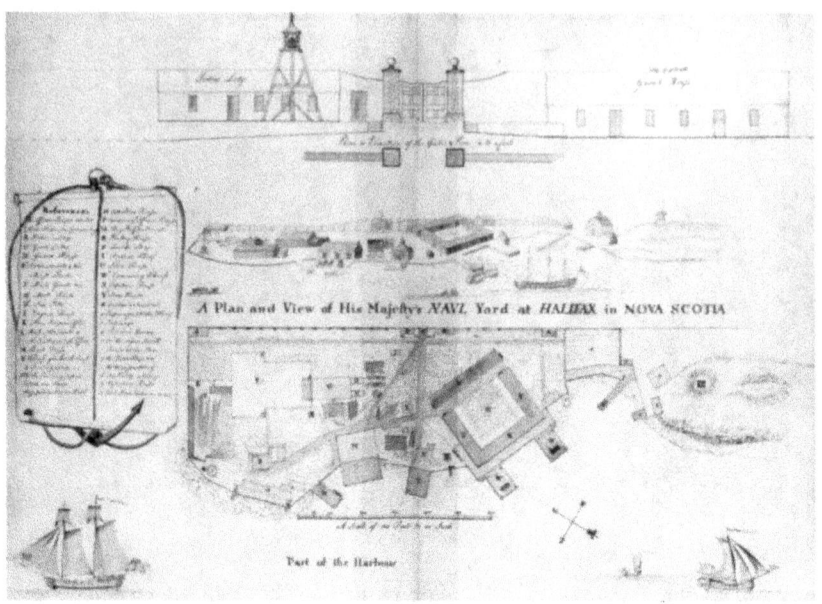

4 "Plan and View of the Nav[a]l Yard at Halifax, Nova Scotia," inscribed on back: "Hon Hugh Palliser, 30 Sept 1771," NMM, LAD/11/51, neg. B994

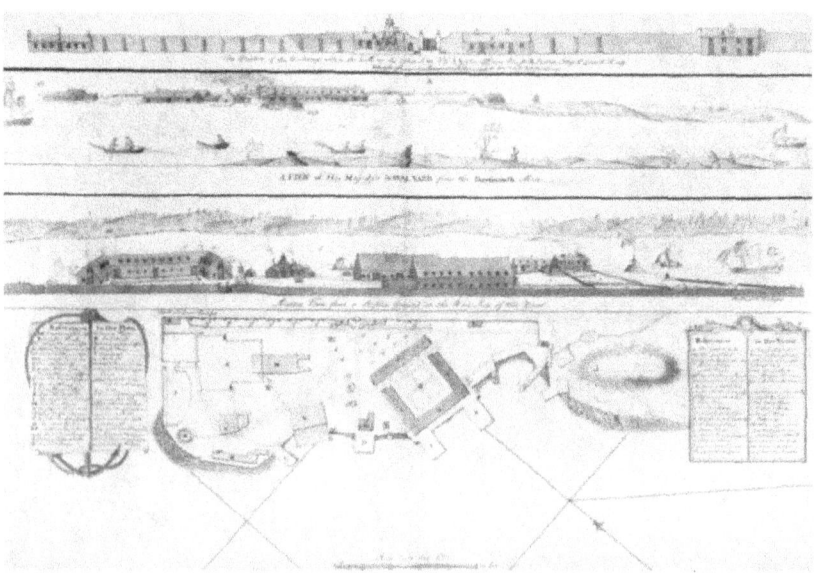

5 "A View of His Majesty's Naval Yard from the Dartmouth Shore, Elevation of Buildings; View from the West Side of the Yard and General Plan," c.1771, NMM, LAD/11/52, neg. B995

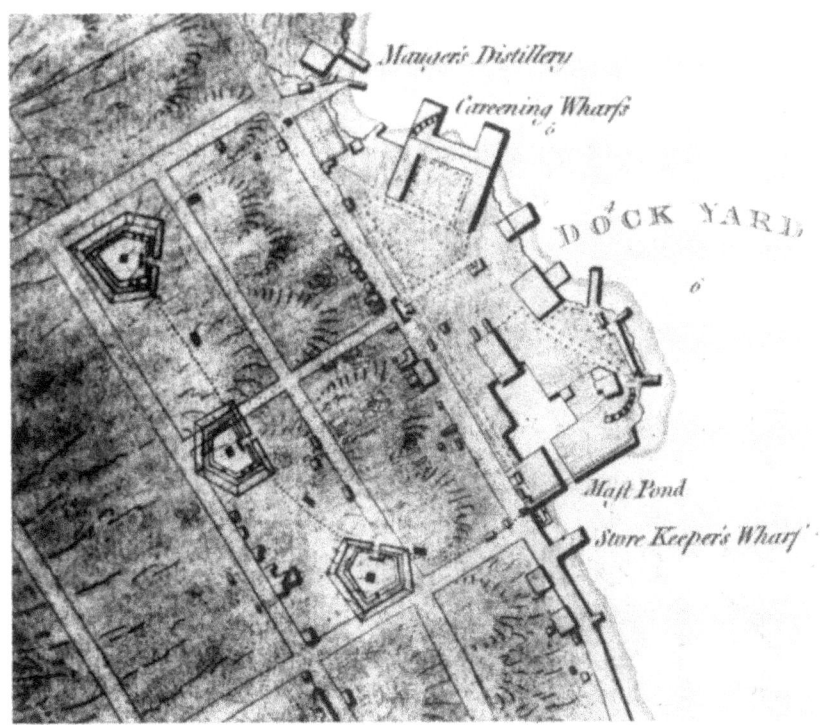

6 "Halifax Harbour" J.F.W. DesBarres, *Atlantic Neptune*, II, pt. 1 #48, NA, NMC-134837 [detail of newly-erected defences at naval yard, c.1776]

7 "Halifax Harbour," J.F.W. DesBarres, *Atlantic Neptune, Atlantic Neptune*, II, pt. 1 #48, NA, NMC-134837 [detail of *Anson* at the careen]

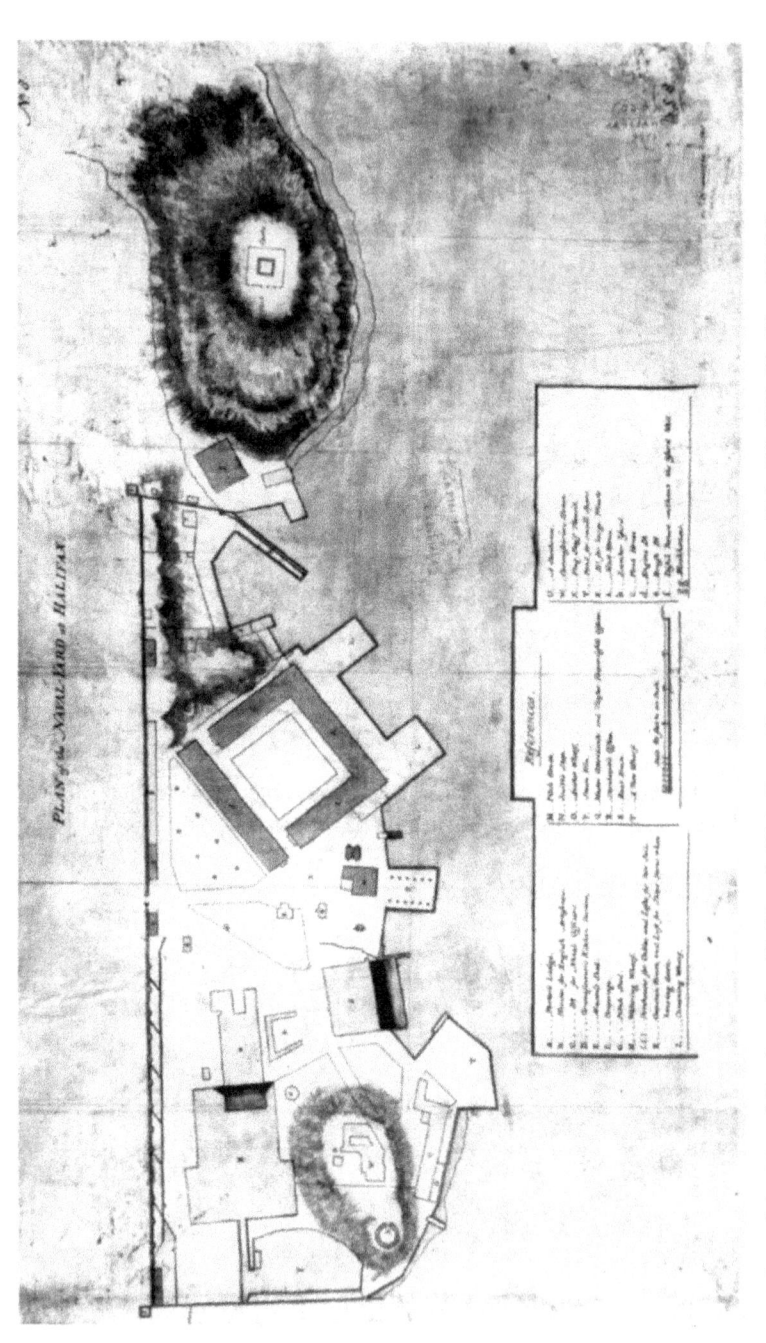

8 "Plan of the Naval Dockyard at Halifax," 1784, Capt. Charles Blaskowitz, NA, H2/250/Halifax/[1784]

9 "The Careening Yard, Halifax, Oct 5–25, 1786," James S. Meres, in log of *Pegasus*, 141, NA, c-002557

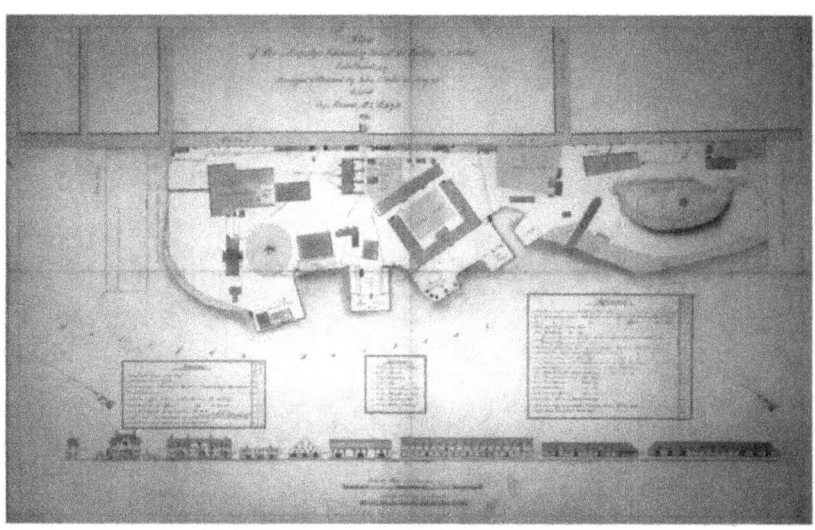

10 "Plan of Her Majesty's Careening Yard at Halifax, Nova Scotia, Established in 1759. Surveyed and Planned by John G. Toler in May 1815, copied by James McKenzie, 1839," Admiralty Library, Pfo B 23

11 "View of Halifax from Davis's Mill, 1800," George I. Parkyns, NA, c-040311 [detail of naval hospital]

12 "View from Fort Needham near Halifax," 29 April 1801, George I. Parkyns, NA, c-000984, [detail of naval yard and hospital].

13 "Instructor's Model of Sheer Legs, Halifax Careening Yard" c.1880, MMA, M49.8

14 "Halifax Dockyard Bell," MMA, M60.6.1

15 "Masthouse, 1759–60," Naval Historical Library, DA034NHL-4-16

16 "Storehouse, 1760," Naval Historical Library, DA040NHL-1-28, [South Wing rebuilt in stone, 1768–9]

17 "Capstan House and North Wing, 1760," MCM [rebuilt 1768–9]

18 "Respective Officers' Offices, 1760s," MCM, Naval Historical Library, DA034, [pitched roof added at a later date]

19 "New Storehouse, 1771," Naval Historical Library, DA034NHL-4-4

20 "Resident Commissioner's House, 1785," Naval Historical Library, DA034NHL-3-9

21 "Admiral's House, Halifax NS," NL, CIN, 4 August 1878

22 "Respective Officers' Tenements, 1793," NSARM, acc. 6835

23 "Boatswain's House, 1814," MCM, Naval Historical Library, DA034NHL-4-26

24 "Provo Featherstone Wallis, 1813," Robert Field, AGNS, 1979.17

25 "Jacob Hurd," William Johnston, The Metropolitan Museum of Art, acc. 64.114.1

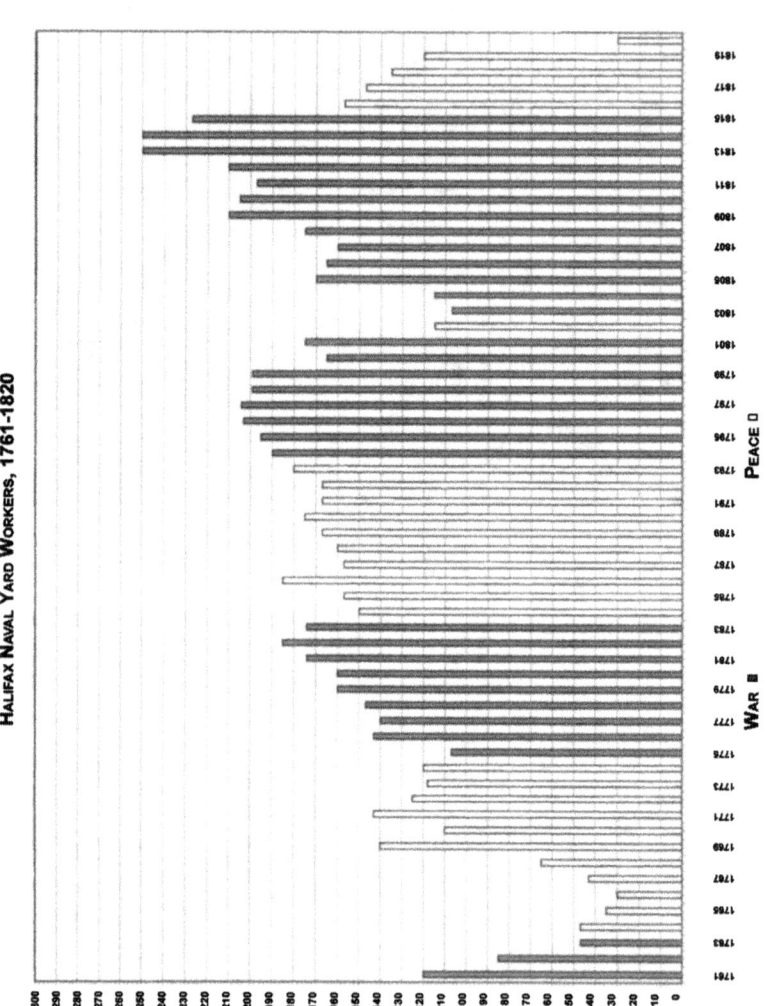

26 Halifax Naval Yard Employment During Periods of War and Peace, 1761–1820

Notes to pages 3–5   239

Chapter 1   Building the Yard, 1758–1783

1. Hood to NB, 7 Aug. 1769. PRO, ADM106/1179.
2. Daniel A. Baugh, *British Naval Administration in the Age of Walpole* (Princeton: Princeton University Press, 1965), 344–5.
3. A yard at Port Antonio, Jamaica, had begun to be erected in 1729, but within a decade was in decay, only to be replaced by the Port Royal yard, begun in 1735. English Harbour had been started in 1728 with a careening wharf, storehouse, and masthouse. Rot was so rapid that, within a decade, the careening wharf had been replaced three times. Capt. Charles Knowles relocated some of the buildings and rebuilt the entire yard on an expanded scale beginning in 1743. See Duncan Crewe, *Yellow Jack and the Worm: British Naval Administration in the West Indies, 1739–1748* (Liverpool: Liverpool University Press, 1993), 213–39.
4. Exceptional cases like yards in Kingston, Upper Canada, or at Madras in British India, and Trincomalee in Ceylon, acquired drydocks early.
5. Warren to Admiralty, 23 Nov. 1745, Julian Gwyn, ed., *The Royal Navy and North America: The Warren Papers, 1736–1752* (London: Navy Records Society, 1973), 118: 191.
6. Gwyn, *Royal Navy and North America*, xxvi–xxvii, 167, 172, 177, 187, 256, 262, 291. Admiralty to NB, 2 Nov. 1745. PRO, ADM2/208, fol. 39. Douglas reminds us that Trincomalee likewise became a temporary base between 1745 and 1749 in the same manner as Louisbourg, and the recently-built careening yards in Jamaica and Antigua, as well as those at Gibraltar and Port Mahon, began as temporary facilities. W.A.B. Douglas, "Nova Scotia and the Royal Navy, 1713–1766" (PhD thesis, Queen's University, 1973), 106.
7. As the careening wharf at Louisbourg was out of repair, Commodore Charles Knowles cleaned his ships at Boston. To Corbett, 20 Jan. 1747. PRO, ADM1/1008.
8. The Turtle Bay facilities, now the site of the headquarters of the United Nations, had been purchased by Capt. Robert Long when he commanded *Shoreham* at New York in 1728–30 and 1732–5. He sold them to Vice Admiral Peter Warren in 1750, and they were eventually sold by his heirs in 1791. See Julian Gwyn, *The Enterprising Admiral: The Personal Fortune of Admiral Sir Peter Warren* (Montreal: McGill-Queen's University Press, 1974), 37, 46–8, 65.
9. Knowles to NB, 28 June & 20 Nov. 1747. PRO, ADM106/1044; Knowles to Corbett, 27 June 1747. PRO, ADM1/234.
10. Knowles to Corbett, 20 Nov. 1747. PRO, ADM106/1044; see also 28 Nov. 1747. PRO, ADM1/234.

240   Notes to pages 5–7

11. Harmar to Corbett, 1 Mar. 1748. PRO, ADM1/1886.
12. 17 Aug. 1748, 19 Aug. 1749. PRO, ADM106/2184; 19 Jan. 1750. PRO, ADM106/2185.
13. Warren to Corbett, 3 Oct. 1745. PRO, ADM1/480; Warren to NB, 11 Oct. 1745. PRO, ADM106/1021; Warren to NB, 16 Jan. 1746. ADM106/1038; Gwyn, *Royal Navy and North America*, 172, 177, 205. Harmar's only other distinction, when in command of *Eagle* (60) in 1755, was to have had on board as a volunteer, able seaman James Cook who had just joined the navy and whom the captain had the wisdom to promote master's mate within a month. Victor Suthern, *To Go Upon Discovery: James Cook and Canada, from 1758 to 1779* (Toronto: Dundurn Press, 2000), 38.
14. 27 July 1749. PRO, ADM2/510.
15. Campbell to Clevland 8 Nov. 1756. PRO, ADM1/1605.
16. Hutchenson to Clevland, 31 July 1753. PRO, ADM1/1888.
17. Barton to Clevland, 6 Dec. 1756. PRO, ADM1/2607; Rous to Clevland, 23 May 1757. PRO, ADM1/2385.
18. Rous to Clevland, 13 Oct. 1757. PRO, ADM1/2385.
19. Spry to Clevland, beginning 22 Nov. 1755. PRO, ADM1/480, fol. 663. In the winter of 1752–3 Rous had unrigged sloop *Albany* "to the standing masts," and hauled her alongside a wharf to avoid damage from ice floating out of Bedford Basin. Hutchenson to Rous, 1 Oct. 1752. ADM1/480.
20. Milnes to NB, 6 Oct. 1756. PRO, ADM2/528, fol. 194.
21. Holmes to Clevland, 7 Nov. 1757. PRO, ADM1/1892.
22. Admiralty to Holburne. PRO, ADM2/1331, fol. 213; Holburne to Clevland, 4 Nov. 1757. PRO, ADM1/481, fol. 454.
23. Colvill kept men at work on George's Island levelling the ground and making an abutment. He planned to build a wharf in the spring, 50–65 feet further out to bring it into three fathoms of water. Colvill to Clevland, 7 Dec. 1757. PRO, ADM1/1606.
24. Gerrish accounts, 1757–73. PRO, ADM17/150, fol. 143.
25. Colvill to Clevland, 1 Jan. 1758. PRO, ADM1/1606.
26. Holburne to Clevland, 4 Nov. 1757. PRO, ADM1/481, fol. 454–5.
27. "As the wharf for careening ships is to be either George's or Cornwallis's [McNab's] Island." Boscawen to Clevland, 26 Feb. 1758. ADM1/481, fol. 504.
28. Pitt was then thinking of Cornwallis Island "or any other place Admiral Boscawen shall find more proper for the service." Pitt to Admiralty, 27 Jan. 1758; Admiralty to NB, 30 June 1758. NMM, ADM/A/2482; NB to Clevland, 7 Feb. 1758.
29. Durell has "pitched on a proper place to build the careening wharf, store-

house, etc. in this harbour ... where are already a piece of a dwelling house and two barns." Gerrish to NB, 20 Nov. 1758. PRO, ADM106/1167.
30. Durell to Clevland, 29 Nov. 1758. PRO, ADM1/1701.
31. With six feet of sea water at low tide, fresh water from a spring-fed stream entered four spouts that had been fashioned on the wharf, from which barrels carried in four longboats could simultaneously be filled. Spry to Clevland, 24 Jan. 1756 & 18 May 1762. PRO, ADM1/480, fol. 682, 778.
32. Evaluation on 16 Dec. 1758 of Gorham's Point improvements: H£100. Lawrence to Morris, Mauger & Francklin, 9 Dec. 1758. Receipts dated 22–3 Dec. 1758 by Joseph Gorham and George Suckling for title and improvements to two adjoining lots. PRO, ADM106/1167. The deeds of conveyance were drawn by William Nesbitt for £6.6.8. Gerrish accounts, 1757–73. PRO, ADM17/150.
33. From William Gorham, truckman, and his wife, Mary, H£120, 1781. HP, IX, 38–9.
34. 20 Dec. 1756. PRO, ADM3/65.
35. Gerrish to NB, 30 Nov. 1758. PRO, ADM106/1167; Durell to Clevland, 19 Mar. 1759. PRO, ADM1/481, fol. 595–6. To house the remainder, six warehouses were hired temporarily, costing £123.2.11. Gerrish accounts, 1757–73, PRO, ADM17/150, fol. 179.
36. Gerrish to NB, 20 Sept. 1760. PRO, ADM106/1121.
37. Colvill to Clevland, 30 Nov. 1759. PRO, ADM1/482, fol. 95–6.
38. Colvill to Clevland, 1 Aug. 1761. PRO, ADM1/482, fol. 152.
39. NB to Stephens, 9 Dec. 1762. NMM, ADM/B/170.
40. Spry to Clevland, 18 May 1762. PRO, ADM1/480, fol. 777–8.
41. Unfortunately for historians, he did not "trouble their lordships with a tiresome or minute detail of Halifax yard." Colvill to Stephens, 27 Nov. 1764. PRO, ADM1/483, fol. 414v–5.
42. NB to Stephens, 26 Apr. 1765. NMM, ADM/B/176.
43. Three had been hanged for desertion, two more were executed for robbery and murder, their bodies hanging in chains. "The most severe corporal punishments, I ever knew, have been inflicted; even up to six & seven hundred lashes a man, have been given from ship to ship ... The criminals declared in general at their trials and execution that drunkenness was the cause of their misfortunes." Colvill to Stephens, 12 Nov. 1765. PRO, ADM1/483, fol. 495–6.
44. PRO, ADM106/1145.
45. Gerrish to Vincent, 13 Jan. 1767. PRO, ADM106/1145.
46. Deposition #4: Michael Geasey, 17 Jan. 1767; 2d deposition, #6: Sgt. Michael Geasey, 20 Jan. 1767. PRO, ADM106/1145.

47. Deposition #7: William Francis, 20 Jan. 1767. PRO, ADM106/1145.
48. Gerrish to NB, 24 Feb. 1767. PRO, ADM106/1153.
49. Deposition #1: 15 Jan. 1767. PRO, ADM106/1145.
50. Including a Mrs Gunnels, "who lived at the sign of the Globe." Deposition #5: Charles Higgins, 19 Jan. 1767, PRO, ADM106/1145.
51. Some 260 bales of woollens and linens, together with sixty-four cases of stockings and shoes. Deposition #8: Moses Clark, 25 Feb. 1767. PRO, ADM106/1145.
52. Gerrish to NB, 24 Feb. 1767. PRO, ADM106/1153.
53. Hood to Stephens, 23 July 1767. PRO, ADM1/483, fol. 8. None of Hood's biographers is aware of his useful role in rebuilding parts of the Halifax yard. See Daniel A. Baugh, "Sir Samuel Hood: Superior Subordinate," in *George Washington's Opponents: British Generals and Admirals in the American Revolution*, ed. George A. Billias (New York: Morrow, 1969) or Michael Duffy, "Samuel Hood, First Viscount Hood, 1724–1816," in *Precursors of Nelson: British Admirals of the Eighteenth Century*, ed. Peter Le Fevre and Richard Harding, 249–278 (London: Chatham, 2000), or Lee Bienkowski, *Admirals in the Age of Nelson* (Annapolis, MD: Naval Institute Press, 2003), 52–77.
54. Hood to NB, 13 Oct. 1767. PRO, ADM106/1153.
55. Hood to Stephens, 1 Oct. 1767. PRO, ADM1/483, fol. 31.
56. Hood to Stephens, 5 Sept. 1767. NMM, ADM/A/2601.
57. John, Marshall & Lee's survey. 7 Sept. 1767. PRO, ADM1/1153.
58. Hood to NB, 18 Sept. 1768. PRO, ADM106/1166.
59. Hood to NB, 7 Aug. 1769. PRO, ADM106/1179. "Have not yet begun slating, as it is thought necessary to lay a foundation in the middle of the building for wood pillars to stand on to support the floors and roof" before slating. Gerrish to NB, 31 Aug. 1769. ADM106/1179.
60. Hood to NB, 18 Sept. 1768. PRO, ADM106/1166.
61. Hood to Stephens, 23 Nov. 1769. PRO, ADM1/483, fol. 236–8.
62. Hood to Stephens, 10 Mar. 1768. PRO, ADM1/483, fol. 50.
63. Hood to Stephens, 4 Apr. 1768. PRO, ADM1/483, fol. 73–4; Hood to NB, 4 Apr. 1768. PRO, ADM106/1166; NMM, ADM/B/181.
64. NB to Stephens, 21 Dec. 1767. NMM, ADM/B/180.
65. NB's permission to finish in stone and slate was not received until December.
66. Hood to NB, 5 Aug. 1768. PRO, ADM106/1167.
67. Gerrish to NB, 7 Aug. & 31 Dec. 1768. PRO, ADM106/1167.
68. Feb. 1769. PRO, ADM42/2149.
69. August 1768 pay list. PRO, ADM42/2149.

70. Gerrish to NB, 5 Aug. 1769. PRO, ADM106/1179.
71. Hood to NB, 7 Aug. 1768. PRO, ADM106/1179.
72. Hood to Stephens, 23 Nov. 1769. PRO, ADM1/483, fol. 236–8.
73. Hood to NB, 2 Sept. 1769. PRO, ADM106/1179.
74. Hood to Stephens, 23 Nov. 1769. PRO, ADM1/483, fol. 236.
75. This repeated a suggestion he had made the year before. Hood to NB, 5 Aug. 1768. PRO, ADM106/1167.
76. "At 317 cubic feet to the rod the cost will be H£13 14s. per rod." Hood to NB, 2 Sept. 1769. PRO, ADM106/1179.
77. In preparing the wall's foundation, a small house that stood on the west side near the southwest corner of the yard that had been used by ships' captains when their warships were at the careening wharf, was removed. In its place he erected a two-room shed. Hood to NB, 11 Oct. 1769. PRO, ADM106/1179.
78. Hood to Stephens, 17 Jan. 1770. PRO, ADM1/483, fol. 259.
79. Gambier to Stephens, 29 Oct. 1770. PRO, ADM1/483.
80. *Lizard*'s "frame was much out of order from lying 8 months ashore at Quebec." Collier to Stephens, 15 Jan. 1777. PRO, ADM1/1611.
81. Collier to Stephens, 22 Jan. 1778. PRO, ADM1/484.
82. Jonathan G. Coad, *Historic Architecture of the Royal Navy: An Introduction* (London: Gollancz, 1983), 20, 55.
83. Barrie to NB, 25 Aug. 1819, NB to Croker, 8 Oct. 1819. NMM, ADM/BP/39b.
84. Jonathan G. Coad, *The Royal Dockyards, 1690–1850: Architecture and Engineering Works of the Sailing Navy* (Aldershot: Scolar Press, 1989), 345–6.
85. Coad, *The Royal Dockyards*, 367.
86. Discussions continued for several years about building a drydock in the harbour. 22 Oct. 1849, *Novascotian*. The next proposal came in 1882. 20 July 1882, *Acadian Recorder*. The first successful plan was presented by the Halifax Graving Dock Company in 1886, incorporated by statute with capital of £160,000 [$800,000]. It opened at the foot of Young Street in 1889. 21 Sept. 1889, *Morning Herald*. It was first used by *Canada*. The Admiralty provided an annual subsidy of £10,000 for twenty years, in return for a stipulated access to the drydock, while the Dominion government and the City of Halifax each provided an annual subsidy of $10,000. Some 567 feet long and eighty-nine feet wide, it could handle ships drawing almost twenty-seven feet of water. Blasted out of rock and lined with concrete, its 100 by twenty-three-foot thick gate with five watertight compartments, built in Glasgow, was towed across the Atlantic. Damaged by the Halifax harbour explosion in 1917, it was again fully operational within two months. A year later it was expropriated for $1.5 million by the Dominion govern-

ment, and renamed the Halifax Shipyards Limited. It was then capable of handling four hulls up to 10,000 tons.
87. Montagu to Stephens, 7 Oct. 1772. PRO, ADM1/484, fol. 155.
88. At the time they made use of the capstan house, which as it lacked a proper "Dutch stove," the sailors brought in their pails of hot coals. Montagu to Stephens, 9 Dec. 1772. PRO, ADM1/484, fol. 158, 161.
89. NB to Gerrish, 1 May 1773. PRO, ADM106/2470, fol. 117.
90. With a small fireplace. NB to RO, 13 Jan. 1775. PRO, ADM106/2470, fol. 176–8.
91. Montagu to Stephens, 16 Dec. 1772. PRO, ADM1/484, fol. 188v.
92. Montagu to Stephens, 28 June 1773. PRO, ADM1/484, fol. 229–9v.
93. NB to Stephens, 24 Mar. 1774. NMM, ADM/B/189.
94. Graves to Stephens, 19 Aug. 1775. PRO, ADM1/485, fol. 328.
95. Arbuthnot to NB, 1 Dec. 1775. PRO, ADM106/1226.
96. A gunner's mate was later borne on each. Each ship carried naval stores to Halifax. NB to Arbuthnot, 27 Apr. 1776. PRO, ADM106/2470, fol. 235–6.
97. Warrants of 26 Apr. & 19 June 1776. Gerrish accounts, 1757–73. PRO, ADM17/150, fol. 357.
98. Shuldham to Stephens, 1 Sept. 1775. PRO, ADM1/484, fol. 329.
99. NB to Arbuthnot, 24 Sept. 1775. PRO, ADM106/2470, fol. 212. Names of volunteer artificers. NB to RO, 23 Oct. 1775. ADM106/2470, fol. 213.
100. NB to Stephens, 20 Oct. 1775. PRO, ADM106/2470, fol. 214.
101. Arbuthnot to NB, 19 Apr. 1776. PRO, ADM106/1233.
102. Arbuthnot evaded their demands for candle and fuel money. The Board merely noted that "it did not think the allowance should be made at the yard's expense." NB to Arbuthnot, 18 June 1776. PRO, ADM106/2470, fol. 241–2.
103. Hamond to NB, 25 Nov. 1781. HP, VII, 47. He asked for ten shipwrights, four house carpenters, and a blockmaker. The Board offered to advertise for artificers to go to Halifax, but the "wants of the fleet" did not allow them to send any. NB to Hamond. PRO, ADM106/2471, fol. 190.
104. The schooner, "either too large or too small," had been on shore once and nearly drowned the crew "several times." Arbuthnot to NB, 26 Jan. 1776. PRO, ADM106/1233.
105. Fowler to NB, 27 Jan. 1776. PRO, ADM106/1233. He complained of a shortage of blocks, and that the one blockmaker in Halifax would not necessarily work exclusively to fill the navy's needs. Arbuthnot to NB, 8 Feb. 1776. ADM106/1233.
106. Arbuthnot to Sandwich, 11 Oct. 1777. G.R. Barnes and J.H. Owen, eds.,

The Private Papers of John, Earl of Sandwich, First Lord of the Admiralty 1771–1782, 4 vols. (London: Navy Records Society, 1932–8) 1: 305.
107. Admiralty to NB, 23 Dec. 1777. NMM, ADM/A/2722.
108. NB to Stephens, 13 Jan. 1778. NMM, ADM/B/195.
109. John Dewar Faibisy, "Privateering and Piracy: The Effects of American Privateering upon Nova Scotia during the American Revolution" (PhD diss., University of Massachusetts, 1972).
110. New works or alterations in the yard could be undertaken only when plans and estimates had first been submitted and approved. NB to Stephens, 11 Aug. 1775. NMM, ADM/B/190.
111. Coad, *Historic Architecture*, 20.
112. Inglefield to RO, 1 Oct. 1807. NMM, HAL/E/38, fol. 237–41.
113. For workforce size, see pay lists. PRO, ADM42/2147–71 & 2177–8.
114. NB to Stephens, 9 Dec. 1762. NMM, ADM/B/170.
115. RO to NB, 15 Apr. 1761. PRO, ADM1/1121.
116. NB to Stephens, 26 Apr. 1765. NMM, ADM/B/176.
117. Colvill to Gerrish, 15 Aug. 1766. PRO, ADM1/482, fol. 532–3.
118. NB to Arbuthnot, 3 Oct. 1775. PRO, ADM106/2470, fol. 211–2.
119. NB to RO, 23 Oct. 1775. PRO, ADM106/2470, fol. 214; Duncan to NB, 24 Jan. 1784. NMM, HAL/F/2, fol. 81–6.
120. Admiralty to NB, 23 Dec. 1777. NMM, ADM/A/2722. On 13 Jan. 1778 the Board responded with suggested establishments for any such yard. NMM, ADM/B/195.
121. NB to Stephens, 16 Dec. 1782. NMM, ADM/BP/3.
122. NB to Stephens, 24 Oct. 1783. NMM, ADM/BP/4.
123. NSARM, MG13/1, #486.

Chapter 2   Development and Expansion, 1783–1819

1. Anthony A. Lockwood, *A Brief Description of Nova Scotia with plates of the principal harbors including a particular account of the Island of Grand Manan* (London: Hayden, 1818), 18.
2. The land – farm lot No. 2 – was escheated and granted to the government for a fee of H£20. Duncan to Thomas, 28 June 1785. NSARM, MG13/1, #555.
3. Wentworth to Duncan, 7 June 1787. NSARM, MG13/2, fol. 460–1.
4. Duncan to NB, 3 Dec. 1787. NSARM, MG13/2, fol. 517–8.
5. Mauger had died in 1788. "To John Butler Dight for the purchase of the distill house lot ... H£555.11.1." Thomas accounts, 1773–80. PRO, ADM17/150; NB to Duncan, 4 Nov. 1789. PRO, ADM106/2472, fol. 302–3.

6. Wodehouse to Smith, 9 Oct. 1816. NMM, HAL/E/21, fol. 439-40.
7. Wentworth to Duncan, 23 Feb. 1786. NSARM, MG13/2, fol. 411-2.
8. It was located 150 feet from a grant made the yard in 1800. H£250 was paid in 1815 to William Gray for the purchase of a house of ill-repute situated on the water lot adjoining the south boundary of the yard and of the unexpired term of the lease – four years – at H£70 a year. Wodehouse to NB, 4 & 25 Oct. 1815. PRO, ADM106/2029, fol. 245-6, 249. When the tenant failed to pay the rent, the house was pulled down. NB to Wodehouse, 16 Sept. 1816. NMM, HAL/C/2, fol. 167. In 1815 H£18.15.6. was paid for the customary fees on the grant of a water lot adjoining. Dawes accounts, 1815. PRO, ADM17/162.
9. As the Admiralty wanted no additional expenses, the plan to establish an additional mastpond there was rejected, even as it approved the purchase of the land. NB to Wodehouse, 6 & 21 Nov. 1815. NMM, HAL/C/2, fol. 87-8, 93.
10. Wodehouse to RO, 13 June 1817. NMM, HAL/E/41, fol. 391.
11. Coffin to Wentworth, 11 Feb. 1800. NSARM, MG13/6, fol. 520-1.
12. Duncan to NB, 16 Sept. 1800. PRO, ADM106/2027.
13. Hidden today, it runs under Brookside Street. In 1807 the master shipwright submitted an estimate for building a wharf and erecting watering spouts there, on government ground in Dartmouth, for the berthing of watering boats, for £125. Hughes to Inglefield, 31 July 1807. NMM, HAL/E/38, fol. 160-2.
14. Formerly Kavanagh's Island, renamed when the navy acquired it in 1804, after First Lord of the Admiralty Henry Dundas, Lord Melville. It was turned first into a prisoner-of-war compound. In 1815 it housed up to 800 black refugees brought by order of Vice Admiral Cochrane from Amelia Island, off the Georgia coast. Of the buildings on Melville Island, the guardhouse and the wharfs needed a general repair by 1811. Three years later Rear Admiral Griffith wanted to erect a building for an officer and twenty men having the command of a field piece on an island to the northwest of Melville Island, and a shed on both sides of the prison yard to hang up hammocks in wet weather. A small store was converted to a steward's room for issuing provisions. The cook-house required repairs, while the prison wall was crumbling.
15. NB to RO, 9 May 1785. NSARM, MG13/1, #565.
16. See Gerrish to NB, 20 Sept. 1760 & 12 Sept. 1772. PRO, ADM106/1121, ADM1/484, fol. 161. Identified in the earliest extant plan of the yard, "A View of his Majesty's Dockyard at Halifax 21 May 1760." Royal Ontario Museum.

Notes to page 30   247

17. In the summer of 1764 this house, intended for the storekeeper, was being fitted. In November–December, sashes and shutters were made for the "house and office intended for the storekeeper." PRO, ADM42/2148.
18. Durell was given permission to use it when he replaced Colvill, but died on his passage to Halifax. See Minute to Durell to NB, 16 Apr. 1766. PRO, ADM106/1144.
19. Hood to NB, 24 Oct. 1767. PRO, ADM106/1153.
20. Built by Hood "about 35 years earlier." Marshall and Hughes to Inglefield, 12 Nov. 1802. PRO, ADM106/2027; Marshall to Coffin, 30 Dec. 1799. NSARM, MG13/6, fol. 407. Coffin ordered the alterations. 31 Dec. 1799.
21. Hood to NB, 19 Dec. 1767. PRO, ADM106/1153. In 1771, Rear Admiral Montagu, who succeeded Hood in command of the North American squadron, also received permission to use the house, but being based in Boston he never came to Halifax. Montagu to NB, 8 Mar. 1771. ADM106/1201. Throughout 1779 carpenters worked on it, a wooden fence was put up, and the drains repaired. When Duncan arrived in 1783 the chimneys were rebuilt. PRO, ADM42/2152.
22. NB to RO, 25 Nov. 1783. NSARM, MG13/1, #521; NB to Duncan. PRO, ADM106/2471, fol. 308.
23. Admiralty to NB, 23 Feb. 1785; NB to RO, 8 Mar. 1785. NSARM, MG13/1, #529.
24. While under construction £53.2.6. was paid to rent a house in town for Duncan, owned by Messrs Cochrane, from 15 Sept. 1786 to 1 June 1787 @ £75 a year. Livie accounts, 1780–90. PRO, ADM17/150; Duncan to Thomas, 22 June 1787. NSARM, MG13/2, fol. 486.
25. The cupola, seen in two paintings made in 1786 and 1800, had disappeared in an elevation made in 1815, and is absent also in the photographs made of the house in the 1880s.
26. "Several alterations and additions laid down in the plan delivered to the Master Shipwright of the Yard appear to be materially necessary to be executed, previous to the house being inhabited." Gordon to RO, 7 Sept. 1799. PRO, ADM106/2027; NSARM, MG13/6, fol. 425–6.
27. Two original plans are dated 14 Nov. 1799. NMM, ADM/BP/19b. There are excellent floor plans and plan of the elevation of the house made 16 Mar. 1872. See PRO, MPI, 284. See estimate for alterations to the commissioner's house, with the master shipwright's plan. Coffin to Richard Nelson, 16 Oct. 1799. PRO, ADM106/2027. It was consumed by fire in November 1909. Marilyn Gurney Smith, *The King's Yard: An Illustrated His-*

248 Notes to pages 30–31

tory of the Halifax Dockyard (Halifax: Nimbus, 1985), 27. The cost of repairs came to £1,122. Duncan to NB, 28 Aug. 1800. ADM106/2027.

28. Extra work done on the commissioner's house amounted to 711½ hours for six carpenters, three masons, and three smiths from 18 Dec. to 1799 and 5 Jan. 1800. Marshall to Coffin, 6 Jan. 1800. NSARM, MG13/6, fol. 428–9; Coffin to Anderson, 11 Jan. 1800. MG13/6, fol. 435. In addition, "four rough partitions" were "run up in the coach house with a small sash in each," while the four stalls in the "cow house," were repaired. In 1812, Commissioner Wodehouse, newly-arrived in Halifax, ordered from London for the dining room and drawing room of the commissioner's house two stoves with grates "upon the newest and most approved principles." Wodehouse to Hartshorne & Boggs, 22 Dec. 1812. NA, I, 18. In January 1814 an inspection found the sills, joints, and all the other woodwork connected with the ground flour of the house "in such a state of general decay as to render an immediate repair absolutely necessary." Hawkes to Wodehouse, 11 Jan. 1814. NA, I, 458–60.

29. Unpainted wood exposed to the weather in Halifax never lasted more than three years. Inglefield to NB, 13 Nov. 1803. NSARM, MG13/3.

30. The Board claimed they lacked the power to comply with the request. NB to RO, 30 Nov. 1786. NSARM, MG13/2, fol. 449; MG13/1, #714.

31. Admiralty orders 10 Nov. 1787; NB to RO, 13 Nov. 1787; received 29 Feb. 1788. NSARM, MG13/2, fol. 328.

32. Duncan to NB, 12 Nov. 1790. PRO, ADM106/2027.

33. Admiralty's approval 19 Apr., NB to RO, 22 Apr. 1788. NSARM, MG13/2, fol. 560.

34. "Officers houses have been built 7 years." Elias Marshall's testimony, 6 May 1800. PRO, ADM106/2027.

35. The houses "were of wood, brick knocked, with brick foundations." RO to NB, 31 July 1793. PRO, ADM106/2027.

36. With such wooden buildings, repairs inevitably followed. In the winter of 1803–4 the floors and floor joists of the kitchens, cellars, and lower passages and the lining of the foundations were all found to be rotten. The front and back steps, the banisters, and the handrails had decayed in part; floors and joists of the backyards were rotten; the lower parts of the back steps needed to be replaced. New shingle roofing was needed. Eaves troughs, called "spouts," were needed on all three tenements. RO to Inglefield, 24 Oct. 1803. NSARM, MG13/9.1, fol. 58–9. In 1817 I. Taplin received H£2.8.9. for making tape ladders for Venetian blinds for the houses: thirty-nine pairs @ 1s.3d. per pair. Dawes accounts, 1817. PRO, ADM17/164. By 1815 the yard officers observed that posts and studs of the houses were

Notes to pages 31–32   249

totally decayed; the buildings still standing only because they had been brick-nogged. RO to Wodehouse, 6 Sept. 1815. NMM, HAL/E/21, fol. 303. The following year new kitchen ranges were installed in each house. "Between the price paid by Dawes to Messrs Starr & Co in Feb. and Mar. 1816 for a kitchen range purchased for the commissioner's and each of the three yard officers' houses and the price which the Board consented by their letter of 6 Apr. 1816 to allow for the same as instead of being purchased on the spot they should have been demanded from home in the usual manner." H£141 4s., Dawes accounts, 1816. ADM17/163.

37. Wodehouse to NB, 10 Feb. 1813. PRO, ADM106/2029, fol. 7–9; for Board's response, see Minute.
38. Duncan to NB, 19 June 1784. PRO, ADM106/1297; Minute "Approve." NB to Duncan, 3 Oct. 1783. ADM106/2471, fol. 301–2.
39. The building was enlarged "by adding the south end of the capstan house thereto by taking in the door which will not only secure the stores abovementioned, but also the staircase of the east sail loft, which I have witnessed myself seamen getting up into by these stairs. I find that the present store called the Careening House not sufficiently large to contain the careening gear, working hawsers &ca and that the latter are obliged to be coiled in the Capstan House exposed to the frequent irregularities committed by the crews of ships alongside the wharf." Jackson to Coffin, 24 Dec. 1799. NSARM, MG13/6, fol. 392; approval, Coffin to Marshall, 26 Dec. 1799. MG13/6, fol. 393.
40. NB to RO, 14 May 1806. NMM, HAL/E/34; NB to RO, 13 July 1809. NMM, HAL/C/1, fol. 111; Inglefield to RO, 28 Mar. 1809. PRO, ADM106/2028; NSARM, MG13/5, fol. 57. In 1807, £130 was required to pay for the cost of repairing the beams, joists, and floor of the cable storehouse and for additional underpinning. Besides the wear and tear on its flooring, the capstan house, like all the yard buildings, suffered periodically from leaks in the roof. First noted in 1803, only in 1806 did Parliament allocate £941 for its reshingling as well as that of the sail loft and hawser house. The sum also applied to the repair of beams, joists, and the floor of the cable store. RO to Inglefield, 4 Mar. 1803. MG13/3. The extreme pressure of refitting work prevented the work being undertaken for several years. In 1818, the whole of the capstan house, with two bays in the cable storehouse, needed new floors and sleepers. The careening room and floor also needed repair. RO to Wodehouse, 21 Oct. 1818. ADM106/2029, fol. 405–6.
41. At an estimated £787 15s. NB to Duncan, 3 Oct. 1783. PRO, ADM106/2471, fol. 301–2.
42. Duncan to NB, 9 June 1786. MG13/2, fol. 406.

250   Notes to pages 32–34

43. Duncan to RO, 28 Nov. 1785. NSARM, MG13/1, #597.
44. Duncan to NB, 29 June 1786. NSARM, MG13/2, fol. 413–5; NB to Duncan, 23 Aug. 1786. MG13/2, fol. 447; received 17 Dec. 1786.
45. In 1787 the Navy Board allowed a budget of £80 to make four staircases to the sail and slop loft, and £295 to repair the south storehouse. NB to RO, 22 Jan. 1787. NSARM, MG13/1, #721. In 1800, all the window shutters in the north wing were decayed and many of the casings needed shifting. New sashes in the sail loft were wanted, many being decayed and others could no longer be opened in warm weather. Estimated cost was £327, which included plastering and whitewashing the sail loft. Jackson and Andrew to Coffin, 1 Feb. 1800. MG13/6, fol. 496–7. In 1808, the officers were ordered to engage four additional house carpenters on the extra list to begin shingling the roofs of the stores. Inglefield to RO, 5 May 1806. NMM, HAL/E/34, fol. 11.
46. Hawkes to Wodehouse, 11 Jan. 1814. NA, I, 458–60.
47. Hawkes to Wodehouse, 8 Jan. 1814. NA, I, 461–2; directed to seek tenders, Wodehouse to RO, 8 Jan. 1814. NSARM, MG13/9.3, fol. 35.
48. The first third was to be paid in 1814, and the balance in 1815. Only Finnerty tendered. Wodehouse to NB, 3 Feb. 1814. PRO, ADM106/2029, fol. 143; Minute "Approve." Messrs Finnerty & Hill in 1814 were paid H£850 for the initial one-third part. Dawes accounts, 1814. PRO, ADM17/161. H£1,700 was paid on their contract of 16 Feb. 1814. Dawes accounts, 1815. ADM17/162.
49. Gerrish to NB, 20 Apr. 1760. ADM106/1121.
50. RO to Wodehouse, 21 Oct. 1818. PRO, ADM106/2029, fol. 405.
51. Oct.–Dec. 1774. PRO, ADM42/2150.
52. NB to RO, 22 Jan. 1787. NSARM, MG13/1, #721.
53. RO to Wodehouse, 21 Oct. 1818. PRO, ADM106/2029, fol. 405–6.
54. NB to Duncan, 3 Oct. 1783. PRO, ADM106/2471, fol. 301–2; Duncan to RO, 1 July 1785. NSARM, MG13/1, #556; Sawyer to Admiralty, 25 July 1785. PRO, ADM1/491, fol. 286v.
55. Inglefield to RO, 3 Jan. 1811. NMM, HAL/E/36, fol. 192–3.
56. NB to RO, 4 Sept. 1811. NMM, HAL/C/1, fol. 150. By 1818, the boathouse roof was again out of repair. RO to Wodehouse, 21 Oct. 1818. PRO, ADM106/2029, fol. 405–6.
57. NB to RO, 22 Jan. 1787. NSARM, MG13/1, #721.
58. The 1805 estimates allowed £340 for its repair. RO to Inglefield, 4 Mar. 1803. NSARM, MG13/3.
59. RO to Wodehouse, 21 Oct. 1818. PRO, ADM106/2029, fol. 405–6.
60. Hamond to masters of *Assurance, Allegiance, Atalanta*, 31 Aug. 1781. HP, IX, 21, 25.

61. April–June 1784. PRO, ADM42/2153.
62. NB to RO, 22 Jan. 1787. NSARM, MG13/1, #721.
63. In 1797 Duncan permitted workers then occupying a house at the watering ground to remain, but in case during his absence in England, "of the removal of any of them, no others to be admitted, as I intend either to pull the house down or turn it into a cooperage, when it will not distress the people." Inglefield to RO, 15 June 1804. NSARM, MG13/9.1, fol. 136. The Board approved. Inglefield to RO, Sept. 1804. MG13/9.1, fol. 174.
64. 7 Sept. 1806. NMM, HAL/A/3b, fol. 169–70.
65. Wodehouse to NB, 15 Nov. 1817. PRO, ADM106/2029, fol. 356.
66. Montagu to Stephens, 12 Dec. 1772. PRO, ADM1/484, fol. 184.
67. Pay lists with descriptions of work. PRO, ADM42/2148.
68. PRO, ADM42/2150; RO to Inglefield, 19 Aug. 1807. NMM, HAL/E/38, fol. 184.
69. NB to Duncan, 3 Oct. 1783. PRO, ADM106/2471, fol. 301–2.
70. Inglefield to RO, 24 Oct. 1803. NSARM, MG13/9.1, fol. 59.
71. PRO, ADM42/2152.
72. Its dimensions were sixty by fifteen feet. PRO, ADM42/2150.
73. PRO, ADM42/2152.
74. Rainy weather had so prevented any outside work that the equipping of his squadron was delayed. He ordered the yard officers to prepare an estimate for erecting a shed in which to fit, rig, and paint hammock covers, hitherto nailed in summer to the yard wall. Berkeley had suggested using the space between the tank and the yard wall extending from the commissioner's garden wall to the partition fence separating the yard from the hospital ground, with which suggestion they concurred. The lumber was to come from condemned masts and spars, a typical example of recycling to keep down costs. The estimate, made 13 Nov. 1807 and amounting to £106.5.10., included 8,468 feet of pine board, 2,900 feet of two to two-and-a-half inch plank, the frame to be made of old studding sail booms, topgallants, masts, and yards returned from the squadron, equal to 1,000 feet of ranging timber, to be built in a month by two house carpenters, two masons working full time, and a sawyer and smith working half the month only, the work performed in the winter months. Berkeley to Pole, 14 Nov. 1807. PRO, ADM1/497, fol. 458; Berkeley to RO, 11 Nov. 1807. PRO, ADM106/2028; for a drawing of the shed. NMM, HAL/A/1.
75. In 1793, a request of £1,345 was made for a watering tank to be dug and set up in place of the watering pond. RO to NB, 31 July 1793. PRO, ADM106/2027. In 1806, £126 was assigned to repair the "cap rail, land ties, port and rails of the tank and for cleaning." NB to RO, 14 May 1806. NMM, HAL/E/34 and HAL/A/3a, fol. 54–6. The tank was also painted regularly.

252   Notes to pages 35–37

76. In response to letters from Berkeley and Warren, the Board approved Warren's order to erect the shed. NB to RO, 23 July 1808. NMM, HAL/C/1, fol. 70.
77. July–Sept. 1783. PRO, ADM42/2152.
78. RO to Wodehouse, 21 Oct. 1818. PRO, ADM106/2029, fol. 405–6.
79. PRO, ADM42/2152.
80. £60 was allocated to fashion a new crane on the slip. NB to RO, 22 Jan. 1787. NSARM, MG13/1, #721.
81. Jackson & Andrew to Coffin, 1 Feb. 1800. NSARM, MG13/6, fol. 496–7.
82. NB to RO, 14 May 1806. NMM, HAL/E/34.
83. RO to Wodehouse, 21 Oct. 1818. PRO, ADM106/2029, fol. 405–6.
84. "On 11–12 Sept. 1783 employed 5 fire engines at His Majesty's coal magazine at request of the Commissary General Roger Johnson Esq.," July–Sept. 1783. PRO, ADM42/2152.
85. Sawyer to Duncan, 27 Apr. 1787. NSARM, MG13/2, fol. 454.
86. Wodehouse to NB, 14 Nov. 1815. PRO, ADM106/2029, fol. 255.
87. NB to Wodehouse, 6 May 1815. NMM, HAL/C/2, fol. 33–4.
88. "To pay James Dickman 10s. a day for twelve days for putting up and regulating the yard clock." Wodehouse to RO, 18 Nov. 1816. NMM, HAL/E/41, fol. 334.
89. RO to Inglefield, 14 Aug. 1811. NMM, HAL/E/25, fol. 81.
90. Wodehouse to NB, 3 June 1815; NB to Wodehouse, 5 July 1815. NMM, HAL/C/2, fol. 60.
91. Wodehouse to NB, 8 Apr. 1816. NMM, HAL/A/5, fol. 398–9.
92. NB to Wodehouse, 5 June 1816. NMM, HAL/C/2, fol. 147.
93. Wodehouse to NB, 14 Nov. 1815. PRO, ADM106/2029, fol. 255.
94. RO to NB, 20 Sept. 1760. PRO, ADM106/1121.
95. Duncan to NB, 19 June 1783, NB to Duncan, 3 Oct. 1783. PRO, ADM106/2471, fol. 301–2.
96. Duncan to RO, 1 July 1785. NSARM, MG13/1, #556.
97. NB to RO, 22 Jan. 1787. NSARM, MG13/1, #721.
98. Inglefield to RO, Jan. 1803; from the low water mark on the southwest side; Inglefield to NB, 25 Feb. 1803. PRO, ADM106/2027.
99. Paid £85.18.2. to officers and seamen to help make a new mastpond from 1 Sept.–30 Nov. 1800 and in collecting stones for the pier. Anderson accounts. PRO, ADM17/152.
100. Inglefield to RO, 4 Aug. 1809. NSARM, MG13/5, fol. 100.
101. Wodehouse to NB, 19 Mar. 1816. PRO, ADM106/2029, fol. 289–90. Board approved. NB to Wodehouse, 19 Apr. 1816. NMM, HAL/C/2, fol. 136.
102. April–June 1784. PRO, ADM42/2153.

Notes to pages 37–39   253

103. Estimates of £526.17.6. for the wood wharf. RO to NB, 31 July 1793. PRO, ADM106/2027.
104. NB to RO, 4 Sept. 1811. NMM, HAL/C/1, fol. 150.
105. Admiralty order 13 July 1784, NB to Duncan, 15 July 1784. PRO, ADM106/2471, fol. 343.
106. Duncan to NB, 29 June 1786. NSARM, MG13/2, fol. 413.
107. Board warrant, 13 July 1809. NSARM, MG13/9.3, fol. 213; NB to RO, same date. NMM, HAL/C/1, fol. 111.
108. The Navy Board was reminded that the problem had first been brought to its attention in 1807. Wodehouse to NB, 27 Mar. 1815. NMM, HAL/A/5, fol. 209–10. The Saint John contractor was George Andrews.
109. Hawkes to Wodehouse, 11 Jan. 1814. NA, I, 458–60.
110. Duncan to RO, 13 Sept. 1787. NSARM, MG13/1, #744.
111. Duncan to NB, 3 Dec. 1787. NSARM, MG13/2, fol. 517–8.
112. NB to RO, 22 Jan. 1787. NSARM, MG13/1, #721.
113. Estimate £700, NB to RO, 13 July 1809. NMM, HAL/C/1, fol. 111.
114. Hawkes to Wodehouse, 11 Jan. 1814. NA, I, 458–60. His first letter dated 14 Jan. 1814. Wodehouse to NB, 28 Nov. 1815. PRO, ADM106/2029, fol. 258. Minute 9 Jan. 1816, "Approve." NB to Wodehouse, 12 Jan. 1816. NMM, HAL/C/2, fol. 108.
115. NB to RO, 15 July 1784. NSARM, MG13/1, #506.
116. Duncan to NB, 27 June 1785 & 2 June 1786. NSARM, MG13/2, fol. 335, 406.
117. RO to NB, 31 July 1793. PRO, ADM106/2027; NB to RO, 14 Jan. 1795. NSARM, MG13/6, fol. 60–1; NB to Duncan, 22 Dec. 1795. MG13/1, fol. 9.
118. Hamond to Morden, 17 Nov. 1781. HP, VIII, 10–11. In 1809 a working party of seamen, under the master attendant, laid down moorings for the floating powder magazine between McNab's Island and George's Island. Inglefield to RO, 21 Aug. 1809. PRO, ADM106/2028; NSARM, MG13/5, #105.
119. Thomas James, acting storekeeper, to Wodehouse, 19 July 1816. NMM, HAL/E/21, fol. 415.
120. Wodehouse to RO, 22 June 1815. NMM, HAL/E/41, fol. 153.
121. Wodehouse to NB, 15 July 1816. PRO, ADM106/2029, fol. 298.
122. Nicolls to Wodehouse, 9 June 1813. NA, I, 177.
123. NB to Arbuthnot, 27 Apr. 1776. PRO, ADM106/2470, fol. 235–6.
124. The Admiralty directed that *Centurion* receive men raised for the service, convalescents from the hospital, and serve as a hulk for ships needing to be hove down; complement of thirty-six men. Warren to Inglefield, 16 June 1809. NMM, HAL/E/39a, fol. 192–3.
125. PRO, ADM42/2152.

254   Notes to pages 39–43

126. PRO, ADM42/2153.
127. Coffin to RO, 22 Jan. 1800. NSARM, MG13/6, fol. 481.
128. Estimate £370. Jackson & Andrew to Coffin, 1 Feb. 1800. NSARM, MG13/6, fol. 496–7. The work was carried out by yard masons using soldiers from the 24th Foot as labourers from 29 Mar. to 8 Sept. 1800. PRO, ADM17/150.
129. RO to Inglefield, 19 Aug. 1807. NMM, HAL/E/38, fol. 184. By 1811 the yard wall from the porter's lodge to the roundhouse needed to be rebuilt. As there were not sufficient masons available, army artificers were asked to assist. Hughes to Inglefield, 5 Apr. 1811. HAL/E/27, fol. 346.
130. Wodehouse to NB, 14 Nov. 1815. PRO, ADM106/2029, fol. 251; Wodehouse to RO, 1 Aug. 1816, 2 Nov. 1816, 4 Aug. 1817. NSARM, MG13/9.3, fol. 206, 221, 223, 233. The Navy Board granted £1,500, the work being undertaken in 1817 by contract with Peter Hay, the yard's mason, for H£2,343.2.9½. 4 Feb. 1817. Dawes accounts, 1817. PRO, ADM17/164.
131. Vandeput to Admiralty, 30 Sept. 1798. PRO, ADM1/494, fol. 144–5; Inglefield to NB, 10 Oct. 1811. PRO, ADM106/2028; Warren to Croker, 13 Nov. 1813. ADM1/504, fol. 351.
132. Inglefield to RO, 15 Mar. 1806. PRO, ADM106/2028.
133. Details on ice conditions are found in Halifax newspapers.
134. Wodehouse to NB, 26 May 1815. NMM, HAL/A/5, fol. 245–6; to RO, 1 June 1815. NSARM, MG13/9.3, fol. 170; NMM, HAL/E/41, fol. 143; NA, II, 288.
135. Minute 9 Jan. 1816, "Approve." Wodehouse to NB, 28 Nov. 1815. PRO, ADM106/2029, fol. 258.
136. Wodehouse to NB, 21 Nov. 1815. NMM, HAL/A/5, fol. 320–5.
137. Wodehouse to RO, 23 Apr. 1817; report 25 Apr. 1817. NSARM, MG13/9.3, fol. 213.
138. NB to Wodehouse, 14 Feb. 1817. NMM, HAL/C/2, fol. 203–4.
139. Wodehouse to NB, 15 Mar. 1819. PRO, ADM106/2029, fol. 444.

Chapter 3   Hospital Complex and Admiral's House

1. Jonathan G. Coad, *Historic Architecture of the Royal Navy: An Introduction* (London: Gollancz, 1983), 17.
2. Allan Everett Marble, *Surgeons, Smallpox, and the Poor: A History of Medicine and Social Conditions in Nova Scotia, 1749–1799* (Montreal: McGill-Queen's University Press, 1993), 48.
3. Oct.–Dec. 1776. PRO, ADM42/2150.
4. Sir George Collier, *A Detail of Some Particular Services Performed in America*

during the Years 1776, 1777, 1778, and 1779 by Commodore Sir George Collier ... compiled from Journals & Original Papers by G.S. Rainier; NMM, Collier papers. The incident is corroborated by the surgeon, James Dickson to Collier, 16 May 1777; printed in *Nova Scotia Gazette and Weekly Chronicle*, 6 Oct. 1778; cited in Marble, *Surgeons*, 113.

5. They built a dispensary with patient wards and 300 feet of shelves. April–June 1779. PRO, ADM42/2152.
6. Hamond to Sick & Hurt Board, 6 Aug. 1781. HP, VII, 6–8; inmates kept to their beds "for want of cloathing." Hamond to Handasyde, 21 Jan. 1782. HP, IX, 10.
7. His estimate later rose to £3,000. Hamond to Digby, 26 Dec. 1781. HP, VII, 56–8.
8. Purchased from truckman William Gorham for £120. Hamond to Thomas, 13 Aug. 1781. HP, IX, 38–9. He also paid Robert Grant £40 for a lot of land adjoining. HP, IX, 120.
9. NB to Hamond, 16 Oct. 1781. PRO, ADM106/2471, fol. 177.
10. Hamond to Digby, 26 Dec. 1781. HP, VII, 56–8.
11. 11 Dec. 1781.
12. Hamond to Thomas, 1 Jan. 1782. HP, IX, 77–8.
13. The offer of Israel Andrews of Windsor arrived too late. Hamond to Thomas, 1 Jan. 1782. HP, IX, 106; Hamond to Israel Andrews, 7 Jan. 1782. HP, VII, 61.
14. Hamond to Stephens, 13 Nov. 1782. HP, VII, 152.
15. Sawyer to Duncan, 4 Aug. 1786. NSARM, MG13/2, fol. 423.
16. Sawyer to Duncan, 21 June 1785. NSARM, MG13/2, fol. 338.
17. Halliburton to Duncan, 15 Aug. 1796. NSARM, MG13/6, fol. 176.
18. These were converted into wards in 1815; contract, 31 Jan. 1815. PRO, ADM106/2029, fol. 217. As the penalty for reneging on the contract was so high, the "tenements" as they were known, were built. Plank, board, and other materials came from New Brunswick, at half Halifax prices. There are errors in a pamphlet by B.A. Winters, *A Brief History of the Dockyard Terrace* (Halifax: privately printed, 1989).
19. Hamond to Halliburton, 15 Dec. 1782. HP, IX, 200.
20. Sawyer to Admiralty, 25 July 1785. PRO, ADM1/491, fol. 287v.
21. Sawyer to Stephens, 12 Oct. 1785. PRO, ADM1/491, fol. 349–50.
22. A "box to be furnished for the said sentinel." Berkeley to Inglefield, 23 Aug. 1806, Inglefield to Berkeley, 24 Aug. 1806. NMM, HAL/A/3b, fol. 161–2.
23. Halliburton to Murray, 21 Aug. 1794. PRO, ADM1/492, fol. 440; survey by Hughes and Andrews. ADM1/492, fol. 438–9.

24. Halliburton to Murray, 20 Aug. 1794. PRO, ADM1/492, fol. 434–5.
25. Perhaps on Kavanagh's Island in the North West Arm. Marble, *Surgeons*, 155.
26. Inglefield to NB, 17 Apr. 1806. PRO, ADM106/2028.
27. Directed master shipwright to report on feasibility of erecting another storey for patients' beds and clothing. Inglefield to RO, 8 Nov. 1809. NSARM, MG13/5, fol. 5; PRO, ADM106/2028.
28. RO to Inglefield, 10 Nov. 1802. NMM, ADM/B/207.
29. Berkeley to Inglefield, 25 Sept. 1806. NMM, HAL/A/3b, fol. 184.
30. Tender £170 2s. from Messrs Henderson and Brynor. Inglefield to Eppes, 27 Oct. 1810. NMM, HAL/E/36, fol. 161.
31. Eppes to Wodehouse, 28 Dec. 1812. NA, I, 20–1.
32. Rowlands to Wodehouse, 3 May 1813. NA, I, 129–31.
33. Halliburton to Duncan, 29 Mar. 1784. NMM, HAL/F/2, fol. 135–7.
34. Inglefield to NB, 17 Apr. 1806. PRO, ADM106/2028.
35. Reported by Halliburton, Inglefield to RO, 4 Sept. 1804. NSARM, MG13/9.1, fol. 173.
36. After Sawyer had brought this to Inglefield's attention, he ordered a survey prepared. 22 Aug. 1811. NMM, HAL/E/36, fol. 303–4.
37. Rowlands to Wodehouse, 5:30 a.m., 17 June 1813. NA, I, 178–9.
38. Sawyer to Admiralty, 25 July 1785. PRO, ADM1/491, fol. 287; Sawyer to Duncan, 4 Aug. 1786. NSARM, MG13/2, fol. 423; Murray to Duncan, 19 Nov. 1795. MG13/6, fol. 119; RO to Inglefield, 10 Nov. 1802. NMM, ADM/B/207.
39. RO to Inglefield, 23 Dec. 1802. NSARM, MG13/3.
40. Inglefield to RO, 16 June 1804. NSARM, MG13/9.1, fol. 138.
41. Estimate £520 5s., 22 Feb. 1813. NA, I, 59–67. In addition, a lead cistern attached to a water closet in the surgeon's hospital apartment burst from ice pressure. Rowlands to Wodehouse, 10 May 1813. NA, I, 143.
42. Marshall & Hughes to Inglefield, 22 June 1804. PRO, ADM106/2028; Inglefield to RO, 27 Aug. 1804. NSARM, MG13/9.1, fol. 172; Berkeley to Inglefield, 4 Oct. 1806. NMM, HAL/A/3b, fol. 189–90; Inglefield to RO, 4 Oct. 1806. ADM106/2028; Inglefield to RO, 25 July 1806. NMM, HAL/E/34, fol. 25.
43. John Hay for H£80, Inglefield to RO, 8 June 1812. NMM, HAL/E/36, fol. 435; Eppes to Wodehouse, 28 Dec. 1812. NA, I, 20–1.
44. Sawyer to Admiralty, 25 July 1785. PRO, ADM1/491, fol. 287.
45. Halliburton to Duncan, 10 Aug. 1796. NSARM, MG13/6, fol. 174–5.
46. Rowlands & Eppes to Wodehouse, 10 May 1813. NA, I, 146.
47. Duncan to Thomas, 18 Apr. 1784. NSARM, MG13/1, #433.

48. A request for £312 10s. was made in 1794 to cover the cost of erecting a 160-foot-long breastwork at the waterside from the lower part of the hospital, ten feet high at the outer end, and three feet high at the upper end, with a picket fence on it to "prevent people coming into the yard." RO to NB, 31 July 1793. PRO, ADM106/2027.
49. RO to Inglefield, 25 Nov. 1803. NSARM, MG13/9.1, fol. 70.
50. Warren to Wodehouse, 30 Nov. 1812. NA, I, 3.
51. Rowlands & Eppes to Wodehouse, 20 Apr. 1813. NA, I, 111–2; Wodehouse to RO, 20 Apr. 1813. NA, II, 8. The surgeon and the agent wrote a joint letter complaining of the mason, John Hay, contractor for building a wall round the hospital. Instead of pointing the wall as his contract required, Hay ignored their request. His reason was, the surgeon believed, that his men were then engaged in "erecting a still for the distillation of spirits within thirty yards of the dockyard and hospital walls, which will have a most injurious tendency not only to the patients under my care but also the working parties within the yard walls." Rowlands to Wodehouse, 14 May 1813. NA, I, 155–6.
52. The structure, now known as Buildings 77, 78, and 79, along with the admiral's mansion are the only two pre-1820 yard structures to survive the effect of the 1917 Halifax harbour explosion and the destruction, especially in 1941, of the historic yard buildings by the wartime Royal Canadian Navy.
53. Except the matron's apartments. Dawes accounts, 1815. PRO, ADM17/162.
54. Wodehouse to NB, 7 Mar. 1815. NMM, HAL/A/5, fol. 193–4; NB to Wodehouse, 10 Apr. 1815. NMM, HAL/C/2, fol. 25.
55. Wodehouse to RO, 11 Sept. 1815. NA, II, 311.
56. Not in 1815, as stated by Winters, *Dockyard Terrace*, 5; contract, 31 Jan. 1815. PRO, ADM106/2029, fol. 217; NMM, HAL/E/41, fol. 393 and HAL/E/1; advance payments amounted to H£3,465.17.6. Dawes accounts, 1814. PRO, ADM17/161.
57. Shipped in transports *Abundance* (200 tons) and *Coromandel* (201 tons). Wodehouse to NB, 15 Sept. 1815. NMM, HAL/A/5, fol. 290–1; Wodehouse to RO, 6 & 9 Oct. 1815. NSARM, MG13/9.3, fol. 185; Wodehouse to NB, 27 Mar. 1815. HAL/A/5, fol. 209–10. For two months in the spring of 1816 a working party of at least twenty sailors with officers earned £56 to dig and level earth and to make a road to the structure. Wodehouse to Locke, 3 Apr. 1816. NMM, HAL/E/21, fol. 392; from 4 Apr. to 3 June 1816. Dawes accounts, 1816. PRO, ADM17/163. The contractors also received H£87.15.8. for putting up closets, fitting three storerooms, and finishing two coal sheds in the houses. For brick nogging the lower storey, Peter Hay

received H£195, as doing so both made the houses warmer "and a great harbour for rats, which are so numerous everywhere contiguous to the yard as to be a very great nuisance, will be prevented." RO to Wodehouse, 6 Sept. 1815. HAL/E/21, fol. 303; H£159.7.6. between March and September 1816 to sink a well, set thirty grates, and build three ovens. 10 Mar. to 29 Sept. 1816. Dawes accounts, 1816. ADM17/163.
58. In 1818 these new buildings nearly burned down. One of the chimneys in the agent's house caught fire on 7 March. When some of the mortar between the bricks collapsed under the heat, flames passed through into the garret "threatening the building with very great danger. As I believe we shall never be secure from fire unless the work I allude to is plastered I have thought it right to make this communication to you." Charles Martyr to Wodehouse, 9 Mar. 1818. NMM, HAL/E/26, fol. 90.
59. Wodehouse suggested to the Board that they consult Hawkes, the former master shipwright for another explanation. Wodehouse to NB, 22 June 1818. PRO, ADM106/2029, fol. 374–5.
60. Admiralty decision, 26 May 1819, VB to Wodehouse, 3 June 1819. NMM, HAL/E/3a, fol. 216.
61. Wodehouse to Jones, 11 June 1819. NSARM, MG13/9.3, fol. 246.
62. Griffith to Croker, 16 Nov. 1819. PRO, ADM1/511, fol. 214–5. For a published account of the fire which incurred losses estimated at £12,000 see 13 Nov. 1819, *Acadian Recorder.*
63. £60 a year, Warren to Pole, 8 Sept. 1809. PRO, ADM1/499, fol. 241.
64. Montagu to Stephens, 19 Jan. 1773. PRO, ADM1/484.
65. Digby to Stephens, 19 Mar. 1782. PRO, ADM1/490, fol. 74.
66. Hamond to surgeons on *Chatham*, *Hussar*, and *Allegiance*, 17 Apr. 1782. HP, IX, 98; Halliburton to Thomas, 1 Mar. 1787. NSARM, MG13/1, #728; Berkeley to Pole, 12 Dec. 1807. PRO, ADM1/497, fol. 488.
67. PRO, ADM1/506, fol. 107.
68. The Board's minutes and deposition have not been located. Warren to Croker, 26 Oct. 1813. PRO, ADM1/504, fol. 285–7.
69. Hume's statement. PRO, ADM1/506, fol. 99.
70. Hume's statement. PRO, ADM1/506, fol. 100.
71. Hume's statement. PRO, ADM1/506, fol. 104.
72. Wodehouse to Griffith, 6 Sept. 1813. NA, I, 366.
73. 12 Jan. 1814. PRO, ADM1/506, fol. 111.
74. Hume's statement. PRO, ADM1/506, fol. 104v.
75. Hume's statement. PRO, ADM1/506, fol. 106.
76. Hume's statement. PRO, ADM1/506, fol. 108.
77. 26 Mar. 1814. PRO, ADM1/506, fol. 111.

78. 26 Mar. 1814. PRO ADM1/506, fol. 115.
79. 26 Mar. 1814. PRO, ADM1/506, fol. 117.
80. On 6 Mar. 1814. Cochrane to Croker, 21 Apr. 1814. PRO, ADM1/506, fol. 97. Enclosed was Hume's "statement of facts" sworn before two Halifax justices.
81. Requested permission to rent a house, as Commodore Douglas had done before him. Sawyer to Admiralty, 26 June 1785. PRO, ADM1/491, fol. 280v; Sawyer to Duncan, 21 June 1785. NSARM, MG13/2, fol. 338.
82. Berkeley to Inglefield, 1 Aug. 1806. PRO, ADM106/2028; NMM, HAL/A/3b, fol. 144.
83. Inglefield to RO, 1 June 1810. NMM, HAL/E/36, fol. 70.
84. Warren to Pole, 18 Aug. 1809. PRO, ADM1/499, fol. 191v; Warren to Sir William Rich, 22 June 1810. PRO, ADM106/1438.
85. NB to RO, 4 Sept. 1811. NMM, HAL/C/1, fol. 150.
86. Sawyer to Admiralty, 6 Aug. 1811. PRO, ADM1/501, fol. 193; allowed £200 per annum, Pole to Sawyer, 9 Sept. 1811. PRO, ADM2/932, fol. 139. The same offer was made to Warren and Griffith, Pole to Warren, 8 Mar. & 27 May 1813. ADM2/932.
87. Warren to Wodehouse, 7 Dec. 1812. NA, I, 8. Board warrant, 4 Sept. 1811.
88. He sent back Merriot's "plan of the house." Wodehouse to Warren, 20 Jan. 1813. NA, I, 23–4.
89. Warren to Wodehouse, 28 Sept. 1813. NA, I, 408.
90. Wodehouse to RO, 29 Oct. 1813. NA, II, 60.
91. Warren to Croker, 5 Mar. 1813. PRO, ADM1/504.
92. Barrow to Cochrane. PRO, ADM2/933, fol. 129–30.
93. Messrs Finnerty & Hill, for H£5,530, undertook to complete the house by October 1814; Thomas Kinnear & John Hay for H£4,550 by July 1814. The Kinnear & Hay tender excluded the costs of painting and glazing, excavating for the foundation, and installing the copper roof. See their letter 24 Oct. 1813. PRO, ADM1/504. Tenders were printed only on 30 Oct. 1813, *Acadian Recorder*. The architectural drawings could be seen by applying to Plaw. Warren sent Croker both tender and completed plans proposed by Thomas Kinnear and John Hay. 5 Nov. 1813. ADM1/504, fol. 298–302 [removed to PRO, MPI, 116]. At Rear Admiral Griffith's initiative, Governor Sherbrooke asked the house of assembly for a subsidy to meet the additional cost above £3,000. Sherbrooke's address to the house of assembly, 28 Feb. 1814. NSARM, RG1/288, doc. 96 and RG1/304.
94. In July he sent "a new plan of the house" with "many architectural improprieties in it, which have chiefly arisen from the changes which I have

thought necessary to make in the original plan by omitting things wherein most of the offices were to be included." Griffith to Croker, 30 July 1815. PRO, ADM1/509, fol. 467; Griffith to Wodehouse, 16 Nov. 1815. PRO, ADM106/2029, fol. 276-7. The foremen "have been diligent in their tasks." Rates of daily pay (H£) for tradesmen working on the house included: working foreman of house carpenters 12s.6d.; masons from 6s.2d. to 7s.6d.; house carpenters 5s.6d.; painters 7s.6d.; a horse, cart, and driver 8s. PRO, ADM17/165, fol. 12. Allowances of H£36.17.5. were paid to soldiers and seamen in November and December 1815 assisting at the house: house carpenter and mason at 2s.6d. (H£) per day, a sergeant of the 99th Foot at 2s.6d., staff corps mason, seamen, and marines at 1s. sterling; two soldiers of the 99th Foot, one of whom was a mason, Pat Ruth, at 2s. Town artificers included John McKenzie and foreman of masons Duncan Alexander, each paid 12s.6d.; two masons at 7s.6d. and 7s.; a plasterer at 8s.; and a house carpenter, John Rigby, at 4s. Dawes accounts, 1816. ADM17/163.
95. NB to Dawes, 27 Dec. 1816. NMM, HAL/E/30, fol. 201.
96. Cochrane to Croker, 5 Oct. 1814. PRO, ADM1/507, fol. 245. The Admiralty refused to send them; NB suggested other building materials: local rubble in the basement, pitch pine timber plastered inside, and chimneys to be of local brick. NB to Wodehouse, 29 Dec. 1814. NMM, HAL/C/2, fol. 41-3.
97. Received Inglefield's letter of 4 Nov. that day; Andrew Belcher to Inglefield, [Dec. 1814] Denmark Hill, Camberwell. PRO, ADM106/1365.
98. NB to Wodehouse, 26 Aug. 1815. NMM, HAL/C/2, fol. 71-3.
99. NB to Wodehouse, 11 Mar., 12 Apr., 15 June & 29 Dec. 1814; NB to Wodehouse, 26 Aug. 1815. NMM, HAL/C/2, fol. 71-3.
100. Griffith to Croker, 4 July 1815. PRO, ADM1/509, fol. 436.
101. *Attentive* was sent to Pictou to take on a cargo of coal and stone for the admiral's house "as Mr E[dward] Mortimer may have caused to be prepared." Wodehouse to Lieut Thomas Smith, 21 June 1816. NMM, HAL/E/41, fol. 295. That men went to Lunenburg to quarry stones is clear from the fact that H£10 8s. was paid a surgeon at Lunenburg, John Bolman, for board and medicines furnished a seaman from *Centurion* employed in quarrying stones for the government there. Dawes accounts, 1817. PRO, ADM17/164.
102. Working party from *Centurion* was paid 3s.9d. (H£) per ton delivered. Wodehouse to RO, 29 Dec. 1815. NMM, HAL/E/41, fol. 252.
103. Schooner *Lively*, purchased "for the purpose of bringing Stone from the sea coast for the house," was to be repaired to make her seaworthy. Wodehouse to RO, 1 Aug. 1815. NSARM, MG13/9.3, fol. 179. In October 1816

the sloop purchased by Griffith to freight stone and sand for the house was to be sold. Wodehouse to RO, 26 June & 23 Oct. 1816. MG13/9.3, fol. 206; NMM, HAL/E/41, fol. 297, 324. Griffith sent vouchers for sail and rigging bought for *Lively* and a flat-bottomed boat used to collect and freight stone. NB to Wodehouse, 17 Oct. 1816. NMM, HAL/C/2, fol. 177. By the end of 1816 *Lively* was sold, as the necessary stone, sand, and lime had been gathered. Wodehouse to RO, 23 Oct. 1816. MG13/9.3, fol. 206. Samuel Albro, for instance, was paid £4 10s. for 180 tons of stone collected by working parties of seamen on his land at Dartmouth. In 1816, H£441.9.3. was paid petty officers, seamen, and soldiers in working parties employed on the site. Daily wages varied: 2s.6d. (H£) per day for the house carpenter, mason, and Dyas Beverley, sgt of marines; 2s. sterling for a master's mate, boatswain, masons, sawyers, and smiths; 1s.3d. sterling for the boatswain's mates; and 1s. sterling to seamen, marines, and soldiers. From *Centurion* hulk came Edward Sharp and John White, both house carpenters, James Egleston and Francis Wilson, both masons. Each earned 2s.6d. sterling a day, as did two masons from the 99th Foot, Owen Coil and Martin Conway.
104. Wodehouse to Crofton, 11 Mar. 1816. NMM, HAL/E/21, fol. 369–70.
105. Crofton to Wodehouse, 11 Mar. 1816. NMM, HAL/E/21, fol. 374–5.
106. Griffith to Wodehouse, 16 Nov. 1815, Wodehouse to Griffith, 17 Nov. 1815. NMM, HAL/E/21, fol. 333–5, 336.
107. Cochrane to Griffith, 9 Oct. 1814. PRO, ADM1/509, fol. 438; Griffith to Croker, 4 July 1815. ADM1/509.
108. 7 Apr. 1815, *Acadian Recorder and Weekly Chronicle.*
109. Griffith to Croker, 4 July 1815. PRO, ADM1/509.
110. Wodehouse to NB, 19 June 1816. PRO, ADM106/2029, fol. 294–5.
111. Wodehouse to RO, 27 July 1816. NSARM, MG13/9.3, fol. 202; Dawes accounts, 1816. PRO, ADM17/163.
112. 25 Apr. 1817. NSARM, MG13/9.3, fol. 213.
113. In 1817 petty officers, seamen, and soldiers earned H£295.18.1. for work on the house. Daily rates of pay for ship's crew and the military garrison amounted to 2s. for sawyers and painters; 2s.3d. for carpenters and masons; and 1s. for seamen, all in sterling. Dawes accounts, 1817. PRO, ADM17/164. At work on the house in 1818 were: one working foreman of house carpenters earning 12s.6d. (H£) a day; two painters at 7s.6d.; three masons at 6s.2d. and two at 7s.6d.; several house carpenters at 5s.6d. each; two horses, and a cart and driver at 8s. a day. Dawes accounts, 1818. ADM17/165, fol. 11–12. In addition H£22.4.5. was paid Isaac Rigby, master carpenter of the Royal Engineers, by way of an allowance for his services in superintending the construction. In June Wodehouse had asked

262 Notes to pages 58–59

Rear Admiral David Milne for two parties of thirty men, with officers, to work both at the admiral's house and on yard work, with such masons, bricklayers, sawyers, and painters as could be spared. Wodehouse to Milne, 4 June 1818. NMM, HAL/E/26, fol. 112.

114. In 1817 tradesmen at work on the house received a total of H£275.9.4., while Joseph Wilson earned H£383 from his contract of 9 Aug. 1817 to build a dry-stone wall in front of the house. Dawes accounts, 1817. PRO, ADM17/164.
115. Wodehouse to RO, 6 Nov. 1816, 11 Mar. & 25 June 1817. NSARM, MG13/9.3, fol. 208, 211, 219.
116. Wodehouse to NB, 19 June 1816. NMM, HAL/A/5, fol. 425–6.
117. In 1816 Wodehouse hired four masons: John Rhind in April to work at the admiral's house at 8s.6d.; John Bryant in May at 8s.; Pat Ruth from the 99th Foot in June at 2s.6d. sterling; Thomas Murdock at 8s.6d. Wodehouse to RO, 13 Apr., 15 May, 1 & 27 June 1816. NSARM, MG13/9.3, fol. 200, 202–3. Discharged in July, they were hired anew in November but at lower wages: Bryant at 7s., Murdock and Rhind at 7s.6. Rhind was discharged before the month was out, Murdock and Bryant in January 1817. Wodehouse to RO, 1 & 29 Nov. 1816, 18 Jan. 1817. MG13/9.3, fol. 207–8, 210.
118. Wodehouse to Dawes, 27 July, 10, 15, 31 Aug., 3 Sept. 1818. NSARM, MG13/9.3, 229–232. The yard purchased sixty-one feet of freestone steps, 925 feet of freestone flagstones, fifty-three feet of freestone cornice, 1,138 bushels of sand, 17,433 bricks probably for the chimneys and hearths and, to keep the workers warm, two cast iron stoves. Wodehouse to RO, 3 Oct. & 4 Dec. 1818. NMM, HAL/E/43, fol. 166, 170–1, 173. Bricklayers and plasterers in 1818 received H£828.12.7. Dawes accounts, 1818. PRO, ADM17/165. fol. 11–12.
119. Wodehouse to RO, 28 Oct. 1818. NSARM, MG13/9.3, fol. 234.
120. The Board chastised him for hiring in mid-August a painter at 7s. a day "as the duty should be performed by the yard painter." NB to Wodehouse, 26 Nov. 1818. NMM, HAL/C/2, fol. 387; Wodehouse to RO, 14 Nov. 1818. NSARM, MG13/9.3, fol. 234.
121. Wodehouse to RO, 25 Feb. 1819. NSARM, MG13/9.3, fol. 237.
122. Dawes accounts, 1819. PRO, ADM17/166, fol. 12.
123. These tradesmen were paid "the present town wages" of 6s. (H£) a day. Wodehouse to RO, 13 Apr. 1819. NSARM, MG13/9.3, fol. 241.
124. Three of them in May: George Paulby, William Strickland, and J. Davie. Wodehouse to RO, 1 & 15 May 1819. NSARM, MG13/9.3, fol. 243–4.
125. Griffith to Jones, 7 Aug. 1819. NSARM, MG13/9.3, fol. 248.
126. Griffith to Jones, 15 Sept. 1819. NSARM, MG13/9.3, fol. 249.

127. Wodehouse to NB, 31 Dec. 1817. NMM, HAL/E/1, fol. 144. The Board sent the new stoves, wallpaper, and 112 brass shutter knobs for the house. NB to Wodehouse, 29 May 1818. NMM, HAL/C/2, fol. 344.
128. Milne to Croker, 1 Nov. 1817. PRO, ADM1/511, fol. 3.
129. Plan not located. Wodehouse to RO, 21 July 1819. NSARM, MG13/9.3, fol. 229.
130. Griffith to Croker, 30 July 1815. PRO, ADM1/509, fol. 467.
131. When *Mersey* arrived in May, Wodehouse requested two working parties, each of twelve men. He wanted bricklayers and masons needed to work on the walls and outbuildings at the admiral's mansion. The yard working hours were then 5:00 a.m. to 4:30 p.m. Wodehouse to Collier, 17 May 1819. NMM, HAL/E/26, fol. 256; Griffith to Jones, 23 Sept. 1819. NSARM, MG13/9.3, fol. 249–50.
132. Only squadron artificers were to be used in the work. Griffith to Jones, 20 Oct. 1819. NSARM, MG13/9.3, fol. 250. In wartime it had accommodated women employed to launder for the hospital.
133. N.A.M. Rodger, *The Wooden World: An Anatomy of the Georgian Navy* (Annapolis, MD: Naval Institute Press, 1986), 109–10.
134. Anthony A. Lockwood, *A Brief Description of Nova Scotia with plates of the principal harbors including a particular account of the Island of Grand Manan* (London: Hayden, 1818), 14.
135. NB to Wodehouse, 10 May 1816. NMM, HAL/C/2, fol. 140–1.

Chapter 4   Officers and Their Clerks

1. Roger Morriss, *The Royal Dockyards during the Revolutionary and Napoleonic Wars* (Leicester: Leicester University Press, 1983), vi–vii, 218, 221–2.
2. J.M. Haas, *A Management Odyssey: The Royal Dockyards, 1714–1914* (Lanham, MD: University Press of America, 1994), 44.
3. Haas, *A Management Odyssey*, 65.
4. See appendix 4.
5. Though called the naval officer, I refer to him by the earlier title of naval storekeeper, as the new title is easily confused with those in the customs and naval services.
6. Haas, *A Management Odyssey*, 52.
7. NB to Admiralty, 16 Dec. 1782. NMM, ADM/BP/3.
8. PRO, ADM1/1441.
9. St Vincent to Spencer, 22 Jan. 1799. H.W. Richmond, ed., *Private Papers of George, Second Earl Spencer: First Lord of the Admiralty*, 4 vols. (London: Navy Records Society, 1924), 59: 5.

10. David Syrett, *The Royal Navy in American Waters, 1775–1783* (Aldershot: Scolar Press, 1989), 121.
11. Hamond to Shelburne, 9 Oct. 1782. HP, VIII, 33; Hamond to Stephens, 30 Oct. 1782. HP, VII, 147–8.
12. Thomas to Duncan, 30 May 1786. NSARM, MG13/2, fol. 399–403.
13. Minute, 8 Aug. 1811. PRO, ADM1/3441; Croker to Inglefield, 10 Aug. 1811. NMM, HAL/A/2, fol. 215; Inglefield to Croker, 15 Oct. 1811. PRO, ADM106/2028.
14. Inglefield to Croker, 10 Jan. 1811. PRO, ADM106/2028.
15. Wodehouse to NB, 29 Jan. 1813. NMM, HAL/A/2, fol. 397–9.
16. Wodehouse to NB, 14 Nov. 1817. PRO, ADM106/2029, fol. 354–5.
17. Duncan to RO, 30 May 1797. NSARM, MG13/6, fol. 244–5.
18. Coffin to Parker, 12 Mar. 1800. NSARM, MG13/6, fol. 535.
19. In order to be identified by the various forts defending the harbour, the commissioner's boat flew a blue flag with white diagonal cross, the master attendant a red flag pierced with white, and the boatswain a plain yellow flag. Coffin to Duke of Kent, 31 Jan. 1800. NSARM, MG13/6, fol. 496.
20. Inglefield to NB, 25 May 1808. PRO, ADM106/2028. To carry a coxswain, NB to RO, 31 May 1808. NMM, HAL/C/1, fol. 58.
21. Resigned as lieutenant governor 30 Oct. 1782; Capt. Ludwidge refused his orders on 6 Dec. HP, VII, 147–8, 162–3.
22. Coffin to RO, 17 Oct. 1799. NSARM, MG13/6, fol. 325a–b; PRO, ADM106/2027.
23. To ignore such services out of the "common course of business." See Minute, RO to Nelson, 26 Apr. 1800. PRO, ADM106/2027.
24. Coffin to RO, 22 Jan. 1800. NSARM, MG13/6, fol. 483.
25. Messrs Reynolds and Brown, Coffin to Vandeput, 31 Jan. 1800. NSARM, MG13/6, fol. 495. This charge, unsupported with evidence, was never investigated. Murray to Uniacke, 18 Apr. 1800. PRO, ADM1/2139; Uniacke to Murray, 20 Apr. 1800. ADM1/2139; Murray to Coffin, 25 Apr. 1800. ADM1/2138.
26. Captains Hardy, Pellew, Douglas, Andrew, Evans, Hall, and Spear to Murray asking that the memorial be sent to the Admiralty, 25 May 1780. Murray to Nepean, 26 May 1800. PRO, ADM1/2139.
27. Murray to St Vincent, 19 May 1801. PRO, ADM1/2139.
28. Inglefield to Croker, 16 Sept. 1811. PRO, ADM1/3441; Croker to Inglefield, 6 Oct. 1810. NMM, HAL/A/2, fol. 198–202.
29. Douglas to Croker, 23 Mar. 1802. PRO, ADM1/495, fol. 280–2.
30. Inglefield to NB, 13 Nov. 1803. PRO, ADM106/2027.
31. 11 Oct. 1807 in *Beagle*; returned on 1 Aug. 1808.

32. Inglefield to [Marsden], 25 June 1811. PRO, ADM1/3441.
33. His reputation had been earned by his behaviour in the West Indies, demonstrated by his rapacity for prize money, upon the seizure of Martinique, Guadeloupe, and St Lucia in 1794. Patricia Crimmin, "John Jervis, Earl of St Vincent, 1735–1823," in *Precursors of Nelson: British Admirals of the Eighteenth Century*, ed. Peter Le Fevre and Richard Harding, 325–52 (London: Chatham, 2000).
34. Coffin to RO, 15 Dec. 1799. NSARM, MG13/6, fol. 350.
35. Coffin to RO, 14 Feb. 1800. NSARM, MG13/6, fol. 506.
36. Coffin to RO, 19 Dec. 1799. NSARM, MG13/6, fol. 366. In this he was supported by the admiral. Vandeput to Coffin, 19 Dec. 1799. MG13/6, fol. 375.
37. Coffin to Anderson, 16 Dec. 1799. NSARM, MG13/6, fol. 352.
38. This abuse he believed had begun after Duncan's departure. Coffin to RO, 24 Dec. 1799. NSARM, MG13/6, fol. 391.
39. Crews provided it when their ships were refitting, the so-called junk being issued by the master attendant. Marshall to Coffin, 31 Dec. 1799, Coffin to Marshall, 31 Dec. 1799. NSARM, MG13/6, fol. 412–3.
40. Coffin to RO, 30 Dec. 1799. NSARM, MG13/6, 404.
41. Coffin to RO, 3 Jan. 1800. NSARM, MG13/6, fol. 424.
42. Coffin to RO, 13 Jan. 1800. NSARM, MG13/6, fol. 448.
43. Coffin to RO, 3 Jan. 1800. NSARM, MG13/6, fol. 425.
44. Also applied to horse or cart drivers employed by the yard. Passes were issued by principal officers, foreman of shipwrights, or foreman of sailmakers. Coffin to Cullen, 21 Oct. 1799. NSARM, MG13/6, fol. 341.
45. Coffin to RO, 10 Mar. 1800. NSARM, MG13/6, fol. 533–4.
46. Wodehouse to RO, 29 June 1819. NMM, HAL/E/42a, fol. 271.
47. Wodehouse to RO, 13 June 1817. NSARM, MG13/9.3, fol. 218.
48. Halifax town and Nova Scotia council to Wodehouse, 30 July 1819. NMM, HAL/E/26, fol. [295–7].
49. RO and Bartlett, Anderson, Sherlock, Ritchie, Walkins to Wodehouse, 30 July 1819. NMM, HAL/E/25, fol. 376–7.
50. 30 July 1819. NMM, HAL/E/26, fol. 297–8.
51. These housed the naval officer, master attendant, master shipwright, boatswain, and foreman of shipwrights. Dawes to Wodehouse, 18 May 1818. PRO, ADM106/2029, fol. 269–70. For as was explained, "if unoccupied will fall into ruin." Permission granted to continue "to inhabit the houses although discharged from the yard, provided they undertake to keep the houses in repair, but no person not belonging to the yard is to be allowed to live within its walls." NB to Jones, 26 Aug. 1819. ADM106/2029, fol. 506.

52. NB to Wodehouse, 6 July 1813. NMM, HAL/E/31, fol. 324–5.
53. Admiralty to NB, 29 Jan. 1810, NB to Inglefield, 5 Feb. 1810. NMM, HAL/C/1, fol. 133–4.
54. Digby to Stephens, 30 Sept. 1783. PRO, ADM1/490, fol. 321; Coffin to Read, 16 Oct. 1799. NSARM, MG13/6, fol. 329.
55. Hamond to Admiralty, 16 May 1782. HP, VII, 84–5. He died the next year.
56. Coffin to Nepean, 18 Oct. 1799. NSARM, MG13/6, fol. 330.
57. Halliburton to Capt. John Douglas, 27 July 1781. PRO, ADM106/2027; discharged, RO to Nelson, 29 July 1801. ADM106/2027.
58. Coffin to Nepean, 18 Oct. 1799. NSARM, MG13/6, fol. 330.
59. Inglefield to NB, 29 Mar. 1803. PRO, ADM106/2027; Dawes to Nelson, 2 Apr. 1803. NSARM, MG13/3.
60. Inglefield to Admiralty, 9 Jan. 1810. NMM, HAL/E/36, fol. 5.
61. NB to Dawes, 14 June 1813. NMM, HAL/C/1, fol. 198; NB to Wodehouse, 27 Nov. 1816. HAL/C/2, fol. 188.
62. NB to Arbuthnot, 23 Oct. 1775. PRO, ADM106/2470, fol. [214]; Parker to Nepean, 28 Feb. 1801. PRO, ADM1/495, fol. 212–4.
63. Coffin to Anderson, 11 Jan. 1800. NSARM, MG13/6, fol. 435–6.
64. Of three sons who entered the navy, William James Hughes retired a sea captain and became a governor of Greenwich Hospital, having married into the English gentry.
65. Inglefield to RO, 13 Apr. 1809. NSARM, MG13/5, fol. 9.
66. NB to Dawes, 12 Aug. 1809. NMM, HAL/C/1, fol. 123.
67. NB to Wodehouse, 9 Mar. 1815. NMM, HAL/C/2, fol. 13–4.
68. Colvill to Stephens, 27 Nov. 1764. PRO, ADM1/482, fol. 414v.
69. Colvill to NB, 26 Dec. 1763. PRO, ADM106/1123.
70. Anderson accounts, 1799–1803. PRO, ADM17/152.
71. Inglefield to RO, 27 July 1807. NMM, HAL/E/27, fol. 54.
72. Dawes to Inglefield, 1 Oct. 1811. NMM, HAL/E/25, fol. 89.
73. Admiralty to NB, 28 Sept. 1757. PRO, ADM2/222, fol. 467; NMM, ADM/B/170.
74. Dawes accounts, 1807–10. NMM, HAL/E/31, fol. 178; NB to Dawes, 11 Feb. 1809. NMM, HAL/C/1, fol. 104; Evans to RO, 25 Nov. 1813. PRO, ADM106/1322; boatswain's new salary rate from 26 Dec. 1809, NB to Inglefield, 5 Feb. 1810. HAL/C/1, fol. 133–4.
75. Morriss, *Royal Dockyards*, 127.
76. Morriss, *Royal Dockyards*, 148.
77. Morriss, *Royal Dockyards*, 128.
78. Thomas to Duncan, 30 May 1786. NSARM, MG13/2, fol. 399–403.
79. RO to Duncan, 3 Aug. 1795. NSARM, MG13/6, fol. 99.

80. Dawes to NB, 30 July 1808. PRO, ADM106/2028.
81. Jackson to NB, 7 Nov. 1800. PRO, ADM106/2027.
82. NB to Hamond, 12 July 1782. PRO, ADM106/2471, fol. 225.
83. Hamond to NB, 12 Nov. 1782. HP, VII, 151–2.
84. Agrees to decline "all such private concerns" if it threatens to "interfere with his duties at the yard." Livie to NB, 1 May 1793. PRO, ADM106/2027.
85. Received 29 Nov. 1802; Inglefield to NB, 29 Mar. 1803; read, 25 Apr. 1803. PRO, ADM106/2027.
86. NB to RO, 23 June 1775. PRO, ADM106/2470, fol. 200–1.
87. Embezzlement meant theft of goods or money received by a servant of an employer from a third party. In law it was a civil breach of trust. A 1724 British statute made stealing the king's stores a capital felony, punishable by transportation. Receivers were also subject to transportation, a fine, public whipping, time in jail, or the pillory.
88. David Wilson, "Government Dock-Yard Workers in Portsmouth, 1793–1815" (PhD thesis, University of Warwick, 1975), 408.
89. Morriss, *Royal Dockyards*, 93–4.
90. Wilson, "Government Dock-Yard Workers in Portsmouth," 429 .
91. Morriss, *Royal Dockyards*, 94.
92. NB to RO, 23 June 1775. PRO, ADM106/2470, fol. 200–1.
93. Detailed complaints against the master shipwright were lodged by the foreman of house carpenters, William Lee. Constable enclosed a narrative of his case [not located], which he asked to be investigated. Admiralty to NB, 2 Apr. 1779. NMM, ADM/A/2738. Upon his death in 1795, his son complained to the Board that his father should have been tried in 1775. Abraham Constable Jr to NB, 22 June 1795. PRO, ADM106/1479.
94. To NB, 1 Dec. 1775. PRO, ADM106/1226.
95. See James E. Candow, "Sir Isaac Coffin and the Halifax Dockyard 'Scandal,'" *Nova Scotia Historical Review* 1 (1981): 50–63.
96. 7 & 9 Jan. 1800. NSARM, MG1/6, fol. 432, 434.
97. "All but five have been located." Enclosed in Coffin to Nepean, 21 Mar. 1800. PRO, ADM1/3364 and ADM106/2027.
98. A search of Samuel Marshall's house revealed a crown property stove which was removed. Coffin to Uniacke, 11 Jan. 1800. NSARM, MG13/6, fol. 443.
99. On one occasion three houses in town owned by William Hughes were also repaired with materials and labour from the yard.
100. Coffin to Anderson, 11 Jan. 1800. NSARM, MG13/6, fol. 436.
101. John King, literate mason, 25 Jan. 1800: No. 15. NSARM, MG13/6, fol. 472,

488; John Brush, literate foreman of smiths, 7 Feb. 1800: No. 20. MG13/6, fol. 502; William McKie, 25 Jan. 1800: No. 16. MG13/6, fol. 490–1.
102. Asa Scott, 2 Apr. 1800: No. 25. PRO, ADM106/2027.
103. Marshall to Coffin, 12 Jan. 1800. NSARM, MG13/6, fol. 444; PRO, ADM106/2027; Coffin to Marshall, 13 Jan. 1800. MG13/6, fol. 447.
104. Marshall's testimony, 6 May 1800. PRO, ADM106/2027, returned with his clerk to Halifax in transport *Duke of Kent*. Marshall to John Kingdom, Portsmouth, 12 June 1800. ADM106/2027.
105. Admiralty's 6 June letter. Duncan to NB, Portsmouth, 9 June 1800. PRO, ADM106/2027.
106. Duncan to NB, 22 Aug. 1800. PRO, ADM106/2027.
107. Marshall was superannuated in May 1805, and died the following year.
108. Sworn 30 Dec. 1799: No. 14. PRO, ADM1/3464.
109. There was a precedent for this. In 1763 when Gerrish went to England to clear his accounts, his first clerk, Jacob Hurd, acted as interim storekeeper. Duncan to Hurd, 15 July 1784, Duncan to Lawson, 15 July 1784. NSARM, MG13/1, #493–4.
110. Duncan departed on 20 July 1784. Douglas to Stephens, 22 Dec. 1784. PRO, ADM1/491, fol. 161v.
111. Douglas to Thomas, 26 July 1784. PRO, ADM1/491, fol. 71.
112. Thomas to NB, 28 Sept. 1784, enclosed in NB to Stephens, 29 Sept. 1784. NMM, ADM/BP/5 and ADM/B/178.
113. Thomas to Douglas, 26 July 1784, Douglas to Thomas, 27 July 1784. PRO, ADM1/491, fol. 73, 75, 77, 79. Douglas ordered the master shipwright, master attendant, and master of *Assistance* to survey stores. See Douglas to Stephens, 5, 7 & 9 Aug. 1784. ADM1/491, fol. 97–8, 102–3; NSARM, MG13/1, #536.
114. Appointed Frederick Edgecombe. Douglas to Thomas, 31 July 1784; Douglas to Edgecombe, 31 July 1784. PRO, ADM1/491, fol. 83, 85.
115. For "neglect of duty and declared disobedience." Douglas to Duncan, 9 Aug. 1784. NMM, HAL/F/2, fol. 230–1; Douglas to Stephens, 10 Aug. 1784. PRO, ADM1/491, fol. 109.
116. "Ever since Sir Charles Douglas appointed Mr Edgecombe to act as storekeeper I have given him all the assistance in my power." Duncan to NB, 6 Dec. 1784. NMM, HAL/F/2, fol. 283–4.
117. Douglas to Stephens, 27 Nov. 1784. PRO, ADM1/491, fol. 159; Admiralty to Douglas, 5 Feb. 1785, Douglas to Stephens, 10 Apr. 1785. ADM1/491, fol. 174.
118. Thomas returned after a ten-months' absence. Duncan to Edgecombe, 10 Apr. 1785. NMM, HAL/F/1, fol. 175.

119. RO to Inglefield, 19 Sept. 1802. NSARM, MG13/3; Inglefield to RO, 19 Sept. 1802. PRO, ADM106/2027.
120. Inglefield to Anderson, 19 & 21 Sept. 1802. PRO, ADM106/2027.
121. Anderson to Inglefield, [twice] 21 Sept. 1802. NSARM, MG13/3; PRO, ADM106/2027.
122. Inglefield to Anderson, 22 Sept. 1802. PRO, ADM106/2027.
123. Anderson to Inglefield, 22 Sept. 1802. PRO, ADM106/2027. Later Anderson assured the commissioner that he could inspect whatever vouchers and receipts he wanted in the storekeeper's office in his presence. Inglefield to Anderson, 15 Oct. 1802, Anderson to Inglefield, 15 Oct. 1802. ADM106/2027; NSARM, MG13/3.
124. Inglefield to NB, 23 Oct. 1802. PRO, ADM106/2027.
125. Anderson to Inglefield, 13 Dec. 1802. NSARM, MG13/3.
126. Anderson to Inglefield, 19 Jan. 1803. NSARM, MG13/3.
127. Inglefield to Anderson, 19 Jan. 1803. NSARM, MG13/3.
128. Anderson to Inglefield, 27 Jan. 1803. NSARM, MG13/3.
129. RO to Duncan, 17 Nov. 1787. NSARM, MG13/2, fol. 507–9.
130. RO to Duncan, 21 Nov. 1787. NSARM, MG13/2, fol. 510–12.
131. Duncan to NB, 26 Nov. 1787. NSARM, MG13/2, fol. 514–5.
132. NB to RO, 29 Mar. 1794. NSARM, MG13/6, fol. 6–8.
133. NB to RO, 27 Sept. 1794. NSARM, MG13/6, fol. 36–40.
134. NB to RO, 26 Mar. 1795. NSARM, MG13/6, fol. 70–4.
135. NB to RO, 5 Mar. 1795. NSARM, MG13/6, fol. 65.
136. NB to Read & Marshall, 22 Apr. 1795. NSARM, MG13/6, fol. 76.
137. NB to Livie, 23 Apr. 1795. NSARM, MG13/6, fol. 7.
138. Before Hurd, Gerrish hired Thomas Palmer at £40 a year in December 1756, then William Sheppard, who boarded with Gerrish. A second clerk, John Neal, was paid 4s. daily. He hired Jacob Hurd Jr and Edward Nicholas in December 1758 at £80 and £60 respectively; reduced in 1759 to £60 and £50 for the balance of the war. Gerrish to NB, 15 Apr. 1761. PRO, ADM106/1121.
139. Hurd to Duncan, 1 Dec. 1794. NSARM, MG13/6, fol. 52; Duncan to NB, 7 Jan. 1795. MG13/6, fol. 53–4.
140. Gerrish to NB, 12 Jan. 1760. PRO, ADM106/1121.
141. *Nova Scotia Gazette*, 1773; cited in T. Watson Smith, "The Slave in Canada," *Collections of the Nova Scotia Historical Society* 10 (1898): 12.
142. 28 Feb. 1797. *Royal Gazette and Nova Scotia Advertizer*.
143. Appointed when Hurd retired. NB to Duncan, 29 Sept. 1795. NSARM, MG13/6, fol. 122.
144. Inglefield to Anderson, 21 Sept. 1804. NSARM, MG13/9.1, fol. 181.

270 Notes to pages 91–94

145. Board refused. Anderson to Wodehouse, 29 Jan. 1813. PRO, ADM106/2029, fol. 5–6.
146. Wallis to Duncan, 7 Nov. 1800. PRO, ADM106/2027.
147. Inglefield to Wallis, 17 Feb. 1810. NMM, HAL/E/36, fol. 27–8.
148. Wallis to NB, 6 Feb. 1816, 14 Mar. & 26 Apr. 1817. PRO, ADM106/1657.
149. The portrait of Wallis is on display in the Art Gallery of Nova Scotia, Halifax. Hurd's portrait and that of his wife holding his eldest child by William Johnston are owned by New York's Metropolitan Museum of Art. See John Caldwell and Oswaldo Rodriguez Roque, *American Paintings in the Metropolitan Museum of Art: A Catalogue of Artists Born by 1815* (New York and Princeton: Metropolitan Museum of Art and Princeton University Press, 1994), 1: 51–3.
150. PRO, ADM36/17229.
151. Entered as an extra clerk in storekeeper's office. Inglefield to Dawes, 2 Aug. 1803. PRO, ADM106/2027; NSARM, MG13/9.1, fol. 22–3. By 1807 he had become second clerk. Clerks' petition to Inglefield, 20 Feb. 1807. NMM, HAL/E/38, fol. 237–41.
152. James to Coffin, 4 Apr. 1800. PRO, ADM106/2027.
153. Farquharson to Inglefield, 30 Aug. 1802. PRO, ADM106/2027.
154. Inglefield to RO, 13 June 1811. PRO, ADM106/2028.
155. Dawes to NB, 8 Mar. 1811. NMM, HAL/B/1, fol. 69.
156. Coffin to RO, 21 Oct. 1799. NSARM, MG13/6, fol. 361.
157. Coffin wrote of the "gross abuses that have been committed not only in your office but in every other department relating to extra attendance." Anderson to Coffin, 28 Dec. 1799, Coffin to Anderson, 28 Dec. 1799. NSARM, MG13/6, fol. 400–1. Coffin refused to appoint another master shipwright's clerk, stating, "No power is lodged with me to comply with your request. State your case to the Board." Marshall to Coffin, 1 Jan. 1800, Coffin to Marshall, 1–2 Jan. 1800. MG13/6, fol. 417.
158. Anderson to Nelson, 27 May 1800. PRO, ADM106/2027.
159. Dawes to Inglefield, 20 Feb. 1809, Inglefield to Dawes, 27 Feb. 1809. NSARM, MG13/5, fol. 44; Inglefield to NB, 6 Nov. 1809. PRO, ADM106/2028.
160. Morriss, *Royal Dockyards*, 131.
161. Gerrish to NB, 1 June 1768. PRO, ADM106/1167.
162. Thomas to Duncan, 30 May 1786. NSARM, MG13/2, fol. 399–403.
163. Clerks to NB, 25 Aug. 1796. PRO, ADM106/2027.
164. Duncan to NB, 26 Aug. 1796. NSARM, MG13/6, fol. 179.
165. Anderson earned about £35 extra in each of the two previous years, the second clerk almost £38. The day's work could be quite short even in war-

time. In 1814 Wodehouse reminded the officers that their normal office hours were from 9:00 a.m. to 4:00 p.m., when clerks were free to depart, unless overtime was required. Wallis to Duncan, 7 Nov. 1800. PRO, ADM106/2027.
166. Duncan to RO, 2 May 1797. NSARM, MG13/6, fol. 233.
167. "Great abuses having taken place, from no account being kept of the fuel that is supplied to the officers' houses, offices, and blacksmith's shop." Coffin to Anderson, 10 Jan. 1800. NSARM, MG13/6, fol. 441.
168. Duncan to RO, 28 May 1797. NSARM, MG13/6, fol. 241.
169. Bartlett, Anderson, James, and Hughes to Inglefield, 20 Feb. 1807. NMM, HAL/E/38, fol. 237–41; in Inglefield to NB, 20 Feb. 1807. HAL/E/38, fol. 28–30; PRO, ADM106/2028.
170. Bartlett, Anderson, James, and Hughes to NB, 20 Feb. 1807. NMM, HAL/E/38, fol. 31–3.
171. Admiralty order 18 Sept. 1808. NB to Dawes, 11 Feb. 1809. NMM, HAL/C/1, fol. 101–4.
172. Inglefield to NB, 1 Nov. 1809. PRO, ADM106/2028.
173. Supported both by Dawes and Inglefield. Sherlock to Inglefield, 20 July 1809. PRO, ADM106/2028.
174. Haas, *A Management Odyssey*, 44.
175. In August 1788 micromanagement reached absurd lengths when the Board told Duncan to inform his officers "to be less wasteful of stationery," by writing "across the whole paper and in a more compact hand." NB to Duncan, 20 Aug. 1788. NSARM, MG13/2, fol. 580.
176. Haas, *A Management Odyssey*, 4.

Chapter 5   Artificers and Labourers

1. R.J.B. Knight, "The Royal Dockyards in England at the Time of the American War of Independence" (PhD thesis, University of London, 1972); David Wilson, "Government Dock-Yard Workers in Portsmouth, 1793–1815" (PhD thesis, University of Warwick, 1975).
2. RO to Inglefield, 10 Jan. 1803. NSARM, MG13/3.
3. Two sailmakers to help. Duncan to RO, 10 Apr. 1789. NSARM, MG13/2, fol. 616. All artificers. Inglefield to RO, 5 Apr. 1806. PRO, ADM106/2028.
4. Duncan to RO, 13 Oct. 1783. NMM, HAL/F/1, fol. 14; Warren to RO, 26 June 1808, Warren to Inglefield, 4 July 1809. NMM, HAL/E/35b, fol. 7. "As has been customary." Inglefield to RO, 3 Oct. 1809. HAL/E/37. Transport *Magnet* to be fitted to carry cattle to Bermuda for squadron. Wodehouse to RO, 1 Mar. 1813. HAL/E/40, fol. 422.

272   Notes to pages 103–104

5. RO to Duncan, 15 Sept. 1784. NMM, HAL/F/2, fol. 238–9.
6. RO to Duncan, 30 Mar. 1785. NMM, HAL/F/2, fol. 311. 100 seamen to assist in stowing cables. Inglefield to Warren, 6 Sept. 1809. NMM, HAL/E/35b, fol. 60.
7. Duncan to Thomas, 4 May 1784. NMM, HAL/F/1, fol. 108; Duncan to Thomas, 31 Jan. 1786. NSARM, MG13/1, #613; received 3 Oct. 1788, NB to Duncan, 16 July 1788. MG13/2, fol. 578.
8. Duncan to RO, 25 Mar. 1789, R0 to Duncan, 26 Mar. NSARM, MG13/2, fol. 610.
9. Master attendant applied for working party "to assist in heaving down the *William* storeship, overhauling careening blocks, filling buoys for the moorings & shoals." Inglefield to RO, 30 Jan., 31 May & 21 Aug. 1809. NMM, HAL/E/37 and HAL/E/39b, fol. 190. Replace and refill the sheers on the sheer wharf. Inglefield to RO, 8 Apr. 1811. HAL/E/40, fol. 342. Forty-five seamen to assist at moorings. Wodehouse to Bart, 9 Mar. & 27 Apr. 1818. HAL/E/26, fol. 89, 106.
10. *Flora* to Antigua. Inglefield to RO, 7 Oct. 1805. NMM, HAL/E/34, fol. 8. Forty seamen to help with Vice Admiral Mitchell's approval. NMM, HAL/A/3b, fol. 47–8. To help unload plank and other materials to build *Halifax*. Inglefield to Commodore Beresford, 16 June 1806. HAL/A/3b, fol. 121–2.
11. Inglefield to Berkeley, 17 Oct. 1806. NMM, HAL/A/3b, fol. 193.
12. Inglefield to RO, 14 May 1807. NMM, HAL/E/38, fol. 82.
13. Douglas to RO, 16 May 1808. NMM, HAL/E/37.
14. RO to Inglefield, 20 Jan. 1809. NMM, HAL/E/39b, fol. 61; Inglefield to Laurie, same date. HAL/E/39a, fol. 81.
15. Bricklayers, sawyers, masons, and painters. Wodehouse to Milne, 4 June & 9 Oct. 1818. NMM, HAL/E/26, fol. 112, 162.
16. Inglefield to RO, 5 & 19 Dec. 1806. NMM, HAL/E/28.
17. Summoned back to their units, Bowyer to Inglefield, 26 Oct. 1808. NMM, HAL/E/39a, fol. 34; ten house carpenters and four smiths, Inglefield to Prevost, 7 Dec. 1809. HAL/E/35b, fol. 190; four blacksmiths, 3 Mar. 1810. HAL/E/27, fol. 13; four house carpenters to fit transports to receive troops at 2s. a day. Wodehouse to [RO], 10 May 1815. HAL/E/41, fol. 124.
18. Article 24, Chapter 2, Section 9 of *New Naval Instructions*; NB to Dawes, 26 Nov. 1805. NMM, HAL/A/3a, fol. 37.
19. Guy Fawkes Day on 5 November was a half-holiday, but often "the people" worked when the squadron was refitting as in 1807. Berkeley to RO, 4 Nov. 1807. NMM, HAL/E/37, fol. 11.
20. Duncan to RO, 30 May 1797. NSARM, MG13/6, fol. 242.

21. NB to RO, 6 Oct. 1814. NMM, HAL/E/29, fol. 60. In 1806 the Navy Board inquired about the hours men worked daily in the yard. NB to Dawes, 3 June 1806. NMM, HAL/E/34.
22. 1 Oct. 1807. NMM, HAL/E/38, fol. 237–41.
23. 1 Oct. 1807. NMM, HAL/E/35a, fol. 156–9.
24. Hawker to Inglefield, 16 Aug. 1805. PRO, ADM106/2028.
25. Inglefield to NB, 19 Aug. 1805. PRO, ADM106/2028.
26. The Board awarded £100 to be divided among the six. NB to Admiralty, 24 Sept. 1805. NMM, ADM/B/220.
27. Oct.–Dec. 1776. PRO, ADM42/2150; July–Sept. 1777 and Jan.–Dec. 1778, July–Sept. 1780. ADM42/2152.
28. See J.K. Laughton and J.Y.F. Sullivan, eds., *Journal of Rear-Admiral Bartholomew James, 1752–1828* (London: Navy Records Society, 1896), 6: 24–5. "As there were no masts in store at this period, we were obliged to cut our own masts in the woods about ten miles from Halifax, which piece of duty was as disagreeable as severe and employed us several days." Feb. 1776.
29. Berkeley to RO, 29 Oct. 1807. PRO, ADM106/2028.
30. Launches commanded by master attendant Atkinson, shipwrights Parr and Dugwell, boatswain Ridgeway. Berkeley to RO, 1 Dec. 1807. NMM, HAL/E/38, fol. 341–2.
31. Inglefield to RO, 21 Apr. 1812. NMM, HAL/E/36, fol. 408–9.
32. Inglefield to RO, 27 Apr. 1812. NMM, HAL/E/36, fol. 410; for individual companies with names, see PRO, ADM106/2028.
33. Commanded by master attendant with rank of lieutenant colonel, with names and appointments, Inglefield to RO, 16 & 20 May 1812. NMM, HAL/E/36, fol. 420–5.
34. Beckwith to Wodehouse, 24 May 1814. NMM, HAL/E/21, fol. 67; lists eighteen officers with dates of their commissions in 1807, 1812, and 1814, fol. 71.
35. Discharged shipwright John Smith and blacksmith James Weeks. Hamond to NB, 25 Nov. 1781. HP, VII, 43, 47.
36. NB to Hamond, 27 Dec. 1781. PRO, ADM106/2471, fol. 190. When Hamond departed Halifax he offered passage to yard workers who wished to return to England as "the severity of the climate had very much injured their health." On board were: carpenters Thomas Smith, John Vaughan, wife and child, John Stanley, wife, four children, and John Mantz, wife and child; watchman John McDonald and wife; and labourer Patrick Poor. Hamond to Fisher of *Caton*, 4 Dec. 1782. HP, IX, 201.
37. They arrived via Bermuda, where for months they worked on the naval

base. Wodehouse to RO, 13 July 1815. NSARM, MG13/9.3, fol. 176. Most departed Halifax before their contracts expired. The painter was discharged as incompetent.
38. Julian Gwyn, *Excessive Expectations: Maritime Commerce & the Economic Development of Nova Scotia, 1740–1870* (Montreal: McGill-Queen's University Press, 1998), 28.
39. Wodehouse to NB, 31 July 1815. NSARM, MG13/9.3, fol. 181–2.
40. Wodehouse to NB, 2 Dec. 1814. NMM, HAL/1/5, fol. 150–4.
41. J.M. Haas, *A Management Odyssey: The Royal Dockyards, 1714–1914* (Lanham: University Press of America, 1994), 23.
42. The first required a shipwright apprentice in his final year to work as a caulker to learn a second trade. Roger Morriss, *The Royal Dockyards during the Revolutionary and Napoleonic Wars* (Leicester: Leicester University Press, 1983), 109–10.
43. Dawes accounts, PRO, ADM17/162, fol. 39–40.
44. "Rule at Home," [June 1809]. NMM, HAL/E/39a, fol. 189.
45. Wilson, "Government Dock-Yard Workers in Portsmouth," 308–402.
46. Philip MacDougall, *Royal Dockyards* (Newton Abbot, Devon: David & Charles, 1982), 103–4.
47. RO to Duncan, 6 July 1795. NSARM, MG13/6, fol. 91.
48. Duncan to RO, 26 July 1795. NSARM, MG13/6, fol. 91–2. Board approved. NB to Duncan, 3 Nov. 1796. MG13/6, fol. 217.
49. First tried at the Antigua yard. NB to RO, 28 Oct. 1806. NMM, HAL/E/28. Inglefield thought it "a great saving and advantageous to gov't, as work time was lost on the days when provisions were issued." Inglefield to NB, 12 Feb. 1807. PRO, ADM106/2028.
50. NB to Inglefield, 23 Apr. 1807, Inglefield to RO, 15 June 1807. NMM, HAL/E/38, fol. 115.
51. Inglefield to NB, 12 Feb. 1807, Minute 21 Apr. 1807, "Approve." PRO, ADM106/2028.
52. Order-in-council of 21 May 1801. Morriss, *Royal Dockyards*, 104. NB warrant, 5 Dec. 1809. NB to RO, 5 Dec. 1809. NMM, HAL/C/1, fol. 128–9.
53. For shipwrights, 6d. a day; their apprentices, 4d. to 6d; for caulkers, house carpenters, sawyers, and smiths, 4d.; their apprentices, 2d. in the first four years, 4d. in last three; labourers, 3d.
54. Jackson to Inglefield, 21 Nov. 1801. PRO, ADM106/2027.
55. Since the 1795 pay increase, retail prices at Halifax, excluding tobacco, rose 48.7 per cent for fourteen other items. If tobacco was added, the price rise was nearly 75 per cent. Examples of commodity price inflation between 1795–6 and 1814 are found in Gwyn, "The Culture of Work in the Halifax

Naval Yard before 1820," *Journal of the Royal Nova Scotia Historical Society*, 2 (1999): 118–43, Table 1, 139n49, "The price of firewood, considering the much greater call for it than there is in England, owing to the extreme severity and length of the winters, is scarcely within the reach of any working man." Wodehouse to NB, 2 Nov. 1814. PRO, ADM106/2029, fol. 190.

56. NMM, HAL/E/29, fol. 16–19.
57. Sixteen literate watchmen signed and twenty-four illiterate labourers marked the memorial. Wodehouse to NB, 6 Aug. 1813. PRO, ADM106/2029, fol. 56–7.
58. Board warrant, 6 Oct. 1813. Wodehouse to NB, 31 Dec. 1813. NSARM, MG13/9.3, fol. 32.
59. Wodehouse to NB, 27 Oct. 1813. PRO, ADM106/2029. Petitions signed by twenty-seven shipwrights, fol. 95; fourteen sailmakers, fol. 101; seventeen house carpenters, fol. 103; and thirteen smiths, fol. 105. The Board noted: "before the present American war [they] were enabled on their present pay and allowances to support their families with the comforts and conveniences of life, but from the great enhancement on every article of subsistence as well as fuel, cloathing and house rent, which in every respect is nearly double since that period, many of them with all their care and economy (having large families) can scarcely obtain the common necessaries of support."
60. NMM, HAL/E/26, fol. 10–13.
61. Board letter was dated 4 Jan. 1815. Wodehouse to NB, 29 July 1815. PRO, ADM106/2029, fol. 233–4.
62. NB to Wodehouse, 6 Sept. 1815. NMM, HAL/C/2, fol. 75–6.
63. Wodehouse to NB, 21 May 1816. NMM, HAL/A/5, fol. 419; Board's letter, 12 Mar. 1816.
64. Shipwrights, with between thirteen and forty-one years of service, averaged thirty years; smiths, with between nine and thirteen years, averaged eleven years; the two sawyers had an average of sixteen years between them; and the two sailmakers an average of twenty-four years.
65. Potatoes were "an article of very principal dependence." Wodehouse fully endorsed the accuracy of their petition. "I have greatly to lament that the whole of it is strictly true." Wodehouse to NB, 8 Apr. 1817. NMM, HAL/E/1, fol. 50.
66. [April, 1817]. NMM, HAL/E/26, fol. 10–13. Petition signed by thirteen shipwrights, three smiths, two sailmakers, and two sawyers.
67. Wodehouse to NB, 12 June 1817. PRO, ADM106/2029, fol. 332–3.
68. NB to Wodehouse, 17 July 1817. NMM, HAL/C/2, fol. 274.
69. Pay rates for apprentices were still set in London, NSARM; Wodehouse to

276 Notes to pages 112–115

RO, 17 & 28 June 1817. NMM, HAL/E/41, fol. 393–3, HAL/E/43, fol. 7; NSARM, MG13/9.3, fol. 219–20. In 1818, Wodehouse reduced yard wages, to match decline of those in Halifax.

70. Duncan McQueen, literate joiner, 5 Feb. 1800: No. 19. NSARM, MG13/6, fol. 501–2.
71. Peter Artz, 14 Jan. 1800: No. 13. NSARM, MG13/6, fol. 469–70; Lawrence Keating, 28 Jan. 1800: No. 17. He gave identical testimony. MG13/6, fol. 493–4; PRO, ADM1/3364.
72. Gordon to Coffin, Fort Edward, Windsor, 22 Jan. 1800. NSARM, MG13/6, 492; to pay the deputy sheriff 20s. to search for Benjamin Marshall, Coffin to Anderson, 24 Jan. 1800. MG13/6, fol. 486; H£23.6.8. to H. Rutherford, Esq., on behalf of Pickle & Post "two men who went in pursuit of Benjamin Marshall and safely lodged him in Annapolis Gaol." Coffin to Anderson, 13 Mar. 1800. MG13/6, fol. 537; to pay Uniacke's account for Marshall's trial, against whom a "bill of indictment has been found by the grand jury of the county of Halifax." Coffin to Anderson, 13 Mar. 1800. MG13/6, fol. 536.
73. Barrow to Inglefield, 2 Sept. 1810. NMM, HAL/A/2/47; Fairfax and Hughes to Inglefield, 10 May 1810. NMM, HAL/E/27, fol. 70–1.
74. RO to Inglefield, 5 Aug. 1812. NMM, HAL/E/25, fol. 128; Inglefield to RO, 6 Aug. 1812. HAL/E/40, fol. 387.
75. Inglefield to RO, 8 June 1812. NMM, HAL/E/36, fol. 435–6.
76. Wodehouse to Croker, 15 Aug. 1817. NMM, HAL/E/1, fol. 104–5.
77. Haas, *A Management Odyssey*, 33.
78. Hamond to Thomas, 1 Jan. 1782. HP, IX, 106.
79. NB to Inglefield, 12 June 1810. NMM, HAL/A/2, fol. 80.
80. Hamond to NB, 4 July 1782. HP, VII, 94.
81. Duncan to NB, 6 Dec. 1784. NMM, HAL/F/2, fol. 277–8.
82. Duncan to NB, 10 Oct. 1785. NSARM, MG13/2, fol. 356–7.
83. RO to Inglefield, 31 Aug. 1802, in Inglefield to NB, 23 Oct. 1802, received 23 Nov. 1802. NSARM, MG13/3; PRO, ADM106/2027.
84. Inglefield to NB, 19 Mar. 1807. PRO, ADM106/2028.
85. Inglefield to RO, 1 Feb. 1810. NMM, HAL/E/36, fol. 19–20; 1 Dec. 1814. PRO, ADM106/2029, fol. 210.
86. Wodehouse to RO, 21 Apr. 1814. NSARM, MG13/9.3, fol. 73.
87. Dr Rowlands's report on the "health and infirmities" of those on the invalid establishment. 1 Dec. 1814. PRO, ADM106/2029, fol. 212.
88. Admiralty awarded him a pension of £20. NB to Dawes, 30 Sept. 1814. NMM, HAL/C/1, fol. 289.
89. Petition 29 Mar. 1814. Wodehouse to NB, 29 Apr. 1814. PRO, ADM106/2029, fol. 160.

90. Wodehouse to NB, 16 May 1814. PRO, ADM106/2029, fol. 169, 171; Dr Rowlands described him as "nearly worn out." 1 Dec. 1814. ADM106/2029, fol. 211.
91. Rowlands's report, 1 Dec. 1814. PRO, ADM106/2029, fol. 210–2.
92. To Inglefield, 17 Oct. 1810, memorial supported by Dawes and Hughes, Inglefield to NB, 3 Nov. 1810. PRO, ADM106/2028.
93. Coffin to Anderson, 16 Mar. 1800. NSARM, MG13/6, fol. 532; H£31 15s. annually.
94. Discharged in January 1800, Jackson and Anderson to Coffin, 23 Jan. 1800. NSARM, MG13/6, fol. 484; re-entered two months later, Coffin to Anderson, 3 Mar. 1800. MG13/6, fol. 518; RO to Inglefield, 4 Sept. 1802. MG13/3; Inglefield to RO, 16 Aug. 1804. MG13/9.1, fol. 165.
95. Lee to Coffin, 21 Mar. 1800. PRO, ADM106/2027.
96. Wodehouse to RO, 1 Mar. 1814. NA, II, 96.
97. NB to Wodehouse, Oct. 1814; referred to in Wodehouse to RO, 1 Dec. 1814. NSARM, MG13/9.3, fol.144–6.
98. £20 for shipwrights, caulkers, masons, wheelwrights, coopers, blockmakers, treenail makers, carvers, oarmakers, plumbers, glaziers, braziers, founders, sailmakers, and painters; £15 for house carpenters, smiths, bricklayers, storehouse labourers, riggers, watermen, and sawyers; £10 for messengers, labourers of every description except ropemakers, labourers, and pitch heaters.
99. Memorial in Inglefield to NB, 19 May 1807. PRO, ADM106/2028.
100. He had the "happiness of witnessing in his time the baptism of 56 children, grandchildren, and great-grandchildren in the protestant faith of the Established Church of England all proceeding from his loins in lawful wedlock." Enclosed in Inglefield to NB, 13 June 1807. PRO, ADM106/2028.
101. To Inglefield, 9 Nov. 1810. Dawes described him as "worn out and unfit for service." Inglefield to NB, 13 Nov. 1810. PRO, ADM106/2028.
102. NB to Dawes, 3 Oct. 1814. NMM, HAL/C/1, fol. 291.
103. Wall to Thomas, [1785]. NSARM, MG13/1, #532.
104. Inglefield to RO, 16 June 1809. NSARM, MG13/5, fol. 56. The culprits were: John Blackadar 6½ days, Edward Maddocks 9 days, William Wills 11 days, Tim Ross 6½ days, John Dunn, labourer, 7½ days.
105. Wodehouse to RO, 8 Dec. 1813. NSARM, MG13/9.3, fol. 25.
106. Wodehouse to Jones, 11 Nov. 1818. NSARM, MG13/9.3, fol. 233.
107. Wodehouse to RO, 5 Dec. 1818. NSARM, MG13/9.3, fol. 234. When the yard was reduced in 1819 he was given a £20 annual pension. NB to Jones, 15 Nov. 1819. NMM, HAL/C/3, fol. 24–5.
108. Coffin to Anderson, 22 Jan. 1800. NSARM, MG13/6, fol. 482.

278 Notes to pages 118–124

109. Coffin to Anderson, 17 Jan. 1800. NSARM, MG13/6, fol. 456.
110. Inglefield to RO, 13 Aug. 1805. NMM, HAL/E/34, fol. 33.
111. Inglefield to RO, 5 Oct. 1803. NSARM, MG13/9.1, fol. 52.
112. Berkeley to RO, 2 Nov. 1807. PRO, ADM106/2028.
113. Fairfax to Inglefield, 10 Mar. 1810. NMM, HAL/E/36, fol. 35–6. A disputed case brought the same verdict. In 1810, the commander of the guard complained that a watchman, Alexander Grant, had treated him with contempt at the gate one night. Though evidence from a second watchman, the only other witness, did not support the lieutenant's charge, the yard officers believed that Grant, "from his behaviour while before us," had indeed conducted himself in the manner represented to them. RO to Inglefield, 10 Sept. 1810. NMM, HAL/E/25, fol. 37; Inglefield to RO, 10 & 12 Sept. 1810. HAL/E/36, fol. 130, 132.
114. Berkeley to RO, 31 Oct. 1807. PRO, ADM106/2028.
115. RO to Inglefield, 14 Nov. 1810. NMM, HAL/E/25, fol. 44.
116. Wodehouse to RO, 8 Dec. 1813. NSARM, MG13/9.3, fol. 25.
117. Wodehouse to RO, 12 May 1815. NMM, HAL/E/41, fol. 126.
118. Wodehouse to RO, 5 Nov. 1817. NSARM, MG13/9.3, fol. 225.
119. Wodehouse to RO, 8 Jan. 1819. NMM, HAL/E/42a, fol. 234.
120. RO to Inglefield, 23 Dec. 1802. NSARM, MG13/3.
121. Wodehouse to RO, 26 May 1815. NSARM, MG13/9.3, fol. 169.
122. Wodehouse to RO, 22 July 1815. NSARM, MG13/9.3, fol. 176.
123. Haas, *A Management Odyssey*, 25.
124. Haas, *A Management Odyssey*, 28.
125. Morriss, *Royal Dockyards*, 109–10.

Chapter 6   The Work of the Yard

1. Rear Admiral Sir William Parker to Evan Nepean, 19 Dec. 1800. PRO, ADM1/491, fol. 100.
2. See appendices 1 & 2 for details of establishment and workforce.
3. George to Admiralty, 26 June 1792. PRO, ADM1/492, fol. 266; muster list of 11 June 1792 enclosed.
4. Complements amounted to about 1,100 men. Owing to huge quantities of stores from New York and Charleston, requiring much labour, continuing work on warships, and preparing transports to ship troops home, Duncan explained, "these matters giving full employment to every person in this Yard I hope will appear a sufficient reason for not immediately making the Reduction directed by the Board." NB to Duncan, 18 July 1783, Duncan to NB, 22 Oct. 1783. NMM, HAL/F/2, fol. 2, 12–13.

5. Murray to Nepean, 30 Oct. 1795. PRO, ADM1/493, fol. 278.
6. Warren to Wodehouse, 27 Nov. 1812. NA, I, 1–2; Wodehouse to RO, 30 Nov. 1812. NMM, HAL/E/40, fol. 407.
7. Griffith to Croker, 16 Nov. 1814. PRO, ADM1/507, fol. 367.
8. Wodehouse to RO, 20 Nov. 1815. NMM, HAL/E/41, fol. 235–7.
9. Pay lists. PRO, ADM42/2152–71.
10. Wodehouse to NB, 21 Nov. 1815. NMM, HAL/A/5, fol. 320–5.
11. Chads to Duncan, 1 Oct. 1783. NMM, HAL/F/2, fol. 3–5.
12. Duncan to Seager, master of transport *Friendship*, and Davison, master of *Stoddy*, 18 Oct. 1783, Duncan to Pearson, master of transport *John*, 21 Oct. 1783, Duncan to Rodd, master of transport *Thetis*, 22 Oct. 1783. NMM, HAL/F/1, fol. 1–3, 6–8.
13. Parr to Duncan, 6 Apr. 1784, Duncan to Parr, 7 April 1784. NMM, HAL/F/2, fol. 148–50. See many letters wherein Duncan gave directions for passengers to be embarked for England or for other parts of Nova Scotia, such as Chedabucto Bay and Shelburne. HAL/F/1, fol. 93ff.
14. Inglefield to NB, 25 May 1809. NMM, HAL/A/4b, fol. 140–1.
15. Inglefield to Warren, 30 June 1809. NMM, HAL/E/39b, fol. 236–7.
16. Dawes to Inglefield, 24 July 1809. NMM, HAL/A/1.
17. Berkeley to Inglefield, 16 Aug. 1806. NMM, HAL/A/3b, fol. 158–9.
18. Inglefield to Berkeley, 17 Aug. 1806. NMM, HAL/A/3b, fol. 159.
19. Inglefield to Mitchell, 18 Aug. 1805. NMM, HAL/A/3b, fol. 27–8.
20. Some 612 men in mid-June 1803 and 800 men in Jan. 1807. NMM, ADM/BP/23b and ADM/BP/27.
21. When the Board sent Inglefield's suggestion, the Admiralty minuted the letter: "Do not approve of any increase." NB to Marsden, 24 Nov. 1806. NMM, ADM/B/224.
22. Inglefield to NB, 10 Oct. 1811. NMM, HAL/A/2, fol. 220–2; NB to Inglefield, 6 Nov. 1811. HAL/A/2, fol. 249.
23. Same allowance rate as for artificers from the warships. Warren to RO, 26 June 1808. NMM, HAL/E/37.
24. Inglefield to RO, 11 Nov. 1808. NMM, HAL/E/37.
25 Inglefield to Pole, 23 Aug. 1808. NMM, HAL/A/4b, fol. 6–7.
26. Inglefield to Pole, 25 Oct. 1808. NMM, HAL/A/4b, fol. 41.
27. RO to NB, 16 Dec. 1807. PRO, ADM106/2028. In 1812 storeship *Spy* had a lucky escape when on her passage from Bermuda during a violent gale she was struck five times by lightning, "each exploding like a bombshell, which hurt some of the people and set fire to main fore-gallant sail and main topmast stay-sails, altho' raining hard." Anderson to NB, 12 May 1812. ADM106/1301.

28. Inglefield to NB, 28 Nov. 1808. NMM, HAL/A/4b, fol. 67–9.
29. Inglefield to Warren, 29 May 1809. NMM, HAL/E/39a, fol. 163.
30. Inglefield to Pole, 21 Aug. 1809. PRO, ADM1/3441.
31. Warren to Inglefield, 5 Oct. 1809. NMM, HAL/E/35b, fol. 103.
32. "Not advantageous to government." Inglefield to Warren, 6 Oct. 1809. NMM, HAL/E/35b, fol. 103.
33. Inglefield to NB, 1 Jan. 1810. NMM, HAL/A/4b, fol. 298.
34. In 1806 Cochrane sent brig *Nimble* to Halifax. Her needed repairs were so extensive that she was patched up for a summer's passage to England. Inglefield to NB, July 1806. PRO, ADM106/2028.
35. Warren to RO, Bermuda, 15 Apr. 1808. PRO, ADM106/2028.
36. To repair and paint boat belonging to naval prisoners of war department. Inglefield to RO, 1 Mar. 1806. NMM, HAL/E/34, fol. 8. Survey sloop *Examiner* to be used by Lockwood, the Admiralty nautical surveyor. Griffith to Wodehouse, 16 Nov. 1815. HAL/E/21, fol. 332.
37. To copper *Voltigeur*, purchased by the Ordnance department as powder vessel. NB to RO, 22 Sept. 1808. NMM, HAL/E/31, fol. 29; Inglefield to RO, 3 Apr. 1810. HAL/E/36, fol. 44.
38. For example: brigantine *Maria*, used for Nova Scotia's coastal survey to be repaired. Duncan to RO, 21 Oct. 1783. NSARM, MG13/1, #392. Governor's schooner *Greyhound* to be fitted. Duncan to NB, 25 Dec. 1785. MG13/2, fol. 371–2. Survey vessel for superintendent of trade and fisheries on Nova Scotia's coasts. Inglefield to RO, 22 May 1807. NMM, HAL/E/38, fol. 93–4. Revenue schooner *Hunter* lately on shore at Canso to be surveyed. Inglefield to RO, 15 Nov. 1811. HAL/E/36, fol. 343.
39. Defects of hired storeship *Ranger* to be examined. Duncan to RO, 4 Jan. 1784. NMM, HAL/F/1, fol. 50.
40. Making masts for transports *Henry* and *Constant Friends*. Duncan to RO, 20 Sept. 1784. NSARM, MG13/1, #515. In transport *Sally* berths built for troops. Hughes and Andrew to Duncan, 20 June 1796. MG13/6, fol. 161. Survey transport *Seahorse*, lately on shore, unfit for foreign service. Inglefield to RO, 20 June 1809. NMM, HAL/E/37.
41. Transports *Lady Delaval* & *Magnet*, the former carried thirty-five bullocks. Wodehouse to RO, 27 Nov. 1812 & 1 Mar. 1813. NMM, HAL/E/40, fol. 407, 422.
42. *Comet* from Newfoundland to repair defects, "I should wish this work may not interfere with the repairs of the ships already in this harbour." Warren to Inglefield, 4 June 1809. NMM, HAL/E/39a, fol. 171. The vessel owned by the military based at St John's and used to fetch coal from Cape Breton was also refitted at the Halifax yard. Treasury vessel schooner *Endeavour* to

be repaired, as "we have no recourse at this station of giving the vessel any repair or improvements of consequence without incurring very heavy expenses." Moore to Inglefield, St John's, 2 Dec. 1810. HAL/E/27, fol. 291–2. Cost H£1,666.12.3, Inglefield to Moore, 16 May 1811. HAL/E/27, fol. 377. "As the garrison here depend entirely upon her for their supply of coal, which article the king's fuel yards are now extremely deficient of and should we be obliged to revert to the market, would cost ... upwards of ten guineas a chaldron." Moore to Wodehouse, St John's, 26 Feb. 1814. HAL/E/21, fol. 21.

43. All cordage and cables not likely to be used to be sent home. NB to Inglefield, 10 Dec. 1807. NMM, HAL/C/1, fol. 25.
44. Storeship *Spy* not "well calculated to carry timber owing to her being both short and narrow naught so sharp forward that to stow a piece straight in the hold, she will not take longer than 48 feet." Richard Anderson to NB, 12 May 1812. PRO, ADM106/1301. They also provided passage home to invalids from the garrison and squadron.
45. NB to RO, 21 May 1788. NMM, HAL/F/1, fol. 293–4.
46. NB to RO, 27 Sept. 1794. NSARM, MG13/6, fol. 36–40.
47. Inglefield to NB, 6 Nov. 1809. PRO, ADM106/2028.
48. For the range of these see appendix 4.
49. NB to RO, 27 Sept. 1794. NSARM, MG13/6, fol. 36–40.
50. NB to RO, 29 Mar. 1794. NSARM, MG13/6, fol. 6–8.
51. Dawes to Inglefield, 24 July 1809. NMM, HAL/A/1.
52. Squadron with "those that have occasionally arrived & received supplies of stores." 3 Apr. 1806 to 10 Mar. 1807. NMM, HAL/E/38, fol. 36–7, NMM, HAL/A/1; Dawes to Dunsier, 13 Dec. 1808.
53. Arrived 27 Sept. 1807, ready to unload 28 Sept.; began unloading 29 Sept.; completed task 11 Oct.; arrived 18 June 1808; ready to unload Sunday 19 June; began unloading 20 June; completed task 27 June, RO to Nelson, 15 Oct. 1807, 29 July 1808. NMM, HAL/A/1.
54. They netted the yard H£2,726.7.6. Gerrish accounts, 1757–73. PRO, ADM17/150.
55. Chips "to be sold on Saturday," along with broken and unserviceable old casks and cases. Inglefield to RO, 18 June 1806. NMM, HAL/E/34, fol. 6, 7; chips "to be sold as customary on Monday." Berkeley to RO, 16 Oct. 1807. HAL/E/38, fol. 275.
56. Inglefield to RO, 1 Aug. 1811. NMM, HAL/E/36, fol. 289.
57. Inglefield to RO, 31 Mar. 1810. NMM, HAL/E/36, fol. 42.
58. NB to Wodehouse, 31 Oct. 1811. NMM, HAL/A/2, fol. 257.
59. Coffin to Alexander, 13 Feb. 1800. NSARM, MG13/6, fol. 506.

282 Notes to pages 136–138

60. RO to Berkeley, 16 Oct. 1807. PRO, ADM106/2027, NMM, HAL/E/38, fol. 277, 279; Dawes and Hughes to Inglefield, 8 Sept. 1809. HAL/E/36, fol. 23.
61. Wodehouse to Transport Board, 1 Feb. 1816. NMM, HAL/E/3b, fol. 15.
62. NB to RO, 13 Oct. 1783. NSARM, MG13/1, #469.
63. Sterling to Thomas, 12 Mar. 1785. NSARM, MG13/1, #605; one was purchased by Tremaine, MG13/1, #606.
64.

Name	Built	Age	Keel length	Breadth of hold	Depth	Tons
Felicity	Bermuda	5	64'	19'1"	7'6"	80
Mackerel	Virginia	4	54'	16'6"	6'	57
Hussar	Philadelphia	7	68'	14'6"	4'8"	39

Duncan to NB, 3 Dec. 1785. NSARM, MG13/2, fol. 370.
65. Duncan to NB, 23 Jan. 1795, NB to Duncan, 31 Mar. 1795. NSARM, MG13/6, fol. 55, 69.
66. Duncan to NB, 7 Nov. 1795, NB to Duncan, 15 Dec. 1795. NSARM, MG13/6, fol. 118, 148.
67. NB to Wodehouse, 15 Apr. & 16 May 1815. NMM, HAL/C/2, fol. 26–7, 36–7.
68. Barrow to Wodehouse, 30 May 1817. NMM, HAL/C/2, fol. 259; NB to Wodehouse, 2 & 20 June 1817, 12 June 1818, 18 Apr. 1819. HAL/C/2, fol. 266–7, 271, 358, 407; Wodehouse to Dawes, 1 Sept. 1817 & 18 June 1819. NMM, HAL/E/42a, fol. 163, 266; *Hibernia* buoy boat sold for H£130 to Samuel Cunard. Dawes accounts, 1819. PRO, ADM17/166.
69. Inglefield to RO, 16 Sept. 1808. NMM, HAL/E/37.
70. Inglefield to NB, 5 May 1809. PRO, ADM106/2028; NB to Inglefield, 7 June 1809. NMM, HAL/A/4b, fol. 175.
71. NB to Wodehouse, 7 Jan. 1817. NMM, HAL/C/2, fol. 197; Wodehouse to NB, 18 Apr. 1817. NMM, HAL/E/1, fol. 54.
72. See Julian Gwyn, "Shipbuilding for the Royal Navy in Colonial New England," *American Neptune* 48 (1988): 22–30; Bernard Pool, *Navy Board Contracts 1600–1832: Contract Administration under the Navy Board* (London: Longmans Green, 1966), 84–5.
73. NB to Stephens, 30 Oct. 1773. NMM, ADM/B/187.
74. It "will be necessary to send out ... pintles and braces, copper fastenings, and sheathing." Inglefield to NB, 24 Aug. 1804. PRO, ADM106/2028.
75. 23 Aug. 1804. NMM, ADM/B/216; PRO, ADM106/2028.
76. Admiralty order 1 Oct. 1804, Minute to Inglefield's letter of 24 Aug. 1804, "send copies of these papers to the Admiralty." 25 Sept. 1804. PRO, ADM106/2028.

Notes to pages 138–140   283

77. Inglefield to RO, 14 July 1806. NMM, HAL/E/34, fol. 20.
78. She was 106 feet 6 inches in length and 28 feet 6 inches in breadth; sixteen 32-lb. carronades, two six-pounders, on the quarterdeck six 12-lb. carronades, and on the forecastle two 12-pounders. NB to RO, 10 Sept. 1805. NMM, HAL/E/34. In 1790 the estimated cost of building a 300-ton sloop of war at an English yard was £6,794, with cordage valued at £36 a ton. HAL/E/27, fol. 436.
79. She was 80 feet in length and 22 feet 6 inches in breadth; main deck: two 12-lb. long guns for the bows and ten 18-lb. carronades. NB to RO, 10 Sept. 1805. NMM, HAL/E/34.
80. Permission to advertise for materials. RO to Berkeley, 7 Dec. 1807. NMM, HAL/E/38, fol. 358–61; Douglas to RO, 17 Mar. 1808. NMM, HAL/E/40, fol. 25; RO to Inglefield, 9 Dec. 1808. HAL/E/39a, fol. 71–2.
81. By order of the general commanding the expedition, George Prevost. Inglefield to NB, 22 Sept. 1808. PRO, ADM106/2028.
82. Inglefield to Warren, 5 Oct. 1808. PRO, ADM106/2028.
83. Inglefield to NB, 4 May 1809. PRO, ADM106/2028.
84. Inglefield to NB, 28 Nov. 1808. PRO, ADM106/2028.
85. Warren to Inglefield, 20 Jan. 1809. NMM, HAL/E/39a, fol. 89; Inglefield to RO, 10 Mar. 1809. NSARM, MG13/5, fol. 52; PRO, ADM106/2028.
86. Minute 27 Sept. 1809, "Approve." Inglefield to NB, 31 Aug. 1809. NMM, ADM106/2028.
87. *Naval Instructions*: Section 1, Chapter 2, Article 31, "Commander-in-Chief, when he orders a prize ship to be purchased is to direct that only three-fourths of the appraised value be paid to the agents of the captors the remaining fourth part being reserved until the commissioners of the navy shall have either approved of the appraised value or made such deductions from it as they shall think necessary." NB to Dawes, 22 Oct. 1808. NMM, HAL/C/1, fol. 83–6.
88. £5,739.1.7. Taken by *Rainbow*. Williams accounts, 1773–80. PRO, ADM17/150; NB to Arbuthnot, 12 May 1778. ADM106/2471, fol. 14.
89. Prize to *Raven*, worth H£1,322.4.5½. Williams accounts, 1773–80. PRO, ADM17/150.
90. Worth H£1,076 11s. and H£1,240, taken by *Amphitrite* and *Milford* respectively. Hamond to RO, 29 Jan. 1782, Hamond to Thomas, 11 Apr. 1782. HP, IX, 63, 90; Williams accounts, 1773–80. PRO, ADM17/150.
91. Brig *Yankee Hero* renamed *Postillion* prize to *Milford*, worth H£890. The rest appear not to have been prizes of war: schooner *Sandwich* H£60; pilot sloop *Jane*, purchased for H£75 to replace schooner *Assistance*; schooner *Arbuthnot* H£350; prize of schooner *Betsey* H£520; brig *Black Snake* H£600; schoo-

ner *Nelly* H£270; schooner *Friends*; sloop *Lord Cornwallis* H£1,793 15s. Williams accounts, 1773–80. PRO, ADM17/150.
92. With a gun deck: 87 feet 4 inches, keel 84 feet, breadth 24 feet, depth of hold 9 feet 6 inches, length of quarterdeck 18 feet, 213 tons, H£3,252.17.2. RO to Inglefield, 24 Aug. 1812, Sawyer to NB, 29 Aug. 1812. PRO, ADM106/1422.
93. Some 294 tons, £3,300.6.7. Inglefield to NB, 25 Sept. 1812. NMM, HAL/A/2, fol. 339.
94. Wodehouse to NB, 2 Aug. 1814. NMM, HAL/A/5, fol. 27, 94–5.
95. Some 548 tons, £8,237.10.4. Wodehouse to RO, 24 Aug. 1814. NMM, HAL/E/41, fol. 22–3; revalued by Board for £8,211.1.7. NB to Wodehouse, 5 May 1815. NMM, HAL/C/2, fol. 31–2.
96. Cochrane to Wodehouse, 31 July 1814. NMM, HAL/E/21, fol. 126.
97. £3,879.2.2. NB to Wodehouse, Sept. 1814. NMM, HAL/A/5, fol. 92–3.
98. Halifax valuation, £1,950.10.10½., Board valuation, £1,933.12.11½.; the difference was less than 1 per cent. Wodehouse to RO, 2 Apr. 1816. NMM, HAL/E/41, fol. 271–2.
99. Halifax valuation £1,949.9.7., Board valuation £1,940.11.5. NB to Wodehouse, 23 Jan. 1816. NMM, HAL/C/2, fol. 111–2.
100. For H£338.17.10. and H£333.6.8. respectively. Livie accounts, 1790–9. PRO, ADM17/151.
101. At H£10,147.17.10. taken by *Chatham*. Thomas to NB, 31 Mar. 1782. PRO, ADM106/2027.
102. In 1794 two small French vessels used as despatch boats, *Little Republican* renamed *Prince Edward* and *Jeu* renamed *Dispatch*, for £305 and £130 respectively. RO and Andrew to Duncan, 9 Dec. 1794. NSARM, MG13/6, fol. 44.
103. For £2,679.13.6. Duncan to Livie, 22 June 1795. NSARM, MG13/6, fol. 75.
104. H£7,236.13.4. and H£2,661.2.2. respectively. Livie accounts, 1790–9. PRO, ADM17/151; Duncan to Livie, 9 July 1795. NSARM, MG13/6, fol. 84.
105. NB to RO, 23 Sept. 1805. NMM, HAL/E/34 and HAL/A/3a, fol. 22–3.
106. Main deck, twenty-eight 18-lb. guns; quarterdeck, twelve 32-lb. carronades; forecastle, two 12-lb. long guns. NB to RO, 3 Oct. 1805. NMM, HAL/E/34 and HAL/A/3a, fol. 24–5.
107. H£5,121 1s. Dawes accounts, 1806–7. PRO, ADM17/155; NB to RO, 30 Sept. 1806. NMM, HAL/E/28.
108. Warren to RO, 28 July 1808. NMM, HAL/E/37.
109. Warren to Inglefield, 10 June 1809. NMM, HAL/E/39a, fol. 185; Warren to Inglefield, 1 Sept. 1809. HAL/E/35b.
110. £7,828 7s. Dawes accounts, 1809. PRO, ADM17/157.

111. For £8,740 10s. Dawes accounts, 1809. PRO, ADM17/157; Inglefield to Dawes, 27 Nov. & 18 Dec. 1809. NMM, HAL/E/40, fol. 293; PRO, ADM106/2028.
112. £2,183.6.2. NB to Inglefield, 1 Aug. 1810. NMM, HAL/A/2, fol. 96–7.
113. £3,870 5s. Inglefield to Dawes, 22 Aug. 1810. NMM, HAL/E/36, fol. 120.
114. Douglas to RO, 9 Feb. 1808. NMM, HAL/E/40, fol. 11.
115. Duncan's 1785 orders. NSARM, MG13/2, fol. 341–2.
116. The commissioner's sole responsibility was to determine the nightly password, which doubtless became the task of one of his gentlemen clerks.
117. When not in use, these arms were stored in the guardhouse.
118. Wodehouse to RO, 5 Dec. 1812. NMM, HAL/E/40, fol. 408. Sent also to Captains Pigot, Graham, Gordon, and Hickey of *Orpheus, Laurestinus, Rattler,* and *Atalanta.* NA, I, 5.
119. PRO, ADM106/2027.
120. Inglefield to Nelson, 18 June 1802. PRO, ADM106/2027.
121. Inglefield to NB, 24 July 1802, enclosed in Board to Admiralty, 30 Aug. 1802. NMM, ADM/B/205.
122. Gerrish & Constable to NB, 12 Sept. 1772. PRO, ADM1/484, fol. 161.
123. Campbell to Duncan, 5 June 1786. NSARM, MG13/2, fol. 408.
124. Duncan to Parr, 31 July 1789. NSARM, MG13/2, fol. 650–1.
125. Wentworth to Duncan, 22 Mar. 1797. NSARM, MG13/6, fol. 225–6.
126. Coffin to RO, 31 Dec. 1799. NSARM, MG13/6, fol. 409.
127. Warren to RO, 24 Aug. 1809. NSARM, MG13/5; NMM, HAL/E/37.
128. Murray to Nepean, 30 Oct. 1795. PRO, ADM1/493, fol. 278–9.
129. Mitchell to Nepean, 19 Oct. 1802. PRO, ADM1/495, fol. 349–52.
130. Warren to Pole, 12 Jan. 1809. PRO, ADM1/499, fol. 17; Warren to Inglefield, 8 Sept. 1809. NMM, HAL/E/35b, fol. 73.
131. Jack C. Arnell, *The Bermuda Maritime Museum and the Royal Naval Dockyard, Bermuda* (Hamilton: Bermuda Press, 1979).
132. Yard officers estimated the cost at £1,004, while the three tenders were more than twice this: Messrs Finnerty £2,390; John Clark £2,298; and Kinnear & Sentill £2,275. Inglefield to RO, 1 Nov. 1809. NMM, HAL/E/35a, fol. 168; NSARM, MG13/5, fol. 1.
133. Dawes accounts, 1814. PRO, ADM17/161.
134. Sawyer to NB, 1 Apr. 1811. PRO, ADM106/1421.
135. Inglefield to NB, 12 July 1811. PRO, ADM106/2028. He proposed that a 250-ton vessel should be purchased and attached to the yard as a transport–storeship to freight materials to Bermuda. As the merchant freight prices appeared so excessive to him, he reckoned to recoup the capital

286 Notes to pages 146–153

cost of the vessel within a year. Inglefield to NB, 23 June 1810. ADM106/2028.
136. Admiralty's order received 23 Sept. NB to Wodehouse, 2 Oct. 1815. NMM, HAL/C/2, fol. 81–3.
137. NB to Wodehouse, 7 Oct. 1815. NMM, HAL/C/2, fol. 85, 145.
138. Transport Board to W.J. Hughes, 11 Nov. 1815, Wodehouse to Transport Board, 1 Feb. 1816. NMM, HAL/E/3b, fol. 11–12, 16–17.
139. Transport Board to W.J. Hughes, 11 Nov. 1815, Wodehouse to Transport Board, 1 Feb. 1816. NMM, HAL/E/3b, fol. 11–12, 16–17.
140. NB to Wodehouse, 31 May 1819. NMM, HAL/C/2, fol. 420–1.
141. Griffith to NB, 5 Apr. 1820. PRO, ADM106/1349.
142. Jones to Griffith, 29 Nov. 1819. PRO, ADM106/1349.
143. Douglas and Jones to Griffith, 19 June 1820, Griffith to NB, 20 June 1820. PRO, ADM106/1349.
144. Griffith to NB, 17 July 1820. PRO, ADM106/1349.
145. Thomas Maynard to NB, 4 Jan. 1822, received 6 Mar. 1822. PRO, ADM106/1384.
146. "The climate of the country ... has been found rather unfavourable to European constitutions. They are wrapt up in the gloom of a fog during great parts of the year, and for four or five months it is intensely cold. But though the cold in winter, and the heat in summer are great, they come so gradually, so as to prepare the body for enduring both ... From such an unfavourable climate, little can be expected." William Guthrie, *A System of Modern Geography*, 7th ed. (London: 1811), 881.

Chapter 7   Suppliers and Tradesmen

1. NB to Thomas, 10 June 1788. NMM, HAL/F/1, fol. 294–5.
2. See Julian Gwyn, *Excessive Expectations: Maritime Commerce & the Economic Development of Nova Scotia, 1740–1870* (Montreal: McGill-Queen's University Press, 1998), 14–42.
3. RO to Inglefield, 27 Feb. 1807. NMM, HAL/E/38, fol. 68.
4. Warren to Inglefield, 26 June 1809, Inglefield to Warren, 27 June 1809. NMM, HAL/E/39a, fol. 207–10.
5. Inglefield to NB, 19 June 1809. NMM, HAL/A/4b, fol. 153–6.
6. Inglefield returned to the subject the following November. "I have always understood that for long voyages, the Irish is to be preferred to the American, that not being so well cured." Yet American beef and pork could be imported into Nova Scotia only with the governor's special license, either for the use of the military and the fleet, or "at particular times to prevent

distress to the colonists." Owing to non-intercourse, there was then no American beef or pork in the Halifax market. Inglefield to VB, 4 Nov. 1809. NMM, HAL/A/2.
7. Warren to Inglefield, 28 June 1809. NMM, HAL/E/39a, fol. 212–3.
8. For an account of the difficulties of John Avery, an earlier purveyor of fresh beef to the squadron, see Julian Gwyn, "Capitalists, Merchants and Manufacturers: The Tangled Affairs of John Avery, James Creighton, John Albro and Joseph Fairbanks," in *Intimate Relations: Family and Community in Planter Nova Scotia 1759–1800*, ed. Margaret Conrad, 190–212 (Fredericton: Acadiensis Press, 1995). Earlier still, Joshua Mauger made his fortune in 1755–6 by buying confiscated Acadian cattle cheaply in a glutted market, and then supplying it to the squadron at contract prices. Julian Gwyn, "Joshua Mauger: The Man and the Myth" (Paper read before the Royal Nova Scotia Historical Society, 2003).
9. Hians also held the contract with the Board of Transport for the supply of meat to prisoners of war. Cochrane to Inglefield, 21 June 1811. NMM, HAL/E/27, fol. 415; Warren to Inglefield, 27 June 1809. HAL/E/39a, fol. 214–5.
10. Inglefield to Warren, 29 June 1809. NMM, HAL/E/39a, fol. 219–20.
11. Inglefield to Hians, 19 Dec. 1809. NMM, HAL/E/35a, fol. 239–41.
12. Inglefield to VB, 10 Oct. 1811. NMM, HAL/A/2, fol. 218.
13. VB to Inglefield, 20 Jan. 1812. NMM, HAL/A/2, fol. 281.
14. Inglefield to VB, 11 May 1812. NMM, HAL/A/2, fol. 293–4.
15. Contract awarded to Starr & Shannon. Inglefield to VB, 17 July 1812. NMM, HAL/A/2, fol. 321.
16. Wodehouse to VB, 21 Nov. 1817, 2 Dec. 1818, 12 May 1819. NMM, HAL/E/3a, fol. 159, 172, 188, 205.
17. For the final quarter, 1810: 300 bushels of potatoes, 250 bushels of turnips, twenty-five bushels of carrots, fifteen bushels of beets, 200 dozen cabbages, and 5,000 bunches of onions. James Proud to Inglefield, 27 Nov. 1810. PRO, ADM106/2029.
18. VB to Inglefield, 19 Apr. 1811. NMM, HAL/A/2.
19. Potatoes and turnips, 1d.; cabbages 2d.; onions 5d.; and for two lbs carrots and beets 1½d. Four "respectable inhabitants of the town" acknowledged that such prices were lower than those then obtaining in Halifax; "the bushel of potatoes weighing about 60 lbs." Inglefield to VB, 16 Sept. 1812. NMM, HAL/A/2, fol. 328–9.
20. New tender per lb: potatoes 1½d. (2 lbs), turnips ½d., beets ¼d., carrots 2¼d., cabbage 1¼d., onions 3d., payable in bills of exchange on London. In January 1819, as "the price of vegetables having fallen," Wodehouse gave

the usual six months' notice to tender the contract, which McNab again won. VB to Wodehouse, 1 Oct. 1816. NMM, HAL/E/3a, fol. 135–6; Wodehouse to VB, 2 Jan. & 10 July 1819. HAL/E/3a, fol. 189, 218. There was also a contract for the supply of tobacco to seamen. In 1817 it was held by Henry Austen, a Halifax importer, who bid 1s.8d. per lb. VB to Wodehouse, 9 May 1817. HAL/E/3a, fol. 148.
21. In the winter of 1760–1 coal cost £3–£4 per chaldron in Halifax. Gerrish to NB, 6 Jan. 1761. PRO, ADM106/1121.
22. George to Hamond, 29 July 1781. HP, VII, 2–6; 11 June 1806. PRO, ADM1/2151. There is an inaccurate print of the engagement in the Beverley R. Robinson Collection, Annapolis, Maryland. See Robert Gardiner, ed., *Navies and the American Revolution 1775–1783* (London: Chatham Publishing, 1996), 149–50.
23. "*Allegiance* has arrived with her colliers." Hamond to Graves, 29 Aug. 1781. HP, VII, 19.
24. The last such shipment to New York took place in November 1783 in the brig *Lark*. Duncan De Brockenback, master of *Castor*, 15 Nov. 1783.
25. Commissioner Hughes in 1781 hired the brig *British Queen* to bring coal from Spanish River. Hamond to Thomas, 27 Jan. 1782. HP, IX, 62; Williams accounts, 1773–80. PRO, ADM17/150.
26. Forsyth to Thomas, 21 Apr. 1785. NSARM, MG13/1, #543.
27. *Lilly*'s owner, James Lowey, was paid for 117 chaldrons.
28. As DesBarres explained "The coals shipped ... in the brig *Lilly*, are the best, at present to be procured here. A new pit is now sinking from whence extraordinary good ones are expected, but they cannot be got out for some time." DesBarres to Duncan, Spanish River, Sydney, 30 June 1785. NSARM, MG13/2, fol. 337–8; Duncan to DesBarres, 30 May 1785. NMM, HAL/F/2, fol. 327.
29. Supplied by James Kavanagh. DesBarres to Thomas, 6 July 1785. NSARM, MG13/1, #558; Forsyth to Thomas, 19 July 1785. MG13/1, #562.
30. From transport *Sceptre*, Inglefield to RO, 30 Nov. 1811. NMM, HAL/E/36, fol. 350.
31. Owing to the "very inclement season ... none could be purchased in town." Inglefield to Dawes, 1 Apr. 1809. NMM, HAL/E/35a, fol. 13.
32. In 1812 a loan of forty chaldrons was repaid to the army from a cargo arriving from Sydney in *Lady Delaval*. Inglefield to RO, 15 July 1812. NMM, HAL/E/40, fol. 381.
33. As coal then sold at Barbados for $1 a bushel, Cochrane wanted twenty to thirty chaldrons sent from Halifax. There were thirty-six bushels per chaldron. Inglefield to RO, 9 Sept. 1807. NMM, HAL/E/38, fol. 212.

34. In 1814 a coal vessel to Bermuda, *Hebe*, was captured by the enemy. Wodehouse to Cochrane, 2 Aug. 1814. NMM, HAL/E/21, fol. 119–20. In 1816 John Leaver was paid H£140 for 140 chaldrons of coal, delivered from Sydney on board hired brig *Lucretia* for the Bermuda yard. Wodehouse to Dawes, 30 Oct. 1817. HAL/E/42a, fol. 151.
35. Transport *Fairey*, Douglas to Dawes, *Bellona*, 16 May 1808. NMM, HAL/E/37.
36. Inglefield to RO, 2 June 1809. NMM, HAL/E/37.
37. In 1808 contract prices rose by 5.25 per cent to 41s.7d. a chaldron over the year before, or about the average price that obtained in 1793–5. For 1798–1807 the average contract price was 35s., but in 1810 it rose to 45s.8d. NSARM, RG1/304/79. By January 1813, wholesale prices had reached 70s., *Acadian Recorder*; Inglefield to RO, 30 July 1811. NMM, HAL/E/40, fol. 353; Inglefield to Ritchie, 19 and 28 June 1810. HAL/E/36, fol. 84, 262.
38. Cash carried by sloop *Clinker* to pay for 150 chaldrons loaded at colliery on transport *Bellona* for Bermuda. Wodehouse to RO, 21 Sept. 1814. NMM, HAL/E/41, fol. 93. The 150 chaldrons cost H£172 10s. Dawes to Nelson, 8 Feb. 1816. NMM, HAL/B/1, fol. 372–3.
39. To collect as much coal as she could stow. Wodehouse to Lieut Thomas Smith, *Attentive*, 21 June 1816. NMM, HAL/E/41, fol. 295.
40. Cordwood: full 4 feet long each stick, the pile to be solid, 4 feet high, 8 feet long; cost for surveying, 2d. per cord. *An Act for Regulating the Exportation of Fish, and the Assize of Barrels, Staves, Hoops, Boards, and all other kind of Lumber; and for appointing Officers to survey the same.* 2 Geo. 3, c.8 [1762]. Richard John Uniacke, ed., *The Statutes at Large, passed in the Several Assemblies held in His Majesty's Province of Nova Scotia from ... 1758, to ... 1804* (Halifax, 1805), 85.
41. NSARM, MG13/1, #443, #541–2, #544–5, #639, #650, #652.
42. Duncan and Sawyer to Stephens, 27 June 1786. NSARM, MG13/2, fol. 412–3.
43. King to RO, 12 Aug. 1801. NSARM, MG13/3.
44. Inglefield to RO, 26 Sept. and 27 Oct. 1806. NMM, HAL/E/28.
45. Williams accounts, 1773–80, Livie accounts, 1790–9. PRO, ADM17/150–1.
46. Coal and firewood prices were always highest in the late-winter months. *Acadian Recorder*.
47. Gerrish accounts, 1757–73. PRO, ADM17/150.
48. Contract with William Shaw, owner of the schooner *Dispatch* (40 tons; Ebenezer Porter, master), 4 May 1781, valued at H£306 by the yard officers. NSARM, MG13/1, #602.
49. Foster Sherlock, owner of a cartel, received payment at the rate of H£50 a

month from 22 June to 31 Oct. Hamond to Thomas, 31 Oct. 1781. HP, IX, 37.

50. James Kerr, master; 150 tons, with 100 prisoners, Hamond to Sick & Hurt Board, and Hamond to NB. 17 Sept. 1781. HP, VII, 23, 25–6; other examples: sloop *Olive* (John Baker, master) to Boston, Hamond to Baker. HP, VIII, 4–5; schooner *Observer* (Lemuel Goddard, master) 70 tons, Hamond to Goddard, 27 Oct. 1781. HP, VIII, 6–7; sloop *Albion* (William Black, master; Alexander Brymer, owner), Hamond to Black, 100 prisoners, 23 Dec. 1781. HP, VIII, 16; Hamond to Thomas, 17 Apr. 1782. HP, IX, 100; brig *Otter* (Ephraim Farnam, master; John Prince, owner), 120 rebels, Hamond to Farnam, 3 Jan. 1782. HP, VIII, 16; Hamond to Thomas, 5 May 1782. HP, IX, 131.
51. Hamond to Thomas, 30 Nov. 1782. HP, IX, 189–91.
52. On *Stanislaus*, see Allan Everett Marble, *Surgeons, Smallpox, and the Poor: A History of Medicine and Social Conditions in Nova Scotia, 1749–1799* (Montreal: McGill-Queen's University Press, 1993), 133, 135.
53. Hamond to Sick & Hurt Board, 25 Nov. 1781. HP, VIII, 11–13.
54. Hamond to RO, 10 Aug. 1781. HP, IX, 23–4; Hamond to Loader, 15 Aug. 1781. HP, IX, 32; Hamond to RO, 9 Dec. 1781. HP, IX, 46.
55. Stoves were also purchased. Hamond to Turnbull, 12 Dec. 1781. HP, VIII, 19.
56. Thomas accounts 1780–84, 1785–90. PRO, ADM17/150, fol. 274; Hamond to Thomas, 29 Dec. 1781, 14 May, 14 Dec. 1782. HP, IX, 54, 119, 186.
57. Hamond to Turnbull, 25 Nov 1781. HP, VIII, 19; to Brigadier Campbell, 23 Jan. 1782. HP, VIII, 26–7; to Capt. Russell, *Hussar*, 23 Jan. 1782. HP, X, 61; to Campbell, 2 Feb. 1782. HP, VIII, 65.
58. Hamond to NB, 1 July 1782. HP, VII, 125–6.
59. Daily rate 10s. Edgecombe accounts, 1784–5. PRO, ADM17/150.
60. Coffin to RO, 12 Feb. 1800. NSARM, MG13/4, fol. 505.
61. To build a 30-foot cutter on the same contract terms as formerly. Inglefield to RO, 13 Apr. 1805. NSARM, MG13/9.1, fol. 262.
62. Inglefield to RO, 30 Sept. 1807. NMM, HAL/E/38, fol. 235–7.
63. Inglefield to RO, 6 Mar. & 5 June 1812. NMM, HAL/E/36, fol. 384–5, 432.
64. RO to Inglefield, 2 Mar. 1802. NSARM, MG13/3.
65. 1809. NSARM, MG13/5, fol. 104.
66. Some 10d. per square yard for hangings and 8d. for borders for the commissioner, 9d. and 6d. respectively for other officers. 1809. NSARM, MG13/5, fol. 104.
67. Incidentally as far as glazing was concerned, window panes could be replaced "when found necessary, but not on account of cracks in the panes." Received 17 Aug. 1809. NSARM, MG13/5, fol. 104.

68. See Hezekiah Reynolds, *Directions for House and Ship Painting Shewing in a Plain and Concise Manner The Best Method of Preparing, Mixing and Laying the Various Colours Now in Use, Designed for the Use of Learners* (New Haven, 1812, reprint ed. Worcester, MA: American Antiquarian Society, 1978). I am grateful to Dr Karen Diadick Casselman for this reference.
69. It "will require at least 8 cwt red ochre to mix with tar and 5 cwt of white lead ground in oil for the doors and windows." Gerrish to NB, 6 Jan. 1762. PRO, ADM106/1121.
70. PRO, ADM42/2147.
71. With tar and red ochre. PRO, ADM42/2149, fol. 20–1.
72. NB to Duncan, 3 Oct. 1783. PRO, ADM106/2471, fol. 301–2.
73. Coffin to RO, 24 March. 1800. NSARM, MG13/6, fol. 560; Lawlor and his father before him had earned about H£250 annually to paint the weatherwork, cabins, arms chests, fire engines, and boats belonging to warships and yard vessels. His terms to 1780 had been: for one coat 2½d. and 3d. per yard; for two coats 4½d.; for three coats 6d.; to paint log boards 5s.; and boats of the commissioner, storekeeper, master attendant, and master shipwright as well as those in storage, 15s. each. Williams accounts, 1773–80. PRO, ADM17/150.
74. The proposed rates were for woodwork: painted once 6d. per yard, twice 8d., thrice 10d.; new canvas for hammock cloths painted three times, 14d. per yard. Lawlor to Coffin, 15 Jan. 1800, Coffin to NB, 17 Jan. 1800. NSARM, MG13/6, fol. 456–7.
75. Douglas to RO, 29 Mar. 1808. PRO, ADM106/2028.
76. Inglefield to RO, 17 Oct. 1808. NMM, HAL/E/37; PRO, ADM106/2028.
77. Inglefield to RO, 21 Oct. 1808. NMM, HAL/E/40, fol. 133.
78. Inglefield to Prevost, 19 May 1809. NMM, HAL/A/4b, fol. 140–1; Inglefield to Pole, 25 May 1809. NMM, HAL/E/39a, fol. 146.
79. Inglefield to RO, 14 July 1809. NMM, HAL/E/37.
80. RO to Wodehouse, 25 Apr. 1814. NMM, HAL/E/25, fol. 202–3. "To get Merrick's proposals for a new one-year contract for glazing and painting, for which they are to take his bond." Wodehouse to RO, 27 Apr. 1814. NA, II, 125.
81. Merrick to Wodehouse, 14 July 1814. NMM, HAL/E/21, fol. 111–12.
82. RO to Wodehouse, 22 July 1814. NMM, HAL/E/25, fol. 215–16.
83. Wodehouse to RO, 11 Aug. 1814. NA, II, 190.
84. Wodehouse to RO, 1 July 1815. NSARM, MG13/9.3, 175. In 1817 men engaged to paint the yard buildings were ordered to work three and a half hours extra per day and to be paid an extra 8½d. an hour. Wodehouse to RO, 9 June 1817. MG13/9.3, fol. 216.

292 Notes to pages 163–166

85. Specific mention was made of the smiths' shop, pitch house, storehouses, and internal fences once they had been repaired. RO to Wodehouse, 21 Oct. 1818. PRO, ADM106/2029, fol. 405–6.
86. Coffin to RO, NSARM, MG13/6, fol. 533–4.
87. Inglefield to RO, 15 Mar. 1806. PRO, ADM106/2028.
88. RO to Inglefield, 8 Feb. 1803. NSARM, MG13/3.
89. Douglas to Duncan, 25 Sept. 1784, 12 Oct. 1785. NMM, HAL/F/1, fol. 155, 194; Dawes to Berkeley, 14 Oct. 1807. NMM, HAL/E/38, fol. 270–1; Inglefield to Dawes, 4 Nov. 1808. HAL/E/37; Dawes to Inglefield, 25 Nov. & 20 Dec. 1809. HAL/E/35a, fol. 202, 243; Wodehouse to RO, 26 Nov. 1814. HAL/E/41, fol. 87; Wodehouse to RO, 31 Jan. 1818. HAL/E/43, fol. 89.
90. Dawes to Inglefield, 3 July 1811. NMM, HAL/E/25, fol. 72–4, 77–8, 86, 96.
91. Duncan to Thomas, 10 Apr. and 15 July 1789. NSARM, MG13/2, fol. 616, MG13/2, fol. 646; Mitchell to Inglefield, 3 Jan. 1806. NMM, HAL/A/3b, fol. 73; Douglas to RO, 12 Feb. 1808. NMM, HAL/E/40, fol. 13; Inglefield to Dawes, 31 Oct. 1809. HAL/E/37.
92. Inglefield to RO, 16 Feb. 1807, 27 Nov. 1809, 26 Nov. 1811. NMM, HAL/E/38, fol. 13, HAL/E/40, fol. 358; RO to Berkeley 18 Nov. 1807. HAL/E/37; Wodehouse to RO, 9 Dec. 1812. HAL/E/40, fol. 410.
93. Details in RO to Inglefield, 22 Nov. 1809. NMM, HAL/A/1.
94. Williams accounts, 1773–80. PRO, ADM17/150.
95. Colvill to Gerrish, 19 Jan. 1761, Gerrish accounts, 1756–73. PRO, ADM17/150, fol. 157.
96. Hamond to Thomas, 1 Aug. 1781. HP, IX, 84.
97. Williams accounts, 1773–80, Livie accounts, 1790–9. PRO, ADM17/150–1.
98. Warren to Dawes, 11 July 1808. NMM, HAL/E/37.
99. Duncan to Thomas, 8 Feb. 1784. NMM, HAL/F/1, fol. 60–1.

100.	Master		Men	Tons	Days	Paid H£
	Shallop	David Munrow	3	12	4	8
	Fortune	Edward Jones	4	25	4	12
	Lidde	A. Chaponan	6	30	4	17
	Peggy	Thomas Benson	9	70	3	22 5s.
	Shallop	D. Bigsley	3	12	3	6
	Shallop	John Redden	3	12	3	6

Duncan to RO, 15 June 1786. NSARM, MG13/1, #629–30; Duncan to Thomas, 15 June 1786. MG13/1, #641.
101. Warren to Dawes, 16 June 1808. NMM, HAL/E/40, fol. 69–70.
102. Livie accounts, 1790–99. PRO, ADM17/151, items 39, 52.

103. Hussey to Inglefield, 4 Nov. 1809. NSARM, MG13/5, fol. 3.
104. Wodehouse to RO, 20 Oct. 1817. NMM, HAL/E/42a, fol. 145.
105. Hamond to Thomas, 3 June 1782. HP, IX, 129.
106. He boarded her on 16 Dec. Inglefield to Dawes, 26 Dec. 1809. NSARM, MG13/5, fol. 41.
107. Wodehouse to NB, 17 Apr. 1813. NMM, HAL/A/2, fol. 439; Wodehouse to RO, 10 Feb. 1813. NA, I, 27.
108. She had asked for £15. William Drummond, Major Commandant, Saint John, to Capt. Godfrey of *Emulous*, 12 Dec. 1812, forwarded to Wodehouse by Capt. Pigot, *Orpheus*, 18 Jan. 1813. NA, I, 25.
109. Wodehouse to RO, 17 Dec. 1814. NA, II, 230.
110. Thomas Turpel entered as a labourer in 1810. 17 Sept. 1810. NMM, HAL/E/36, fol. 136; Wodehouse to RO, 1 Dec. 1815. HAL/E/41, fol. 244–5.
111. Inglefield to RO, 21 Feb. 1806. NMM, HAL/E/34, fol. 6.
112. Julian Gwyn, *Excessive Expectations*, 28–30.
113. Some H£3,422.13.1¼. was paid in 1790–9 to Lawlor. Livie accounts, 1790–9. PRO. ADM17/151, item #4.
114. Dawes accounts, 1806–7. PRO. ADM17/155; 1809. ADM17/157; 1810–11. ADM17/158.

Chapter 8   Mast Contractors and Wood Merchants

1. Wentworth to NB, 14 June 1806. PRO, ADM106/1653.
2. Roger Morris, *The Royal Dockyards during the Revolutionary and Napoleonic Wars* (Leicester: Leicester University Press, 1983), 73.
3. The timber supply, from Maine south, has been well-studied especially by Joseph J. Malone, *Pine Trees and Politics: The Naval Stores and Forest Policy in Colonial New England 1691–1775* (Seattle: University of Washington Press, 1964). Pre-1815 timber exports from Nova Scotia remain virtually unstudied, though Albion supplied some data for 1799–1815, Robert Greenhalgh Albion, *Forests and Sea Power: The Timber Problem of the Royal Navy 1652–1862* (Cambridge, MA: Harvard University Press, 1926), appendix D, 420–2.
4. Mauger to John Butler, 22 Nov. 1760. The Pierpont Morgan Library, Gilder Lehrman Collection, GLC3902/262.
5. 4 June 1755, NB and Henniker. NSARM, MG13/3.
6. 2 Geo. 2, c.35. An additional contract in 1757, also won by Henniker, called for the delivery of two shiploads to the naval yards at Antigua and Jamaica, of New England masts, yards, bowsprits, cheeks for masts, spars, rafters, capstan bars, sheathing board, pitch, tar, turpentine, and other stowage goods.

7. Julian Gwyn, "Shipbuilding for the Royal Navy in Colonial New England," *American Neptune* 48 (1988): 22–30. The Board responded in the same tone to an offer from Messrs Begbie & Manson, shipbuilders at Hobeau, South Carolina, who offered to build a 32-gun ship with oak and pine timber. "We cannot by any means think it advisable to accept their offer of building any abroad." NB to Stephens, 30 Apr. 1773. NMM, ADM/B/187.
8. Some twenty-eight such warships were commissioned by the end of 1781, nine as frigates, fourteen as sloops, one fireship, and four brigs. NB to Stephens, 22 Jan. 1782. NMM, ADM/BP/3.
9. 28 Oct. 1768. NMM, ADM/B/181.
10. NB to Admiralty, 5 July 1775. NMM, ADM/B/190.
11. Middleton to Sandwich, 4 May 1781. NMM, ADM/BP/2. As the cargoes were still largely intact six years later, Middleton wanted a water-borne assault made on the mast pond to recover the sticks.
12. Albion, *Forests and Sea Power*, 290.
13. Albion, *Forests and Sea Power*, 297–8; others called it "ill-luck," David Syrett, *The Royal Navy in American Waters 1775–1783* (Aldershot: Scolar Press, 1989), 101; others referred to Byron's "costly wild goose chase," N.A.M. Rodger, *The Insatiable Earl: A Life of John Montagu, 4th Earl of Sandwich 1718–1792* (New York: Norton, 1993), 278; none seems to have considered, let alone challenged, Albion's contention.
14. Nova Scotia's Mast Exports to Great Britain

	Great	Middling	Small
1751–7	16	125	210
1766–75	216	178	740
1776–83	220	456	177

Also exported were several hundred spars, at least twenty-five bowsprits, and 283 yards. PRO, CUST3/49–71; CUST16/1; CUST17/1–8.
15. Gerrish to NB, 18 July 1760. PRO, ADM106/1121.
16. Hurd to NB, 7 May 1763. PRO, ADM106/1134.
17. Before the outbreak of hostilities Wentworth had "pushed out far into Nova Scotia" to survey forest tracts for the navy. Malone, *Pine Trees and Politics*, 135.
18. Sir George Collier, *A Detail of Some Particular Services Performed in America, during the Years 1776, 1777, 1778, and 1779 by Commodore Sir George Collier ... compiled from Journals & Original Papers by G.S. Rainier* (New York, 1833).
19. Oct.–Dec. 1779. PRO, ADM42/2152.
20. NB to Hughes, 9 Dec. 1778. PRO, ADM106/2471, fol. 34–7.
21. Acknowledged letters of 15 and 17 May from Hughes. NB to Hughes, 12 Aug. 1779. PRO, ADM106/2471, fol. 66–7.

22. NB to Hughes, 30 Dec. 1779. PRO, ADM106/2471, fol. 87.
23. The contract called for the supply of eighty sticks. Hamond amended the contract to 150 to be delivered to Fort Howe by the end of June 1782. Hamond to Davidson, 27 Aug. 1781. HP, VII, 32. "Having had that country accurately examined to the distance of ninety miles from the mouth, it is reported to me that a very considerable quantity of masts from 26 inches downwards may be cut annually for many years to come." Hamond to NB, 25 Nov. 1781. HP, VII, 45–6.
24. W.A. Spray, "William Davidson, c.1740–1790," *DCB* (Toronto: University of Toronto Press, 1979), 4: 195–7.
25. Davidson to [Duncan], 29 July 1784. NMM, HAL/F/2, fol. 240–3.
26. Thomas to NB, 18 Nov. 1784. NMM, HAL/F/2, fol. 312–5.
27. They completed their contract in September 1783. Hamond to John Hayes, surveyor to attend the contractor at 10s. a day, 9 Aug. 1781. HP, IX, 17; Hazen & White to Duncan, 8 Apr. 1784. NMM, HAL/F/2, fol. 155–9.
28. Hayes to Hazen & White, 5 and 11 Feb. 1782; Samuel Peabody to White, 18 Aug. 1782, and Davidson to Peabody, 9 Dec. 1782. NBM, White papers, Shelf 5, A3.
29. 25 Apr. 1782. NBM, White papers, Shelf 5, A3.
30. The Admiralty provided escorts to convoy the mastships involved from Fort Howe either to Halifax or New York and thence to the English yards. NB to Hamond, 28 Sept. 1781. PRO, ADM106/2471.
31. NB to Stephens, 25 Aug. 1783, NMM, ADM/BP/4.
32. Duncan to Wentworth, 15 Nov. 1783. NMM, HAL/F/2, fol. 38.
33. NB to Duncan, 1 May 1784. NMM, HAL/F/2, fol. 234–6.
34. Duncan to NB, 2 Nov. 1784. NMM, HAL/F/2, fol. 261–6.
35. William Davidson may have built the first such ship in the Maritime colonies in 1784–5. "There is not water here for ships of a large draft, but one or two might be built to answer the purpose. I intend to build one here this winter for the lumber trade from this place. She will be fit to take in the largest masts." Davidson to Thomas, 20 Aug. 1785. NSARM, MG13/1, #568.
36. In 1788 he travelled as far east as the Miramichi River. Duncan to Andrew, 9 Aug. 1788. NSARM, MG13/2, fol. 568.
37. Duncan to NB, 11 Oct. 1785. NSARM, MG13/2, fol. 357–8.
38. "On sartching through the woods here I find that better masts may be got and of a larger size than at the River Saint Johns." Davidson to Thomas, Miramichi, 20 Aug. 1785. NSARM, MG13/1, #568.
39. "There is no reason to doubt of the country's furnishing trees fit for masts." He went up both main branches of the rivers "as far as the keel boat could go," using Samuel Holland's not very accurate chart. Duncan to NB, 15 & 25 Sept. 1788. NSARM, MG13/2, fol. 574–6.

40. Duncan to NB, 11 Oct. 1785. NSARM, MG13/2, fol. 357–8.
41. "I have examined a piece of grey oak timber brought from Saint John. It is small grain'd: When green remarkable tough and stringy. In my opinion it is superior in quality to the timber that has been made use of in the king's dockyards in England, called saten timber." Comments by Provo Wallis. 23 Sept. 1784, enclosed in Duncan to NB, 2 Nov. 1784. NMM, HAL/F/2, fol. 266.
42. NB to Duncan, 8 Dec. 1784. PRO, ADM106/2471, fol. 369–70.
43. NB to Duncan, 15 Mar. 1787. NSARM, MG13/2, fol. 457–8.
44. NB to Duncan, 3 Oct. 1787. NSARM, MG13/2, fol. 506.
45. Duncan to NB, 28 May 1787. NSARM, MG13/2, fol. 459.
46. NB to Duncan, 2 May 1788. NSARM, MG13/2, fol. 562.
47. Duncan to NB, 16 June 1788. NSARM, MG13/2, fol. 563.
48. Andrew to Thomas, 17 Dec. 1783. NSARM, MG13/1, #415.
49. Andrew to Thomas, 18 Mar. 1784. NSARM, MG13/1, #432.
50. Andrew to Thomas, 28 Dec. 1783. NSARM, MG13/1, #417; Andrew to Duncan, 11 Sept. 1784. NMM, HAL/F/2, fol. 302–3.
51. The same problem limited the value of both *Prudent* and *Diana*. The former was "not calculated for masts, as the greatest length she can take on the upper tier in the hold will not exceed 81 ft. and 25" in diameter with not 10½ feet in the hold. There is a ship *Diana* with provisions, whom her agent wants used as a mastship, but as her raft port is only 22" and so near the deck that she could not take in more than 18" or 19" of which there are not many." Andrew to Duncan, 13 Jan. 1784. NSARM, MG13/1, #421; Andrew to Thomas, 1 July 1784. MG13/1, #481.
52. McGee, master. Andrew to Thomas, 17 Mar. 1784. NSARM, MG13/1, #431.
53. Thomas to NB, 18 Nov. 1784. NMM, HAL/F/2, fol. 312–5.
54. Davidson's memorial, 29 July 1784. NMM, HAL/F/2, fol. 240–3.
55. Duncan to Davidson, 18 Apr. 1785. NSARM, MG13/1, #548. In 1786 Davidson, who was struggling to avoid insolvency, supplied about ninety sticks before the fishing season began, "which I must attend." Davidson to Thomas, 15 Apr. 1786. MG13/1, #617.
56. Memorial to Duncan, 28 Aug. 1786. NSARM, MG13/2, fol. 429–30; Davidson to Thomas, 16 Feb. 1787. MG13/1, #711.
57. "From different unexpected disappointments in trade I am at present obliged to adopt the method of making partial payments to those I'm due. They are sufficiently safe in the whole and will instantly receive one half and in some months after the whole, when I can convert some part of my propertie into cash for that purpose. But in the meantime it's reasonable

every one should be put on the same footing." Though he claimed his assets were four times greater than his H£2,700 debts, "yet ... I cannot immediately convert so much of it into ready money as will discharge them." Davidson to Thomas, 28 Aug. 1786. NSARM, MG13/1, #668.
58. Thomas to NB, 18 Nov. 1784. NMM/HAL/F/2, fol. 312–5.
59. Hazen & White to Duncan, 8 Apr. 1784. NMM, HAL/F/2, fol. 155–9; NB to Duncan, 8 June 1784. HAL/F/2, fol. 227.
60. Eventually the Navy Board allowed the sticks cut in wartime and undelivered to be paid 10 per cent above the 1784 contract prices. NB to Thomas, 9 Mar. 1786. NSARM, MG13/1, #627; same day to Duncan. MG13/2, fol. 415–6.
61. Duncan to Hazen, 13 Sept. 1784. NMM, HAL/F/2, fol. 237–8; Hazen to Duncan, 5 Oct. 1784. HAL/F/2, fol., 243–5.
62. It required, among other things, that the "head is to be 4¾" for every yard the mast is long. The diameter was to be measured in each quarter, and wrought in a workmanlike manner in one-eighth squares, to be free of large knots, or sudden bites below the tongue or any defects, one-quarter of all masts between 22" and 27" shall not be 'tongued.' All bowsprits shall be at the upper end in the four squares for the better putting in the caps and bees, that the length of the square from the upper end shall be three times the diameter of the bowsprit, and that one-third of the bowsprits from 26" to 31" in diameter shall be left from the bed to the heel in the four squares, and the same diameter in the bed where there is proper room for it." 5 Oct. 1784. NSARM, MG13/2, fol. 351–4.
63. Duncan to Andrew, 27 May 1786. NMM, HAL/F/1, fol. 213–8; "deficiencies to be good," masts £28.12.4., yards £5 5s., bowsprits £164.17.9½., topmasts £72, in total £270.15.1½., 23 Dec. 1784. HAL/F/2, fol. 295.
64. Hazen & White also agreed to make good the deficiency in their 9 Aug. 1781 contract with Hamond. Permission to cut had first to be granted by the surveyor general. Duncan to Wentworth, 18 Oct. 1784. NMM, HAL/F/2, fol. 253. It was late in 1786 before the contractors received their final payments. Hazen & White to Duncan, 16 Oct. & 28 Nov. 1787. NSARM, MG13/2, fol. 600–01.
65. NB to Duncan, 16 Oct. 1787. NSARM, MG13/2, fol. 520–1.
66. Deadline was delayed by two months. NSARM, MG13/2, fol. 521.
67. Duncan to NB, 26 Nov. 1787. NSARM, MG13/2, fol. 512–3.
68. Ship *Admiral Parker*. NB to Duncan, 31 Jan. 1788. NSARM, MG13/2, fol. 550–1. She arrived at Fort Howe the following July. Andrew to Duncan, 13 Sept. 1788. MG13/2, fol. 572.
69. Duncan to NB, 19 Dec. 1788. NSARM, MG13/2, fol. 590.

298   Notes to pages 180–182

70. Wallace, Holmes & Davidson to Duncan, 30 Dec. 1788. NSARM, MG13/2, fol. 592–3; Duncan to NB, 1 Jan. 1789. MG13/2, fol. 591.
71. NB to Duncan, 17 Feb. 1789. NSARM, MG13/2, fol. 614.
72. NB to Duncan, 27 Mar. 1789. NSARM, MG13/2, fol. 625.
73. Forsyth to Duncan, 24 Sept. 1787. NSARM, MG13/2, fol. 516.
74. For details of the Blair-Glenie contract difficulties, see Wentworth letter-books, NSARM, RG1/49–54; W.G. Godfrey, "James Glenie, 1750–1817," *DCB* (Toronto: Toronto University Press, 1983), 5: 347–58.
75. NB to Duncan, 17 Apr. 1789. NSARM, MG13/2, fol. 642.
76. Glenie to Duncan, 4 July 1789. NSARM, MG13/2, fol. 652–3.
77. Especially Arthur R.M. Lower, *Great Britain's Woodyard: British America and the Timber Trade, 1763–1867* (Montreal: McGill-Queen's University Press, 1973) and Graeme Wynn, *Timber Colony: A Historical Geography of Early Nineteenth Century New Brunswick* (Toronto: University of Toronto Press, 1981).
78. Wentworth to NB, London, 12 Dec. 1791. PRO, ADM106/1653.
79. Wentworth to NB, 10 Jan. 1794. PRO, ADM106/1653.
80. Robertson to O'Brien, 2 Oct. 1791; copy sent to the owners Hunter, Robertson & Forsyth in Greenock. PRO, ADM106/1531; crew list of *Earl of Mansfield*, 15 Oct. 1791 numbered thirty-two including six "black men who had never been to sea before" – Roberts, Rogers, Terrey, Will, Smith, and Davie – six discharged soldiers and four apprentices, with only four capable of "taking the wheel." Affidavit sworn in Greenock, 5 Apr. 1792 by Robertson. James Hunter to NB, London, 11 Nov. 1791. ADM106/1531.
81. They considered inaccurate the captain's description of the events relating to the pressing of seven men from their ship *Earl of Mansfield* in October 1791. O'Brien to Stephens, 19 Dec. 1791 enclosed in NB's letter to them of 7 Mar. 1792, Hunter & Robertson to NB, 19 Apr. 1792. PRO, ADM106/1531.
82. One retained was a 16-year-old apprentice, expressly exempted by act of Parliament. Forsyth & Smith to Inglefield, 10 May 1805. NSARM, MG13/9.1, fol. 295–6.
83. "The *Busy* has got three of *Governor Carleton*'s men from the jail, and one of the *Lilly*'s. But Capt. Bryant rendered assistance to carry both ships to Halifax." John Black to Forsyth & Smith, 28 June 1805. NSARM, MG13/4, fol. 52–3.
84. Forsyth & Smith to Inglefield, 13 Aug. 1806. NMM, HAL/A/3b, fol. 155–7.
85. Forsyth & Smith to Inglefield, 24 Sept. 1808. NMM, HAL/E/39a, fol. 5; Warren to Inglefield, 26 Sept. 1808. HAL/E/39a, fol. 6.
86. The escort was *Maidstone* (32). Vandeput to Marsden, 31 Oct. 1797. PRO, ADM1/494, fol. 83–4. In 1798 it was sloop Dasher. Vandeput to Marsden, 23 June 1798. ADM1/494, fol. 118.

87. Forsyth to Duncan, 15 May 1797. NSARM, MG13/6, fol. 235.
88. Berkeley to Inglefield, 13 Sept. 1806. NMM, HAL/A/3b, fol. 173; Inglefield to Berkeley, 14 Sept. 1806. HAL/A/3b, fol. 174.
89. Forsyth & Smith to Inglefield, 15 Sept. 1806. NMM, HAL/A/3b, fol. 155-7.
90. Some 176 masts from seventeen to thirty-three inches in diameter, 146 yards from sixteen to twenty-four inches in diameter, twenty-five bowsprits from seventeen to thirty-three inches in diameter, and 1,106 spruce spars mainly from ten to fourteen inches in diameter. 20–24 Aug. 1801. PRO, ADM106/2027.
91. He had just arrived from Gibraltar, where "immense prices are demanded." Inglefield to NB, 25 Aug. 1801. PRO, ADM106/2027.
92. NB to Nepean, 27 June 1803. NMM, ADM/B/209. The problem recurred in 1805; "as there is a considerable surplus of masts and spars at Halifax, in part of what was deposited there in the late war." Storeship *Dolphin* on her way to Antigua to bring them to England. NB to Marsden, 7 June 1805. ADM/B/219.
93. Two each of 27", 26", 25", and 24" diameter. RO to Inglefield, 12 Aug. 1807, RO to Forsyth & Smith, 15 Aug. 1807. NMM, HAL/E/38, fol. 178-9; Forsyth & Smith to RO, 18 Aug. 1807. HAL/E/28.
94. NB to Inglefield, 11 Sept. 1807. NMM, HAL/C/1, fol. 5.
95. NB to Inglefield, 26 Aug. 1807. NMM, HAL/E/28.
96. Scott & Idle to supply masts: two 24"–24½"; six each 22"–22½" and 21"–21½", fifteen 20"–20½", eighteen 19"–19½", twenty each of 18"–18½", 17"–17½", 11"–11½", 10"–10½", 9"–9½", and thirty each of 8"–8½", and 7"–7½". NB to RO, 6 Oct. 1807. NMM, HAL/C/1, fol. 9.
97. Inglefield to NB, 20 June 1807. PRO, ADM106/2028.
98. Forsyth & Smith to Inglefield, 26 Aug. 1807. PRO, ADM106/2028.
99. NB to Inglefield, 2 Oct. 1807. NMM, HAL/C/1, fol. 8.
100. Forsyth to Duncan, 15 Aug. 1793, Duncan to NB, 27 Aug. 1793. PRO, ADM106/2027.
101. This is a rare document: Capt. Robert Murray's *Convoy Instructions*, 28 Oct. 1795. PRO, ADM1/2130.
102. John Oakes Hardy to Nepean, 25 Nov. 1795. PRO, ADM1/1913. In 1792-4, Hardy spent at least two years in New York on leave. ADM1/1910-11.
103. Inglefield to NB, 10 May 1804. PRO, ADM106/2028.
104. At 13°10'N, 57°10'W on 2 Aug. The sloop suffered one killed and eleven wounded. Keily to Berkeley, 2 Aug. 1806. PRO, ADM1/496, fol. 446-8; Berkeley to Marsden, 17 Sept. 1806. ADM1/496, fol. 443.
105. Inglefield to RO, 11 Nov. 1801. PRO, ADM106/2027; Anderson to Forsyth & Smith, 21 Apr. 1802. NSARM, MG13/3.

106. NB to RO, 23 Nov. 1807. NMM, HAL/C/1, fol. 19.
107. Belcher to Inglefield, 7 Jan. 1809. NMM, HAL/E/37.
108. Dawes to Inglefield, 9 Jan. 1809. NMM, HAL/E/39b, fol. 51–3.
109. Belcher to Inglefield, 10 Jan. 1809. NMM, HAL/E/39b, fol. 54–6.
110. Douglas to RO, 12 May 1808. NMM, HAL/E/37.
111. Twenty-six black spruce spars from sixteen to twenty-two inches diameter and from fifty-eight to seventy feet in length were purchased for H£123, supplied by John & James Feely of Windsor Road. Douglas to RO, 29 Mar. 1808. NMM, HAL/E/37, fol. 98.
112. Several persons from England had recently arrived who "are now employed going over the country to buy up large quantities of timber ... the Baltic being shut ... the benefit which the provinces would derive from supplying Great Britain with timber ... would be advantageous to the general service." Warren to Pole, 16 June 1808. PRO, ADM1/498, fol. 260–1.
113. Formerly "obtained from Norway." NB to Inglefield, 8 June 1808. NMM, HAL/A/4b, fol. 1.
114. Fraser & Thom, Halifax merchants, made the offer. Warren to RO, 20 July 1808. NMM, HAL/E/40, fol. 87–8.
115. 49 Geo. 3, c.98 and 50 Geo. 3, c.77; See Albion, *Forests and Sea Power*, 355–7.
116. David Roberts, "John Mure, d.1823," *DCB* (Toronto: University of Toronto Press, 1987), 6: 531–5.
117. Mure & Joliffe to Warren, 2 July 1808, enclosed in Warren to NB, 20 July 1808. PRO, ADM106/1437.
118. PRO, CUST17/30 and CUST4/1–3. See Bryan Latham, *Timber* (London: Harrap, 1957), 48.
119. Inglefield to Warren, 5 Dec. 1808. NMM, HAL/E/39a, fol. 66; Inglefield to Mure & Joliffe, 8 Dec. 1808. HAL/E/39a, fol. 69.
120. Inglefield to Mure & Joliffe, 8 July 1809. NMM, HAL/E/35b, fol. 6; Mure & Joliffe to Inglefield, 17 Aug. 1809. HAL/E/35b, fol. 74–5.
121. Reached Halifax only on 14 Oct. 1809. Mure & Joliffe to Inglefield, 11 Sept. 1809. NMM, HAL/E/35b, fol. 94; NB to Inglefield, 28 Nov. 1809. NMM, HAL/A/4b, fol. 322.
122. Arrived on 23 July, and took sixteen days to unload. Mure & Joliffe to Inglefield, 12 July 1810, Inglefield to Mure & Joliffe, 7 Aug. 1810. NMM, HAL/E/27, fol. 118–9, 136–7.
123. Inglefield to NB, 14 Sept. 1811. NMM, HAL/A/2, fol. 196.
124. Inglefield to NB, 10 Oct. 1811. NMM, HAL/A/2, fol. 219–20.
125. NB to Inglefield, 16 Jan. 1812. NMM, HAL/A/2, fol. 277.
126. Inglefield to NB, 6 Nov. 1809. PRO, ADM106/2028.
127. The warships included *Horatio, Milan, Guerrière, Junon, Cherub, Cleopatra,*

Thetis, Melampus, and *Pompey.* For cargo details for storeship *Eisdale,* armed ship *Diligence* in 1808, *Dawson,* and armed storeship *William,* which departed Halifax for England in Apr. 1809, see NMM, HAL/A/4b, fol. 112–3. Another 2,002 spars went with *Ajax* in August 1809, for cargo details, HAL/A/4b, fol. 201. Transport *Eliza* sailed in August 1809 with 893 spruce spars from 16½" downwards, two 14' & 15' spruce bowsprits, 3,166 feet of oak plank from 1½–4½", HAL/A/4b, fol. 208.

128. Fraser to Inglefield, 7 Sept. 1809. HAL/E/35b, fol. 63–4; W.A. Spray, "James Fraser, c.1760–1822," *DCB* (Toronto: University of Toronto Press, 1987), 6: 262–3.
129. Cargo listed. Inglefield to RO, 14 May 1810. NMM, HAL/A/2, fol. 37–8; Inglefield to NB, 14 Sept. 1809. HAL/A/4b, fol. 215–7; Inglefield to RO, 26 & 28 Oct. 1809. NMM, HAL/E/40, fol. 286; HAL/E/37.
130. Cargo for transport *Ariel* was completed in part from spars supplied by Andrew Blair of Windsor Road. Inglefield to RO, 13 Nov. 1809. NMM, HAL/E/35a, fol. 189. On 8 Jan. 1810 *Diligent* and transport *Robert,* armed storeship *William* sailed with cargoes mainly of spars up to 16½" & 18½". NMM, HAL/A/4b, fol. 295–7.
131. As examples, see Forsyth & Black to Inglefield, 2 Jan. & 11 Oct. 1810. PRO, ADM106/2028.
132. Wodehouse to Oviatt, 12 Feb. 1813. NA, I, 51; William Oviatt to Wodehouse, 31 Mar. 1813. NA, I, 134–5.
133. Wodehouse to Capt. Hawkins, 6 May 1813. NA, I, 132–3. In fact, they were not shipped until August in the ship *Sir George Prevost* (William Barratt, master); Oviatt to Wodehouse, Quebec, 12 July and 8 Aug. 1813. NA, I, 332–3 and NA, II, 352–4.
134. From Messrs Usborne Benson. NB to RO, 6 Apr. 1813. NMM, HAL/E/29, fol. 6.
135. Wodehouse to NB, 18 Aug. 1813. PRO, ADM106/2029, fol. 65, Minute, fol. 64, "pleased that masts have been found growing so near Halifax, but fear they might be of yellow pine, which they fear are not strong enough to serve as topmasts."
136. Wodehouse to NB, 5 Nov. 1813. PRO, ADM106/2029, fol. 107, Minute, "will not send any more."
137. NB to Wodehouse, 6 Oct. 1813; Wodehouse to RO, 3 Jan. 1814 NSARM, MG13/9.3, fol. 33; NA, II, 79.
138. NB to Wodehouse, 17 Mar. 1814; Wodehouse to RO, 24 May 1814. NSARM, MG13/9.3, fol. 85; NA, II, 137.
139. Alexander Gardiner to NB, 9 Aug. 1813. Minute, 12 Sept. 1813. PRO, ADM106/1524.

140. Joseph Scott to Thomas, 24 May 1784. NSARM, MG13/1, #461.
141. Duncan to Andrew, 11 Sept. 1785. NSARM, MG13/1, fol. 343. There was "no mill, at present, in the river, [which] saws longer" than thirty-two feet. Andrew to Duncan, 3 Oct. 1785. NSARM MG13/2, fol. 364–5.
142. Timber was to be fourteen inches squared. Duncan to Thomson, 9 Mar. 1786. NSARM, MG13/2, fol. 375.
143. Thomas & Samuel Mercer, Leonard Dunn & Asa Scott, 3 Mar. 1788. NSARM, MG13/2, fol. 529.
144. Duncan to Parr, 22 Dec. 1788. NSARM, MG13/2, fol. 602.
145. NB to Duncan, 26 Mar. 1789. NSARM, MG13/2, fol. 624–5.
146. Elphinstone to Murray, 31 Oct. 1795, Cape of Good Hope, 31 Oct. 1795. NSARM, MG13/6, fol. 132.
147. Duncan to NB, 19 Feb. 1796. NSARM, MG13/6, fol. 136; Duncan to Elphinstone, 26 Feb. 1796. MG13/6, fol. 137–8.
148. Some 200 tons, Joshua Shephard, master, Forsyth to Duncan, 18 Feb. 1796. NSARM, MG13/6, fol. 133–4.
149. NB to Coffin, 28 Aug. 1799. NSARM, MG13/6, fol. 326–7.
150. RO to Berkeley, 30 Nov. 1807. NMM, HAL/E/38, fol. 342–6.
151. See, for instance, details of a cargo purchased from James Fraser of Halifax in brig *Spence* (John Pain, master) shipped from Miramichi in October 1809. NMM, HAL/E/35a, fol. 139.
152. Inglefield to NB, 1 Sept. 1807. PRO, ADM106/2028.
153. To be delivered at the same price as in the former 1805 contract with Robertson & Forsyth for delivery to Halifax. Inglefield to NB, 11 May 1812. NMM, HAL/A/2, fol. 288–9.
154. Wodehouse to RO, 7 Mar. 1815. NMM, HAL/E/41, fol. 100–01.
155. NB to Wodehouse, 14 June 1815. NMM, HAL/C/2, fol. 53.
156. Wodehouse to NB, 15 May 1815. NMM, HAL/A/5, fol. 239–41.
157. Last noted before 1820, and resulted from an advertisement for a vessel to load wharf logs and other timber from LaHave. Wodehouse to RO, 20 Apr. 1818. NMM, HAL/E/42a, fol. 182.
158. Wentworth's certificate, 3 Jan. 1805. PRO, ADM106/1580.
159. George Brinley's certificate, 3 Jan. 1805; at "all times fulfilled their engagements to the entire satisfaction of the lieutenant general commanding and to mine." John Butler's certificate, 3 Jan. 1805; Horton, ordnance storekeeper's certificate, 3 Jan. 1805; they are "men in whom I can at all times place every confidence both as to their fairness as merchants, and their ability and punctuality to perform any contract they might offer to enter into with me as agent of his Majesty." PRO, ADM106/1580.
160. Miller & Miller to NB, 21 Jan. 1805. PRO, ADM106/1580.

161. Miller & Miller to NB, 29 Jan. 1805. PRO, ADM106/1580.
162. NSARM, RG36a/93.
163. Inglefield to RO, 30 June 1809. NMM, HAL/E/40, fol. 237. They offered seasoned plank for repairs to the squadron. RO to Inglefield, 21 Apr. 1810. HAL/E/36, fol. 52–3.
164. Fraser & Thom to RO, offered 6,769 feet, RO to Inglefield, 30 Oct. 1804. NSARM, MG13/9.1, fol. 197–8.
165. Inglefield to RO, 4 Apr. 1805. NSARM, MG13/9.1, fol. 241.
166. Forsyth & Smith, Fraser & Thom to Inglefield, 25 Sept. 1805. NMM, HAL/A/3b, fol. 41–4.
167. Ordered to pay their final account. Inglefield to RO, 14 July 1806. NMM, HAL/E/34, fol. 20.
168. Protection for the crew of *Hannah*. Fraser & Thom to Inglefield, 7 May 1806. NMM, HAL/A/3b, fol. 96.
169. Completed the following August. RO to Inglefield, 15 Aug. 1807. NMM, HAL/A/1.
170. Inglefield to RO, 14 Oct. 1808. NMM, HAL/E/37.
171. 16 Dec. 1808. NMM, HAL/E/39b, fol. 57.
172. Inglefield to RO, 3 July 1809. NMM, HAL/E/40, fol. 276.
173. Inglefield to RO, 29 Apr. 1809. NMM, HAL/E/40, fol. 276.
174. Inglefield to RO, 7 June 1811. NMM, HAL/E/36, fol. 250.
175. Roger Morriss, *The Royal Dockyards during the Revolutionary and Napoleonic Wars* (Leicester: Leicester University Press, 1983), 73.
176. From Moose Island and St Andrews. Wodehouse to NB, 27 Mar. 1815. NMM, HAL/A/5, fol. 209–10; NB to Wodehouse 24 Apr. 1815. NMM, HAL/C/2, fol. 28; Wodehouse to Oake, master commanding *Abundance*, 7 Sept. 1815. NMM, HAL/E/41, fol. 183, HAL/E/35a, fol. 228–9.
177. Julian Gwyn, "Nova Scotia's Shipbuilding and Timber Trade: David Crichton of Pictou and His Liverpool Associates, 1821–1840," *Canadian Papers in Business History* 2 (1993): 211–33.

Chapter 9   Paying Bills and Raising Cash

1. 29 Sept. 1841, *Mechanic and Farmer*.
2. Julian Gwyn, "The Impact of British Military Spending on the Colonial American Money Markets, 1760–1783," *Historical Papers* (1980): 77–99, and Gwyn, "British Government Spending and the North American Colonies, 1740–1775," *Journal of Imperial and Commonwealth History* 8 (1980): 74–84.
3. Dawes to T.I. Howe, postmaster, T.N. Jeffery, collector of the customs, J.B.

304   Notes to pages 202–207

Haliburton, receiver for Greenwich Hospital, T.C. Morris, registrar of the vice-admiralty court, 16 Aug. 1809. NMM, HAL/A/1.
4. P.G.M. Dickson, *The Financial Revolution in England: A Study in the Development of Public Credit 1689–1756* (London: Macmillan, 1967).
5. Gambier to Stephens, 12 May 1771. PRO, ADM1/483, fol. 397. Malachy Salter led the search. In all £891.9.4. was lost and £188.13.11. spent in recovering the balance. Gerrish accounts, 1756–73. PRO, ADM17/150, fol. 338.
6. Julian Gwyn, "Financial Revolution in Massachusetts: Public Credit and Taxation, 1692–1774," *Histoire sociale-Social History* 17 (1984): 59–77.
7. Julian Gwyn, "Private Credit in Colonial New York: The Warren Portfolio, 1745–1795," *New York History* 54 (1973): 268–93.
8. Inglefield to VB, 13 Jan. 1810. NMM, HAL/A/4b, fol. 314–6.
9. See Julian Gwyn, "Economic Fluctuations in Wartime Nova Scotia, 1755–1815," in *Making Adjustments: Change and Continuity in Planter Nova Scotia, 1759–1800*, ed. Margaret Conrad, 60–88 (Fredericton: Acadiensis Press, 1991).
10. Inglefield to NB, 13 Jan. 1811. NMM, HAL/A/2, fol. 121–4.
11. Dawes accounts, 1817. PRO, ADM17/164.
12. Julian Gwyn, *The Enterprising Admiral: The Personal Fortune of Admiral Sir Peter Warren* (Montreal: McGill-Queen's University Press, 1974).
13. Montagu to Gerrish, 23 June 1772. PRO, ADM17/150, fol. 143.
14. Gerrish accounts, 1757–73. PRO, ADM17/150, fol. 392.
15. His share would have been one-eighth. Gerrish accounts, 1757–73. PRO, ADM17/150, fol. 387–9.
16. In response to the Board's letter of 4 Apr. 1772, Montagu to NB, 25 June 1772, enclosed in NB to Stephens, 12 Aug. 1772. NMM, ADM/B/186. What Montagu failed to refer to was the fact that he held back in Boston part of the money raised for the Halifax careening yard. Significant sums were then disbursed "without being subject to the ... control of this Board, according to the rules and customs of the navy, as the secretaries only transmit an account of their receipts and payments every quarter to the naval officer, which are inserted in his accounts with a charge of 6.5 per cent commission for their trouble in transacting this business, and have no further account to pass, which deprives us of the means of checquing any irregular expenses." In future, they suggested, commanders-in-chief should be instructed to follow the regulations and "make use of their own credit and authority upon all future occasions in taking up money" where no naval yard is established. NB to Stephens, 11 Mar. 1774. ADM/B/188.
17. Williams to NB, 12 Nov. & 31 Dec. 1773, NB to Williams, 19 Apr. 1774. PRO, ADM106/2470, fol. 139–40. A summary of the matter is found in NB to Stephens, 15 Nov. 1774. NMM, ADM/B/189.

18. NB to Stephens, 8 Aug. 1775. NMM, ADM/B/190.
19. Gerrish accounts, 1757–73. PRO, ADM17/150.
20. In *Roebuck*. NB to Williams, 25 Aug. 1775. PRO, ADM106/2470 fol. [204].
21. Williams accounts, 1773–80. PRO, ADM17/150.
22. Rejected Governor Legge's request for a £1,000 loan, enclosed in NB to Stephens, 9 Feb. 1776, Arbuthnot to NB, 28 Dec. 1775. NMM, ADM/B/191.
23. In *Emerald*. NB to Williams, 23 Apr. 1776. PRO, ADM106/2470, fol. [234].
24. In *Ardent*. NB to Stephens, 19 Feb. 1778. NMM, ADM/B/195.
25. Hughes to NB, 15 May 1780. PRO, ADM17/150, fol. 374–6.
26. Edgecombe's accounts, 1784–5. PRO, ADM17/150.
27. Exchange rate on drawing bills: 23–25 Apr. 1785 at 3 per cent premium, 19–30 Aug. 1785 at 2 per cent premium. Duncan to NB, 30 Aug. 1785. NSARM, MG13/2, fol. 356.
28. Thomas to Duncan, 30 June 1786. NSARM, MG13/2, fol. 422; Duncan to NB, 3 May 1787. MG13/2, fol. 455.
29. Ogilvie to Duncan, 12 May 1794. NSARM, MG13/6, fol. 1.
30. Inglefield to Dawes, 16 & 23 Sept. 1805. PRO, ADM106/2028.
31. Admiralty immediately agreed. NB to Marsden, 15 Nov. 1805. NMM, ADM/B/220.
32. From Jamaica, Dilkes to Inglefield, 20 Feb. 1806. NMM, HAL/A/3b, fol. 88.
33. Inglefield to RO, 26 Sept. 1805. PRO, ADM106/2028. This order was cancelled only nine months later, when the yard had sufficient cash. Inglefield to RO, 21 June 1806. NMM, HAL/E/34, fol. 4.
34. Inglefield to NB, 14 Oct. 1805. NMM, ADM/B/220.
35. Inglefield to Dawes, 12 Nov. 1805. NMM, HAL/E/34, fol. 11. Under "existing circumstances we approve of the deviation which has taken place from the practice of accepting only the lowest tenders received on days appointed by advertisement for that purpose." NB to Dawes, 22 Jan. 1806. NMM, HAL/A/3a, fol. 42.
36. Inglefield to MacKellar, agent for prisoners of war, 19 May 1806, enclosed in Inglefield to NB, 20 May 1806. PRO, ADM106/2028.
37. Inglefield to MacKellar, agent for prisoners of war, 19 May 1806, enclosed in Inglefield to NB, 20 May 1806. PRO, ADM106/2028.
38. Dawes to Inglefield, 25 Aug. 1807. NMM, HAL/E/38, fol. 187–8.
39. Dawes to Inglefield, 8 Oct. 1807. NMM, HAL/E/38, fol. 261; Berkeley to Dawes, 23 Nov. 1807. HAL/E/37, fol. 19.
40. Reject tenders for £4,000 at 1.25–1.5 per cent. Berkeley to Dawes, 11 Dec. 1807, payable at 30 days' sight to Charles Morris, for £10,000 or H£11,111.2.2. Dawes to NB, 11 Dec. 1807. PRO, ADM106/2028. In May 1808, Morris of the vice-admiralty court offered the yard another £5,000,

and in July another £4,000, both offers being accepted. Douglas to Dawes, 20 & 21 May 1808. NMM, HAL/E/40, fol. 59; Warren to Dawes, 30 July 1808. HAL/E/37.
41. Also suggested that a suitable chest be fashioned to hold the money, with two separate keys, one held by the commissioner. Berkeley to NB, 30 Nov. 1807. PRO, ADM106/1308.
42. Berkeley to RO, 9 Dec. 1807, order cancelled in June 1807. NMM, HAL/E/37.
43. Admiralty's order, 3 May 1808. NB to RO, 5 May 1808. NMM, HAL/E/29, fol. 62–5.
44. NB to Inglefield, 24 June 1808. NMM, HAL/A/4b, fol. 3–4.
45. Equivalent of H£7,000 or £5,000. Dilkes to Dawes, Jamaica yard, 2 July 1808, Inglefield to Dawes, 12 Aug. 1808. NMM, HAL/E/40, fol. 96; Yates to Dawes, Jamaica yard, 2 Sept. 1808. HAL/E/40, fol. 135.
46. Inglefield to NB, 22 Nov. 1806. NMM, HAL/A/4b, fol. 70.
47. NB to Inglefield, 3 June 1808. NMM, HAL/A/4b, fol. 11.
48. Warren to Inglefield, 13 Oct. 1808. NMM, HAL/E/39a, fol. 25; Dawes to John Dunsier at Bermuda, 29 Nov. 1808. NMM, HAL/A/1.
49. £3,000 in bills needed in both January and February. Inglefield to Dawes, 16 Jan. 1809. NMM, HAL/E/37; Dawes to Inglefield, 16 Feb. 1809. NMM, HAL/A/1; Dawes to Inglefield, 18 Apr. 1809. HAL/E/39b, fol. 143.
50. On 13 May received $42,000 or £9,450. Wolley to Inglefield, 15 Apr. 1809. NMM, HAL/E/39a, fol. 139; Inglefield to NB, 19 May 1809. NMM, HAL/A/4b, fol. 137.
51. Warren to Inglefield, 15 June 1809. NMM, HAL/E/39a, fol. 191; Inglefield to Dawes, 16 June 1809. HAL/E/37.
52. Inglefield to NB, 13 Aug. 1809. NMM, HAL/A/4b, fol. 204–5.
53. Requested £15,000, Inglefield to Wolley, 8 Sept. 1809, shipped $48,037, or £10,800, Wolley to Inglefield, 9 Nov. 1809. NMM, HAL/E/35b, fol. 86, 191.
54. Inglefield to Croke, 7 Oct. 1809, Croke to Inglefield, 8 Oct. 1809. NMM, HAL/E/35b, fol. 106, 115.
55. Inglefield to Prevost, 9 Oct. 1809, Prevost to Inglefield, 10 Oct. 1809. NMM, HAL/E/35b, fol. 114, 118–9; Inglefield to NB, 10 Oct. 1809. NMM, HAL/A/4b, fol. 232.
56. Inglefield to VB, 13 Jan. 1810. NMM, HAL/A/4b, fol. 314–16.
57. Inglefield to NB, 13 Apr. 1810. NMM, HAL/A/2, fol. 11–13.
58. $63,000 at 5s. equivalent of H£15,750 or £14,175. Inglefield to NB, 3 Oct. 1810. NMM, HAL/A/2, fol. 99.
59. Prevost to Inglefield, 3 Oct. 1810. NMM, HAL/E/27, fol. 203; Inglefield to

Dawes, 3 Oct. 1810. HAL/E/36, fol. 150; repaid when *Emulous* was sent to Vera Cruz on behalf of the army, Inglefield to Dawes, 20 Feb. 1811. HAL/E/36, fol. 205.
60. Wolley to Inglefield, 31 Jan. 1811. NMM, HAL/E/27, fol. 337. Some coins were defaced, light dollars, some types of silver coins were not accepted in Halifax, while others were made of base metal, that were cut to pieces "to prevent their further circulation," the metal then sold by weight. Inglefield to Dawes, 21 Mar. 1811. HAL/E/36, fol. 218; HAL/E/25, fol. 58.
61. Inglefield to Wolley, 30 July 1811. NMM, HAL/E/27; Inglefield to NB, 28 Aug. 1811. NMM, HAL/A/2, fol. 190.
62. NB to Inglefield, 15 Oct. 1811. NMM, HAL/A/2, fol. 247.
63. Inglefield to NB, 7 Nov. 1811. NMM, HAL/A/2, fol. 229.
64. Inglefield to NB, 12 Nov. 1811, NB to Inglefield, 3 Jan. 1812. NMM, HAL/A/2, fol. 232, 276–7.
65. NMM, HAL/E/36, fol. 257.
66. Inglefield to Dawes, 4 Feb. 1812. NMM, HAL/E/36, fol. 373–4; Inglefield to Dawes, 14 Apr. 1812. HAL/E/36, fol. 404.
67. Inglefield to RO, 23 Mar. 1812. NMM, HAL/E/36, fol. 392.
68. Inglefield to RO, 13 Oct. 1812. NMM, HAL/E/40, fol. 402; Inglefield to [NB], 28 June 1812. NMM, HAL/A/2, fol. 304–6.
69. NB to Inglefield, 4 Aug. 1812. NMM, HAL/A/2, fol. 336.
70. Inglefield to NB, 25 Aug. 1812. NMM, HAL/A/2, fol. 324–5.
71. Inglefield to Wolley, 16 Oct. 1812. NMM, HAL/A/2, fol. 353–4.
72. Dawes to Wodehouse, 20 Jan. 1813. NMM, HAL/E/25, fol. 152–5.
73. Wodehouse to NB, 29 Jan. 1813. NMM, HAL/A/2, fol. 397–9.
74. Wodehouse to RO, 8 Feb., 17 Feb., and 23 Mar. 1813. NMM, HAL/E/40, fol. 417, 421, 424.
75. Wodehouse to NB, 26 Oct. 1814. NMM, HAL/A/5, fol. 80–1.
76. $150,000, the equivalent of H£50,000 or £33,750. Woodriffe to Wodehouse, 8 Feb. 1815. NMM, HAL/E/21, fol. 221; Wodehouse to RO, 3 Apr. 1815. HAL/E/21, fol. 111; Wodehouse to NB, 14 Apr. 1815. NMM, HAL/A/5, fol. 220.
77. Sherbrooke to Wodehouse, 8 Apr. 1815, Wodehouse to Sherbrooke, 10 Apr. 1815. NMM, HAL/E/21, fol. 225–7.
78. $63,000. Woodriffe to Wodehouse, 18 Apr. 1815, Wodehouse to Sherbrooke, 6 June 1815. NMM, HAL/E/21, fol. 250, 261.
79. NB to Dawes, 17 June 1813. NMM, HAL/E/31, fol. 299–303; NB to Dawes, 29 Apr. 1814. NMM, HAL/A/5, fol. 6–8.
80. Dawes to Wodehouse, 15 Oct. 1817. NMM, HAL/E/25, fol. 314–5.
81. Starr & Shannon to Wodehouse, 4 Nov. 1814. NMM, HAL/E/21, fol. 164.

308 Notes to pages 213–228, 327

82. Manby to Wodehouse, 8 Nov. 1814. NMM, HAL/E/21, fol. 166–7.
83. NB to Wodehouse, 11 Jan. 1815. NMM, HAL/C/2, fol. 1–3.
84. NB to Stephens, 12 Feb. 1783. NMM, ADM/BP/4.
85. 14 Mar. 1839. *Journals and Proceedings of the House of Assembly for 1838* (Halifax, 1839).

Conclusion

1. *Book of Wisdom* 5: 10.
2. Wodehouse to NB, 2 Dec. 1814. PRO, ADM106/2029, fol. 196–8.
3. See Appendix three.
4. Wodehouse to NB, 21 Nov. 1815. PRO, ADM106/2029, fol. 279–81.
5. NB to Stephens, 16 Dec. 1782. NMM, ADM/BP/3.
6. NB to RO, 10 Sept. 1805. NMM, HAL/A/3a, fol. 18–9.
7. NB to RO, 16 Jan. 1808. NMM, HAL/C/1, fol. 34.
8. Jack C. Arnell, *The Bermuda Maritime Museum and the Royal Naval Dockyard, Bermuda* (Hamilton: Bermuda Press, 1979), 22–48.
9. Wodehouse to NB, 21 Apr. 1817. NMM, HAL/E/1, fol. 49.
10. Wodehouse to RO, 7 Oct. 1816. NMM, HAL/E/41, fol. 318, HAL/E/42a.
11. At the request of the chief justice. Wodehouse to RO, 15 Mar. 1817. NMM, HAL/E/41, fol. 355.
12. Roger Morriss, *The Royal Dockyards during the Revolutionary and Napoleonic Wars* (Leicester: Leicester University Press, 1983), 3.
13. NB to Admiralty, 14 Dec. 1814. NMM, ADM/BP/34b.
14. Thomas Chandler Haliburton, *The Old Judge; or, Life in a Colony* (Ottawa, ON: Tecumseh Press, 1978), 93.

Biographical Directory

1. Petition, 9 Feb. 1801, Adams to Thornborough, 28 Nov. 1801; Wallace, Belcher & Morris to Parker, 10 Jan. 1801; Inglefield to Thornborough, 28 Nov. 1801. PRO, ADM106/1654.
2. Wallace to Duncan, 20 Nov. 1804. PRO, ADM106/1654.
3. 31 Jan. 1823, *Novascotian*.
4. NB to Thomas, 5 Sept. 1783. NSARM, MG13/1, #424.
5. NB to Duncan, 29 Sept. 1795. NSARM, MG13/6, 122.
6. Vandeput to Anderson, 7 Sept. 1799. NSARM, ADM106/2027.
7. Anderson to Inglefield, 24 May 1802. PRO, ADM106/2027.
8. Inglefield to Anderson, 21 Sept. 1804. NSARM, MG13/9.1, 181.
9. Dawes to Inglefield, 29 Aug. 1811. NMM, HAL/E/25, fol. 82.

10. Anderson to Wodehouse, 29 Jan. 1813. PRO, ADM106/2029, fol. 5–6.
11. NMM, HAL/E/25, fol. 376–7.
12. 6 Feb. 1833, *Nova Scotia Royal Gazette*.
13. NB to RO, 6 Feb. 1776. PRO, ADM106/2470, fol. [226].
14. Paid 19s. a day from 20 June 1781. Hamond to Thomas, 18 Sept. 1782. HP, IX, 164.
15. Coffin to Marshall, 11 Jan. 1800. NSARM, MG13/6, 436–7.
16. Inglefield to NB, 9 Sept. 1802. PRO, ADM106/2027.
17. Inglefield to RO, 1 Mar. 1806. NMM, HAL/E/34, fol. 9.
18. NB to Stephens, 11 Aug. 1775. NMM, ADM/B/190.
19. PRO, ADM1/1441.
20. Hughes to Stephens, 19 Aug. 1778. PRO, ADM1/1904.
21. Inglefield to Admiralty and NB, 9 Jan. 1810. NMM, HAL/E/36.
22. Griffith to NB, 13 Sept. & 22 Oct. 1819. PRO, ADM106/1396, NMM, HAL/C/3, fol. 24–5.
23. NB to RO, 23 Oct. 1775. PRO, ADM106/2470 fol. [213].
24. £7 12s. monthly. PRO, ADM42/2150–53.
25. Will, NSARM, RG48, reel 358/2, 80; Marsh to Thomas, 24 Aug. 1785. NSARM, MG13/1, #593; Fitzgerald to Thomas, 14 Nov. 1785. MG13/1, #596.
26. Griffith to NB, 8 Sept. 1819. PRO, ADM106/1349.
27. Griffith to NB, 8 Sept. 1819. PRO, ADM106/1349.
28. At 3s. daily; then 3s.6d.,1782. PRO, ADM42/2150.
29. PRO, ADM42/2148.
30. PRO, ADM42/2148.
31. 14 Oct. 1783, *Nova Scotia Royal Gazette*. NSARM, RG48, reel 397.
32. 1 Oct. 1782, *Nova Scotia Royal Gazette*.
33. At 3s.6d. daily. PRO, ADM42/2153.
34. Blackadar to Inglefield, 17 Oct. 1810; supported by Dawes and Hughes. Inglefield to NB, 9 & 13 Nov. 1810. PRO, ADM106/2028.
35. Inglefield to RO, 29 Oct. & 24 Dec. 1810. NMM, HAL/E/36, fol. 162.
36. NB to Wodehouse, 30 Mar. 1815. NMM, HAL/C/2, fol.18–21.
37. PRO, ADM42/2155.
38. NB to Wodehouse, 30 Mar. 1815. NMM, HAL/C/2, fol. 18–21. Will, NSARM, MG100/111, #32.
39. 14 Mar. 1818, *Acadian Recorder*.
40. Charles Stayner, "The Blackadar Family of Halifax," *Nova Scotia Historical Review* 1 (1981): 67.
41. PRO, ADM42/2147.
42. Will, 7 May 1791. NSARM, MG100/111, #34; RG48/3, 131.
43. At 2s.6d. daily. PRO, ADM42/2154.

44. Hawkes to Wodehouse, 3 Jan. 1814. PRO, ADM106/2028, fol. 127.
45. Griffith to NB, 13 Sept. & 22 Oct. 1819. PRO, ADM106/1396, NMM, HAL/C/3, fol. 24-5.
46. Duncan to Livie, 1 Jan. 1795. NSARM, MG13/6, 51.
47. Wodehouse to NB, 30 Nov. 1815, PRO, ADM106/2029, fol. 267, 270; NB to Wodehouse, 20 Jan. 1816. NMM, HAL/C/2, fol. 109-10; Wodehouse to RO, 2 Apr. 1816. NA, III, 447.
48. Wodehouse to Douglas, 19 May 1817. NMM, HAL/E/41, fol. 380-1.
49. [30 July 1819]. NMM, HAL/E/26, fol. [297-8].
50. PRO, ADM42/2147.
51. Duncan to Livie, 3 Aug. 1796. NSARM, MG13/6, 172.
52. Brush to Wodehouse, 23 Feb. 1814. PRO, ADM106/2029, fol. 147.
53. 24 Feb. 1815, *Weekly Chronicle*.
54. Allan C. Dunlop, "John Burbidge, 1718-1812," *DCB* (1983), 5: 121-2.
55. Duncan to NB, 10 Oct. 1785. NSARM, MG13/2, 356-7.
56. Griffith to NB, 13 Sept. & 22 Oct. 1819. PRO, ADM106/1396, NMM, HAL/C/3, fol. 24-5.
57. Charlton to NB, 20 Sept. 1760. PRO, ADM106/1121.
58. Clark to Duncan, 23 Sept. 1785. NSARM, MG13/2, 355-6.
59. Duncan to NB, 14 Oct. 1785. NSARM, MG13/2, 362.
60. Lois K. Yorke, "Duncan Clifford, 1759-1808," *DCB* (1983), 5: 187-8.
61. PRO, ADM102/256.
62. Coffin to Nepean, 16 Oct. 1799. NSARM, MG13/6, 328.
63. RO to Nelson, 26 Apr. 1800. PRO, ADM106/2027.
64. Roger Morriss, *The Royal Dockyards during the Revolutionary and Napoleonic Wars* (Leicester: Leicester University Press, 1983), 123.
65. Coffin to Admiralty, 13 Apr. 1801. PRO, ADM106/1844.
66. Colvill to Clevland, 24 Oct. 1752. PRO, ADM1/1604.
67. Will. PRO, PROB11/960, #34.
68. Hurd to NB, 22 Sept. 1763. PRO, ADM106/1134.
69. PRO, ADM42/2150.
70. Constable to NB, 27 June 1760. PRO, ADM106/1121.
71. NB to Arbuthnot, 14 Aug. 1776. PRO, ADM106/2470, 247; Lee to Arbuthnot, 10 Nov. 1775. NMM, ADM/B/192.
72. Abraham Constable Jr to NB, Lewisham, 22 June 1795. PRO, ADM106/1479.
73. Memorial to Inglefield, 9 Nov. 1810; Inglefield to NB, 13 Nov. 1810. PRO, ADM106/2028.
74. NSARM, RG48, reel 400.
75. Livie accounts, 1790-9. PRO, ADM 17/151.

76. At 3s. daily. PRO, ADM42/2154.
77. Da Costa to Stephens, 18 June 1790. PRO, ADM1/5120; Broderick to Clevland, 19 Feb. 1759. ADM1/926; PRO, ADM49/1, fol. 125.
78. E. Alfred Jones, *The Loyalists of Massachusetts* (London, ON: Saint Catherine Press, 1930), 109–10.
79. Dawes to NB, 22 July 1808. PRO, ADM106/2028.
80. Hamond to Dickson, 1 Aug. 1781. HP, IX, 38.
81. Hamond to Thomas, 5 Nov. 1781. HP, IX, 107.
82. Hamond to Digby, 15 Feb. 1782. HP, VII, 65.
83. NB to Dawes, 8 Mar. 1815. HAL/E/30, fol. 33.
84. Inglefield to RO, 12 Oct. 1809. NSARM, MG13/5, #155.
85. 20 Dec. 1823, *Acadian Recorder*. Sarah d. 1827 at Harrietsfield, aged 28.
86. 13 Dec. 1828, *Acadian Recorder*.
87. 19 May 1838, *Acadian Recorder*.
88. PRO, ADM42/2153.
89. Coffin to Anderson, 11 Jan. 1800. NSARM, MG13/6, 435.
90. Douglas to RO, 5 Apr. 1808. PRO, ADM106/2029.
91. Wodehouse to RO, NSARM, MG13/9.3, 81; Griffith to Wodehouse, 30 Nov. 1814. NMM, HAL/E/21, fol. 72–3.
92. Wodehouse to RO, 6 June 1816. NSARM, MG13/9.3, 201; NMM, HAL/E/41, fol. 291.
93. Wodehouse to Nelson, 5 Sept. 1819. PRO, ADM106/2029, fol. 508.
94. 23 May 1836, *Halifax Journal*.
95. Inglefield to RO, 15 June 1809. NSARM, MG13/5, #53.
96. Wodehouse to RO, 14 June 1816. NSARM, MG13/9.3, 201.
97. 23 Feb. 1828, *Acadian Recorder*.
98. 27 Nov. 1830, *Acadian Recorder*.
99. In transport *Britannia*. Duncan to Stephens, 22 July 1783. PRO, ADM1/1710.
100. Sawyer to Stephens, 1 Aug. 1784. PRO, ADM1/491, fol. 90.
101. Edgecombe to NB, 21 Jan. 1791. PRO, ADM106/1338.
102. Wodehouse to RO, 1 Dec. 1814. NSARM, MG13/9.3, 155; NA, II, 240.
103. Petition, 12 June 1820. PRO, ADM106/1349.
104. PRO, ADM104/1; *Naval Chronicle* 36 (1816): 439.
105. Supporting documents signed by two dozen men including the collector of customs, judges of the court of pleas, JPs, and the rector of St George's parish. Petition to Inglefield, Shelburne, 6 Sept. 1802. PRO, ADM106/2027.
106. NB to Dawes, 12 Aug. 1809. NMM, HAL/C/1, fol. 123.
107. NB to Wodehouse, 9 Mar. 1815. NMM, HAL/C/2, fol. 13–4.

108. Farquharson to Coffin, 6 Apr. 1800. PRO, ADM106/2027.
109. Inglefield to Fernie, 27 Apr. 1805. NSARM, MG13/9.1, 274–5.
110. Fernie to NB, 3 Oct. 1806. PRO, ADM1/1447.
111. Griffith to Croker, 8 Aug. 1815. PRO, ADM1/510, fol. 17.
112. Wodehouse to NB, 3 Feb. 1814. PRO, ADM106/2029, fol. 143; Minute: "approve." Finnerty & Hill in 1814 were paid H£850 for one third part. Dawes accounts, 1814. PRO, ADM 17/161. H£1,700 paid on their contract of 16 Feb. 1814. Dawes accounts, 1815. PRO, ADM17/162. The tenements cost H£7,144.
113. Hamond to NB, 4 July 1782. HP, VII, 94.
114. Minute: "Acquaint him that we shall be glad to see him here tomorrow at 1 o'clock," Forsyth to NB, at Mr Livie's Copthall buildings, 15 Dec. 1792. PRO, ADM106/1514.
115. David Sutherland, "William Forsyth, c.1749–1814," *DCB* (1983) 5: 327–9.
116. 27 Jan. 1752, *Halifax Gazette*.
117. PRO, ADM42/2147–50.
118. NSARM, RG48, reel 405.
119. Gerrish to NB, 15 Apr. 1761. PRO, ADM106/1121.
120. Gerrish to NB, 10 Oct. 1761. PRO, ADM106/1121.
121. Gerrish to NB, 9 Sept. 1763. PRO, ADM106/1123.
122. Hood to Stephens, 7 Oct. 1768. PRO, ADM1/483, fol. 143.
123. Owned three slaves at the time of his death, T. Watson Smith, "The Slave in Canada," *Collections of the Nova Scotia Historical Society* (1898), 10: 13.
124. 2 June 1774, *Nova Scotia Gazette and Weekly Chronicle*.
125. PRO, ADM42/2154.
126. Duncan to NB, 10 Oct. 1785. NSARM, MG13/2, 356–7.
127. Montagu to Stephens, 19 Jan. 1773. PRO, ADM1/484.
128. Byron to Stephens, 30 Nov. 1778. PRO, ADM1/486, fol. 139v.
129. Digby to Stephens, 19 Mar. 1782. PRO, ADM1/490, fol. 74.
130. Hamond to surgeons on *Chatham*, *Hussar*, and *Allegiance*, 17 Apr. 1782. HP, IX, 98; Halliburton to Thomas, 1 Mar. 1787. NSARM, MG13/1, #728.
131. Halliburton to Mitchell, 21 June 1803. PRO, ADM1/495, fol. 420.
132. Berkeley to Marsden, 11 June 1807. PRO, ADM1/497, fol. 175.
133. Berkeley to Pole, 12 Dec. 1807. PRO, ADM1/497, fol. 488.
134. Hurd to NB, 22 Sept. 1763. PRO, ADM106/1134.
135. Arrived Halifax on storeship *Recovery*; Hamond to NB, 6 Aug. 1782. HP, VII, 8.
136. NSARM, RG1/136, 307. PRO, CO217/56, fol. 261.
137. Parr arrived on 5 Oct. and moved into the governor's mansion when Hamond was absent. Hamond to Admiralty, 7 Dec. 1785. PRO, CO217/

57, 184; Hamond to Shelburne, 9 Oct. 1782. HP, VIII; Hamond to Stephens, 30 Oct. 1782, VII, 147–8.
138. Digby to Stephens, 15 Mar. 1783. PRO, ADM1/490, fol. 233v.
139. For H£684 16s. Lee's memorial to Parr, 31 Oct. 1787. NSARM, RG5, ser. A/2.
140. H£300 reimbursed by the house of assembly, 1787; Uniacke led opposition. NSARM, MG100/153, #16.
141. Hamond to Handasyde, 4 Aug. 1781. HP, IX, 4; Hamond to Thomson, 14 Jan. 1782. HP, VII, 62.
142. To follow orders of the surgeon and agent @ £100. Hamond to Handasyde, 1 Jan. 1783. HP, IX, 202.
143. Hamond to Digby, 15 Feb. 1782. HP, VII, 67.
144. 26 Sept. 1783, *Halifax Journal*.
145. Griffith to NB, 14 Oct. 1819. PRO, ADM106/1349.
146. 6 Nov. 1819, *Acadian Recorder*.
147. NB to Dawes, 14 June 1813. NMM, HAL/C/1, fol. 198.
148. Wodehouse to Hutchinson, 2 June 1817. NMM, HAL/E/41, fol. 387.
149. Holburne to Clevland, 4 Nov. 1757. PRO, ADM1/481, fol. 455.
150. At 8s.4d. a day. PRO, ADM42/2152; "to superintend coppering of ships bottoms at Halifax," embarked 14 Apr., landed 30 July 1781. Thomas accounts, 1790–99. PRO, ADM17/150.
151. Wodehouse to RO, 1 Dec. 1814. NSARM, MG13/9.3, 155.
152. From 5 Dec. 1781. PRO, ADM42/2152.
153. NB to Graves. PRO, ADM106/2470, fol. 176–7; Williams accounts, 1773–80. PRO, ADM17/150.
154. PRO, ADM42/2148.
155. Colvill to Stephens, 27 Nov. 1764. PRO, ADM1/482, fol. 414v.
156. Hurd to NB, 15 Nov. 1763. PRO, ADM106/1123; PRO, ADM42/2147.
157. Gerrish accounts, 1757–73. PRO, ADM17/150.
158. Colvill to Stephens, 27 Nov. 1764. PRO, ADM1/483, fol. 414v.
159. Colvill to NB, 26 Dec. 1763. PRO, ADM106/1123.
160. At 3s. daily. PRO, ADM42/2154.
161. Arrived Aug. 1778 in armed storeship *Pacific* having been waiting a passage at Portsmouth since March. Hughes to Stephens, 3 June & 19 Aug. 1778. PRO, ADM1/1904.
162. Hughes to Hall, 3 Aug. 1781. HP, IX, 2.
163. Parker to Nepean, 28 Feb. 1801. PRO, ADM1/495, fol. 212–14.
164. NB to Arbuthnot, 23 Oct. 1775. PRO, ADM106/2470, fol. [214].
165. NB to RO, 3 Mar. 1778. PRO, ADM106/2470.
166. Coffin to Anderson, 11 Jan. 1800. NSARM, MG13/6, 435–6.

314   Notes to pages 336–338

167. Hughes to Hamond, 23 Mar. 1800. PRO, ADM106/1531.
168. Halliburton to Hamond, 20 Jan. 1800. PRO, ADM106/1531.
169. Hughes to NB, 30 Aug. 1800; Duncan's note, 26 Sept. 1800. PRO, ADM106/1531.
170. Parker to Nepean, 28 Feb. 1801. PRO, ADM1/495, fol. 212.
171. NSARM, MG100/235, #2.
172. Wodehouse to RO, 17 Mar. 1813. NMM, HAL/E/40, fol. 424; NSARM, MG100/235, #1–2.
173. Hughes to Croker, No. 7 Walbroke Row, City Road, Hoxton Fields, 5 & 15 Oct. 1813; salary advance and instructions as governor. PRO, ADM1/1948.
174. Transport Board to Hughes, 11 Nov. 1815. NMM, HAL/E/3b, fol. 11–12.
175. Had eight children living in 1813. ADM1/506, fol. 107.
176. 2 May 1853, *Novascotian*.
177. 10 Dec. 1758 at H£80 annually. Gerrish to NB, 15 Apr. 1761. PRO, ADM106/1121.
178. Gerrish to NB, 12 Jan. 1760. PRO, ADM106/1121.
179. NB to Gerrish. PRO, ADM106/2470, 46.
180. *Nova Scotia Gazette*, 1773, cited in Smith, "The Slave in Canada," 12.
181. Hurd to Duncan, 1 Dec. 1794. NSARM, MG13/6, 52; Duncan to NB 7 Jan. 1795. MG13/6, 53–4.
182. 28 Feb. 1797, *Royal Gazette and Nova Scotia Advertizer*.
183. NMM, HAL/E/31, fol. 178.
184. Returned to Halifax on 1 Aug. 1808. Inglefield to RO, 18 Feb. 1808. NMM, HAL/E/37; Inglefield to [Marsden], 25 June 1811. PRO, ADM1/3441.
185. Croker to Inglefield, 19 Aug. 1811. NMM, HAL/A/2, fol. 215; Inglefield to Croker, 15 Oct. 1811. PRO, ADM106/2028.
186. Inglefield to [Marsden], 25 June 1811. PRO, ADM1/3441.
187. Transport Board to Wodehouse, 28 June 1816. NMM, HAL/E3b, fol. 25.
188. NSARM, RG48, reel 409.
189. Coffin to Nepean, 18 Oct. 1799. NSARM, MG13/6, 330.
190. Inglefield to NB, 29 Mar. 1803. PRO, ADM106/2027; Dawes to Nelson, 2 Apr. 1803. NSARM, MG13/3.
191. James to Coffin, 4 Apr. 1800. PRO, ADM106/2027.
192. PRO, ADM36/1729.
193. Storekeeper's extra clerk. Inglefield to Dawes, 2 Aug. 1803. NSARM, MG13/9.1, 22–3.
194. PRO, ADM42/2148.
195. Hood to Stephens, 6 Nov. 1770. PRO, ADM1/483, fol. 304.
196. At H£8.7.3. monthly. PRO, ADM42/2150.

197. Jones to NB, 9 Nov. 1816. PRO, ADM106/2029, fol. 308.
198. NB to Wodehouse. 27 Nov. 1816. NMM, HAL/C/2, fol. 188.
199. Colvill to Gerrish, 28 Oct. 1763. PRO, ADM106/1123.
200. NSARM, RG48, reel 410.
201. PRO, ADM1/490; PRO, ADM104/1.
202. Kavanagh to Wodehouse, 23 Mar. 1815. Wodehouse to NB, 27 Mar. 1815. ADM106/2029, fol. 220, 222.
203. Hamond to Kennedy, 1 Jan. 1783. HP, IX, 203.
204. 13 Nov. 1819, *Acadian Recorder*.
205. Williams accounts, 1773–80. PRO, ADM17/150.
206. Affidavit #15, 25 Jan. 1800. PRO, ADM1/3364.
207. Jackson and Anderson to Coffin, 23 Jan. 1800. NSARM, MG13/6, 484.
208. 8 July 1837, *Acadian Recorder*.
209. PRO, ADM2/222, fol. 467.
210. PRO, ADM42/2147.
211. Williams accounts, 1773–80. PRO, ADM17/150.
212. Lee to Coffin, 21 Mar. 1800. PRO, ADM106/2027.
213. Hamond to Thomas, 1 Jan. 1782. HP, IX, 106.
214. Hamond to Thomas, 1 Jan. 1782. HP, IX, 106.
215. Lee to Coffin, 21 Mar. 1800. PRO, ADM106/2027.
216. Lee to Coffin, 21 Mar. 1800. PRO, ADM106/2027.
217. Lee to Coffin, 28 Mar. 1800. PRO, ADM106/2027.
218. Wodehouse to NB, 7 Mar. 1814. PRO, ADM106/2029, fol. 156.
219. 28 Aug. 1819, *Acadian Recorder*.
220. 21 Sept. 1816, *Acadian Recorder*.
221. PRO, ADM49/1, fol. 12
222. Coffin to Nepean, 18 Oct. 1799. NSARM, MG13/6, 330.
223. NB to Livie, 22 Aug. 1799. NSARM, MG13/6, 344. Anderson to Nelson, 17 Sept. 1799. PRO, ADM106/2027.
224. Livie to Vandeput, 9 Sept. 1799, PRO, ADM1/494, fol. 209; Vandeput to Livie, 28 Sept. 1799. ADM1/494, fol. 208.
225. Dawes to NB, 8 Mar. 1811. NMM, HAL/B/1, fol. 69.
226. Inglefield to RO, 13 June 1811. PRO, ADM106/2028.
227. 27 Apr. 1821, *Weekly Chronicle*.
228. Allowed three apprentices. NB to RO, 6 Feb. 1776. PRO, ADM106/2470, fol. [226].
229. NB to Arbuthnot. PRO, ADM106/1479; ADM106/2470, fol. 247.
230. Hamond to Stephens, 16 May 1782. HP, VII, 84–5.
231. Hamond to NB, 24 Sept. 1782. HP, VII, 142.
232. 1 Dec. 1821. NSARM, MG10/22, #25.

233. 7 Feb. 1853, *Novascotian*.
234. NSARM, RG36a/93.
235. 15 Feb. 1817, *Halifax Journal*.
236. Contract: land sale NSARM, MG100/144, #25H, cost H£116, 1 May 1818.
237. July 1847, *Novascotian*.
238. Griffith to NB, 14 Oct. 1819. PRO, ADM106/1349.
239. PRO, ADM42/2153.
240. PRO, ADM42/2147.
241. Colvill to NB, 26 Dec. 1763. PRO, ADM106/1123.
242. Hurd to NB, 15 Nov. 1763. PRO, ADM106/1123.
243. Arbuthnot to NB, 1 Dec. 1775. PRO, ADM106/1226.
244. NB to Arbuthnot, 14 Aug. 1776. PRO, ADM106/2470, fol. 247.
245. Hamond to Marshall and Johnson, 4 May 1782. HP, IX, 115; Hamond to Admiralty, 16 May 1782. VII, 84–5.
246. Duncan to NB, 1 May 1793. PRO, ADM106/2027.
247. Coffin to Marshall, 11 Jan. 1800. NSARM, MG13/6, 436–7.
248. Marshall to Coffin, 4 Feb. 1800. NSARM, MG13/6, 503.
249. Minute, 27 Apr. "to receive pension," Elias Marshall to NB, 22 Mar. 1805. PRO, ADM106/2028.
250. Inglefield to Dawes, 2 May 1805. NSARM, MG13/9.1, 287.
251. 19 Apr. 1806, *Weekly Chronicle*.
252. From 10 Feb. 1785. PRO, ADM42/2153.
253. NSARM, MG100/235, #1.
254. PRO, ADM42/2155.
255. Coffin to Uniacke, 11 Jan. 1800, Coffin to RO, 11 Jan. 1800. NSARM, MG13/6, 443.
256. 12 Oct. 1799, *Weekly Chronicle*.
257. D.A. Story, "An Interesting Relic of Halifax School Days," 1 June 1925, *Morning Chronicle*.
258. 29 Mar. 1791, *Royal Gazette and Nova Scotia Advertizer*.
259. Hamond to Stephens, 25 Nov. 1781. HP, VIII, 43.
260. PRO, ADM104/1.
261. NMM, HAL/E/26, fol. [297–8].
262. PRO, ADM102/255.
263. PRO, ADM102/256.
264. Griffith to NB, 13 Sept. & 22 Oct. 1819. PRO, ADM106/1396, NMM, HAL/C/3, fol. 24–5.
265. At £7 12s. monthly, PRO, ADM42/2152.
266. Duncan to Thomas, 13 Oct. 1783. NSARM, MG13/1, #391.
267. The key to the Inverness Jail, which he brought from Scotland, is in NSARM. 30 Nov. 1829, *Halifax Journal*.

Notes to pages 341–342   317

268. PRO, ADM106/1349.
269. Griffith to NB, 13 Sept. & 22 Oct. 1819. PRO, ADM106/1396, NMM, HAL/C/3, fol. 24–5.
270. Inglefield to RO, 21 Oct. 1808. NMM, HAL/E/37.
271. Inglefield to RO, 6 July 1810. NMM, HAL/E/36, fol. 94.
272. NB to Wodehouse, 30 Mar. 1815. NMM, HAL/C/2, fol. 18–21.
273. 2 May 1835, *Acadian Recorder*.
274. Griffith to NB, 13 Sept. & 22 Oct. 1819. PRO, ADM106/1396, NMM, HAL/C/3, fol. 24–5.
275. 27 Aug. 1842, *Acadian Recorder*.
276. Norwood to Wodehouse, [Nov. 1815]. PRO, ADM106/2029, fol. 263.
277. 6 Jan. 1800. PRO, ADM1/3364.
278. 7 Feb. 1817, *Weekly Chronicle*.
279. Wodehouse to RO, 19 May 1817. NSARM, MG13/9.3, 215.
280. PRO, ADM42/2150.
281. Inglefield to RO, 29 Nov. 1805. NMM, HAL/E/34, fol. 1.
282. Thomas accounts, 1780–90. PRO, ADM17/150.
283. Hamond to Thomas, 14 May 1782. HP, IX, 119.
284. Wodehouse to NB, 30 July 1819. PRO, ADM106/1349.
285. 1 Sept. 1821, *Acadian Recorder*.
286. 20 June 1840, *Acadian Recorder*.
287. 2 May 1843, *Halifax Times*.
288. Oben to Nelson, 30 Jan. 1800. PRO, ADM106/2027.
289. Arrived 26 Nov. 1800 on storeship *Foster Burham*; Anderson to NB, 16 Dec. 1800. PRO, ADM106/2027.
290. Halliburton to Douglas, 27 July 1781; RO to Nelson, 29 July 1801. PRO, ADM106/2027.
291. Inglefield to NB, 25 Aug. 1801. PRO, ADM106/2027.
292. PRO, ADM104/1; requested passage, 15 Jan. 1814. PRO, ADM98/28, fol. 85.
293. Griffith to NB, 13 Sept. & 22 Oct. 1819. PRO, ADM106/1396, NMM, HAL/C/3, fol. 24–5.
294. 24 Apr. 1841, *Acadian Recorder*.
295. NSARM, RG48, reel 418; 20 Oct. 1795, *Nova Scotia Royal Gazette*.
296. Inglefield to Dawes, 2 May 1805. NSARM, MG13/9.1, 287.
297. Inglefield to RO, 6 Jan. 1806. NMM, HAL/E/34, fol. 12.
298. Inglefield to RO, 13 Apr. 1809. NSARM, MG13/5, #9.
299. NA, RG8, IV/72, 34740–82.
300. Inglefield to NB, 27 Apr. 1805. NSARM, MG13/9.1, 275.
301. Patterson to NB, 14 Dec. 1805. PRO, ADM106/2028.
302. PRO, ADM42/2147–8.

318   Notes to pages 342–345

303. Allan Everett Marble, *Surgeons, Smallpox, and the Poor: A History of Medicine and Social Conditions in Nova Scotia, 1749–1799* (Montreal: McGill-Queen's University Press, 1993), 93, 108, 215.
304. Will, RG48, reel 712/2, 75; 8 Dec. 1772, *Nova Scotia Royal Gazette*.
305. 30 Aug. 1773. NSARM, O/S, #266.
306. Irene L. Rogers, "John Plaw, 1746–1820," *DCB* (1983), 5: 678–80.
307. PRO, ADM102/256.
308. Williams accounts, 1773–80. PRO, ADM17/150.
309. Livie accounts, 1790–9. PRO, ADM17/151.
310. Coffin to Read, 16 Oct. 1799. NSARM, MG13/6, 329.
311. Duncan to NB, 10 Oct. 1785. NSARM, MG13/2, 356–7.
312. Petition, 11 May 1820. NSARM, ADM106/1349.
313. 15 Feb. 1841, *Halifax Journal*.
314. David Rowlands, 13 May 1818. PRO, ADM106/1349.
315. Griffith to NB, 6 Mar. 1820. PRO, ADM106/1349.
316. 9 Dec. 1840, *Nova Scotia Royal Gazette*.
317. Wodehouse to Douglas, 19 May 1817. NMM, HAL/E/41, 380–1.
318. Duncan to Livie, 17 Aug. 1794. NSARM, MG13/6, 21–2; 27 June 1798–30, June 1799. Livie accounts, 1790–99. PRO, ADM17/150.
319. Mitchell to Nepean, 20 Feb. 1804. PR0, ADM1/495, fol. 455, 457.
320. Douglas to RO, 5 Apr. 1808. PRO, ADM106/2028.
321. [30 July 1819]. NMM, HAL/E/26, fol. [297–8].
322. 23 Oct. 1819, *Acadian Recorder*; see estate papers, NSARM, RG5, GP/10, #9.
323. Ritchie to Inglefield, 16 Nov. 1810. Dawes to Inglefield, 17 Nov. 1810; Inglefield to NB, 17 Nov. 1810. PRO, ADM106/2028; NMM, HAL/E/27, fol. 257–9; HAL/E/36, fol. 192.
324. Dawes accounts, 1815. PRO, ADM17/162.
325. Rowlands to Wodehouse, 12 Jan. 1814. PRO, ADM1/506, fol. 111.
326. Epworth to Croker, 5 Mar. 1814. PRO, ADM1/1771.
327. Inglefield to RO, 13 June 1811. NMM, HAL/E/36, fol. 253.
328. 13 Sept. 1817, *Acadian Recorder*.
329. 25 Jan. 1875, *Halifax Chronicle*.
330. £61.13.4. at 10s. sterling daily, Dawes accounts. 1815. PRO, ADM17/162; Wodehouse to RO, 14 Oct. 1814. NA, II, 208–9.
331. [30 July 1819]. NMM, HAL/E/26, fol. [297–8].
332. 13 Mar. 1851, *Novascotian*.
333. Duncan to Livie, 30 June 1796. NSARM, MG13/6, 167.
334. Sherlock to Inglefield, 20 July 1809. PRO, ADM106/2028.
335. Inglefield to RO, 13 June 1811. NMM, HAL/E/36, fol. 253.

336. 1 Mar. 1834, *Acadian Recorder*.
337. Petition, Inglefield to NB, 30 Nov. 1805. PRO, ADM106/2028.
338. Same rate as shipwrights and caulkers; Dawes, Hughes, and Fairfax to Inglefield, 30 Apr. 1811. NMM, HAL/E/27, fol. 423–4.
339. Griffith to NB, 14 Oct. 1819. PRO, ADM106/1349.
340. Warren to Pole, 8 Sept. 1809. PRO, ADM1/499, fol. 241; Warren to Croker, 19 June 1810. ADM1/500, fol. 94; Admiralty approved, 29 Oct. 1810; Warren to Croker, 8 Jan. 1811. ADM1/500, fol. 4.
341. Transport Board to Wodehouse, 28 June 1816. NMM, HAL/E/3b, fol. 25.
342. 10 Mar. 1829, *Free Press*.
343. Stewart to Wodehouse, 1 Sept. 1815; Wodehouse to NB, 2 Sept. 1815. PRO, ADM106/2029, fol. 241, 243.
344. NB to Wodehouse, 30 Mar. 1815. NMM, HAL/C/2, fol. 18–21.
345. PRO, ADM106/2029, fol. 211.
346. NB to Wodehouse, 30 Mar. 1815. NMM, HAL/C/2, fol. 18–21.
347. Griffith to NB, 22 Oct. 1819. NMM, HAL/C/3, fol. 24–5.
348. Thomas to White, 15 Apr. 1783. NBM, White papers, Shelf 5, A4.
349. NB to Thomas, 24 Apr. 1784. PRO, ADM106/2471, fol. 324.
350. Thomas to Hamond, 27 June 1786. PRO, CO42/51, fol. 69.
351. Daily allowance 10d. Collier to Dickson, 3 Nov. 1778. PRO, ADM98/11, fol. 310.
352. NSARM, RG48, reel 423.
353. Duncan to Thomas, 4 May 1784. NSARM, MG13/1, #435.
354. Turpel to Thomas, 25 Apr. 1785. NSARM, MG13/1, #551.
355. Digby to Stephens, 30 Sept. 1783. PRO, ADM1/490, fol. 321.
356. NB to Duncan, 23 Apr. 1792. PRO, ADM106/2473, 80.
357. 8 Aug. 1797, *Royal Gazette and Nova Scotia Advertizer*.
358. Duncan to Livie, 14 Oct. 1795. NSARM, MG13/6, 122.
359. 30 Sept. 1788, *Nova Scotia Royal Gazette*.
360. Inglefield to Wallis, 17 Feb. 1810. NMM, HAL/E/36, fol. 27–8.
361. Departed in storeship *Abundance*. Wodehouse to Oakes, 11 Oct. 1815. NMM, HAL/41, fol. 204; Wodehouse to NB, 27 Oct. 1815. PRO, ADM106/2029, fol. 250; Wodehouse to RO, 27 Oct. 1815. NA, II, 323.
362. Wallis to NB, 6 Feb. 1816, 14 Mar. & 26 Apr. 1817. PRO, ADM106/1657.
363. Wodehouse to NB, 18 June 1816. PRO, ADM106/2029, fol. 292.
364. NB to Wodehouse, 11 Sept. 1816. NMM, HAL/C/2, fol. 16.
365. Williams to NB, 10 Feb. 1779. NMM, ADM/B/198.
366. NB to Admiralty, 3 Apr. 1779. NMM, ADM/B/198.
367. PRO, ADM42/2149.
368. Wills to Coffin, 10 Mar. 1800. NSARM, MG13/6, 530.

369. Wodehouse to Croker, 14 Oct. 1812. NMM, HAL/A/2, fol. 353.
370. NMM, HAL/E/26, fol. [290–8].
371. Duncan to Livie, 15 Oct. 1795. NSARM, MG13/6, 112.
372. Petition to NB, 30 Aug. 1800. PRO, ADM106/1654.
373. Petition to Duncan, 27 Dec. 1803. PRO, ADM106/1654.
374. 5 June 1781, *Nova Scotia Gazette and Weekly Chronicle*; NSARM, RG48, reel 425; d. 1781.
375. At 4s.6d. daily. PRO, ADM42/2150–2.

Glossary

Admiral a flag rank, attained through seniority from among serving captains, for those in command of a squadron or fleet
Afloat when a ship is swimming on the water
Amidships in the middle of a ship
Anchor, bower one of two anchors stowed farthest forward, or near the bows
Anchor, sheet independent resource, used only when either of the bowers part, for which purpose the cable is always kept ready bent with a long range to be let go in an emergency
Ballast additional weight added to a ship, usually in the form of stones or iron, placed in the ship's hold to give it greater stability by increasing her draught
Ballast basket stout baskets to carry ballast in the form of stones in a ship's hold
Base a facility where expendable stores were replenished; where damaged or worn masts, yards, spars, rigging, and sails were replaced; where careening occurred; and where all but the most radical repairs carried out
Beam the width of the ship
Bees of the bowsprit pieces of hard wood bolted to the outer end of a bowsprit through which are wove the fore topmast stays before they are brought in to the bows and secured
Boatswain pronounced bo'sun; inferior officer in charge of sails, rigging, cordage, and boats
Bowsprit spar extending forward from the stem above the ship's bow to which headsails were secured
Breaming to clean a ship's bottom with lighted brush faggots; a task undertaken before caulking could begin, also called graving; to burn off the filth, such as grass, ooze, shells, or seaweed, from a ship's bottom, that has gathered to it in a voyage, or by lying long in a harbour. This operation is performed by holding kindled furze or faggots to the bottom, so that the flame incorporating with the pitch, sulphur, and so on that had formerly covered it, immediately loosens and throws off whatever filth may have adhered to the planks. After this, the bottom is covered anew with a composition of sulphur, tallow, and other material that not only makes it smooth and slippery, so as to spread the fluid more readily, but also poisons and destroys the teredo worms which eat through the planks in the course of a voyage
Breastwork barrier between twenty and twenty-five feet wide, breast-high,

built against the encroachments of the sea on the harbour side of the yard, constructed of earth, stones, and wharf timbers

Brick nogging to use poor quality or broken bricks to fill the space between exterior and interior walls to produce a stronger and more stable wall; sometimes referred to as knocking

Brush house building to store brush used in breaming ships

Bulwarks the upper section of the frames and side planking, which extends above and around the upper deck

Capstan a vertical winch or barrel, used to weigh anchors, or to hoist heavy sails, raise heavy hawsers, or chains attached to anchors

Capstan bars stout wooden bars inserted in the capstan head to heave the capstan around, each bar manned by one or more sailors

Careen to heave a vessel over on her side by applying cables to the upper masts, in order to clean, caulk, or repair the exposed side of her bottom

Careening capstan one of a set of capstans built in the side of a wharf and used to heave down a sailing ship before being cleaned

Careening pit a ditch dug in the side of a wharf, and lined with timbers, and so situated that the lower yardarms of a ship could be lodged, thus avoiding the necessity of having to lower the yardarms

Carronade a short, light muzzle-loading cannon, throwing a very heavy ball a relatively short distance

Cat strong tackle or machine formed by a combination of pulleys which serves to hook and pull the anchor up to the cathead without tearing the ship's side with it's flukes

Cathead large piece of timber or a crane, projecting over the bow for drawing up the anchor clear of the ship's side; also serves to suspend the anchor clear of the bow; when it is necessary to let it go it is supported by a sort of knee, which is generally ornamented with sculpture

Caulker an artificer whose special tools makes watertight a seam between two planks, either on a ship's bottom or deck planking by forcing in strips of hot tarred rope fibres or oakum, before paying with pitch

Caulking the filling of the seams of the planks with oakum, made of old junk, to prevent a ship from leaking

Chain moorings most efficient method of establishing permanent moorings for a ship in harbour, where anchors are fixed to the bank and connected by a chain, in the middle of which was a square link attached to a cable, to hold a ship at anchor

Cheek large horizontal knee on either bow which supports transversely the knee of the head

Chips the wastage occurring when timber was converted to specific uses, to which certain artificers, until 1809 in Halifax, had a right to remove from the yard under certain conditions

Clean see breaming

Colours flag, banner, or insignia flown by a ship at sea

Commodore a captain in command of a detached squadron, with the right to fly a broad pendent, usually red

Convoy a group of merchant ships, transports, naval storeships, etc. escorted by warships; sometimes also used to denote the escorting war- ship

Coppering to place thin copper sheeting over a ship's bottom planking, below the waterline, dating from the 1770s; held with copper fastenings, first applied to warships and later to merchant vessels, to resist teredo worm damage and to reduce the rate of accumulation of weeds and molluscs; to enable the ship to sail faster

Cutter a small, single-masted vessel, fore-and-aft-rigged; two were built in the Halifax yard

Deal fir or pine board used especially for ship's decking, cut three inches or so thick

Draught depth of a body of water sufficient for a ship to float

Drydock an excavated area in a yard often referred to as a graving dock, separated from water by watertight gates into which a ship was floated. The water was then pumped out, in order to inspect, clean, and repair the ship. When a new hull or hull repairs were completed, water was then admitted to float the hull and tow it out

Escort a warship sailing with and protecting a convoy

Fearnaught a stout, thick, woollen cloth first developed in 1772; textile used chiefly as coats for hulksmen and watchmen in the naval yard; also used on warships as a covering for portholes and powder magazines

Forecastle upper deck forward of the foremast

Foremast the mast nearest the bow, when there is more than one mast in a ship

Frigate square-rigged three-masted ship, with a single covered gun deck, carrying from 20 to 60 guns

Futtlings or foot-waling all the inside plank or lining of a ship's bottom, used to prevent any part of the ballast or cargo from falling between the floor-timbers

Futtocks curved or straight parts of a ship's frame timbers, situated between the keel and the top-timbers, to give strength to the sides

Gun brig a small vessel, built to carry an unusually heavy armament; the Halifax yard built one such, *Plumper*

Half pay portion of pay, received by statutory right by naval officers, and by

Admiralty regulations by pilots on warships during periods when not actively engaged in the naval service

Handskoons   sailors' woollen mittens

Heel   the after-end of a ship's keel; the lower part of a mast or any timber

Hulk   an old or rotting, large warship stripped of its masts, spars, and rigging, used to house yard workmen, prisoners of war, crews whose ships were at the careening wharf or to serve as a naval hospital

Hulksmen   sailors appointed to the hulk's establishment

Impressment [sometimes referred to as the press, or to press]   a statutory system of compulsory service by seamen, and later by landsmen, to man the fleet

Keel   the lowest longitudinal timber, the backbone of a ship from which the ribs start

Keelson   longitudinal timber laid inside a vessel on the floor timbers, parallel to the keel and bolted to it, to give additional strength

Kersey   a coarse narrow cloth, woven from long wool; textile often used for making colours

Knee   a crooked piece of timber, having two branches, or arms, and generally used to connect the beams of a ship with her sides or timbers

Leeward   downwind side of a vessel

Letter-of-marque   either a vessel or the commission authorizing a private vessel to operate against enemy vessels, at its own risk, while still carrying freight

Magazine   place where ammunition is stored either on board a warship, or on a specially designated vessel in harbour, or in a purpose-built structure ashore

Mainmast   the middle mast in a three-masted ship; the aftermast in a two-masted vessel

Marines   soldiers serving aboard ships, raised especially for sea duty

Mastpond   pond where mast timbers are kept submerged to prevent decay until they are fashioned into masts, bowsprits, yards, or spars

Oakum   loose, stringy, hemp fibre, picked from old ropes called junk, used in caulking ships and boat seams

Pay   to daub or smear the surface of a vessel body, in order to preserve it from the injuries of the water, weather, and other agents; thus the bottom of a ship is paid with a composition such as tallow, sulphur, and rosin; to pay a ship's bottom with pitch and tar, known as "black stuff" in the ratio of two parts pitch to one part tar, or with oil, rosin and brimstone, known as "white stuff"

Pendent   a sort of long narrow banner, displayed from the mast-head of a ship of war, and usually terminating in two ends or points. There are pendents of a larger kind used to distinguish the chief of a squadron of ships

People of the yard those less skilled than artificers; mainly labourers, watchmen, sheer hulksmen, boats' crews, porters

Pettyauger a Trinidad-designed gondola or flat-bottomed open boat, with sail and oars, mounting a few light guns, between fifty and eighty tons; some were built in the Halifax yard in 1808–09

Pintle pin or bolt

Privateer a privately-owned vessel, heavily-armed and crewed, with a government commission to sail against enemy shipping

Prize a captured enemy warship or merchant vessel, later condemned by a vice-admiralty court

Prize money the net proceeds accruing to the captors from the process of bringing a capture before a vice-admiralty court, distributed by shares determined by parliamentary statute when a warship, or by contractual agreement when a privateer or letter-of-marque ship

Quarterdeck the after part of the upper deck, usually raised above it

Quick-work a general name given to all that part of a ship which is under the surface of the water when she is laden fit for a sea-voyage; also applied, occasionally, to that part of the side which is above the sheer-rail, and which is usually painted with trophies on the outside

Rigging, running ropes to work sails and yards

Rigging, standing ropes supporting the masts

Rounder one who makes the rounds of the watchmen and sentinels

Sheer hulk hulk equipped with lifting gear, an arrangement of stout poles (sheers) and tackle for stepping or unstepping a ship's masts, using a central pole incorporated into the hulk like a stunted mast, with a second pole attached to it at a point near the top known as sheer legs

Shipwright a ship's carpenter

Slip sloping planked surface to ease the hauling or landing of boats, masts, and other stores

Sloop of war a small three-masted full-rigged ship, with guns on a single deck, with usually sixteen or eighteen light cannon

Slops ready-made clothing and bedding supplied to a warship for seamen

Standard an inverted knee which is placed above the deck instead of beneath it, and having its vertical branch pointed upwards from that which lies horizontally

Store(s) general term for provisions, materials, and supplies used aboard ship for the maintenance of the crew, and for the navigation, propulsion, and upkeep of the vessel and its equipment

Swivel gun a light, easily-handled cannon on a non-recoiling swivel mount, firing a projectile as light as a half-pound, and mounted on a ship's bulwarks or in the tops

Timber a squared log; later sawn into boards

Topmen active men stationed in the tops to attend to the sails on the three masts above the lower yard

Tops platform located high on a mast, manned in action by seamen and marines, armed with muskets or swivel guns to fire down into the enemy's crowded deck

Transport a vessel converted to conveying soldiers and their officers, refugees, or others

Treenail long, cylindrical hardwood pin employed to connect securely the planks of a ship's side and bottom to the corresponding timbers

Trestletree and crosstree the former of these are two strong bars of timber, supported by two prominences, which are like shoulders on the opposite sides of the mast, a little under its upper end; athwart the trestletrees and the cheeks are fixed the crosstrees, upon which the frame of the top is supported

Upper works part of a vessel above the main deck

Victualler a ship, owned or hired by the Victualling Board, to carry barrelled provisions, provided by contractors, principally of bread and biscuit, beef and pork, beer, butter, and peas, for the use of ships in commission

Waist portion of the deck between the forecastle and quarterdeck

Wharf a substantial structure of timber, earth, and stone secured with pilings, built usually at right angles to the shore to enable ships to lie alongside to load, unload, or careen

Windward toward the wind

Yard spar on which a square sail is set

Biographical Directory

ADAMS, Daniel   commander of rebel privateer *Lively*; rescued survivors of *Blonde* wrecked on Seal Island, and landed them on the Nova Scotian mainland, before sailing to Boston, 1782; "in resentment for his action, he became hateful to his countrymen and for want of employment;" British naval pilot 1782–d.; widow Sarah, as she and her five children were in great distress, petitioned for help,[1] with support from Michael Wallace;[2] she died in Saint John 23 Jan. 1828, aged 74.[3]

ANDERSON, Alexander   b. c.1758; entered yard from England as storekeeper's 2d clerk, 1783;[4] suspended in 1784; reinstated, 1785; 1st clerk when Hurd was superannuated, 1794;[5] acting storekeeper for forty-three months, 1799–1803;[6] granted leave "not having been at home for near twenty years," 1801; leave delayed when Oben collapsed;[7] superseded by Dawes, Jan. 1803; accused by Inglefield of insubordination when he requested that his conduct be officially investigated; visited England, 1804–5;[8] confined by sickness to his house, 1811;[9] requested house to be built for him as "comfortable dwelling houses not to be procured on almost any terms within a reasonable distance from the yard;"[10] pensioned, 1819;[11] d. at Halifax, 1833, aged 75.[12]

ANDREW, George   entered from Plymouth yard, 1776;[13] surveyor of masts, Saint John 1781–5;[14] acting master shipwright, when Coffin suspended Marshall, 1800;[15] retired to England, 1802; "a man of good character."[16]

ANDREW, George   shipwright-caulker; 1806, entered yard in place of Robert Baker, dismissed.[17]

ARBUTHNOT, Marriot   commissioner, Halifax 1775–8;[18] lieut gov., 1776–8; served in North American sqdn under Boscawen and Spry, 1755; Virginia and New York stations, 1757;[19] departed Halifax, when replaced by Hughes, Aug. 1778;[20] rear admiral and c-in-c North American sqdn, 1779–81; vice admiral, 1779; admiral, 1793; at siege of Charleston, 1780; failed to attack inferior French sqdn at Newport, 1780; squandered chance to defeat Destouches's sqdn off Virginia Capes, March 1781; fell out with Rodney and Clinton at New York; retired on half pay, 1781; d. 1794.

ATKINSON, Thomas   master of *Victory*, 1803–05; master attendant, 1807–9; "conducted himself with propriety and attention was always obedient to command;"[21] 3d master attendant at Portsmouth yard, 1809–10; 2d master attendant at Portsmouth, 1810–23.

AYRES, Richard   entered 26 Oct. 1795, shipwright-caulker; £20 pension, 1819.[22]

328 Biographical Directory

BADCOCK, John smith; volunteered for Halifax yard from Plymouth, 1775;[23] master smith, 1776–83;[24] d. 28 Feb. 1783; his widow in England applied for effects and servants' wages, which he left by his will to Elizabeth Roberts of Halifax "a matter unsatisfactory to his widow."[25]

BALL, Thomas from England as yard's painter, 1817; "very indifferent workman and ignorant beyond anything beyond the very commonest work, not being able to letter (as it is termed) in the plainest manner," discharged 1819.[26]

BELL, James "an expert workman and strongly recommended" by Wodehouse as yard painter to replace Ball, 1819.[27]

BEST, Henry yard stewart, 1775–89;[28] d. 1789.

BEST, John mason's labourer in Halifax yard, 1767–73;[29] d. 1778; survived by widow, Dorcas.

BEST, William b. c.1707; settler arrived with Cornwallis, 1749; master mason in Halifax yard, 1767–73;[30] slave owner;[31] MHA for Halifax, 1758–9, 1761–70; d. 1782;[32] survived by s., Richard, and dau., Mrs. Richard [Jane] Tritton.

BLACKADAR, Charles entered yard as apprentice to master carpenter, Lee, 1784;[33] s. John Oaks, d. aged 24 in 1824; s. George d. aged 24 in 1826; his son, James, d. aged 20 in Demerara in 1826.

BLACKADAR, Christopher entered yard as house carpenter, 1790; "health now impaired by hurts received in the yard, with rheumatism ... after consulting his physician despairs of ever being able to return to his duty," 1815;[34] temporary clerk in the storekeeper's office, 1810; discharged at his own request;[35] £20 pension, 1815;[36] dau. Mary, Sarah, Mary Eleanor, Rebecca (d. in Portsmouth, aged 19, in 1822); from whom the Yarmouth NS Blackadars derive; one s. Henry Nicol, became MHA for Pictou.

BLACKADAR, Hugh b. Halifax 1773; entered as master shipwright's apprentice, 1792;[37] £24 pension, 1815;[38] d. at Halifax, 1818;[39] widow, Amy, d. aged 42, in 1823.

BLACKADAR, James Christopher b. 1738, Boston;[40] among the original yard shipwrights, 1758;[41] d. 23 May 1791; by his will he left a house in Dutch Village north suburbs of Halifax to his wife, Catherine, during her life, whom he named his sole executrix, and thereafter to his children: Christopher, Charles, Hugh, John, Mary, Catherine, and Elizabeth;[42] his dau. Mary married John Dugwell, 1787; his widow d. 1794, aged 53.

BLACKADAR, John entered yard as apprentice blockmaker, 1790;[43] later shipwright-caulker; volunteered to refloat sloop *Tartar*, Bermuda, 1805; praised by Hawkes in repairing *Victorious*, after Nov. 1813 hurricane; merited "the strongest recommendation I can give on behalf of a good and faithful servant to his country;" Blackadar requested an apprentice under him;[44] granted £20 pension, 1819.[45]

BRIDGE, Benjamin Halifax founder and coppersmith; retained by yard at H£10 yearly with provisions, 1781–3; re-entered yard, 1795.[46]

BROCKWELL, Henry foreman of sailmakers; apprenticeship at Portsmouth dockyard; leading man of sailmakers, Portsmouth 1794–1804; foreman of sailmakers, Halifax 1804; successfully protested reduction to leading man of sailmakers, 1815;[47] warned for leaving the loft unattended, when a theft occurred, 1817;[48] co-signer of greetings to Wodehouse, 1819.[49]

BROWN, Ephraim first foreman of the yard, 1759–63;[50] d. Halifax, 1775.

BRUSH, John foreman of smiths, 1796–1814; b. Westchester, New York; served apprenticeship as blacksmith; joined Orange Rangers Regiment as sgt., 1776; disbanded from engineers' branch, 1783; evacuated to Nova Scotia; foreman of yard's blacksmith shop, 1786; yard foreman, replacing McKay "discharged for neglect of duty," 1796;[51] very severe illness, 1812; applied for pension, 1814;[52] d. 1815.[53]

BURBIDGE, John b. 1718, Cowes; contractor built north careening wharf, and prepared ground for capstan house and two storehouse wings, 1759–60; built masthouse and slip, 1760; foreman of artificers at Louisbourg, 1747; evacuated to Halifax, 1749; established 300-acre farm, Bilkington Park, in Cornwallis township; JP, Halifax County, 1761; capt., Halifax militia, 1762; major, King's County militia; justice inferior court of common pleas, 1776; MHA, 1759–70; devoted Anglican; m. secondly, Rebecca, widow of Benjamin Gerrish; d. 1812 worth H£1,500.[54]

BUTLER, John b. 1728; entered yard 1768 as shipwright; worn out & discharged in 1785 into *Pembroke* hulk.[55]

CARLETON, Matthew entered yard as shipwright-caulker, 1804; discharged 1819; £20 pension.[56]

CHARLTON, John master house carpenter sent from England to superintend building of yard, 1758–60; in dispute with Gerrish over wages and allowances.[57]

CLARK, Duncan b. c.1759; Edinburgh University, 1777–8; formerly surgeon 82d Foot Regt.; replaced Rutherford as yard surgeon;[58] called by Duncan "a very able Surgeon;"[59] acting surgeon at naval hospital, 1783–7; m. Justina Bayer, Halifax 1789; 5 sons; physician-in-ordinary in Halifax to the household of HRH Prince Edward; pres. North British Society, 1789 & 1797; free mason; d. Halifax 1808, leaving a net estate of H£208.[60]

CLIFFORD, John surgeon of *Leopard*; appointed surgeon agent of Halifax naval hospital when Halliburton retired, 1807–11;[61] d. 1811, leaving widow, four children.

COFFIN, Isaac b. 1759 Boston; as lieut survived shipwreck of armed vessel *Pinson*, Labrador coast, 1779; Arbuthnot's signal lieut on *Royal Oak* off Virginia Capes, 1781; volunteered under Hood in action off St Kitts; capt. 1782; commanded *Thisbe* taking Lord Dorchester to Quebec; court-martialled for signing false ship's musters; dismissed from his ship; gave passage to Dorchester to England, 1790; commissioner Halifax yard, 1799–1800;[62] returned to England, 1800;[63] commissioner of Sheerness dockyard, 1801–5, where he "imposed a vigorous reorganization,"[64] with "little regard for artificers' interests;" when he impressed a yard man for insolence and disobedience, a large number of artificers, riggers, and labourers threatened his life and forced him to revoke his order, 1801;[65] rear admiral 1805; created baronet 1804; vice admiral 1808; admiral 1814; MP 1818–26; gov. Greenwich Hospital, 1832; m. Elizabeth Browne Greenly, 1811; granted seigneury of Madeleine islands, 1798; tried in vain to remove twenty-two families who had settled there in 1792 from St Pierre & Miquelon, 1806; d. Cheltenham, 1839.

COLVILL, Lord Alexander capt. 1744; rear admiral, 1762; at Halifax and Boston, 1750–2; received public addresses of thanks in Boston, to express people's "great satisfaction;"[66] c-in-c North American sqdn 1757–8, 1759–63; at siege of Louisbourg 1758; never married; fathered four children, Charles b. Boston, 1751, two s. in Exeter by 1762, dau. by Elizabeth Green of Halifax;[67] d. 21 May 1770.

CONSTABLE, Abraham master shipwright, Halifax yard; carpenter on *Invincible*; arrived Halifax with Gen. Amherst, May 1758 as master shipwright, 1758–63, 1771–5; in England, 1763–71;[68] s. Richard, acted as his clerk;[69] recommended by Boscawen;[70] accused by Lee of corruption; suspended by Arbuthnot, 1775;[71] Admiralty neither tried nor re-employed him; d. 1795 when s., Abraham, complained of his father's treatment.[72]

COOK, John literate sawyer; in 70th Foot to 1783; entered yard, 1785; sought pension from "hurts he has received and from the cold and damps of the laborious trade of sawing timber has become feeble, with pains in the breast, indicative of an approaching consumption;" by 1810 "worn out and unfit for service."[73]

COX, Joseph yard's first foreman of caulkers, 1759–63, thereafter caulker, 1763–d.; d. Halifax, 1785;[74] survived by s., Joseph and Francis.

CULLEN, Stephen yard's gate porter, succeeding Gleeson, 1787–99; leased horses and carts to yard from 1790–d. for H£5,180;[75] d. 1799;[76] one s. set fires in the yard and his home, 1799.

DA COSTA, Isaac s. of successful Boston merchant; at defence of Annapolis Royal, 1744; volunteered at Louisbourg, 1745; in Williams's regiment at first battle of Fort William Henry, 1755; master mason at Halifax yard, 1758–60;[77] worked on Annapolis Royal fort, 1761; fled Boston, 1776; returned to Boston from England, 1778; arrested and banished; in debtors' prison, England 1782–3; loyalist claimant.[78]

DAWES, Daniel Butler   entered naval service 1778; purser on *Dreadnaught* before becoming storekeeper at Halifax yard, 1803;[79] returned to England, 1819.

DICKSON, James   first surgeon appointed to new Halifax naval hospital, 1781–2;[80] responsible for POWs;[81] health "has long been declining;"[82] d. 1782.

DOUGLAS, John   master of the fleet under HRH Duke of Clarence; master attendant at Halifax, 1815–9.[83]

DUGWELL, Hugh   b. 1793; entered yard as temporary clerk @ £50 a year, 1809; son of John;[84] m. Sarah Mariett, 1823;[85] secondly Mary Marlin of Harrietsfield;[86] d. 1838.[87]

DUGWELL, John   b. in Kent; entered as master shipwright's apprentice, 1784;[88] yard foreman, 1800;[89] helped get storeship *William* off rocks at Canso, 1808;[90] praised for his exertions during 1813 Halifax harbour hurricane; "whilst *Epivier* lay on shore in Bedford Basin after the hurricane ... Dugwell was employed for three successive days and nights in getting her off; I have seldom witnessed greater exertions, directed by better judgement. The same was manifest in getting *Manby* off – both these sloops were laying on shore above high water mark, and I am persuaded that we are principally in debt for their safety to this Man's exertions;"[91] sent to New Brunswick to survey compass timber for building "buoy boat now in progress at the yard," 1816;[92] co-signed message upon Wodehouse's departure, 1819; Wodehouse ensured that he was looked after for his "long and meritorious service;"[93] d. 1836[94] leaving widow and four children; younger dau., Mary Ann, d. 1835; elder dau., Catherine, wife of John Smith, d. aged 49 in 1839.

DUGWELL, Joseph   entered as Lee's apprentice, 1809;[95] house carpenter, 1817; John's 3d s.;[96] m. Catherine Butter, 1828;[97] d. 1830.[98]

DUNCAN, Henry   b. Dundee; entered navy as able seaman in 1739; served with Holburne off Louisbourg, 1757; Howe's flag capt., 1776–8; selected careening yard site on Manhattan Island, 1776; commissioner at Halifax yard, 1783–99, 1800, under Howe's patronage;[99] MLC; deputy comptroller of the navy 1801–6; superannuated captain 1811 with £900 pension; m. at Dartmouth, Mary French, 1761; retired to Dartmouth; d. 1814; widow received a £300 pension and inherited his Newfoundland estate.

EDGECOMBE, Frederick   acting naval storekeeper, 1784–5; described by Sawyer as "a gentleman of publick merit and private virtue, who was regularly brought up as a clerk in the commissioner's office at Plymouth, and who came out with Admiral Pigot to the West Indies"[100] in 1782; encountered "heavy expences" to "procure some papers ... which I had repeatedly asked for in vain"[101] in 1791; clerk of the survey, Plymouth, 1812–17.

ELDER, William literate blacksmith; entered yard as smith, 1806; leading man of smiths, 1814;[102] discharged, 1819; sought pension, 1820 with wife and six children "having unfortunately lost the little property he had acquired by industry while in the service, is now in indigent circumstances;"[103] recommended as a "faithful, sober and attentive man."

EPPES, W.S. agent to naval hospital at £350 a year, 1808–16; superseded for irregularities in his accounts.[104]

ETHERINGTON, John b. 1733; literate; settled in New York, 1763; imprisoned by rebels, 1776; served as naval pilot, 1776–83; when army left New York, he was imprisoned and his property seized by the Americans; emigrated to Shelburne as half pay pilot, 1784–1802; contracted "a distemper in his loins and limbs, which obliges him to walk with crutches;" petitioned when unable to work, feared ending his days in poverty, being "reduced to the greatest indigence and distress."[105]

FAIRFAX, Edmund yard's master attendant, 1810–15, having been master of the Channel fleet;[106] dismissed for having run *Superbe* on Mars rock.[107]

FARQUHARSON, Alexander commissioner's 2d clerk; requested Coffin's patronage to secure post in Bermuda or pension "in order to enable me in the decline of life to support a large family;"[108] despaired when discharged penniless, 1802; given passage to England with his family.

FERNIE, David master of *Leander*; made acting master attendant, when Patterson went on leave, 1805;[109] departed Halifax, 1806.[110]

FERRYMAN, Rev. Robert interim chaplain to the naval hospital, 1815; appointed by Griffith.[111]

FINNERTY, William yard's master house carpenter; added third storey to 1771 sail loft, 1814–15;[112] with his partners built tenements for the surgeon, dispenser, and agent at the naval hospital, 1815–16.

FLINT, John boatswain of *Pembroke* hulk; entirely worn out; discharged; "has a large family," recommended for pension.[113]

FORSYTH, William Halifax merchant; from Glasgow, 1784; an importer supplied by his Greenock partners, Robertson & Hunter, with whom he shared a mast contract, 1789–1805; partner with his son-in-law, William Smith, 1797–1806, until Smith settled in Liverpool; partner was John Black, manager of his Saint John business interests, 1806–; made first of several trips to England and Scotland, 1792;[114] describing himself as "residing in Nova Scotia, where I superintend the whole of the concern," he asked for an interview before setting out for Scotland; settled in Greenock, 1809.[115]

FRASER, Alexander   literate; after serving three years in the army, served yard as watchman, 1802–19; discharged aged 67, with wife and three children, very poor.

FRASER, James   Halifax wood merchant, c.1804–15; sometime partner with Thom; shipping from Miramichi.

FRAZIER, William   b. 1742; entered yard as blacksmith, 1782; discharged into *Pembroke* hulk, 1785.

GARDNER, John   boatswain of *Adamant*; master sailmaker Halifax yard on Martin's death, 1792; d. 1803.

GERRISH, George   Dartmouth resident, where at his blacksmith shop built a crank weighing 1,700 lbs. for the new Dartmouth saw mill "as well made as any in Holland;"[116] foreman of smiths' yard, 1762–75;[117] d. 1775.[118]

GERRISH, Joseph   b. 1709 Boston; brother of George; officer at Louisbourg siege, 1745; wounded at Grand Pré, 1747; naval storekeeper, 1756–d.;[119] MHA, 1758–9; MLC, 1759–62; deputy judge of the vice-admiralty court, 1769–d.; settled accounts in England, 1763–4, when he failed to secure rights to mine Cape Breton coal;[120] wrongly arrested on account of the insolvency of his former partner, John Barrell, 1763;[121] Hood called him "a man of very great integrity and highly deserving of any trust;"[122] slave owner;[123] m. Mary Brenton; secondly Mary Cradock, 1768; d. 1774.[124]

GLEESON, James   yard gate porter; d. 1787;[125] succeeded by Cullen.

HALEY, Edward   b. 1727; entered yard as watchman, 1782; fractured skull; discharged into *Pembroke* hulk, 1785.[126]

HALLIBURTON, John   b. c.1737; during the Seven Years' War appointed surgeon's mate in *Thames* (32); surgeon in fireship *Prosperine* (12), frigates *Deale Castle* (20) and *Maidstone* (28), and schooner *Sultana*, before settling in Newport, Rhode Island, as a surgeon; m. 1767 Susannah, dau. of Jalheel Brenton; contracted with Rear Admiral Montagu to look after the sick of the sqdn, 1773;[127] at naval hospital during the British occupation of Newport; Admiral John Byron called him "a person of knowledge & experience"[128] as he was "particularly useful to Admiral Arbuthnot and has suffered greatly by being obliged to make his escape with all his family from Rhode Island;"[129] appointed acting surgeon at Halifax naval hospital upon Dickson's death;[130] confirmed upon Handasyde's death, 1783; requested pay raise as unable by 1803 "to supply with common comforts any family however small its number;"[131] application for a pension at full pay, when aged nearly 70, supported by Berkeley, for his "most arduous attention to his duty, accompanied by the highest professional skill and excellence of private character;"[132] resigned owing to his uncertain health and his wish to avoid "the severity of the winter," 1807,[133] MLC, 1787–1807; s. John made a career in navy; dau. Rebecca

m. John Murray, captain of *Oiseau*, at Halifax, 1794; son, Brenton, became chief justice of Nova Scotia; pres. of the North British Society; d. 1808.

HAMILTON, Richard first master attendant, 1758–63, returned to England with his family.[134]

HAMOND, Sir Andrew Snape b. 1738; commanded sloop, *Newfoundland*, 1767–9; capt., 1770; commanded *Arethusa* in North American sqdn, 1771–3; gave Arbuthnot passage to Halifax, 1775; knighted for service in defence of Sandy Hook, 1778; at siege of Charleston, 1780; commissioner Halifax naval yard and commander of ships in Halifax harbour, 1781–82; Nova Scotia's lieut gov., 1781–2;[135] encouraged loyalist settlement in Nova Scotia;[136] resigned when superseded by Parr;[137] departed Halifax in *Caton*, dismasted off Newfoundland and made for Antigua; Digby bewailed his departure "I am afraid that at this critical juncture the absence of so good an officer will be some disadvantage to the service;"[138] in Halifax he hired Lee to build a house and barn[139] on 40 acres at the Narrows on the east side of Gottingen Street and north of Young Street;[140] married secondly Ann Graeme, 1779; baronet 1783; extra commissioner of NB, 1793–4; deputy comptroller of the Navy, 1794; comptroller of the Navy, 1794–1806; MP 1796–1806; superannuated capt., 1806; Fellow of the Royal Society; d. 12 Sept. 1828; both his only s. and a grands. achieved flag rank.

HANDASYDE, John acting asst. surgeon, Halifax naval hospital, 1781–2;[141] dispenser, 1782;[142] "a man of abilities ... appears to have given much satisfaction to the patients as well as to the captains and officers who have visited the hospital;"[143] wife Elizabeth; d. 1783.[144]

HAVERSTOCK, John entered yard, 1794; recommended by Griffith for a £10 pension though he was incapacitated neither by age nor infirmities from earning his livelihood;[145] his wife, Elizabeth, aged 42, d. 1819, leaving eight children.[146]

HAWKES, Thomas Forder master shipwright, 1813–17; formerly foreman of shipwrights at Deptford;[147] superseded by Jones.[148]

HAY, Charles acting master attendant at Halifax, 1757–8, appointed by Holburne.[149]

HAYES, John yard's first copperer, 1781–4.[150]

HEMMENS, Samuel master attendant, 1780–7; 2d master attendant at Plymouth, 1790–99; master attendant at Chatham, 1799–1817.

HINKLE, Frederick foreman of smiths to replace Brush, 1812.[151]

HINES, John yard's first blockmaker, 1781–d.;[152] d. Halifax, 1792.

HOLMAN, John master of *Preston*; acting master attendant, 1774–5.[153]

HOOD, Viscount Samuel b. 1724, Somersetshire; served at Charleston and Philadelphia, 1754–6; capt. 1756; c-in-c North American sqdn, 1767–70;

rebuilt major yard structures; commissioner Portsmouth dockyard, 1778; baronet 1779; rear admiral 1780; created Irish peer, 1782; MP 1784; vice admiral 1787; first lord of Admiralty, 1788–95; admiral 1794; English peer 1796; gov. of Greenwich Hospital 1815; m. Susannah Linzee; d. 27 Jan. 1816.

HOOPER, David   acting master attendant, 1763–5;[154] boatswain of *Romney*, had sailed with Colvill "above twenty years, has had great practice in heaving down ships, and tho' only assistant to Mr Hamilton, late master attendant, was chiefly depended upon in the business of that department."[155]

HOOPER, James   acting master shipwright, 1763–5;[156] as carpenter of *Arc-en-ciel* was paid £5 for his expenses at Piscataqua, while inspecting masts for Holburne, 1757;[157] ship's carpenter of *Romney*; "assistant to Mr Constable ... but is a much better man both in the theory & practice of his business"[158] wrote Colvill, "I could not properly direct the whole business of the yard without the assistance of one of superior skill and genius."[159]

HUGHES, George   b. 1790; s. of William Hughes; entered yard; made later career in commissariat department; m. Mary Ann, dau. of Frederick Major; d. Charlottetown, 1813.

HUGHES, Peter   b. 1775 in Deptford; eldest s. of William Hughes; entered yard as his apprentice, 1788;[160] ended career as naval paymaster; m. widow of Sir de Lacy Evans, equerry to the queen.

HUGHES, Sir Richard, bart.   capt. 1756; commissioner of Halifax yard and Nova Scotia's lieut gov., 1778–81;[161] returned to England in transport *Vernon* after landing provisions for the military detachment at Spanish River;[162] rear admiral 1780; vice admiral 1790; c-in-c Halifax station, 1789–92; admiral 1795; d. 1812.

HUGHES, William   b. 1745 in Merioneth, Wales; "brought up in Deptford yard"[163] where he served for nine years; volunteered for Halifax as shipwright, 1775;[164] allowed an apprentice on Arbuthnot's recommendation "having upon all occasions discharged his duty with much fidelity and as it may prevent him from returning home at the expiration of three years;"[165] acted as "converter" on behalf of the yard for mast contractors, 1777–9; suspended by Coffin as yard foreman for alleged embezzlement of stores, 1800; replaced by Dugwell;[166] sought Hamond's protection, when Sir Andrew became comptroller of the navy, as he "never have had one single angry word from any of my superior officers ... but have always been look'd upon by them as a man deserving preferment ... I have gave universall satisfaction to them and have come forward to offer me their interest unasked for. Since Duncan's departure I have been the most particular officer as could be, which I am sure from the conversation of some of the captains from this station you must have heard the same from them. Particular to, sir, as the builder of the yard [Marshall] has been very infirm and Mr Lee, the foreman of the house carpenters, almost past duty, and Mr George Andrew, part of his time purveying for the mast contractors and at times very much afflicted with the gout, and William Burns, the leading man that superintended the caulkers was dead. So that the duty has rather bore hard on me, and the ships has been in want of great repairs and at the naval hospital last year, by order of the admiral, I superintended the building of a new wharf and have carried it out into the harbour, so that there is water sufficient for a frigate to lay at low water ... For I do most solemnly declare to you that I have been the greatest slave any man could in forwarding the public service;"[167] Halliburton also wrote to Hamond in support of Hughes;[168] reinstated by Murray after three months during which he declined "several lucrative situations;"[169] estimated timber reserves in Nova Scotia and New Brunswick, 1801;[170] superseded Marshall as master shipwright, 1805–d.; said to be "a prime favorite of ... the Duke of Kent, was made by him purveyor of his household, who took him with him on at least one of his visits to Annapolis Royal, 14 June 1794 ... and presented him with a gold-headed staff before he left this station."[171] m. Ann Richards (1750–1812); d. 1813.[172]

HUGHES, William James b. August 1783; youngest s. of William Hughes; entered as able seaman on *Espérance* in Halifax, 1795; wrecked in Gulf of St Lawrence, Aug. 1798, when in command of a prize in the Gulf of Mexico, taken by Spanish letter-of-marque; retaken; lieut 1802; returned to Halifax, 1802–03; took passage on *Lady Hobart* packet for England; navigated prize French fishing schooner to Liverpool, England; while in command of fireship *Phosphorous*, beat off a French lugger privateer; badly wounded in his hand; awarded a £100 sword by the Patriotic Society, as well as an equivalent sum of money; cmdr. 25 Sept. 1806; agent of POWs at Jamaica, 1808; commanded sloop *Ephira* in home waters, 1809–13; agent of transports to Russia and port admiral at Karlscrona, returned to England with a body of Russian seamen; gov. of Halifax naval hospital, 1813–16 at £500 a year, with £100 house rent, and 2s.6d. a day for rations;[173] discharged, 1816;[174] £150 pension on account of his wound, 1815; m. 1803, Elizabeth, dau. of Thomas Clay Esq.; 10 children; d. 21 Mar. 1862.

HUME, Robert entered as surgeon's mate on *Thetis*, under Alexander Cochrane, 1793, before going to London to complete examination as surgeon; surgeon in sloop *Spencer*, 1795–9; dispenser Halifax naval hospital, 1799–1814; served as surgeon, Halliburton "being an old man & living two miles from the hospital;" attended POWs on Melville Island, 1802–13, for which he had to keep a horse, though unable to afford it and "having a large family to support;"[175] helped cure 110 men "with the worst species of ulcer," 1802; by 1813 salary was £300 a year plus 15s. house rent, 2s.6d. for rations; serious dispute with Rowlands over care of Melville Island sick; dismissed; board of inquiry failed to reinstate him; to England to plead his case, 1814; on half pay; entered private practice in Halifax; d. 25 Apr. 1853, aged 71, leaving a widow.[176]

HURD, Jacob b. c.1726; entered the navy, 1756; in *Prince of Orange* which careened at Barnard's wharf, Halifax; "employed here since the first foundation" of careening yard; chief clerk to storekeeper, Dec. 1758;[177] served until 1794; acting naval storekeeper 1763–64, 1779–80; travelled to Quebec to secure admiral's approval of bills drawn by Gerrish;[178] visited England, 1771;[179] slave owner who offered H£5 for the return of Cromwell, a runaway;[180] requested pension as "at my stage of life I am unable to give the attendance or necessary assistance that may be required," 1794;[181] d. aged 71, 1797;[182] left a widow and large family; portrait and that of his wife, Metropolitan Museum of Art, New York.

HURD, Jacob II master attendant's clerk, Apr. 1809 @ H£120.[183]

INGLEFIELD, John N. b. 1748; served on Durell's flagship *Launceston*, 1766; flag capt. of *Barfleur* (90) in 1780 under Hood, with whom he had served on *Romney* at Halifax, 1768–70; commanded *Centaur* (74) in action with De Grasse off Chesapeake, 1781; lost ship in hurricane on homeward passage after she was on her beam ends; escaped to Fayal in pinnace with master, midshipman, and nine seamen after sixteen days at sea; last served at sea as fleet captain in Mediterranean, 1794; retired capt., 1799; commissioner at Corsica, Malta, and Gibraltar, 1795–1801, Halifax, 1801–12; while at Gibraltar, was promised Chatham, whenever it became available; upon arrival at Halifax declined seat at the NB, as "my eye sight was too feeble for that sort of duty;" went on leave in England without permission, 1807; greeted with astonishment by NB; behaviour arose from promises received from Mulgrave;[184] by 1811 Inglefield was "senior commissioner of the navy;" sought appointment to Chatham or Plymouth yards;[185] departed Halifax 1812 on pension; m. dau. of Sir Thomas Slade; published *Narrative of the Loss of HMS Centaur*; d. 1828; one s. was a naval capt. unemployed in 1811, lacking "weight of interest."[186]

INGLIS, Rev. Dr John b. 1777; chaplain to naval hospital, 1816, on Stanser's resignation;[187] third bishop of Nova Scotia with salary and allowances of £2,350; MLC, 1825; d. 1850.

INGOLLS, William built yard boathouse, 1759; d. Halifax, 1786;[188] leaving several children.

JACKSON, John master attendant, 1799 appointed by Coffin; formerly master on *Ville de Paris*;[189] 3d master attendant, Portsmouth dockyard, Apr. 1803–04;[190] 1st master attendant, Plymouth, 1804–29.

JAMES, Benjamin   entered service in commissary general's department, New York 1776–83, paying out almost £500,000, his care saving on oats alone "upwards of £8,000;" 2d clerk, storekeeper's office @ £50 salary with £10 house rent; paid H£30 for house rent, with "small remainder am obliged to struggle hard to support myself and family,"1800;[191] d. 22 July 1803;[192] succeeded by s. Thomas.[193]

JOHNS, William   acting master shipwright, 1767–70;[194] Hood praised his "integrity and cleverness;"[195] undertook partial survey of the woods of Nova Scotia, 1770.

JOHNSON, Thomas   foreman of shipwrights afloat at the Halifax yard, 1776–83.[196]

JONES, Algernon Frederick   master shipwright, 1816–19;[197] formerly assistant to master shipwright at Deptford yard;[198] wife accompanied him to Halifax.

JONES, John   b. c.1722; master sailmaker, 1758–63;[199] d. Halifax 1781; widow, Mercy.[200]

JONES, Richard   acting surgeon Halifax hospital upon Crawford's death, until relieved by Rowlands, 1811–13.[201]

KAVANAGH, James   b. 1750; from Saint John to Halifax yard as foreman of smiths, 1795; hurt leg, 1814; incurable ulcer prevented him from standing at the forge; blind in one eye by a spark while at the yard, 1815; sought pension.[202]

KENNEDY, Jane   b. 1751; first matron of nurses at Halifax naval hospital, 1783;[203] d. Halifax, 1794.

KENNEY, Mrs.   widow; formerly nurse in the naval hospital, d. in hospital fire, 1819.[204]

KILWORTH, John   acting master attendant, 1773–4.[205]

KING, John   literate mason; entered yard from England, 1781; given an apprentice, 1783; occupied a yard house with two cords of wood and provisions for himself and apprentice, 1784–; gave evidence against Marshall, 1800, on whose private houses he worked.[206]

KINNEAR, Thomas Clifford   from Ireland; discharged house carpenter, when Coffin reduced staff, 1800; thereafter Halifax house builder who tendered to build the admiral's mansion, 1814;[207] m. 1837, Sarah Ann Brown.[208]

KITTOE, George   first acting master shipwright at Halifax, 1756.[209]

LAWLOR, Thomas   Boston emigrant to Halifax; yard painter, 1764–;[210] paint contractor to yard; d. Halifax, 1772, aged 52.

LAWLOR, William   s. of Thomas, contractor to paint yard buildings, ships' boats, and yard vessels;[211] m. Elizabeth Paget, 1747; maj. in Halifax County militia; departed for England, 1807; d. Southsea, 1822.

LEE, William   b. 1737; entered military service, 1758; expedition to Fort Ticonderoga and Fort Frontenac, 1758; entered yard 1764 as house carpenter; Colvill admired his "zeal, activity and abilities;"[212] foreman of house carpenters, 1768; gave evidence against Constable, 1775; contracted to erect naval hospital, 1782–3;[213] petitioned Nova Scotia government for payment of materials while superintending house and barn construction at North Farm for Hamond;[214] testified against Marshall, 1800; applied for pension "being now subject to many infirmities incident to old age" with twelve children, 1800;[215] would "starve me and family in this country" if he could not get pension equivalent to full salary;[216] took his last apprentice in 1809;[217] applied for increased pension, which rose from $70 to $84 a year, when he was very infirm and unlikely to live long, 1814;[218] d. 1819;[219] his wife, Mary, d. 1816, aged 72.[220]

LEWIS, George   first acting naval storekeeper, 1756.[221]

LIVIE, Titus   naval storekeeper, 1790–9; "deprived of his reason prior to his departure;"[222] sailed home via Quebec to convoy home the trade, 1799;[223] Anderson replaced him.[224]

LIVINGSTON, John   entered as storekeeper's 2d clerk, 1796; fell into a "state of mental derangement" and "many errors have been discovered in the balance book," 1808;[225] sought pension "as accumulated infirmities render him incapable of performing job;" Inglefield placed him on superannuated list;[226] d. Morristown, SC, 1821.[227]

LOADER, John   master shipwright, 1776–82; from England;[228] formerly carpenter of *Prince George*;[229] seized with a "fit of delirium ... incapable of doing his duty,"[230] sent home; falsely accused by Roger Hambrow of misconduct, the "result of malice and revenge;"[231] d. 1783.

MACKENZIE, John   b. c.1786; working foreman of carpenters; supervised building of admiral's house, 1814–19; bought land from the Tobin brothers in 1821;[232] d. 1853.[233]

MAJOR, Frederick   b. in 1767; his mother, Venetia, d. 15 Oct. 1768, and was buried in St Paul's cemetery; was raised in the Halifax poorhouse and apprenticed to tanner, John Albro;[234] m. secondly, 1819, Marion (1800–71), dau. of Benjamin Marshall, and widow of W.H. Burton of Chatham, New Brunswick; dau. Mary Ann, married s. of William Hughes, the yard's master shipwright; later formed partnership with s., Frederick J., to supply fresh beef to Halifax squadron;[235] bought land, Cow Bay 1818;[236] d. 1847 at Cow Bay.[237]

MANNING, Cornelius   b. 1762; entered yard as labourer, 1794; sawyer; partially lame in left arm injured while on duty, 1819; £15 pension recommended.[238]

MARSHALL, Benjamin b. 1770; s. of Elias Marshall; entered as apprentice to Provo Wallis;[239] shipwright; fled prosecution in 1800; arrested at Annapolis about to leave Nova Scotia; convicted of fraud and theft; m. Mary Ann (1773–1860), dau. of William Hughes; 8 children; d. 1825.

MARSHALL, Elias b. 1737; apprenticed to carpenter of *Grafton*, 1752; carpenter's mate, 1759; carpenter, 1761; foreman of Halifax yard, appointed by Spry, 1763–82;[240] Colvill thought him "very well qualified as a foreman;"[241] and Hurd "an active, stirring man;"[242] deeply implicated in Constable's frauds, 1775; Arbuthnot believed him "really valuable & does more real duty than any person" and asked Board "to overlook past errors;"[243] acting master shipwright, 1776;[244] acting joint-master shipwright with Thomas Johnson, 1782–3;[245] superseded by Wallis, 1783; master shipwright when Wallis retired, 1793–1805;[246] dismissed by Coffin for peculation and fraud, 1800;[247] defended himself in England;[248] Board thought his misdemeanours minor; "greatly afflicted with the gout and asthma and otherwise very infirm;"[249] superannuated, 1805;[250] m. Mary (1737–1813) in England; d. Halifax 1806, aged 68;[251] dau. Elizabeth d. 1792 aged 15; dau., Mary, m. 1803 Daniel Wood, widower; s. John made career in navy.

MARSHALL, Elias, Jr entered yard as his father's apprentice, 1785;[252] deranged; conspired to burn down yard buildings, 1799; d. 1801.

MARSHALL, John Houlton b. 1769, Halifax; eldest s. of Elias Marshall; entered navy as servant on sloop *Albany*, under Mowat; lieut 1794; cmdr. 1810; d. London, 1837; no issue; portrait by Field in Government House Library, Halifax.[253]

MARSHALL, Joseph contractor who built capstan house and the double-winged storehouse, 1759.

MARSHALL, Samuel b. 1776; 3d s. of Elias Marshall; entered yard as his father's apprentice, 1792;[254] shipwright; discharged for embezzlement of a stove, 1800;[255] m. Jane Pryor, 1799;[256] d. 1856; their third child, Elias, won the silver medal awarded by the National School c.1818; master of one of the vessels owned by his father-in-law; lost at sea when s., Edward, was an infant.[257]

MARSHALL, William b. 1767, Halifax; s. of Elias Marshall; entered Halifax yard as Loader's apprentice, 1780; d. 1791; buried from his father's house.[258]

MARTIN, William b. 1737; master sailmaker, 1781–92; appointed by Hughes upon Wynn's death;[259] d. 1794.

MARTYR, Charles replaced Eppes as agent to the naval hospital, 1816–19.[260]

MATTHEWS, Christopher literate mason; b. 1759; entered yard from

England, 1783; on establishment, 1785; leading man of masons, 1804–19; discharged, 1819; unemployed with wife and six children; without savings "the price of every necessary article of living having been for many years very extravagant;" he once went on leave to England, and left at the Board of Admiralty his signed certificates of service under Duncan and Inglefield; co-signed greetings upon Wodehouse's departure; applied for pension.[261]

MCEVOY, John   naval hospital dispenser at £80, 1783–99;[262] salary raised to £100, 1795.[263]

MCEWEN, John   entered yard as caulker-shipwright, 1794; later cabin keeper; granted £24 pension, 1819.[264]

MCKAY, Roderick   *Hector* settler at Pictou, 1773; yard foreman of smiths, 1783–96;[265] appointed by Duncan, 1783;[266] dismissed for neglect of duty, 1796; replaced by Brush; retired to Pictou; d. 22 Nov. 1829.[267]

MCKIE, James   literate; yard apprentice to smith; smith, 1805–19; petitioned for pension; father had served twenty years as a mason and died in the service; m.; two children; unemployed.[268]

MCQUEEN, Duncan   entered as house carpenter, 1798; granted £15 pension, 1819.[269]

MERRICK, John   contractor to supply paint, oil, varnish and turpentine, and to paint yard buildings and warships, 1806–15; supplied products "of unexceptionable quality;"[270] built Province House, Halifax.

MUHLIG, Frederick   yard shipwright; cautioned for being three days' absent without adequate reason, 1810;[271] granted £24 pension, 1815;[272] d. 1835, aged 62;[273] dau., Maria Matilda, m. 1838.

MUHLIG, Thomas   b. c.1762; entered as apprentice, 1785; shipwright-caulker, 1792–1819; £20 pension, 1819;[274] d. 1842, aged 80;[275] wife, Sarah, d. 1836, aged 66.

MURPHY, Matthew   entered yard as labourer, 1770; worn out and discharged in 1785 into *Pembroke* hulk.

NORWOOD, Edward   b. 1760; literate; entered yard, 1781 as labourer and watchman; his father also served "a great number of years;"[276] gave evidence against Elias Marshall, 1800;[277] rheumatism rendered him unfit, 1814; sought pension, 1815; d. Halifax, 1817.[278]

NORWOOD, Edward   entered as apprentice, 1810; shipwright, 1817.[279]

NORWOOD, William   b. 1746; yard stewart, 1771–4,[280] possibly Cork emigrant, s. of Sarah Norwood (1723–1787); d. 1795.

NORWOOD, William II   entered as apprentice to Winckworth Norwood II, 1805.[281]

NORWOOD, Winckworth   master attendant's clerk, 1780–90;[282] leased decked ship *Stanislaus* to navy as a prison ship, 1781–3.[283]

NORWOOD, Winckworth II b. c.1766; shipwright's apprentice, 1785–92; helped to refloat *Tartar* at Bermuda; leading man of shipwrights; suffered "a violent contusion of the right leg and ankle" on board *Hydra* when he fell from the poop deck, 1817; recovered "with a lameness of the ankle;" petitioned for a pension, 1819; recommended by Wodehouse as a man of zeal and ability "when the state of his health would admit of it;"[284] d. 30 Aug. 1821;[285] 3d. s. Winckworth, d. 19 June 1840, aged 46;[286] s. William d. in 1843 in Halifax, aged 50, leaving a widow and six children.[287]

OBEN, Thomas formerly storekeeper at Corsica; travelled from Corsica to Leghorn, Genoa, and Naples "to obtain supplies"[288] for the Mediterranean fleet; storekeeper Halifax yard, 1800;[289] fell into "a damaged state of mind," 1801;[290] Inglefield noted that "when in health was always considered to be a very honest, diligent, and capable man."[291]

O'BRIEN, Michael naval hospital dispenser sent from England to replace Hume, 1814–19.[292]

PARKER, Sacker b. Virginia; loyalist refugee; entered 29 May 1785; yard sawyer and wheelwright; £24 pension, 1819;[293] d. Chatham, NB, 1841.[294]

PARMINTER, John Duncan's 1st clerk, 1783–d.; prepared drawings of yard buildings, 1792; d. Oct. 1795, in Halifax, aged 33; widow, Sophia.[295]

PARRY, John carpenter of *Leander*; appointed foreman of shipwrights by Mitchell;[296] sent to Bermuda to superintend vessels building for government by Messrs Godrich, 1806;[297] "grossly insulted and abused" Atkinson, 1809;[298] foreman of the yard, 1811; served on three-man board appointed by the vice-admiralty court in case of slave schooner *Severn*;[299] acting master shipwright, 1813; signatory of joint letter by artificers and labours upon Wodehouse's departure.

PATTERSON, George entered navy, 1777; off the island of Texel volunteered to go in a Dutch fishing boat to survey the "channel & reconnoitre the Dutch fleet, for which he received Lord Duncan's fullest approbation;" master in *Bath* at Camperdown; acting master attendant Yarmouth yard, 1800–04; Halifax yard master attendant, 1804–05; praised for his "indefatigable attention to his duty and zeal for the service;"[300] retired to England and sought pension, 1805, owing to old wounds in "my neck and arm & the general ill-state of my health, the severity of the climate at Halifax keeps me in a constant pain & incapacity."[301]

PEAKE, Philip foreman of shipwrights, 1759–;[302] s. William, entered as master attendant's apprentice, 1761–3; s. Philip, also a shipwright, served in yard from July 1767; undertook survey of woods at Lunenburg.

PHILLIPS, John had been in Halifax since 1758; MHA, 1770–85; surgeon at naval hospital, 1775–6, and to Loyal Nova Scotian Volunteers.[303]

PIERPONT, Joseph New England contractor who blasted rocks to excavate mastpond, 1759; built boathouse slip and the south pier, 1759; d. 1772 "after a long and lingering sickness;"[304] will mentions a brother, Robert, in Boston, and a sister; widow, Mary, sold a Halifax waterfront lot to Abraham Constable, 1773.[305]

PLAW, John b. London 1745; pres. Incorporated Society of Artists, 1790; established builder and architect in Westminster; circular villa on Belle Isle in Lake Windermere was his most ambitious surviving structure, 1774; in Southampton to design and build barracks, 1795; published *Rural Architecture* (1785), *Ferme ornée* (1787) and *Sketches for country houses, villas and rural dwellings* (1800); emigrated to Prince Edward Island, 1807; prepared plans for the admiral's house, 1813; d. Charlottetown, 1820.[306]

PROUD, James clerk in naval hospital @ £60, 1796–1802.[307]

PROWSE, Richard master attendant, 1773–80.[308]

RAY, George pilot on transport *Burton*, 1797–8; ordered to Little Harbour, east of Halifax to assist in bringing her to port; blown off coast to West Indies; taken by the French; retaken and carried into Montserrat.[309]

READ, Thomas master attendant, 1787–99; superannuated and retired to England, 1799.[310]

REGAN, Timothy entered yard as labourer, 1769; worn out and discharged into *Pembroke* hulk, 1785.[311]

RHODES, H. Melchior b. 1779; literate; entered as apprentice sailmaker, 1795, on establishment, 1802; discharged, 1819; sought pension, had a wife, five children "whom he has with the greatest difficulty supported through the last winter in consequence of the depression of trade;" from his "former savings and economy, undertook and partly completed a small house, but in consequence of the great fall in the value of property here and the incumbrances upon his, from being borrowed money upon mortgage, he is left quite destitute and distressed;"[312] Atkinson described him as "sober, diligent and obedient," 1809; d. 1841; 3d dau., Mary Martha, m. 1836.[313]

RHODES, Jasper b. c.1775; literate shipwright apprentice, 1792; on establishment, 1797–1818; ill-health forced his resignation, threatened with a rupture of his left groin, when attempting to lift an object, suffered from severe pain in the breast and across his loins;[314] recommended for superannuation, 1820;[315] d. 1840; eldest dau., Louisa Catherine, m. 1832.[316]

RHODES, John sailmaker; sold canvas with the king's mark "embezzled by him out of the Sail loft," 1817;[317] discharged and pay mulcted.

RIDGEWAY, David b. 1754; served in Halifax yard on extra list, 1794–9;[318] boatswain on *Pembroke* sheer hulk to 1799; yard boatswain, 1800–d.; retained by Mitchell when ordered home, 1802;[319] secured stores from storeship *Will-*

iam, Canso 1808;[320] house built for him between yard and hospital, 1813; co-signer of joint letter to Wodehouse upon his departure;[321] d. 1819; m. Mary (1762–1832);[322] 2d dau., Mary Ann, widow of Mr Thomas Robinson, RN, m. 1814, secondly a lieut of 98th Foot; 3d dau., Elizabeth, m. 1821; dau., Maria, m. James Irwin, 1831.

RITCHIE, James   store porter to Halifax yard; clerk at £78 a year with another £42 for allowance in lieu of provisions, 1804; paid as issuing clerk with pay of storekeeper's 2d clerk, with house rent and fuel as "all the necessaries of life have risen to near double the price at which they might have been obtained a few years back;"[323] supported by Inglefield and Dawes, who found him "diligent and faithful;" paid £92 10s., with allowance of 15s. sterling per day, to oversee shipping on board transports, materials collected at St Andrews by Gordon Adams on his contract for erecting the three buildings for the Bermuda naval hospital;[324] applied for pension.

ROWLANDS, David   surgeon of the Halifax naval hospital, 1812–19; dismissed Hume; abjectly apologized for slandering Wodehouse.[325]

RUTHERFORD, George   first surgeon at Halifax naval hospital; surgeon of prison hospital, New York; went on leave to England in October 1783 where he d. shortly thereafter.

SELLY, Seth   pilot on *Nymphe*, 1813–14; described as "an exception to the generality of pilots upon the Nova Scotia station. Very few of them, I am sorry to say, have little if any knowledge of the coast. He has a general knowledge of the American coast and a perfect knowledge from Cape Cod through the different channels between the shoals of Nantucket and all the adjacent harbours, from Mount Desert and Cape Cable up the Bay of Fundy and all its harbours, as well as the Gut of Canso and the Gulf and River St Lawrence to Quebec."[326]

SELLON, Edward   yard shipwright; sent to Canso to help get storeship *William* off the rocks, 1808.

SELLON, Edward II   b. 1788; entered yard as a temporary clerk at £70, 1808; £90 as extra clerk, 1809; assistant clerk upon Sherlock's promotion;[327] store porter; petitioned for preferment, 1819; retired as chief clerk quartermaster general's office; m. 1817, Susan Dousley;[328] d. 1875.[329]

SELLON, Samuel   b. c.1765; leading man of shipwrights; volunteered to refloat *Tartar*, Bermuda, 1805; at St Andrews to survey wood purchased to build three framed structures for Bermuda naval hospital, 1814–5;[330] co-signer of joint letter to Wodehouse on his departure;[331] for sixty-five years a "pious member of the Wesleyan Church;"[332] d. 1851, aged 86, at Coffin Island, near Liverpool; wife, Charity (1767–1839), also d. there.

SELLON, Thomas   yard cabin keeper; invalided at £20 a year "on account of his long servitude," 1796.[333]

SHERLOCK, George entered as storekeeper's extra clerk, 1805; applied for pay raise, 1809; support of Dawes and Inglefield;[334] storekeeper's 2d clerk, when Livingston given pension, 1811;[335] d. 1834;[336] two sons, aged 18 and 16 d. en route from Havana to Liverpool in different vessels, Aug. 1842; one was on ship owned by Sherlock's son-in-law, Wentworth Kenny, who m. his dau., Louisa Ann, 1840; his 2d dau., Sarah Lavinia, m. in Yarmouth, 1835.

SHEY, Robert entered Halifax yard, 1767; discharged, 1800; sought relief "being far advanced in life and in indigent circumstances makes him labour under many difficulties at this inclement season, with a family to support."

SIMMONS, John b. c.1746; Pennsylvania loyalist; entered naval service to repair sails in *Roebuck* under Hamond and sloop *Delaware*, 1776–7, "the revolutionists being greatly exasperated at him for it;"[337] when Philadelphia was evacuated, entered the New York yard as sailmaker, 1777; evacuated with family to Halifax yard, 1783; "confined to his bed with an inflammation in his leg," from an accident in the sail loft, a few months earlier, 1805; not yet sixty, he had lost nearly all his family by sickness or accident, who might have supported him; sought pension, 1805; supported by Hughes and Inglefield; "during a long service in this yard as a sailmaker behaved himself with diligence and sobriety, and always bore a good character, and that his present illness is partly owing to an injury he received at his duty."

SMITH, Peter b. 1779; blockmaker and shipwright; volunteered to help refloat *Tartar* at Bermuda, 1805; described by Dawes as "very industrious," with privilege of "taking chips from the yard," 1809; requested allowance in lieu of chips, 1811;[338] "still capable of earning his livelihood," recommended for £15, the lowest rate for a shipwright.[339]

STANSER, Rev. Dr Robert b. 1760; formerly of St John's College, Cambridge; St Paul's, Halifax, 1796–1816; first chaplain to naval hospital, 1810–16;[340] resigned when nominated as second bishop of Nova Scotia, @ £1,000 a year;[341] wife, Mary, d. 1815; retired, 1825; d. 1828 in Hampton.[342]

STEWART, Alexander b. 1751; served in New York naval yard, 1777–83; evacuated to Nova Scotia, 1783; entered Halifax yard as watchman, 1795; injured while on duty, which confined him to his bed, 1814; a wife and family to support;[343] £15 pension, 1815.[344]

STOREY, James b. 1754; illiterate; first served on *Eagle*, under Duncan, 1777; lost the use of two fingers; entered yard as watchman, 1784; invalid list, 1813–15;[345] discharged, 1819; without savings owing to illness and to "extravagant prices of all necessaries;" the late "calamitous reduction" left him destitute; £15 pension, 1815.[346]

SUTTON, Thomas entered 1799 as shipwright and boat builder; pension £20.[347]

THOMAS, George reputed illegitimate s. of Admiral Sir Hugh Palliser; Halifax yard naval storekeeper, 1780–90; in 1783 went to Fort Howe to collect debts owed the yard;[348] went home to clear his accounts and name, 1784–5;[349] exonerated in dispute with Douglas; criticized by NB for deficient reports, 1787–8; one of forty-five proprietors of 9,000 acres of land between Birch Cove and the head of St Margaret's Bay, given the name Hamonds Plains after Sir Andrew Snape Hamond.[350]

THOMSON, Andrew Scottish-born, Halifax merchant; purveyor to Halifax naval hospital, 1778–83 for POWs and sqdn, appointed by Collier;[351] pres., North British Society, 1782; d. Halifax, 1795, leaving a widow, Maria.[352]

TURPEL, John literate smith; discharged 1784;[353] applied to re-enter when unemployed, Apr. 1785.[354]

WALLIS, Provo b. 1735; master shipwright New York yard, 1776–83, appointed by Howe; evacuated to Halifax, 1783–92; appointed by Digby "as a reward for his services here," 1783;[366] retired to England to be "examined for superannuation," 1792;[356] d. 1797.[357]

WALLIS, Provo Featherstone s. of Provo Wallis; carpenter's servant *Eagle*, 1776–8; labourer in New York yard, 1778–83; clerk to master shipwright, New York yard, 1783; clerk to the master shipwright, Halifax yard, 1784–95; commissioner's 1st clerk upon Parminter's death;[359] m. 1788, Elizabeth, dau. of William Lawlor;[359] superintendent Halifax naval cooperage;[360] returned to England to recover his health;[361] sought pension when reluctant to return to Halifax, and after failing to secure an appointment in England, 1817; of Heavitree, near Exeter;[362] portrait Art Gallery of Nova Scotia.

WERLING, John entered yard as labourer, 1793–9; watchman 1799–1803; foreman of labourers, 1805;[363] discharged 1815; £15 pension, 1815.[364]

WILLIAMS, Richard naval storekeeper when Gerrish d. 1773; "terribly afflicted with the rheumatism & other disorders occasioned by this severe & unwholesome clime as to render me incapable of doing my duty;"[365] returned to England to recover his health, 1779.[366]

WILLISON, Thomas acting master shipwright, 1770–1;[367] superseded by Constable.

WILLS, Thomas entered army "early in life;" served twenty-six years in the 62d and 70th Foot Regts., including ten years in Caribbean; invalided from army, 1783; entered as slater Halifax yard until 1789; labourer 1789–1800; discharged by Coffin, 1800; with "large family to support in very indigent circumstances," sought "relief as will prevent his family from suffering in this inclement season."[368]

WODEHOUSE, Hon. Philip younger s. of John, 1st baron Wodehouse; b. 1773; of Kimberley, Wymondham, Norfolk; capt. 1796; commissioner at Halifax, 1812–19;[369] rear admiral 1819; vice admiral 1830; m. 7 May 1814,

Mary Hay, dau. of Charles Cameron, gov. of Bahamas Islands; showered with good wishes upon his departure;[370] s. Edwin, b. Halifax 1817, d. 1838.

WOOD, Thomas   replaced Provo F. Wallis as master shipwright's clerk, 1795;[371] discharged by Coffin, 1800; accompanied Elias Marshall, his father-in-law, to England to clear accounts.[372]

WRIGHT, Benjamin   apprentice to sailmaker; when master sailmaker died, applied to take Gardner's place, 1803.[373]

WYNN, William   first master sailmaker at Halifax yard, 1771–81;[374] succeeded by William Martin.[375]

Bibliography

MANUSCRIPT SOURCES

CANADA:
National Archives, Ottawa
Philip Wodehouse fonds: 3 letterbooks, I, 1812–14; II, 1813–15; III, 1813–16.

New Brunswick Museum, St John
White papers, Shelf 5, A3.

Nova Scotia Archives and Records Management, Halifax
Naval yard: MG13/1–6, 9.1–3: Duncan letterbook, 1782–7; 1784–9; storekeeper's letterbook, 13 Feb. 1801–21 July 1803; out-letterbook, 1805; out-letters from Halifax Yard, 1809; letterbook, 1794–1800; commissioner's orderbook, 1803–05, 1804–05; commissioner's orderbook to master shipwright, 1813–9.

GREAT BRITAIN:
National Maritime Museum, Greenwich
Collier papers.
In-letters (bound) to Navy Board from Admiralty: 1758, 1767, 1776–7, 1779. ADM/A/2482, 2601, 2705, 2722, 2738; 1757–1780, 1800–09. ADM/B/155–235.
In-letters (unbound) from Navy Board to Admiralty: 1780–1819. ADM/BP, 66 vols.
Halifax Dockyard Records, 1783–1819: HAL/–, [microfilm at NSARM and NA].

Public Record Office, Kew
Admirals' despatches, 1745–1819. ADM1/480–511, [microfilm at NA].
Captains' letters, 1745–1820. ADM1/–, [microfilm at NA].
Letters from foreign yards, 1809–39. ADM1/3441, 3443.
Admiralty out-letters to Navy Board, 1757–8. ADM2/222.
Admiralty minutes, 1757–9. ADM3/65–6.
Naval storekeeper's accounts, Halifax 1757–1819, New York, 1775–83. ADM17/150–66, 220, [microfilm at NA].
Halifax yard musterbooks, 1757–1809. ADM36/15490, 17229; ADM37/8602–7, [microfilm at NA].

Halifax yard paybooks, 1761–1819. ADM42/2147–78, 2200–02, [microfilm at NA].
Navy Board in-letters, 1757–1820. ADM106/1123–1657.
Navy Board to Admiralty, 1758–9, 1766–8, 1782–4. ADM106/1021, 1038, 2027–9, 2184–5, 2189, 2191, 2210–11.
Orders to Respective Officers, 1770–96. ADM106/2470–3, 3174, 3218–22, 3364.
Halifax yard photographs, c.1870, c.1880. ADM195/48–9.
CO42/51.
CUST3/49–71, CUST16/1, CUST17/1–8.
MPI, 116, MPI, 284.

UNITED STATES:
The Pierpont Morgan Library, New York City
Gilder Lehrman collection. Joshua Mauger papers.

University of Virginia, Charlottesville
Sir Andrew Snape Hamond papers, vols 7–9, 1781–3, [microfilm at NSARM].

PRINTED SOURCES

Albion, Robert Greenhalgh. *Forests and Sea Power: The Timber Problem of the Royal Navy, 1652–1862*. Cambridge, MA: Harvard University Press, 1926.
Arnell, Jack C. *The Bermuda Maritime Museum and the Royal Naval Dockyard, Bermuda*. Hamilton: Bermuda Press, 1979.
Barnes, G.R., and J.H. Owen, eds. *The Private Papers of John, Earl of Sandwich, First Lord of the Admiralty 1771–1782*. 4 vols. London: Navy Records Society, 1932–8.
Baugh, Daniel A. *British Naval Administration in the Age of Walpole*. Princeton: Princeton University Press, 1965.
——. "Sir Samuel Hood: Superior Subordinate." In *George Washington's Opponents: British Generals and Admirals in the American Revolution*, ed. George A. Billias. New York: Morrow, 1969.
Bienkowski, Lee. *Admirals in the Age of Nelson*. Annapolis, MD: Naval Institute Press, 2003.
Caldwell, John, and Oswaldo Rodriguez Roque. *American Paintings in the Metropolitan Museum of Art: A Catalogue of Artists Born by 1815*. Vol 1. New York and Princeton: Metropolitan Museum of Art and Princeton University Press, 1994.
Candow, James E. "Sir Isaac Coffin and the Halifax Dockyard 'Scandal.'" *Nova Scotia Historical Review* 1 (1981): 50–63.

Coad, Jonathan G. *The Royal Dockyards, 1690–1850: Architecture and Engineering Works of the Sailing Navy.* Aldershot: Scolar Press, 1989.

——. "The Building of the Commissioner's House, Bermuda Dockyard." *Post-Medieval Archaeology* 17 (1984): 163–76.

——. *Historic Architecture of the Royal Navy: An Introduction.* London: Gollancz, 1983.

Collier, Sir George. *A Detail of Some Particular Services Performed in America, during the Years 1776, 1777, 1778, and 1779 by Commodore Sir George Collier ... compiled from Journals & Original Papers by G.S. Rainier.* New York: 1833.

Crewe, Duncan. *Yellow Jack and the Worm: British Naval Administration in the West Indies, 1739–1748.* Liverpool: Liverpool University Press, 1993.

Crimmin, Patricia. "John Jervis, Earl of St Vincent, 1735–1823." In *Precursors of Nelson: British Admirals of the Eighteenth Century*, ed. Peter Le Fevre & Richard Harding, 325–52. London: Chatham, 2000.

Darnton, Robert. *The Great Cat Massacre and Other Episodes in French Cultural History.* New York: Basic Books, 1984.

Dickson, P.G.M. *The Financial Revolution in England: A Study in the Development of Public Credit 1689–1756.* London: Macmillan, 1967.

Douglas, W.A.B. "Nova Scotia and the Royal Navy, 1713–1766." PhD thesis. Queen's University, 1973.

Duffy, Michael. "Samuel Hood, First Viscount Hood, 1724–1816." In *Precursors of Nelson: British Admirals of the Eighteenth Century*, ed. Peter Le Fevre & Richard Harding, 249–278. London: Chatham, 2000.

Dunlop, Allan C. "John Burbidge, 1718–1812." *Dictionary of Canadian Biography.* Toronto: Toronto University Press, 1983, 5: 121–2.

Faibisy, John Dewar. "Privateering and Piracy: The Effects of American Privateering upon Nova Scotia during the American Revolution." PhD diss. University of Massachusetts, 1972.

Falconer, William. *An Universal Dictionary of the Marine: Or, a Copious Explanation of the Technical Terms and Phrases Employed in the Construction, Equipment, Furniture, Machinery, Movements, and Military Operations of a Ship ...* London: Cadell, 1780.

Gardiner, Robert, ed. *Navies and the American Revolution 1775–1783.* London: Chatham Publishing, 1996.

Godfrey, W.G. "James Glenie, 1750–1817." *Dictionary of Canadian Biography.* Toronto: Toronto University Press, 1983, 5: 347–58.

Guthrie, William. *A System of Modern Geography.* 7th ed. London: 1811.

Gwyn, Julian. *Frigates and Foremasts: The North American Squadron in Nova Scotia Waters, 1745–1815.* Vancouver: University of British Columbia Press, 2003.

———. *Excessive Expectations: Maritime Commerce & the Economic Development of Nova Scotia, 1740–1870*. Montreal: McGill-Queen's University Press, 1998.
———. *The Enterprising Admiral: The Personal Fortune of Admiral Sir Peter Warren*. Montreal: McGill-Queen's University Press, 1974.
———, ed. *The Royal Navy and North America: The Warren Papers, 1736–1752*. Vol. 118. London: Navy Records Society, 1973.
———. "The Halifax Naval Yard and Mast Contractors, 1775–1815." *Northern Mariner–Le Marin du nord* 11 (2001): 1–25.
———. "The Culture of Work in the Halifax Naval Yard before 1820." *Journal of the Royal Nova Scotia Historical Society* 2 (1999): 118–43.
———. "Capitalists, Merchants and Manufacturers: The Tangled Affairs of John Avery, James Creighton, John Albro and Joseph Fairbanks." In *Intimate Relations: Family and Community in Planter Nova Scotia 1759–1800*, ed. Margaret Conrad, 190–212. Fredericton: Acadiensis Press, 1995.
———. "Nova Scotia's Shipbuilding and Timber Trade: David Crichton of Pictou and His Liverpool Associates, 1821–1840." *Canadian Papers in Business History* 2 (1993): 211–33.
———. "Economic Fluctuations in Wartime Nova Scotia, 1755–1815." In *Making Adjustments: Change and Continuity in Planter Nova Scotia 1759–1800*, ed. Margaret Conrad, 60–88. Fredericton: Acadiensis Press, 1991.
———. "Shipbuilding for the Royal Navy in Colonial New England." *American Neptune* 48 (1988): 22–30.
———. "Financial Revolution in Massachusetts: Public Credit and Taxation, 1692–1774." *Histoire sociale–Social History* 17 (1984): 59–77.
———. "British Government Spending and the North American Colonies, 1740–1775." *Journal of Imperial and Commonwealth History* 8 (1980): 74–84.
———. "The Impact of British Military Spending on the Colonial American Money Markets, 1760–1783." *Historical Papers* (1980): 77–99.
———. "Private Credit in Colonial New York: The Warren Portfolio, 1745–1795." *New York History* 54 (1973): 268–93.
———. "Joshua Mauger: The Man and the Myth." Paper read before the Royal Nova Scotia Historical Society, 2003.
Haas, J.M. *A Management Odyssey: The Royal Dockyards, 1714–1914*. Lanham, MD: University Press of America, 1994.
Haliburton, Thomas Chandler. *The Old Judge; or, Life in a Colony*. Ottawa, ON: Tecumseh Press, 1978.
Jones, E. Alfred. *The Loyalists of Massachusetts*. London, ON: Saint Catherine Press, 1930.
Knox, Ronald, tr. *The Autobiography of a Saint: Thérèse of Lisieux*. London: Collins, 1958.

Knight, R.J.B., ed. *Portsmouth Dockyard Papers 1774–1783: The American War: A Calendar.* Portsmouth: Portsmouth Record Series, 1987.

———. "The Royal Dockyards in England at the Time of the War of American Independence." PhD thesis. University of London, 1972.

Latham, Bryan. *Timber.* London: Harrap, 1957.

Laughton J.K., and J.Y.F. Sullivan, eds. *Journal of Rear-Admiral Bartholomew James, 1752–1828.* Vol. 6. London: Navy Records Society, 1896.

Lavery, Brian. *Nelson's Navy: The Ships, Men and Organization 1793–1815.* London: Conway Maritime Press, 1989.

Lockwood, Anthony A. *A Brief Description of Nova Scotia with plates of the principal harbors including a particular account of the Island of Grand Manan.* London: Hayden, 1818.

Lower, Arthur R.M. *Great Britain's Woodyard: British America and the Timber Trade, 1763–1867.* Montreal: McGill-Queen's University Press, 1973.

MacDougall, Philip. *The Chatham Dockyard Story.* Rev. ed. Rainham, Kent: Meresborough Books, 1987.

———. *Royal Dockyards.* Newton Abbott, Devon: David & Charles, 1982.

Malone, Joseph J. *Pine Trees and Politics: The Naval Stores and Forest Policy in Colonial New England 1691–1775.* Seattle: University of Washington Press, 1964.

Marble, Allan Everett. *Surgeons, Smallpox, and the Poor: A History of Medicine and Social Conditions in Nova Scotia, 1749–1799.* Montreal: McGill-Queen's University Press, 1993.

Morriss, Roger. *The Royal Dockyards during the Revolutionary and Napoleonic Wars.* Leicester: Leicester University Press, 1983.

Nova Scotia. *Journals and Proceedings of the House of Assembly for 1838.* Halifax, 1839.

Pool, Bernard. *Navy Board Contracts 1600–1832: Contract Administration under the Navy Board.* London: Longmans Green, 1966.

Raymond, Brent. *Tracing the Built Form of HMC Dockyard.* Curatorial Report 88. Halifax: Maritime Museum of the Atlantic, 1999.

Reynolds, Hezekiah. *Directions for House and Ship Painting Shewing in a Plain and Concise Manner The Best Method of Preparing, Mixing and Laying the Various Colours Now in Use, Designed for the Use of Learners.* New Haven, 1812. Reprint ed. Worcester, MA: American Antiquarian Society, 1978.

Richmond, H.W., ed. *Private Papers of George, Second Earl Spencer: First Lord of the Admiralty,* 4 vols. Vol. 59. London: Navy Records Society, 1924.

Roberts, David. "John Mure, d.1823." *Dictionary of Canadian Biography.* Toronto: University of Toronto Press, 1987, 6: 531–5.

Rodger, N.A.M. *The Insatiable Earl: A Life of John Montagu, Fourth Earl of Sandwich 1718–1792.* New York: Norton, 1993.

―――. *The Wooden World: An Anatomy of the Georgian Navy.* Annapolis, MD: Naval Institute Press, 1986.
Roger, Irene L. "John Plaw, 1746–1820." *Dictionary of Canadian Biography.* Toronto: University of Toronto Press, 1983, 5: 678–80.
Smith, Marilyn Gurney. *The King's Yard: An Illustrated History of the Halifax Dockyard.* Halifax: Nimbus, 1985.
Smith, T. Watson. "The Slave in Canada." *Collections of the Nova Scotia Historical Society* 10 (1898): 12.
Spray, W.A. "James Fraser, c.1760–1822." *Dictionary of Canadian Biography.* Toronto: University of Toronto Press, 1987, 6: 262–3.
―――. "William Davidson, c.1740–1790." *Dictionary of Canadian Biography.* Toronto: University of Toronto Press, 1979, 4: 195–7.
Stayner, Charles. "The Blackadar Family of Halifax." *Nova Scotia Historical Review* 1 (1981): 67–72.
Sutherland, David. "William Forsyth, c.1749–1814." *Dictionary of Canadian Biography.* Toronto: University of Toronto Press, 1983, 5: 327–9.
Suthern, Victor. *To Go Upon Discovery: James Cook and Canada, from 1758 to 1779.* Toronto: Dundurn Press, 2000.
Syrett, David. *The Royal Navy in American Waters, 1775–1783.* Aldershot: Scolar Press, 1989.
Uniacke, Richard John, ed. *The Statutes at Large, passed in the Several Assemblies held in His Majesty's Province of Nova Scotia from ... 1758, to ... 1804.* Halifax, 1805.
Wilson, David. "Government Dock-Yard Workers in Portsmouth, 1793–1815." PhD thesis. University of Warwick, 1975.
Winters, B.A. *A Brief History of the Dockyard Terrace.* Halifax: privately printed, 1989.
Wynn, Graeme. *Timber Colony: A Historical Geography of Early Nineteenth Century New Brunswick.* Toronto: University of Toronto Press, 1981.
Yorke, Lois K. "Duncan Clifford, 1759–1808." *Dictionary of Canadian Biography.* Toronto: University of Toronto Press, 1983, 5: 187–8.

Index

Acadiens, 120, 217, 228
Adams, Alfred Gordon, 146, 195, 346
admiral's house, 28, 41, 43, 54–60, 103, 222, 260 n. 94, 263 n. 131, 341; earlier accommodation, 30, 44, 54, 260 n. 81, 259 n. 93; gardens, 60; illus., plans, 260 n. 88, 260 n. 94, 345; stone for, 57, 260–1 n. 101–03, 262 n. 118; walls, 60
Admiralty Board, 5, 6, 7, 8, 10–11, 13, 15, 18, 19, 20, 83, 92, 112, 175, 209, 217; approves new yard buildings, 31; and admiral's house, 55; and Bermuda, 219–20; and deserters, 166; First Lord of, 71, 246 n. 14, 337; impressment, 182; and masts, 177, 295 n. 30; neglect by, 42, 125, 127, 129–30, 132–3, 135; and rum ration ashore, 103; specie shipments, 210 structure, 66; and wage rates, 109
Afro-Nova Scotians, 120–1, 229; to clean necessaries, 47, 225; refugees, 246 n. 14; sailors, 298 n. 80
Albro, John, 47, 342
Albro, Samuel, 260–1 n. 103
Anderson, Alexander, 84, 92, 94, 96, 100, 233, 268 n. 115, 269 n. 123, 270–1 n. 165, 341; career, 90–1, 329; dispute with Inglefield, 85–7
Andrew, George, 174, 175, 233, 329, 338
Andrews, George, 48, 253 n. 108
Antigua, x, xii, 80, 97, 134, 177, 179, 181, 182, 183, 185, 186, 188, 194, 199, 219, 336. *See also* English Harbour
apprentices, 101, 102, 107, 146, 225, 229–30, 274 nn. 42, 53, 298 n. 82, 315 n. 228, 331, 334, 341, 342, 343, 344, 345, 349; in English yards, 107; wages, 275–6 n. 69
Arbuthnot, Marriot, 20–1, 78, 83, 99, 169, 173, 174, 233, 244 n. 102, 332, 336; career, 67, 69, 329–30

artificers, xii, 7, 10–11, 24, 26, 28, 38, 40, 43, 99, 101, 102, 103, 110, 113, 120–1, 126, 129–30, 142, 146, 173, 225; apprentices of, 107; for Bermuda yard, 146; blockmakers, 106, 229, 244 nn. 103, 105, 277 n. 98, 331, 337, 347; caulkers, 6, 10, 17, 20, 21, 22, 25, 26, 77, 102, 107, 110–11, 130, 222, 229, 324–5, 333; English, 20–1, 106, 107, 111, 244 n. 103, 273–4 nn. 36–7, 330, 338, 341; establishment, 229; invalids, 116–17; masons, xv, 15, 16, 35, 40, 57, 58, 59, 72, 82, 107, 110, 126, 229, 254 n. 129–30, 257 n. 51, 341; from New England, 10, 106, 108, 118; military, 103, 138; from Nova Scotia, 99, 107, 111, 112, 130, 138, 148; petition, 111, 275 n. 59; sailmakers, 10, 22, 24, 77, 101, 102, 103, 107, 110, 229, 265 n. 44, 271 n. 3, 275 nn. 64, 66, 277 n. 98, 331, 335, 340, 343, 345, 346, 347, 349; sawyers, 82, 107, 110, 116, 251 n. 74, 260–1 n. 103, 261–2 n. 113, 272 n. 15, 274 n. 53, 275 nn. 64, 66, 277 n. 98, 332–3; shipwrights, 6, 10, 12, 17, 20–1, 22, 24, 25, 26, 38, 77, 78, 82, 84, 91, 102, 104–5, 106, 110–11, 114, 115–16, 118, 119, 121, 130–1, 145, 172, 174, 222, 225, 229, 244 n. 103; smiths, 20, 22, 25, 77, 82, 107, 110, 117, 229, 331; from warships, 129, 131. *See also* carpenters, copperers
Atkinson, Thomas, 78, 96, 233, 330, 346

Baltic, 161, 169–70, 189, 191, 193, 198, 199–200, 223, 300 n. 112
Barbados, xii, 125; masts for, 134, 183, 184, 186
battle, of Fort William Henry (1755), 333; of Fort Ticonderoga (1758), 341; of Fort Frontenac (1758), 341; of Lexington (1775), 171; off the Chesapeake (1781),

Index 355

68; of Yorktown (1781), 68; of the Saints (1782), 68
Belcher, Andrew, 56, 154, 188–9
Berkeley, George Cranfield, 34, 35, 72, 129–30, 183, 209–10, 251 n. 74, 336; and admiral's house, 53–4; and hospital, 45; and sea fencibles, 105
Bermuda, 55, 59, 104, 129, 133, 146, 153, 154, 192, 194, 195, 199, 221, 224, 225, 271 n. 4, 273 n. 36, 279 n. 27, 285–6 n. 135, 289 n. 34, 334, 344, 347; limestone, 136; masts for, 129, 134, 184; Murray's Anchorage, 139, 145, 220; survey, 145; warships built at, 124. *See also* Ireland Island
Blackadar family, Charles, 91, 96, 330; Christopher, 115, 330; Hugh, 115, 330; James, 107, 331
Board of Ordnance, 24, 213
Boscawen, Edward, 6, 7, 67, 240 n. 28, 329
Boston, 4, 18, 67, 68, 78, 84, 108, 118, 158–9, 180, 195, 206, 247 n. 21, 333, 341; careening at, 5, 239 n. 7; money market, 202, 226, 229, 304 n. 16; Tea Party, 19; as temporary naval base, 1774–6, 19, 23
boys, 40, 95
British Isles, 169, 226; Cork, 344; Dundee, 334; Great Britain, 112, 161, 167, 201, 202, 204, 217, 294 n. 14, 300 n. 112; Glasgow, 158; Greenock, 180, 184, 227, 335; Ireland, 341; Liverpool, 200, 335; Wales, 338. *See also* England
British North America, xiii, 121, 126, 134, 135, 137, 175, 181, 189, 200
Brush, John, 117, 331
Burbidge, John, 8, 331
buoys, 80, 126, 137, 222, 272 n. 9
Byron, John, 172, 336

Canada, 162; Ottawa River, 189, 200
Canadiens, 18–19
Cape Breton, 24, 27, 128, 133, 166, 168, 280–1 n. 42; coal mining, 155–7, 226,
335; masts, 174; Spanish River, 155, 166, 337; Sydney, 156, 287 n. 32, 288 n. 34. *See also* coal, Louisbourg
Cape of Good Hope, xii, 31, 80, 194–5, 225
carpenters, house, 22, 39, 44, 54, 58, 59, 77, 79, 106, 110, 116, 229, 244 n. 103, 250 n. 45; petition, 275 n. 59
cartel ships, sloop *Albion*, 290 n. 50; schooner *Betsy*, 158, 283–4 n. 91; *British Queen*, 158; schooner *Observer*, 290 n. 50; sloop *Olive*, 290 n. 50, brig *Otter*, 290 n. 50
Caribbean, 138, 139, 168, 203, 217, 349. *See also* West Indies
Charleton, John, 10, 331–2
chips, 108–9, 136, 281 n. 55, 325, 347
Chesapeake, 23, 184, 195, 339
clerk, xii, xv, 10, 12, 84–5, 90–7, 100, 101, 108, 137, 146, 229, 269 n. 138, 285 n. 116; to Boston, 19; fuel accounts, 94–5; for hospital, 46; petitions by, 94; to St Andrews, 195; salaries, 92–3, 96–7
climate, 286 n. 146, 288 n. 31; winter, x, 6, 8, 13–14, 21, 24, 33, 40, 46, 47, 81, 95, 103, 111–12, 115, 127, 148, 163–4, 173, 218, 222, 274–5 n. 55. *See also* gales, hurricanes
coal, 37, 44, 47, 83, 112, 129, 147, 151, 155–8, 163, 166, 168, 226, 280–1 n. 42, 288 nn. 21–24, 28, 288 n. 32, 289 nn. 34, 38, 335; in Barbados, 288 n. 33; British, 155; for officers, 81. *See also* Cape Breton, colliers, Pictou, prices
Cochrane, Alexander, 133, 160, 183, 246 n. 14, 280 n. 34, 288 n. 33, 339; and hospital, 53, 55–6
Coffin, Isaac, 29, 39, 78, 92, 116, 144–5, 160, 161, 233, 270 n. 157, 334, 340, 349; career, 67–9, 332; detects fraud, 71, 75, 83–4; management style, 70, 73–4, 99, 163; and merchants, 74; and sea officers, 71, 74
coin, 21, 147, 201–15, 226, 228, 289 n. 38,

304 n. 5, 305–6 n. 40, 306 nn. 41, 45, 49, 50, 53, 58, 306–7 n. 59, 307 nn. 60, 76
Coleman, Seth, boat-builder, 160, 168
Collier, Sir George, 17, 43, 173, 348
colliers, *Allegiance*, 288 n. 23; *Attentive*, 260 n. 101; *Bellona*, 289 n. 38; *Castor*, 288 n. 24; *Hebe*, 289 n. 34 *Lady Delaval*, 289 n. 32; *Lark*, 288 n. 24; *Lilly*, 156, 288 nn. 27–8; *Lucretia*, 289 n. 34; *Rebecca*, 156; attacked, 155–6, 288 n. 22. *See also* coal
Colvill, Alexander, 7, 8, 11, 25, 30, 78, 116, 161, 218, 240 n. 23, 247 n. 18, 332, 337, 341, 342
commissioner. *See* resident commissioner
Constable, Abraham, 12, 18, 81, 107, 233, 332, 337, 341, 342, 345; embezzlement, 82, 83, 99, 267 n. 93; pay, 79
Cook, James, 24, 165–6, 240 n. 13
copper (er, ing), 87–8, 101, 113, 116, 129, 141, 223, 280 n. 37, 282 n. 74, 313 n. 150, 325, 331
cordwood. *See* firewood
Cornwallis Island. *See* McNab's Island
Corsica, 68, 78, 339, 344
crime, 11–12
Cullen, Stephen, 84, 143, 164, 333, 335

Dartmouth, xiv, 29, 40, 44, 118, 217, 225, 246 n. 13, 260–1 n. 103; boat-builder, 160, 168; saw mills, 335; slate quarry, 16
Davidson, William, 174–5, 178–9, 180, 295 nn. 23, 35, 38; 296 n. 55, 296–7 n. 57
Dawes, Daniel Butler, 51, 79, 80, 86, 96, 197, 209, 211, 212, 213, 233, 329, 332, 346, 347
DesBarres, Joseph F.W., v, 18–19, 24, 288 n. 28
deserters, 47, 166, 185, 227, 241 n. 43. *See also* stragglers
Digby, Robert, 44, 336, 348
dockyards, xii, xiv, 3, 17, 21, 98, 107, 108, 120, 121, 161, 181, 186–7, 190, 199, 219, 295 n. 30, 296 n. 41; Chatham, 25, 72, 78, 337, 339–40; Deptford, 25, 78, 134, 228, 340; Plymouth, 17, 25, 72, 78, 133, 181, 184, 186, 187, 334, 340; Portsmouth, 17, 25, 78, 81–2, 87, 101, 133, 172, 181, 186, 187, 228, 315, 330, 340; Sheerness, 68, 130, 332; Woolwich, 36, 134
Douglas, Sir Charles, 84–5, 268 nn. 113, 116, 348
Douglas, John, 161, 233, 332
drunkenness, 11, 15, 20, 45, 119, 241 n. 43
drydock, 16–17, 22–3, 325
Dugwell, John, 107, 333, 338
Duncan, Henry, 24, 28, 30, 32, 38, 78, 81, 87, 92, 94, 98, 114, 124, 130, 144, 156, 178, 180, 194, 195, 208, 226, 233, 247 n. 24, 251 n. 63, 338, 343; career, 67, 68, 71, 334; investigates fraud, 83–4; issues orders, 70, 236–7; on leave, 70; management style, 73, 99; salary, 69; supports pay increases, 108; timber tour, 175–7, 178, 295 nn. 36, 39
Durell, Philip, 7, 8, 68, 240–1 n. 29, 247 n. 18, 339

Edgecombe, Frederick, 84, 233, 268 nn. 114–16, 334
embezzlement, 101, 120, 267 n. 87; and Coffin, 71, 83–4; at Halifax yard, 82–4, 99, 346; in Portsmouth, 71–2
England, xii, 3, 4, 6, 7, 10, 17, 19, 21, 23, 30, 37, 50, 56, 59, 70, 72, 73, 77, 80, 83, 84, 88, 90, 91, 93, 120, 128, 131, 136, 146, 170, 174, 175, 180, 182, 186, 187, 192, 200, 209; coin shipments, 202, 204, 205, 207–8, 210–12, 226; Exeter, 349; Liverpool, 200; Thames, 184. *See also* British Isles
English Harbour yard, xi, 3, 23, 80, 97, 103, 127, 225, 228, 239 nn. 3, 6, 274 n. 49; masts for, 134, 177, 179, 181, 186, 194, 219, 293 n. 6
Eppes, William, 52, 53, 334
exchange rate, 106, 139–40, 165, 204, 205–11

Fairfax, Edmund, 79, 96, 100, 119, 233, 334
Farquharson, Alexander, 92, 334
Fernie, David, 233, 334
Finnerty, William, 34, 48, 250 n. 48, 259 n. 93, 334–5
fires, 16, 18, 19, 33, 34, 46, 49, 61, 142–3, 144–5, 158, 227, 247–8 n. 27, 258 nn. 58, 62, 333, 342
firewood, 37, 44, 47, 82, 94, 95, 151, 157–8, 163, 168, 177, 226, 274–5 n. 55, 289 nn. 40, 46, 341. *See also* fuel, prices
Flint, John, 114, 335
Forsyth, William, 156, 180–1, 183, 195, 227, 335; and Black, 195; and Smith, 138, 183, 184, 196–8, 209
Fort Howe, 159, 174, 178, 179, 180, 295 n. 30, 297 n. 68
France, xiii, 22, 128, alliance with Spain, 139; and Cape Breton, 155, 166, 217; naval forces of, 128, 188, 219; relations with Great Britain, 177, 217–18, 220
Francklin, Hazen and White, 175, 179, 180, 298 n. 66
Fraser, James, 191, 302 n. 151, 335; Fraser and Thom, 138, 196–8
fraud. *See* embezzlement
fuel, 47, 71, 81, 94–5, 108, 111, 271 n. 167. *See also* coal, firewood
Fundy, Bay of, 5, 84, 128, 173–4, 176, 180, 182, 185, 192, 199, 219, 347

gales, 15, 17, 37, 39–40, 47–8, 103, 131, 185, 218, 279 n. 27
Gambier, James, 16–17, 23, 206
George's Island. *See* Halifax harbour
Gerrish, Joseph, 8, 12–13, 16, 18, 136, 172, 203, 206, 207, 233, 268 n. 109, 269 n. 138, 339; career, 78, 335; pay, 79
Gibraltar yard, xi, 3, 68, 71, 80, 146, 147, 183, 194, 195, 223, 225, 239 n. 6, 299 n. 91, 339
Graves, Samuel, 18, 19, 20
Greenwich Hospital, 69, 201, 337
Griffith, Edward, 28, 136, 147, 246 n. 14, 260–1 n. 103, 334, 336; and admiral's house, 54, 55–6, 58–60
grog shop, 11, 12, 113, 119, 225
Gulf of Maine, 23, 26, 42, 219
Gulf of Mexico, 42, 338
Gulf of St Lawrence, 6, 22, 128, 203, 226, 338, 346

Halifax, x–xiii, xiii–xiv, 3, 4, 28, 68, 69, 77–8, 80, 91, 93, 95, 97, 98, 106, 108, 118, 154, 166, 169, 172, 173, 175, 179, 180, 181, 182, 185, 188, 193, 196–9, 206–7, 217, 219, 225, 247 n. 21, 301 n. 135; coal use, 155–6; prices, 109; fish market, 29, 75; Hamonds Plains, 348; meat market, 286–7 n. 6; naval cemetery, 44, 54; poverty in, 15; prices, 109; wage rates, 108–9, 110, 221, 262 n. 123. *See also* climate, fires, military garrison
Halifax harbour, 6, 7, 15, 17–18, 23–4, 27, 178, 202; Barnard's wharf, 6, 7; defences, 141; drydock, 243–4 n. 86; felling trees around, 173, 195, 272 n. 28; ice in, 40, 240 n. 19; Bedford Basin, 40, 240 n. 19, 333; Chebucto Head, 15; Eastern Passage, 40; Fort Sackville, 40; George's Island, 7, 36, 43, 240 nn. 23, 27, 253 n. 118; Gorham's Point, 7, 241 n. 32; ice, 40, 218, 254 n. 133; Mars rock, 79; McNab's Island, 38, 40, 158, 240 nn. 27–8, 253 n. 118; Melville Island, 29, 50, 246 n. 14, 339; North West Arm, 29; Sambro lighthouse, 185, 228; Thrum Cap Shoal, 132; Tufts Cove, 29, 167
Halifax squadron. *See* North American squadron
Halifax yard, 6, 10, 19, 22–6, 121, 218, 223; absenteeism, 117–18, 228; artificers' shed, 21, 35; auctions, 136–7, 281 n. 55, 282 n. 64; as banker, xii, 201–15; bell, illus., vi; boats, 102, 159–60; boathouse, 10, 15, 32, 34; boathouse slip, 34, 41, 250 n. 56; boats, 264 n. 19, 273 n. 30, 291 n. 73, 333, 348; boatswain, 20, 76, 79, 91, 142, 145, 222, 229, 233; boatswain's

house, illus., vi, 29, 31, 91; breastwork at, 9, 10, 13, 14, 37–8, 193, 257 n. 48, 324; brush house, 10, 324; cable store, 41; capstan house, illus., vi, 9, 16, 18, 25, 32, 35, 41, 244 n. 88, 249 n. 39–40; clock, 35–6, 252 n. 88; chapel, 120; coal yard, 129, 156; construction at, 8–9, 248–9 n. 36; contractors, 8, 9, 23, 35, 77; cooperage, 8, 34, 35, 91, 251 n. 63, 146, 348; coppersmith's shop, 35; cost of, 22, 221; daily routine, 104, 119, 120, 142–3, 270–1 n. 165, 273 n. 21; damage to, 13, 14; defence of, 19–20, 105, 141–2, 219, 273 n. 33; discharge, 113, 117–18; drydock proposed, 16–18, 222, 243–4 n. 86; establishments of, xiii, 10–11, 22, 24–5, 59, 107, 113, 123–4, 129–30, 143–4, 147, 218, 229–30; extra list, 113; fire engines, 10, 35, 102, 144, 252 n. 84; gardens, 31, 35, 46–7, 59, 60, 72, 75, 82, 102; gate, 36; guardhouse, 10, 18, 35, 36, 285 n. 117; holidays, 104, 272 n. 19; impact of war upon, 125–6, 147–8; invalids, 113–16, 275 n. 64, 277 n. 98; iron store, 35; lamp lighting, 36; lime shed, 35; masons' shed, 35; masthouse, vi, 9, 10, 18, 32, 34, 41; mastpond, 8, 9, 10, 14, 18, 20, 28, 35, 36–7, 103, 144, 167, 246 n. 9, 327; mast supply, 134, 171–92, 223, 273 n. 28, 295 n. 30; meal times, 104; medical care, 113, 120; morale, 73, 99; 'new' storehouse of 1771 [sail loft], illus., v, vi, 16, 25, 32, 33; night watch, 236–7; office, 18, 247 n. 17; officers' lodge, 18, 35, 71; overtime, 104; paint (ers), 9, 35, 78, 101, 106, 110, 129, 151, 160–3, 168, 223, 226, 229, 251 n. 74, 262 n. 120, 273–4 n. 37, 291 nn. 69, 71, 73–4, 80, 84, 330, 343; painters' shed, 35, 251 n. 74; password, 142, 236, 285 n. 116; pitch house, 9, 10, 35, 41, 292 n. 85; plans of, v–vi, 241 n. 41, 247–8 n. 26–9; porter's lodge, 10; prize surveys, 139–40; reduced, xii, 41, 76, 117, 126, 137, 146–7, 222; refitting warships, 101, 125, 129, 148, 220; relative importance, xiii, 40, 99, 147–8, 224–5, 228; reputation, 227; resident commissioner's house, illus., 29, 30–1, 247–8 n. 25–8; respective officers' tenements, illus., vi, 11, 31, 248–9 n. 36, 265 n. 51; returns, 234–5; rounders, 113, 142, 236–7; sea fencibles, 105; seaman's lodge, 18, 35; shingles, 18; shipbuilding, 125, 129, 130, 136, 193, 196; ship hire, 158–9; ship repairs, 127–33, 188, 220, 280 n. 34; ship sales, 136–7, 139; signals, 144; slate roofs at, 16, 18, 32–3, 242 nn. 59, 65; slaters, 106–7, 115, 229; smiths' shop, 9, 32, 35, 41, 112, 292 n. 85; stone for, 15; storehouses, 9, 13, 16, 25, 31, 32, 33, 35, 103, 131, 132, 133, 159, 250 n. 45, 292 n. 85, 335; Sunday work, 129; supplies for, 134–5; taphouse, 119; value to Nova Scotia, 26; volunteer battalion, 105–6; wallpaper, 160, 290 n. 66; walls, 13, 16, 24, 26, 39, 41, 244 n. 77; watchmen's shed, 35; watering tank, 35, 251 n. 75; watering wharf, 8, 34, 38; wharfs, 8, 9, 13, 32, 34, 37–8, 41, 193, 241 n. 31, 253 n. 103; work conditions, 70; workforce, 123–4, 127, 220, 231–2, 260–1 n. 103, 261–2 n. 113, 117. *See also* boatswain, fires, hulk

Halliburton, John, 45, 48, 331, 338, 339; career, 49–50, 335; salary, 80

Hamilton, Richard, 233, 336, 337

Hamond, Andrew Snape, 22, 78, 81, 98, 106, 113, 159, 175, 179, 233, 244 n. 103, 250 n. 60, 273 n. 36, 295 n. 23, 314, 338, 341, 348; career, 67, 68, 69, 71, 336; as comptroller of the navy, 68; and naval hospital, 44, 45, 48, 60; resignation, 72

Harmar, Joseph, 5, 240 n. 13

Hawkes, Thomas Forder, 55, 78, 233, 258 n. 59, 337

Hay, Charles, 233, 337
Hazen and White. *See* Francklin, Hazen and White
Hemmens, Samuel, career, 78, 80, 233, 337
Henniker, John, 170, 293 n. 6
Hians, Capel, 153–4, 287 n. 9
Holburne, Francis, 6, 7, 67, 337
Holland, Samuel, 24, 295 n. 39
Holman, John, 233, 337
Hood, Samuel, 13–16, 18, 25, 30, 68, 128, 161, 193, 242 n. 53, 247 nn. 20–1, 332, 335, 337, 340
Hooper, David, 79, 233, 337
Hooper, James, 233, 337
horses, 31, 46, 50, 74, 84, 147, 163–4, 225, 226
hospital, naval, 24, 27, 29, 39, 43–59, 60, 80, 193, 222, 253 n. 124, 255 n. 5–6, 256 nn. 27, 41, 339, 348; chaplain, 334, 340, 348; destroyed by fire, 49, 258 n. 62; establishment, 146, 334, 343, 345; garden, 46–7; guard, 119; guardhouse, 46; illus., v–vi; lunatic cabin, 44, 46; necessary, 46, 47; nurses, 45, 49, 53, 340–41; officers' tenement, 45, 48, 257 n. 18, 257 n. 52, 257–8 n. 57–8, 335; porter's lodge, 46; staff, 49; stores, 45; walls, 44, 47, 257 n. 51; wash house, 46; water supply for, 47; wharf, 44, 47
Howe, Earl Richard, 21, 22, 25, 67
Hughes, George A., 91, 96
Hughes, Sir Richard, 31, 67, 69, 158, 174, 208, 233, 329, 337, 338
Hughes, William, 78, 83, 96, 107, 138, 145, 233, 266 n. 64, 267 n. 99, 338, 342, 347
hulk, 20, 114, 253 n. 124, 326; sheer, 102, 126, 130, 327, 346
hulksmen, 102, 110, 113, 126, 130, 164
Hume, Robert, 50–3, 339
Hunter, Robertson and Forsyth, 188
Hurd, Jacob, 12, 81, 100, 268 n. 109, 269 n. 138, 342; career, 90, 339; portrait, vi, 91, 270 n. 149

Hurd, Jacob, junior, 91, 96, 339
hurricane, 14, 39, 68, 130, 133, 183; of 1757, 6, 15; of 1813, 331, 333, 339

Idle, Christopher, John, and George & Co., 188, 189
impressment, 182, 198–9, 326
inflation, 70, 80, 93–4, 96, 108, 109, 111, 146, 193, 212, 214–5, 346
Inglefield, John, xv, 30–1, 67, 93, 96, 102, 104, 108, 118, 124, 129–30, 131–2, 143, 153, 163–4, 183–4, 188–9, 195, 195–8, 204–5, 210–12, 233, 274 n. 49, 285–6 n. 135, 329, 341, 343, 344, 346, 347; accused of fraud, 72; career, 68, 339–40; on climate, 81; dispute with Anderson, 84, 85–7, 100; issues orders, 70; lacks a coxswain, 70–1; leave, 70, 72, 209; salary, 69–70; and shipbuilding, 137–8
invalids, 113–16
Ireland Island, 145, 148, 152, 165, 194, 195, 220–1, 224, 228, 273 n. 36, 346; admiral's mansion, 61, 145; naval hospital, 346, 347; naval yard, x, xii, 42, 145; naval yard costs, 41–2, 145–6; proposed drydock at, 17. *See also* Bermuda

Jackson, John, 78, 80, 233, 340
Jamaica, x, xi, 80, 97, 177, 179, 181, 182, 183, 194, 199, 219, 239 n. 3, 6; coin shipments, 202, 204, 205, 209, 211–12, 213, 214, 226, 305 n. 32; squadron, 131, 222. *See also* Port Royal
James, Benjamin, 91, 93, 94; career, 91–2, 340
Johns, William, 233, 340
Jones, Algernon Frederick, 55, 78, 233, 340

Kent, HRH Prince Edward, duke of, 30, 196, 332, 338
King, Samuel, 157–8
Kingston, Upper Canada, xii, 225, 239 n. 4; drydock on Lake Ontario, 17

Kittoe, George, 79, 233, 341
Knowles, Charles, 4–5, 239 n. 3, 7

labourers, local, 10, 25, 26, 30, 32, 40, 45, 72, 76, 77, 80, 82, 85, 92, 103, 107, 109–10, 112, 113, 115, 118, 119, 126, 145, 146, 173, 225, 230; petition, 108, 275 n. 57
Lawlor, William, painter, 161, 168, 291 n. 73, 293 n. 113, 341
Lawson, John, 84, 157
Lee, William, 44, 116, 267 n. 93, 334, 336, 338, 341
Leeward Islands squadron, 131, 133, 156, 160, 183, 184, 222
Lewis, George, 233, 341
liquor. *See* rum
livestock, xv, 70, 133, 170, 178, 271 n. 4, 280 n. 41, 339. *See also* horses
Livie, Titus, 78, 81, 158, 233, 341
Livingston, John, 92, 96, 341
Loader, John, 44, 78, 233, 341–2, 343
London, xii, 17, 19, 20, 37, 44, 50, 56, 79, 89, 97, 134, 155, 175, 184, 188, 192, 200, 201, 227
Louisbourg, ix–x, 239 nn. 6, 7, 331; 1745 siege of, 4, 217, 333; 1757 blockade of, 6, 67, 334; 1758 siege of, 7, 8, 22; careening at, 4, 5
Lower Canada. *See* Quebec
loyalist refugees, 107, 118, 127–8, 152, 180, 193, 279 n. 13, 331, 332, 333, 334, 336, 344, 347
Lunenburg, 3, 217, 219, 260 n. 101, 345

MacKenzie, John, 55, 58, 59
Madras, xii, 41, 127, 225, 228, 239 n. 4
magazine, powder, 38–9, 253 n. 118
Major, Frederick, 154, 196–7, 337, 342
Malta, xii, 17, 41, 68, 71, 127, 225, 228, 339
marines, 12, 60, 113, 164, 166
Marnel, Thomas, 112–13
Marshall, Benjamin, 83, 107, 112, 276 n. 72, 342

Marshall, Elias, 12, 78, 107, 144, 233, 268 nn. 104, 108, 338, 341, 342, 344, 349; embezzlement, 82–3, 99, 112
Marshall, Elias, junior, 143, 342
Marshall, Samuel, 83, 107, 267 n. 98, 343
Marshall, Joseph, 9, 343
master attendant, xv, 11, 18, 22, 25, 26, 78, 101, 145, 146–7, 222, 229, 233, 273 n. 33; authority, 70, 77, 95; vessel for, 21, 273 n. 30
master shipwright, xv, 11, 12, 22, 25, 37, 55, 78, 96, 97, 98, 99, 109, 118, 222, 229, 233; authority, 70, 77, 101; and hospital, 44
masts, xii, 23, 26, 35, 67, 101, 103, 132, 133–4, 163, 223, 272 n. 28, 294 n. 14, 299 nn. 90, 93; contractors, 169–92, 219, 296 n. 62, 299 n. 96, 302 n. 153, 338; New England, 293 n. 6, 11
mastships, 178, 181, 182, 183, 184, 185, 186, 187, 188, 295 n. 30, 300 n. 111; *Admiral Parker*, 181, 186, 297 n. 68; *Ajax*, 187; *America*, 182, 186, 188; *Amphion*, 181; *Ariel*, 187; *Britannia*, 178, 182, 186; *British Tar*, 187; *Brunswick*, 185, 186; *Caledonian*, 186; *Dawson*, 186, 189; *Diana*, 187, 296 n. 51; *Diligence*, 186; *Diligent*, 187; *Dorset*, 190, 300 n. 122; *Duke of Kent*, 183, 186, 299 n. 90; *Earl of Mansfield*, 182, 185, 186, 298 nn. 80–1; *Eliza*, 186; *Elk*, 186; *Governor Carleton*, 182, 184, 186, 298 n. 83; *Hamilton*, 184, 186; *Holderness*, 178; *Keppel*, 178; *Lady Parker*, 186, 188; *Lilly*, 182, 186, 298 n. 83; *Lord Macartney*, 186; *Pallas*, 186, 187; *Penelope*, 187; *Princess of Wales*, 182, 186; *Prudent*, 296 n. 51; *Robert*, 187; *Rosina*, 186, 187; *Selina*, 178; *Sir George Prevost*, 301 n. 133–4; *Trelawny*, 182, 186
Mauger, Joshua, 169, 247 n. 5, 287 n. 8; distillery of, 8, 20; heirs of, 28
McNab's Island. *See* Halifax harbour
meat, fresh, 152, 342; salted, 153–5,

286–7 n. 6; Irish, 153, 286–7 n. 6. *See also* prices
Mediterranean, 135, 183, 339, 344; Malta, xii, 17, 41, 68, 71, 127, 225, 228, 339; Minorca, 3, 68; Port Mahon, xiv, 3, 239 n. 6
Melville Island. *See* Halifax harbour
Merrick, John, painter, 161–3, 168, 291 n. 80
Mi'kmaq, 217, 225
Miller, Jacob and Garret, 196–8
military garrison, 20, 24, 37, 43, 45, 58, 108, 141, 144, 156, 157, 166, 167, 193, 196, 200, 203, 204, 206, 208, 212, 213, 214, 280–1 n. 42, 306–7 n. 59
Miramichi River, 146, 174, 176, 177, 180, 182, 189, 191, 200, 226, 295 nn. 36, 39
Mitchell, Andrew, 72, 130, 346
Montagu, John, 18–19, 49, 206, 247 n. 21, 304 n. 16, 336
Morriss, Roger, xiii, xiv, 169
Muhlig, Frederick, 114, 276 n. 87, 343
Mure and Joliffe, 189–90
Murray, George, 45, 124, 194, 338

Naval Dockyards Society, xiii, xiv
naval storekeeper, 22, 24, 79, 83–4, 98, 99, 103, 129, 135–6, 158, 164, 172, 197–8, 202, 203, 206, 211, 212, 214, 222, 226, 229, 233, 240 n. 14, 247 n. 17; at Halifax, xv, 8, 10, 21, 33; at Boston, 19; at Louisbourg, 4; authority, 77, 201
Navy Board, xii, 4, 5, 7, 15, 20, 30, 31, 34–7, 71, 72, 77, 80, 85, 92, 95, 99, 100, 103, 104, 106, 194, 217, 223; and admiral's house, 57; apprenticeship policy, 107; approves repairs, 33–4, 38; attitude toward Halifax yard, 10, 25, 26, 41, 102; auctions policy, 136, 137; censures, 81; complaint to, 196; disputes with yard officers, 87–90; in error, 109; false economies, 124–5, 148; ignores yard's 1812 wartime needs, 93, 124–30, 132; management style of, 65–6, 87–90, 97–8, 134–5, 189–92, 223, 271 n. 175; on masts, 134, 169–70, 173–80, 190–1, 297 n. 41, 301 n. 135; own needs, 40, 42, 200; painting regulations, 160–2; pay policy, 108; plans of yard requested, 29, 245 n. 110; report on yard required, 21, 41; returns required, 135; shipbuilding policy, 136, 138; specie policy, 209–12, 304 n. 16; stores policy, 134; superannuation policy, 114, 116; and tonnage measurements, 81, 139; wage policy, 110–12, 275 n. 59; and wood shingles, 18
New Brunswick, 27, 48, 110, 152, 180, 181, 193, 194, 195, 198, 199, 225, 333; Chatham, 344; St Andrews, 182, 195, 303 n. 176, 346, 347; timber reserves, 69, 173–7, 189, 200, 302 n. 141. *See also* Fort Howe, Miramichi, Saint John, St John River,
New England, 4, 6, 8, 18, 23, 151–2, 170, 181, 203; Connecticut, 170; Kennebeck River, 171; Machias, 174; Maine, 169, 170; Massachusetts, 10, 18, 19, 170, 203; mast supplier, 169–76, 293 n. 6; Nantucket, 346; New Hampshire, 19, 169, 171; Newport, 23, 49–50, 69, 218, 330, 335–6; Penobscot Bay, 23; Piscataqua River, 78, 169, 337; Rhode Island, 4, 22, 23, 25, 50, 170; settlers in Nova Scotia, 19; threat of invasion from, 173; warships built in, 137
Newfoundland, 17, 153, 168, 217; ships at, 24, 26, 68, 131, 132, 133, 222, 280–1 n. 42, 332, 334, 336; St John's, 280–1 n. 42
New York, x, 4, 22, 23, 44, 69, 77, 87, 91, 107, 112, 117, 156, 158, 170, 171, 180, 184, 209, 218, 278 n. 4, 295 n. 30, 330, 334, 340; coast, 67; Lake Champlain, 179, 224; Manhattan Island, xi, 17, 22; money market, 202, 203, 226; prison hospital, 346. *See also* Turtle Bay yard

North American squadron, 5, 11, 23, 24, 25, 27, 33, 44, 55, 61, 69, 84, 93, 101, 102, 103, 106, 123–4, 125, 126–9, 141, 147–8, 193, 206, 217–18, 220, 222, 223, 228, 303 n. 163, 329, 332, 337
North British Society, 332, 336
Northumberland Strait, 180, 219
Norwood, William, 107, 344
Norwood, Winckworth, 91, 159, 343
Nova Scotia, 4, 91, 97, 128, 133, 183, 184, 194, 217; Albro Lake, 29; Annapolis Royal, 5, 23, 84, 112, 128, 219, 276 n. 72, 333, 342; Canso, 131, 166, 168, 176, 333, 346, 347; Chedabucto Bay, 128, 176, 279 n. 13; Chester, 172; coal use, 155–8; Country Harbour, 128; Cumberland County, 128; currency, 202–3; Digby, 128, 336; economy, 151–2, 153, 167–8, 193, 203–4, 212, 214–5, 218, 225; fisheries, 202, 280 n. 38; fur trade, 174; harbours, 176–7; house of assembly, 113, 330, 331, 335, 345; LaHave River, 34, 172, 302 n. 157; legislative council, 76, 78, 334, 335, 336, 340; Liverpool, 347; Mahone Bay, 172; Merigomish, 176; Minas Basin, 176; money market, 201–15; Pictou, 115, 155, 157, 166, 168, 176, 189, 191–2, 200, 226, 293 n. 3, 294 nn. 14, 17, 300 n. 112, 330, 343; preservation of, 23, 26–7; strategic importance of, 27; timber, 69, 172–4; 189, 191–2, 200, 293 n. 3, 294 nn. 14, 17, 300 n. 112, 340; waters, ix–x, xiii; Yarmouth, 167, 330. *See also* Cape Breton, Dartmouth, Halifax, Halifax harbour, Halifax yard

oakum, 12, 75, 115, 265 n. 39, 327
Oben, Thomas, 78, 233, 329, 344
Ordnance Board, 108, 133, 141, 280 n. 37

Parliament, 113, 170, 177, 189; appropriations, 37, 54; member, 68–9
Parminter, John, 344, 348

Parr, John, 22, 69, 144, 314, 336
Parry, John, 79, 119, 233, 344
Passamaquody Bay, 128, 176
Patterson, George, 233, 334, 345
pay, 109–12; officers, 79; artificers, 106, 108; clerks, 92–7, 99 ship's 6, 17, 20, 22; working parties, 103–4
peace, 26, 30, 40, 42, 48, 60, 126, 157, 191, 192, 195, 208, 214–5, 218, 219
Peake, Philip, 172, 345
pensions, 69, 101
petitions, 80, 91, 94, 95, 99, 108, 109, 110, 111, 115, 116, 120
pettyaugers. *See* shipbuilding
Pierpont, Joseph, 8–9, 345
Pitt, William, 3, 7, 22, 127, 217, 240 n. 28
Plaw, John, 55, 345
Port Royal, Jamaica, 3, 23, 80, 97, 103, 127, 225, 228, 239 n. 3, 6; masts for, 134, 177, 179, 181, 186, 194, 219, 293 n. 6
prices, 109, 275 n. 55; coal, 156–7, 280–1 n. 42, 289 n. 21, 289 nn. 37, 46, 330; firewood, 157–8, 289 n. 46; meat, 153–4; oars, 160; paint, 161
Prince Edward Island, 166, 176; Charlottetown, 337, 345
prisoners of war, 333, 339, 348; American, 158–9; French, 158–9
privateers, 188, 327; American, 128, 140, 145, 219; *Lively*, 329; French, 129, 141, 33
prize agency, 81; vessels, 139, 213–14, 283 n. 87, 327; American, 140–1, 283–4 nn. 88–93, 95, 97–100, 294 n. 8; French, 140–1, 220, 284–5 nn. 101–13; Spanish, 46
Prowse, Richard, 233, 345

Quebec, 90, 154, 214, 243 n. 80, 339, 341, 346; 1759 siege of, 8, 22; currency, 203; Gatineau River, 200; ships at, 26; timber supplier, 152, 180, 188–9, 191, 199, 200

Read, Thomas, 77, 233, 345

resident commissioner, xii, xv, 11, 18, 24, 26, 101, 103, 145, 153, 158, 169, 174, 175–9, 182, 189–90, 191, 192, 199, 211, 222, 223, 224, 227, 229, 233, 285 n. 116, 329, 336, 337; authority, 72; chief clerk, 137; house illus., vi; mansion, 29, 30; partiality, 195–8; pensions, 69; personalities of, 72–3; relations with naval commanders, 71; role, 66–7; salary, 69–7
respective officers, xv, 70, 76–90, 99, 146, 192, 222, 223, 229, 270–1 n. 165; authority, 142; fuel, 94–5; Navy Board's censure, 87–8; rounders, 113, 142, 236–7
Rhodes, Jasper, 119, 346
Ridgeway, David, 233, 346
Ritchie, James, 195, 346
Rowlands, David, 339, 340, 346; career, 50; controversy, 50–3
rum, 11, 16, 36, 45, 103, 113, 119–20; still, 257 n. 51

sails, 5, 7, 24, 32, 87, 260–1 n. 103, 129, 131, 347
Saint John, 167, 181, 182, 185, 200, 253 n. 108, 296 n. 41, 329, 335, 340; harbour, 182
St John River, 23, 128, 159, 174, 175–6, 177, 178, 179, 180, 181, 219, 226, 295 n. 38, 302 n. 141
St Lawrence River, 166, 189, 191, 346
St Vincent, John Jervis, earl of, xiii, 68, 71, 74, 265 n. 33
Sandwich, John Montagu, earl of, 21
Sawyer, Herbert, senior, 4, 54, 334; junior, 54, 146
Scott, Asa, 83, 194
Seal Island, 167, 329
seamen, clothing, 164; working parties of, 6, 10, 14, 16, 24, 37, 40–1, 57, 101, 102, 103, 105, 129, 173, 253 n. 118, 257–8 n. 57, 260–1 nn. 101–03, 261–2 n. 113, 263 n. 131, 272 nn. 6, 9–10. *See also* slops

Sellon, Edward, 91, 96, 347; Samuel, 107, 195, 347
Shelburne, 118, 128, 176, 194, 279 n. 13, 334
Sherlock, George, 96, 347
shipbuilding, Bermuda, 124; New Brunswick, 295 n. 35; New England, 171; New York, 171; Nova Scotia, 193, 196; pettyaugers, 125, 129, 136, 327; sloop, 130, 224, 272 n. 10, 283 n. 79
ships, American: *Amsterdam*, 140; *Anaconda*, 140; *Cabot*, 140; *Chesapeake*, 141; *Curlew*, 140; *Friends Adventure*, 140; *Frolic*, 140; *Hancock*, 140; *Little Republican*, 140; *Lynx*, 140; *Nautilus*, 140; *Racer*, 140; *Rattlesnake*, 140; *Ritterhouse*, 140; *Yankee Hero*, 283–4 n. 91
ships, British: *Adamant*, 335; *Adonis*, 131 *Ajax*, 129, 300–01 n. 127; *Albany*, 5, 140, 342; *Allegiance*, 250 n. 60, 258 n. 66, 312 n. 130; *America*, 137; *Amphitrite*, 283 n. 90; *Amsterdam*, 186; *Anson*, v; schooner *Arbuthnot*, 283–4 n. 91; *Arc-en-ciel*, 6, 7, 337; *Ardent*, 305 n. 24; *Arethusa*, 336 *Assistance*, 268 n. 113; schooner *Assistance*, 283–4 n. 91; *Assurance*, 250 n. 60; *Atalanta*, 166, 250 n. 60, 285 n. 118; cutter *Barbara*, 141; *Barfleur*, 339; *Bellona*, 186, 187; sloop *Betsy*, 166; *Bien Aimé*, 5; brig *Black Snake*, 283–4 n. 91; *Blonde*, 167; *Bonne Citoyenne*, 186; *Boston*, 78, 137, 186; *Boulogne*, 20, 37; brig *Busy*, 182, 186, 188, 298 n. 83, 299 n. 104; *Brothers*, 103; schooner *Caledonian*, 167; *Cambrian*, 182, 186; *Camilla*, 195; *Caton*, 336; *Centaur*, 68, 339; *Centurion*, 54, 132, 136, 253 n. 124, 260 n. 101–2; *Ceres*, 186; *Chatham*, 21, 258 n. 66, 284 n. 101, 312 n. 130; schooner *Chatham*, 136; *Chebucto*, 140; *Cleopatra*, 132, 186, 187, 198, 300–01 n. 127; *Cherub*, 300–01 n. 127; *Colibri*, 132; *Columbia*, 140; *Columbine*, 132; *Comet*, 132, 133, 280–1 n. 42; *Dasher*,

186; *Deale Castle*, 335; sloop *Delaware*, 347 *Diligent*, 136, 301 n. 130; schooner *Dispatch*, 131, 158, 282 n. 64; *Dreadnaught*, 333; *Driver*, 132; *Eagle*, 186, 240 n. 13, 348; *Emerald*, 305 n. 23; *Emulous*, 140, 306–7 n. 59; *Endeavour*, 280–1 n. 42; *Ephira*, 339; *Epivier*, 332; *Espérance*, 186, 284 n. 103, 338; *Eurydice*, 119; survey sloop *Examiner*, 136, 280 n. 36; *Fantôme*, 167; armed tender *Felicity*, 136, 282 n. 64; *Feret*, 132; *Flora*, 272 n. 10; *Florida*, 140; *Forth*, 120, 167; *Fox*, 17; schooner *Friends*, 283–4 n. 91; *Furieuse*, 191; *Glasgow*, 12; *Grafton*, 6, 342; *Granby*, 202, 203, 228; schooner *Greyhound*, 280 n. 38; *Guarland*, 67; *Guerrière*, 300–01 n. 127; *Halifax*, 130, 132, 138, 196, 272 n. 10, 283 n. 78; *Harpy*, 187; *Hector*, 343; buoy boat *Hibernia*, 57, 136, 157; *Hogue*, 119; *Hope*, 113; *Horatio*, 132, 186, 300–01 n. 127; galley *Hussar*, 136; *Hussar*, 132, 186, 258 n. 66, 282 n. 64, 312 n. 130; *Hydra*, 344; *Invincible*, 332; pilot sloop *Jane*, 283–4 n. 91; brigantine *Jennie*, 158; prison ship *Jersey*, 136; *Junon*, 132, 300–01 n. 127; transport *Lady Delaval*, 157; *Latona*, 166; *Launceston*, 68, 339; *Laurestinus*, 285 n. 118; *Leander*, 38, 118, 334, 344, 346; *Leopard*, 141, 332; *Lilly*, 186; *Little Belt*, 132, 167; *Lively*, 57, 260–1 n. 103; *Lizard*, 17, 243 n. 80; sloop *Lord Cornwallis*, 283–4 n. 91; *Lynx*, 186; pilot boat *Mackerel*, 136, 282 n. 64; *Magicienne*, 81; *Maidstone*, 298 n. 86, 335; *Manby*, 333; survey vessel *Maria*, 280 n. 38; *Melampus*, 300–01 n. 127; *Mermaid*, 12, 17; [*Ville de*] *Milan*, 115, 186, 284 n. 106, 300–01 n. 127; *Milford*, 283–4 nn. 90–1; *Musquodoboit*, 140; *Nassau*, 67; schooner *Nelly*, 283–4 n. 91; *Newfoundland*, 336; *Niger*, 136; *Nimble*, 280 n. 34; *Nymphe*, 346; *Observateur*, 284 n. 107; *Oiseau*, 336; *Orpheus*, 285 n. 118; *Pallet*, 119; *Pegasus*, vii; *Pembroke*, 20, 114, 331, 335, 344, 346; *Penzance*, v; *Phosphorous*, 338; *Pinson*, 68, 332; *Placentia*, 68; *Plumper*, 138, 167, 182; *Pompey*, 300–01 n. 127; *Postilion*, 283–4 n. 91; *Preston*, 337; *Prévoyante*, 284 n. 104; armed cutter *Prince Edward*, 136, 140, 282 n. 64; *Prince George*, 342; *Prince of Orange*, 339; *Prosperine*, 335; *Prospero*, 187; *Pyramus*, 60; *Rainbow*, 283 n. 88; *Raison*, 186, 284 n. 104; *Rattler*, 285 n. 118; *Roebuck*, 305 n. 20; *Royal Oak*, 332; *Raven*, 283 n. 89; *Resistance*, 186; *Resolution*, 186, 188; *Rifleman*, 119; *Roebuck*, 21, 67; *Romney*, 68, 337, 339; schooner *Sandwich*, 283–4 n. 91; *Severn*, 185, 186; slave schooner *Severn*, 344; *Shelburne*, 140; *Shoreham*, 239 n. 6; *Sophy*, 198–9; brig *Spence*, 302 n. 151; *Spencer*, 339; *Squirrel*, 132; prison ship *Stanislaus*, 159, 343; *Success*, 38, 136; *Sultana*, 335; *Superbe*, 79, 334; *Sutherland*, 7; *Tartar*, 104, 186, 198, 332, 344, 347; *Thames*, 335; *Thisbe*, 68, 185, 186, 332; *Thetis*, 52, 300–01 n. 127; *Tilbury*, 7; *Tribune*, 166; *Vestal*, 166; *Victorious*, 332; *Victory*, 330; *Ville de Paris*, 340; sloop *Virgin*, 166; *Voltigeur*, 280 n. 37; *Weazle*, 166; *Winchelsea*, 81
ships, French: *Bonne Citoyenne*, 141, 284 n. 110; *Colibri*, 141 *Espérance*, 141; letter-of-marque *Fantôme*, 141, 285 n. 113; *Furieuse*, 141, 285 n. 111; *Jeu*, 284 n. 103; *Junon*, 141; *Little Republican*, 284 n. 102; *Magicienne*, 141; *Matilda*, 141; *Observateur*, 141, 284 n. 107; cutter *Peraty*, 141, 285 n. 112; *Prévoyante*, 141; *Raison*, 141; *Ville de Milan*, 141; *Voltigeur*, 141
Sick and Hurt Board, 45, 80, 225
slaveowner, 312 n. 123, 330, 335, 339
slops, 12, 80, 131, 136, 164, 328
soldier(s), 21, 36, 37, 92, 115, 116, 147; in Cape Breton, 155; disbanded, 127–8, 152; working parties of, 37, 59, 103, 254 n. 128–9
South Carolina, 5, 169, 294 n. 7, 341;

Charleston, 4, 5, 23, 69, 107, 145, 278 n. 4, 336, 337
Spain, 138, 139, 220; letter-of-marque, 338
Spry, Richard, 6, 8, 11, 67, 329, 342
squadron. *See* North American squadron
Stanser, Rev. Robert, 49, 340, 348
Starr and Shannon, 213, 287 n. 15
storeships, 8, 10, 20, 21, 24, 38, 39, 72, 87, 103, 129, 131, 133, 135; *Abundance*, 319 n. 361 ; *Camel*, 186; *Chichester*, 186; *Comet*, 72; *Dawson*, 300–01 n. 127; *Dolphin*, 299 n. 92; *Diligence*, 300–01 n. 127; *Eisdale*, 186, 300–01 n. 127, *Foster Burham*, 317 n. 289; *Hazard*, 136; *Hewson*, 136; *Inflexible*, 38, 129, 132, 135; *Lyon*, 159; *Pacific*, 313 n. 161; *Ranger*, 280 n. 39; *Recovery*, 312 n. 135; *Spy*, 279 n. 27, 281 n. 44; *William*, 131, 132, 166, 168, 186, 272 n. 9, 300–01 nn. 127, 130, 333, 346; *Zephyrus*, 129, 135
storms. *See* gales, hurricanes
stragglers, 166, 227. *See also* deserters
surgeon, hospital, xv, 45, 46, 48, 113, 229, 260 n. 101, 332, 333, 335, 336, 340, 346

theft. *See* embezzlement
Thomas, George, 71, 80, 84, 165, 233, 268 n. 118, 348
timber, 4, 9, 10, 18, 28, 34, 36, 37, 48, 56, 58, 69, 77, 82, 83, 84, 112, 132, 133, 138, 146, 151, 163, 193–200, 212–13; North American, 137–9, 140; New Brunswick, 296 n. 41; Nova Scotia, 293 n. 3, 300 n. 112; Quebec, 134; shortage, 137
Transport Board, 153, 213, 225, 287 n. 9
transports, 102, 127–8, 129, 133, 278 n. 4, 328; *Abundance*, 257–8 n. 57; *Adventure*, 195, *Ariel*, 301 n. 130; *Bellona*, 289 n. 38; *Burton*, 345; *Constant Friends*, 280 n. 40; *Coromandel*, 257 n. 51; *Duke of Kent*, 268 n. 104; *Eliza*, 300–01 n. 127; *Fairey*, 289 n. 36; *Friendship*, 278 n. 4; *Henry*, 280 n. 40; *John*, 278 n. 4; *Lady Delaval*, 280 n. 41; *Magnet*, 271 n. 4, 280 n. 41; *Robert*, 301 n. 130; *Sally*, 280 n. 40; *Sceptre*, 288 n. 30; *Seahorse*, 280 n. 40; *Stoddy*, 278 n. 4, *Thetis*, 278 n. 4; *Vernon*, 337
Treaty of Amiens (1802), 102, 124, 145
Tremain, Messrs Jonathan and John, 156, 158
Trincomalee, xii, xiv, 41, 225, 239 nn. 4, 6
Turtle Bay yard, Manhattan Island, xi, 4, 19, 22, 23, 25, 67, 77, 87, 194, 219, 239 n. 8, 278 n. 4, 334, 348; masts sent to, 26, 219, 295 n. 30

United States, xv, 99, 110, 125, 145, 165, 177, 193, 195, 221, 224; Congress, 128; Florida, 128; Georgia, 217; merchant ships, 129, 140; navy, 219; New Jersey, 170; Pennsylvania, 347; Philadelphia, 4, 22, 194, 337; South Carolina, 5, 169, 294 n. 7, 341; trade, 134, 153, 161, 195, 198, 204–05, 220, 226, 228, 286–7 n. 6; Virginia, 4, 67, 69, 154, 330, 344. *See also* New England, New York, South Carolina, Turtle Bay yard
Upper Canada, 191, 200, 203, 224

vegetables, 155, 275 n. 64, 287 n. 17, 287–8 nn. 19–20
vice-admiralty court, 78, 193, 201–02, 211, 218, 305–6 n. 40, 335
Victualling Board, 49, 153, 155, 213, 225
Vincent, Anthony, 118–19
Virginia, 4, 154; Capes, 67, 69, 330

wages, 275–6 n. 69; of artificers, 7, 20–1, 58, 275 n. 66; of hulksmen, 20, of painters, 163; of soldiers, 58; of tradesmen, 58–9
Wallace, Michael, 158, 180, 329
Wallis, Provo, 77, 80, 84, 233, 296 n. 41, 348
Wallis, Provo Featherstone, 96, 196; career, 91, 348–9; portrait, vi, 91, 270 n. 149
War of American Independence, x, xi, 8,

19–20, 25, 26, 27, 35, 41, 43, 81, 104, 108, 115, 116, 117, 128, 130, 171–2, 193, 194, 199, 202, 207, 218–19, 223, 228
War, Seven Years', 4, 22, 49, 116, 123, 335
War with Revolutionary and Napoleonic France, xiii, 26, 41, 99, 106 108, 124, 126, 140, 145, 147, 156, 184–5, 191, 220, 221
War with the United States, xiii, 23–5, 26, 40, 41–2, 47, 61, 92, 93, 99, 105, 106, 125–6, 147–8; induces inflation, 70, 96, 158, 162, 191, 212, 214–5, 220–1, 224, 275 n. 59
Warren, John Borlase, 72, 125, 131–2, 153, 166, 189; and admiral's house, 54; and Bermuda, 145; and hospital, 48, 49
Warren, Peter, x, 4, 140, 206, 239 n. 8
watchmen, 10, 12, 19, 25, 26, 70, 80, 102, 113, 115, 142, 146–7, 225, 229, 277 n. 100, 278 n. 113, 348, 349; coats for, 164; house, 35; orders, 236; pay, 109–10; 275 n. 57; in Portsmouth, 82
Wentworth, John, 28, 29, 46, 171, 173, 175, 177, 181, 294 n. 17
West Indies, xiv, 135, 153, 184, 192, 217, 222, 226, 345; careening in, 21, 103; masts sent to, 26, 134, 177, 180, 185, 199, 218, 223; Spanish, 138; warships from 10, 24, 89, 93, 125, 131, 132. *See also* Antigua, Barbados, Caribbean, English Harbour, Jamaica, Port Royal
Williams, Richard, 158, 165, 166, 207, 233, 349
Wiswell, Enoch, oarmaker, 160, 168
Wodehouse, Philip, 28, 67, 97, 99, 113, 115, 117, 118, 125, 130, 147, 191, 212, 221–2, 223, 233, 248 n. 28, 261–2 n. 113, 262 n. 117, 270–1 n. 165, 321, 331, 333, 343, 344, 345, 346, 347; and admiral's house, 55–9; career, 68, 349; and hospital controversy, 52–4; and pay rates, 109, 110–11; reputation, 75–6; salary of, 70; and yard structures, 31, 33–4, 35, 36, 37–8, 40–1, 48
women, 121, 165, 168, 225, 242 n. 50; daughters, 330, 331, 332, 333, 336, 337, 342, 346; grog shopkeepers, 11, 12, 113; mistresses, 330, 332; nurses, 45, 49, 53, 340–1; widows, 329, 330, 331, 333, 339, 344, 345, 346, 348; witnesses, 52–3; wives, 331, 332, 333, 334, 335–6, 337, 338, 339, 341, 342, 343, 345, 346, 348, 349